Queer Women and Religious Individualism

Queer Women and Religious Individualism

Melissa M. Wilcox

Indiana University Press
BLOOMINGTON AND INDIANAPOLIS

This book is a publication of

Indiana University Press
601 North Morton Street
Bloomington, IN 47404-3797 USA

www.iupress.indiana.edu

Telephone orders 800-842-6796
Fax orders 812-855-7931
Orders by e-mail iuporder@indiana.edu

♾ *The paper used in this publication meets the minimum requirements of the American National Standard for Information Sciences—Permanence of Paper for Printed Library Materials, ANSI Z39.48-1992.*

MANUFACTURED IN THE UNITED STATES OF AMERICA

Library of Congress Cataloging-in-Publication Data

Wilcox, Melissa M., date-
Queer women and religious individualism / Melissa M. Wilcox.
p. cm.
Includes bibliographical references and index.
ISBN 978-0-253-22116-2 (pbk. : alk. paper) — ISBN 978-0-253-35351-1 (cloth : alk. paper) 1. Lesbians—California—Los Angeles. 2. Lesbians—Religious life—United States. 3. Lesbians—United States—Social conditions. I. Title.
HQ75.5.W56 2009
205'.66—dc22
2009002226

1 2 3 4 5 14 13 12 11 10 09

To everyone who kept me alive—thank you.

Contents

Acknowledgments

That this book project has come to fruition is the result of a great deal of luck and the generosity and support of many people. Keeping a newborn academic career alive in the current market is a difficult task, made even more challenging by my decision to study religion within fields that generally prefer to marginalize or ignore it: queer studies, women's studies, and sociology. Religious studies, for its part, has tended to marginalize or ignore queer studies, women's studies, and sociology. Happily, the past several years have seen increasing interest in this confluence of fields, and a growing number of scholars are turning their attention to sociologically minded queer studies in religion. The road to this point, however, has been paved with generosity, and it is to those who kept this project and my career afloat that I owe great thanks.

As in any ethnographically based work, I wish to thank first and foremost those who shared their time and their lives with me as I was researching and finalizing this project. The core participants of the Los Angeles Women and Spirituality Project welcomed me into their homes, met me in their favorite parks, invited me to their performances, and tolerated not only my tape recorder but also a video camera and microphones for the film project that accompanied this book. Some also kept me updated on the events of their lives, and carefully read through and commented on the interview transcripts I sent to them many months later. Thanks to these participants, I came to understand a great deal about the complexities of queer women's spiritual lives in twenty-first-century Los Angeles. I hope they feel that my understanding accurately reflects them. Likewise, the leaders of the spiritual and religious (and sometimes even secular) organizations where the core participants practiced their spirituality took the time to meet with me and with my research assistants, educated us about their organizations, welcomed us at services and group meetings, and reviewed transcripts of their interviews later on. They, too, contributed significantly to the completion of this book.

The University of California at Santa Barbara supported this project in a number of ways. Thanks to Wade Clark Roof for nominating me for a faculty fellowship at UCSB, and to the religious studies department for housing me during the two years of the fellowship. I still miss the intellectual richness of that large and vibrant department. During the year after the fellowship ended, I was housed and primarily supported by UCSB's women's studies program, where I benefited from the generosity of Jacqueline Bobo and the support of Eileen Boris, and learned much from colleagues such as Alison Kafer and the grassroots antiwar protest group made up of fellow staff and students at UCSB. Support during that year also came from the departments of sociology and black studies and from the Writing Center. This support allowed me to wrap up my research, and kept me afloat long enough to be hired by Whitman College. At Whitman I have enjoyed the company of supportive colleagues, good friends, and incredibly sharp students—including Cole Rathjen, who proved an insightful conversation partner during a particularly stimulating independent study on religious individualism in the fall of 2007. I am deeply grateful to the religion department at Whitman for hiring me on a permanent basis after my two one-year appointments. Had I not been able to find a stable foothold in academia I likely would not have finished this book at all.

Grants to support this project came from UCSB's Interdisciplinary Humanities Center, the Association for the Sociology of Religion, the UCSB Faculty Senate, the American Academy of Religion, and the Whitman College Office of the Dean of Faculty (a grant supported by the Abshire family). Marie Cartier offered early advice on queer women and community in Los Angeles. The staff of the UCSB Learning Labs and the photography office offered advice on video equipment and put me in contact with Anita David and Frederick Backman, whose Zeituna Productions supported the initial phases of the film project.

I was fortunate to have the able help of a number of graduate and undergraduate research assistants in the interview phase of this project. At UCSB, Nancy Arnold and Dan Michon conducted field visits and interviews as well as transcribing other interviews. Marcy Braverman (now Goldstein) conducted the interview at St. Francis. Jennifer Heisler, Sarah Whedon, Leona Smith, and Suzanne Crawford painstakingly transcribed my interviews with core participants. At Whitman, Morgan Ross and Richard Jones put countless hours and incredible effort into finalizing and editing *Each of Us,* the film based on this project. I had begun to lose hope of ever finishing the film, and I am deeply grateful to them for making *Each of Us* a reality.

For assistance during the writing process, I thank Buzz Haughton and Jim Webber at Sacramento's Lavender Library, Archives, and Cultural Exchange for providing me with photocopies of relevant sections of the 2001 Southern California *Gay and Lesbian Community Yellow Pages;* the *Lesbian News* for providing me with a 2001 back issue; and Jen Johnson at Whitman's Penrose Library for satisfying my obscure interlibrary loan requests and using her research expertise to help me connect some important dots.

I have had the honor and pleasure of presenting portions of this work to a number of different audiences, all of whom have been receptive and have offered helpful questions and suggestions. These include the participants in a consultation on religion and sexuality held at Princeton's Center for the Study of Religion in 2003, especially Dawne Moon and Marie Griffith (thanks also to Marie for inviting me to the consultation), the Center for Lesbian and Gay Studies in Religion and Ministry at the Pacific School of Religion, Iowa State University, California State University at Fresno, California State University at Long Beach, Minnesota State University at Mankato, the College of Charleston, the University of South Florida, West Virginia University, the University of Toronto, the University of Waterloo, and of course, Whitman. Audiences at the Association for the Sociology of Religion meetings and the Society for the Scientific Study of Religion meetings have been equally helpful.

Clark Roof, Cathy Albanese, Richard Hecht, Beth Schneider, and Jodi O'Brien have been stalwart supporters and mentors throughout this project. Steve Warner and Nancy Ammerman reached out to me as mentors early in my career—a rare and admirable practice among senior scholars, and an example I try to emulate. Mary Jo Neitz offered encouragement, as well as insight into the framing of the book that helped to jump-start the final revisions. Christel Manning provided helpful comments on a draft of chapter 5; Laurel Schneider read the whole manuscript and was enthusiastic in her encouragement. Heather White has become a friend and colleague, and I thank her not only for her close and thoughtful reading of chapter 2 but also for many insightful and enjoyable conversations over the years.

I am grateful to Indiana University Press for its interest in this book, and especially to Bob Sloan for helping me to move the project from concept to publication and Susanna J. Sturgis for her able copyediting.

Having opened with one of the most important groups of people to thank, I want to close with the other: my family. My parents, Margaret and Wayne Wilcox, and my brother, Wynn Gadkar-Wilcox, provided both emotional and financial support throughout the rocky journey that has led at last to the publication of this book. My partner, Janet Mallen, helped to support me in between annual contracts and gave up a job to brave the move from Santa Barbara to tiny, rural Walla Walla. She has served as my emotional support and the bright spot in my life when things have looked bleakest.

My thanks to all. I hope this book is everything you imagined it would be.

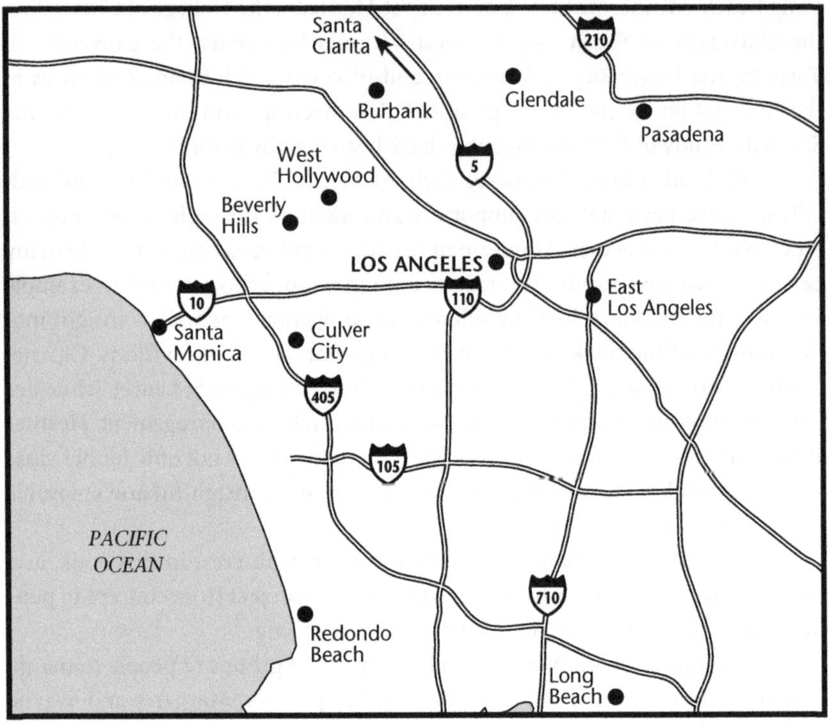
Santa Clarita
210
Glendale
Burbank
Pasadena
West Hollywood
5
Beverly Hills
LOS ANGELES
10
110
East Los Angeles
Santa Monica
Culver City
405
105
PACIFIC OCEAN
710
Redondo Beach
Long Beach

Queer Women and Religious Individualism

1 *Beyond the Congregation*

As Featherstone says, "When religion is defined as providing the most coherent set of answers to . . . core existential questions, a decline in religion must necessarily be seen as providing a threat to social integration and the social bond." *But what if different questions were asked?*
—David Lyon, *Jesus in Disneyland: Religion in Postmodern Times*

Spirituality, Sex, and the Postmodern Self

Spirituality seems to be booming in the twenty-first-century United States. So too, for that matter, is sex—or at least discussions about, debates over, marketing of, and media obsession with sex. Is there a connection between the two? Self-help books and DVDs promote a variety of forms of "sacred sex," most of them severe misinterpretations (or cunning reinterpretations) of nonwestern religious traditions, and the more daring among traditional religious institutions offer workshops on inviting the divine into one's marital intimacy. Yet while there is a niche market for the "spiritual element" of sexuality, to many in the United States sexuality appears as something separate from or even inimical to the life of the spirit.

Despite this clear separation of spheres, the forms taken by spirituality and sexuality in the twenty-first-century United States derive from the same larger cultural pattern, on the rise since at least the early twentieth century but best documented during its midcentury ascendance in Robert Bellah and his colleagues' famed book, *Habits of the Heart.*[1] Individualism, understood variously by commentators as a driving force of entrepreneurial capitalism, the demise of community orientation, freethinking, or a moment of autonomy in the social construction of the self, has long been a powerful force in U.S. culture, albeit one strongly influenced by gender, class status, ethnicity, and other factors.[2]

With the cultural, social, and economic changes of the 1960s and 1970s and the transition from a modern social world to one considered "postmodern" or "high modern" came an increased emphasis on the individual rather than the family or community as the basic unit of social exchange. Though marketing strategies had been focusing on lifestyle and image since at least the 1920s, by the late twentieth century a wide range of products were touted as expressions of the inner self and, ironically, of individualism and uniqueness.

An intrinsic aspect of these social shifts was a growing engagement with the self as what social theorist Anthony Giddens has termed a "reflexive" project.[3] While many writers in the standard canon of western intellectual history have seen the self as an object of reflection, inquiry, and sometimes even active construction, Giddens and others argue that the conscious construction of the self has come to the forefront under postmodernity. Although these consciously constructed selves are still subject to important and sometimes crushing forms of social constraint, they also have opened for some the opportunity to explore alternatives in both sexuality and spirituality, not just as practices but as aspects of identity, parts of the self-in-progress. Thus, although the western concept of sexual orientation as an identity rather than simply an act of sexual object choice has its roots in the nineteenth century, it was in the mid–twentieth century that gay men, lesbians, and bisexuals began to lay open claim to such identities, leading to the rise of the gay liberation and lesbian feminist movements in the 1970s. As the twentieth century drew to a close, sexual identities continued to proliferate, giving rise to the rapidly multiplying "alphabet soup" of sexual and gender identifications and the growing use of "queer" as a catch-all term for those claiming non-normative genders and sexual identities.[4]

Like sexual identity, religious identity has also become increasingly complex and voluntary in the United States during recent decades. Of great interest to contemporary sociologists of religion—beginning, in fact, with a chapter in *Habits of the Heart*—has been the influence of individualism on patterns of religious belief, practice, and commitment in the United States. Though earlier debates over the apparent secularization of the country have mostly died down, concern remains in many circles over the rise of what Grace Davie has termed in the British context "believing without belonging."[5] After the heights of membership and participation reached by U.S. mainline Protestant denominations in the mid–twentieth century, the decline of these denominations in the following decades led to concern that religiosity in the United States as a whole was weakening. As early as Marx, social commentators had predicted the decline of religion as a result of social progress, and as the baby boom generation drifted out of the mainline churches, debates arose among observers of U.S. religion over whether these long-standing predictions were in fact coming true. Since at least the early 1990s these debates have been largely resolved (at least in the

United States) in favor of an alternate explanation: rather than dying out, U.S. religiosities have instead been changing. As new religious movements within or beyond traditional U.S. religions drew adherents, and as less institutional forms of religious practice became increasingly attractive, attendance and membership fell among the mainline denominations, producing the illusion of religious decline.[6] One important influence in these changes has been the rise of individualism.

Robert Bellah and his colleagues described religious individualism through the example of a woman they called "Sheila Larson," who never attended church (though it is perhaps interesting that she used the Christian term "church" to speak of religious institutions). She spoke of her religion as personal, doctrinally inchoate, and focused on love. Yet the reflexive project of the postmodern self is not necessarily an anti-institutional one, as the authors of *Habits of the Heart* feared. Rather, the reflexive self draws on institutions as resources that can provide tools and materials from which the self can be cobbled together in a kind of existential "found art." Robert Wuthnow describes this most clearly when he posits that, between the middle and the end of the twentieth century, the dominant form of religiosity in the United States shifted from a "spirituality of dwelling," in which religious identity is ascribed and permanent, to one of "seeking," wherein religious identity is sought out and negotiated.[7] In studies following the spiritual lives of the baby boom generation, Wade Clark Roof also finds this "seeking" pattern among some participants, though he understands the term more narrowly as describing a form of spiritual quest.[8] Still other commentators have adopted Levi-Strauss's term "bricolage" to speak of the ways in which postmodern religious identities take shape.[9] Regardless of their terms or metaphors, though, it is clear that commentators on contemporary religion, especially in the United States, have repeatedly pointed to a growing pattern of conscious negotiation: the religious self, like the sexual self, is increasingly a reflexive project in at least some social contexts.

Though the authors of *Habits of the Heart* drew on the lives of both male and female participants in demonstrating the prevalence of religious individualism, the prominence of a female participant as an exemplar of this pattern prompts the question of whether such individualism, at least in the case of religious identities, is gendered. On the one hand, women have long been the mainstays of religious congregations in the United States, usually making up well over half of the institutional membership even when they were (or are) forbidden to enter the leadership. With religion so often the province of women in the culture, one might expect religious individualism, too, to be more prominently a female pattern than a male one. On the other hand, in western philosophy and in most of the cultures shaping and shaped by that philosophy, individualism and the project of the self have been distinctly male preserves. On that logic, one might argue for a religious individualism that complements the masculine "rugged individualist" of U.S. mythology. Still, studies of youth who leave their childhood religions show no clearly gendered patterns: boys and girls appear to have departed at equal rates and equal ages for several decades.[10]

Tracking religious individualism in the general population—seemingly the best way to determine whether this pattern is gendered—is a tricky proposition. What questions might one ask in a survey that would concisely capture respondents' tendencies toward religious individualism? Religious membership might be a possibility, but some seekers maintain membership in a religious organization, and some who are not members of a religious organization are simply religiously disinterested. Defining oneself as "religious," "spiritual," or both does not seem to track directly with religious individualism. Active disagreement with the doctrines of one's religion can be a partial measure of religious individualism, but only for those with a single, central religious commitment. Studies like Roof's meticulous longitudinal work on baby boomer spiritualities can demonstrate seekerism through changing patterns of attendance, belief, and commitment. Because of their large scope, even with in-depth interview components these studies are limited in the depth with which they can explore religious identity construction, and thus in the depth to which they can explore the finer points of religious individualism—such as the question of gender. The exemplary case study offers an important complement to such large-scale projects.

To a statistician, the case study may be the nadir of unreliable research. Dependent on small and hopelessly insignificant samples (in quantitative terms), case studies offer rich detail but no hope of statistical generalizability. On the other hand, in situations where larger patterns have already been identified but have not been explored at the desired level of complexity, case studies can be invaluable. An exemplary case study begins with an already-identified cultural phenomenon, selects a context in which that phenomenon is particularly prevalent, and focuses on an in-depth exploration of that context as an exemplar of the broader phenomenon at hand. While the exemplary case study cannot identify national patterns with any statistical accuracy, it can unearth as-yet untapped nuances in those patterns, and on the basis of those nuances it can offer more general hypotheses for theoretical consideration and, when feasible, quantitative evaluation.

Michael Burawoy makes a similar point in his discussion of the extended case method, which he describes as "appl[ying] reflexive science to ethnography in order to extract the general from the unique, to move from the 'micro' to the 'macro,' and to connect the present to the past in anticipation of the future, all by building on existing theory."[11] Though Burawoy's approach involves more complexly layered social phenomena, the underlying argument is essentially the same as the one I am making for the exemplary case study: when grounded in pre-existing theory, case studies can offer generalizable insights without being statistically significant. An exemplary case study, then, should be a particularly fruitful approach to the study of religious individualism at this point in time, when sociologists know quite a bit about the overall patterns of individualism but relatively little about how reflexive spiritual selves are constructed and negotiated over time.[12]

Queer Women and Religious Individualism offers an exemplary case study of religious individualism among women by focusing on a population long known to avoid traditional religious organizations: lesbian, bisexual, and transgendered (LBT) women. In considering specifically LBT women who live in the sprawling tangle of concrete that constitutes greater Los Angeles, the study approaches a widely diverse population that has access to a plethora of religious and spiritual options: LGBT (lesbian, gay, bisexual, and transgender) churches, synagogues, and meditation groups; welcoming religious organizations; numerous new religious movements that are welcoming of, or at least indifferent toward, sexual and/or gender diversity; women-only groups and mixed groups; and even non-religious organizations that nonetheless can serve as sources of spiritual sustenance to some of their members. Despite this wide availability of options, however, and especially the availability across nearly four decades of religious organizations specifically targeting gay men and lesbians, scholars and religious leaders have known for some time that men's attendance at such organizations has been heavily disproportionate to women's attendance—not only in Los Angeles but in Chicago, New York, Denver, Philadelphia, San Francisco, and even Salt Lake City. While no nationwide study has yet been conducted to confirm these observations, they nonetheless suggest that LBT women who consider themselves religious or spiritual are an important exemplary case for the study of religious individualism.

Where Are All the Women?

> Originally, women did not feel particularly welcome at MCC [Metropolitan Community Church] and experienced some difficulty being accepted.
> —E. Michael Gorman, 1980

> At a typical Sunday Mass [at Dignity] with two hundred thirty-five individuals present, perhaps only ten of these would be women.
> —Leonard Norman Primiano, 1993

> Underrepresentation of women characterized most CBST [Congregation Beth Simchat Torah] activities, committees, and leadership positions.
> —Moshe Shokeid, 1995

In 1974 the first in-depth, academic study of a gay religious organization appeared. Written by two sociologists who were also interested in—and often suspicious of—new religious movements more generally, Ronald Enroth and Gerald Jamison's *The Gay Church* presented the Metropolitan Community Church (MCC) congregation of San Francisco in rather skeptical terms, portraying it as little more than a new cruising option for gay men.[13] Although other scholars have since studied MCC congregations in a more nuanced light, what has not received much comment is that in Enroth and Jamison's work, as well as in Paul Bauer's 1976 study of MCC Denver, MCC congregations seem to be composed almost entirely of men.[14] An admirable but unfortunately unpublished dissertation filed at the University of Chicago in 1980 came to a similar conclusion in the case of three different congregations: another MCC church, a chapter of Dignity (an organization for lesbian and gay Catholics that later broadened its ministry to include bisexuals and transgendered people), and a synagogue for gay men and lesbians.[15] Studies conducted in the 1980s and 1990s, some of which included bisexuals and transgendered people at least tangentially, have continued to note significant gender differences in LGBT congregations.[16]

Before the 1990s, the question of gender in LGBT religious communities remained implicit in academic writing; while it is clear in these earlier studies that the congregations involved were heavily male, the authors fail to comment explicitly on this fact or to explore congregational gender dynamics in any depth.[17] The first to consider gender explicitly was Leonard Norman Primiano, who published an article in 1993 focusing on gender dynamics in the Philadelphia chapter of Dignity.[18] Since then, most studies of LGBT religious communities have given at least passing notice to gender. As of 2008, Moshe Shokeid was still the only scholar to have written about an increase in women's participation in such communities; in a follow-up article published several years after his 1995 ethnography,[19] Shokeid traced the tensions and political upheavals accompanying the hiring of a woman rabbi at a large LGBT synagogue in New York City and the subsequent, dramatic rise in women's participation. Tellingly, the article's title is "The Women Are Coming"—a prophecy uttered in the early 1990s by a man who had been a longtime member of the synagogue.[20] Shokeid's article aside, most studies have found a consistent preponderance of men over women in Jewish and Christian LGBT congregations.

Though discussions of the underrepresentation of women in LGBT congregations has often been perfunctory,[21] scholars have offered several possible explanations for this phenomenon. Their main interpretive approaches are cultural and demographic. Primiano points out, for instance, that despite efforts among the leaders of Dignity Philadelphia in the 1980s to make their services more attractive to women, the organization's culture—like its population—remained heavily male.[22] Cultural references and jokes during homilies were often specific to gay male culture, and social activities outside of Dignity frequently took place in all-male surroundings or were attended only by men.[23] Finally, even after incorporating an inclusive-language liturgy, Dignity Philadelphia in the 1980s retained its insistence on having mass conducted by an ordained Roman Catholic priest, making women's presence behind the altar a virtual impossibility. With the congregation less than 5 percent female, it would have been difficult to change its culture sufficiently to attract the women who might have altered the demographics, and thereby the culture as well. While Primiano's study presents an extreme case, other authors have attributed less severe gender disparities to similar combinations of demographics and culture.

Leadership is another possible piece of this puzzle. When Primiano conducted his research in the 1980s, Dignity Philadelphia adhered to Roman Catholic rules of male leadership even while vocally opposing other teachings of the church.[24] Congregation Beth Simchat Torah (CBST), the subject of Shokeid's work, was led by lay people, but its elite was predominantly male before the hiring of Rabbi Sharon Kleinbaum in 1992, and until 2000 the Metropolitan Community Churches had more male than female ministers.[25] Shokeid traces the shift in CBST's gender demographics to the hiring of a female rabbi: "Since the inauguration ceremony of Rabbi Kleinbaum . . . the number of female congregants [has] expanded dramatically and the rabbi [has become] a subject of adulation by women in particular."[26] In my own work with two MCC congregations, I found striking gender differences that mapped directly onto leadership: the congregation led by a woman pastor, though quite small, had almost entirely women in attendance during the course of my fieldwork, while the larger, male-led congregation ranged between 25 percent and 40 percent women at services.[27] Since leaders help to set the tone of a congregation, it is likely that demographics, culture, and leadership intertwine to shape a congregation's attractiveness—or lack thereof—to women, just as women members, in large enough numbers, can in turn shape the congregation's culture and leadership.

In the midst of the admittedly limited scholarly discussion of gender disparities in LGBT congregations, one question has been surprisingly absent: If only a few women are in congregations, then where are the rest? Are queer women simply more likely than queer men to be atheists?[28] Although this is certainly one possibility, even anecdotal evidence from LGBT communities seems to suggest a more complex answer. Gary David Comstock hints at an alternative explanation in his study of lesbians, gay men, and bisexuals in the United Methodist Church (UMC) and the United Church of Christ (UCC):

> Women from the UMC and UCC identified their primary faith communities as their lovers, partners, and families more often than UMC and UCC

> men. . . . Further, UMC men identified the denominational gay organization more often than UMC women; and UCC men identified the Christian church in general more often than UCC women. . . . Women more often than men would appear to have found their primary faith communities outside of institutional and formal religious organizations.[29]

If even women affiliated with two prominent Protestant denominations center their religious experiences outside the context of congregation and church, then women not affiliated with mainstream religions may also be finding their "primary faith communities" outside of religious institutions. Perhaps a similar situation holds for the studies already cited; Shokeid notes that before the arrival of Rabbi Kleinbaum, women were underrepresented at all CBST activities except "High Holiday services and congregational dinners," when the female membership of the synagogue was, in contrast, "overrepresented."[30] Women who were members of CBST, like those in Comstock's study, may have found their day-to-day religious communities and experiences outside of a formal religious setting, returning to the synagogue only for informal social occasions and for the most sacred holidays of the Jewish calendar.

If this is a preliminary answer to the question of what queer women are doing religiously—that some of them maintain ties with traditional and LGBT religious organizations but find their most important religious community elsewhere—the question remains of where exactly that "elsewhere" is, and what women are doing who do not maintain ties with a traditional religious organization. Furthermore, to what extent are queer women's religious beliefs and practices influenced not only by their gender and their sexual orientation or transgender identity but also by other factors such as race, class, or even religious background? Race, class, and gender are so readily seen as mutually influential that the American Sociological Association has a section dedicated specifically to the integrated study of the three; it would be difficult to imagine that religious beliefs and practices fail to reflect this same interaction. Sexual orientation and transgender identity are also likely to be important factors shaping religion; although I have used the term "queer women" and spoken of lesbians, bisexual women, and transgendered people together, it is well worth asking to what extent the religious experiences of these groups differ as well as to what extent they are the same.

This book explores such questions in the religious and spiritual life stories of lesbian, bisexual, and transgendered women who live in the greater Los Angeles area, seeking through these stories to highlight the complexity of the religious, sexual, and gendered reflexive self in the early twenty-first century. Drawing from the long-established sociological model of community studies but updating that model to consider a number of intersecting subcultures within a sprawling and often self-centered metropolis, it presents three interconnected social layers that together form a three-dimensional sketch of queer women's spiritualities in this twenty-first-century city.[31] The twenty-nine core participants who took part in lengthy interviews about their beliefs, their religious and spiritual experiences, and their lives in general serve as one of these layers. These life stories, in turn, influence and are influenced by the dizzying array of organizational options in which lesbian, bisexual, and transgendered women in L.A. can practice their spirituality—including a few organizations whose members might be surprised to hear their group called "spiritual" or "religious."[32] Furthermore, both the women's lives and the organizations in which they participate are fundamentally shaped by the history of Los Angeles—the city's religious history, its queer history, and more recently, its queer religious history. Three chapters of the book lay out these layers in succession, in the process laying the groundwork for the final three chapters of the book, which consider the relationships between the life stories of the women in this study and the rise of sexual and religious individualism in the United States as a whole.

Like its design, the goals of *Queer Women and Religious Individualism* are multilayered. At one level, the book aims to map the religious resources drawn on by some lesbians, bisexual women, and transgendered people in Los Angeles; to trace the ways in which those alternatives are being utilized; and to understand why the participants in the study make the decisions they do in their religious and/or spiritual lives. At a second level, it aims not only to add women more explicitly to the study of LGBT religiosities, but also to bring LGBT people more centrally into the study of contemporary religion, to fold religion into the study of contemporary LGBT lives, and to consider how LGBT identities *and* religious identities affect and are affected by postmodern cultural patterns. I argue throughout this book that contemporary queer women's religiosities are both an integral part of, and subtly distinct from, twenty-first-century religiosities in the United States as a whole. As such, these forms of religiosity and negotiation of religious identity offer significant insights into broader patterns in U.S. religion, especially in the context of religious individualism.

Like many others of all genders in the United States today, the women who participated in this project are engaged in an ongoing process of self-construction and self-maintenance, in which religion plays a part—sometimes positive, sometimes negative, often ambivalent. Like many others, too, these women draw on an "expressive individualism" noted by many cultural commentators as uniquely prevalent in late-twentieth-century and early-twenty-first-century postmodern societies. At the same time, their individualism is both consciously and unconsciously rooted in community—a source of support and rejection, of identity and disidentification, of misunderstanding and deep comprehension. But unlike most people living in the United States today, the women in this study are all quite clearly aware that some religions condemn at least one aspect of what they consider to be their innermost selves: same-sex attraction, transgender identity, or both. Many have experienced that condemnation themselves, either directly or indirectly. With homophobia, biphobia, transphobia, and sexism a part of many traditional religions, for these women religious individualism is more of a necessity than it is for many of their heterosexual, cisgender counterparts. Their processes of identity negotiation, and the religious and spiritual beliefs and practices they have brought together in those identities, are thus exemplary cases of religious practice and identity in the contemporary United States, and of the postmodern self.

Religion and Spirituality

One of the questions nagging at scholars of contemporary religion, especially in the west, is the distinction between "religion" and "spirituality."[33] One reason this is a nagging question is that scholars of religion have never managed to agree on exactly what religion *is*. Though most if not all can concur that Christianity, for instance, is a religion (logically enough, as it was the model or ideal type for early studies in the field), when asked to identify precisely what defines religion, scholars begin to diverge. From the often broad perspective of religious studies, and especially the study of "lived religion,"[34] religion encompasses beliefs and/or practices centered around ultimate meaning. To the devout, sports can function as a religion; so can communism. From this perspective, the personal and largely private forms of experience that most people seem to reference when they use the term "spirituality" are a form of religion. This is not, of course, consistent with the broader, popular usage of the term "religion," which generally implies institutional forms and, when used negatively, smacks of dogmatism and rote behavior. This popular usage is also what most participants in this study mean when they use the term "religion." Through the course of the book it will become apparent that what participants define as "spiritual" practice does not always fall within the boundaries of the "religious," as typically defined in popular discourse or by participants themselves. One participant finds hiking and backpacking spiritual; another takes part in a secular organization that both parodies and emulates the Roman Catholic Church (with, in her opinion, some significant improvements over Roman Catholicism). The challenge here, then, is to negotiate between what scholars mean when we say "religion" and what participants in this study mean.

Peter Berger once claimed that "definitions cannot, by their very nature, be either 'true' or 'false,' only more useful or less so."[35] Because this book is, in part, a study of identity negotiation, how participants define and construct their religious (or spiritual) identities is important. Thus, it would be of little use to place firm boundaries on the definitions of religion or spirituality and to evaluate each participant by those standards, determining from the outside which of her actions are "religious" and which are not. This can be a useful method of analysis and is the focus of one branch of research on contemporary "spirituality" and "religion," but it makes little sense here. Instead, I begin with participants' own definitions.[36] If a participant claims that a certain activity is "spiritual" for her, then I consider that activity a part of her spirituality. I also asked participants to explain how they use the terms "religion" and "spirituality"; where relevant, in the pages that follow, I specify these individual definitions. When I speak generally, comparing across participants, I use the terms "religion" and "spirituality" interchangeably, and in the few instances where this is not the case, I make it explicit that I am doing otherwise.[37]

The entanglement of spirituality and religion in the discussion above is an indication of the ongoing challenges faced by scholars in studying religion as it is lived by everyday people rather than as it is invoked by religious leaders or specialists. In order to study many different aspects of religion, rather than focusing on the texts and leaders that were at the center of earlier scholarship in the field, contemporary religionists may use the term "religion" to describe everything from building home altars to camping at a national park: if a participant considers the activity to connect to the transcendent, to ultimate meaning, then we generally consider it "religious," at least in function. This allows us not only to broaden the study of religion beyond religious elites, but thereby to add a great deal of breadth and nuance to our understanding of religious lives. For those reasons, this book is about "religion." Yet, many of the participants in this study consider themselves spiritual but not religious. Though by my own academic definition of religion this oft-remarked pattern of "spirituality" in postmodern cultures like the contemporary United States is one aspect of the complex phenomenon of religion, as the participants define it "spirituality" is something wholly distinct from "religion." Thus, this book is also about "spirituality." Especially when speaking of individual participants' experiences, I have made an effort to avoid the term "religious" when a participant would not use that term herself.

Identity and (Post)Modernity

It is not an exaggeration to say that this study would not have been the same—indeed, would likely have been impossible—in a different era and a different cultural context. Fifty years ago, gay men, lesbians, and bisexuals kept their heads down, even in Los Angeles. Transsexuals had recently become publicly visible through the high-profile life of Christine Jorgensen, who eventually settled in L.A.,[38] but despite the gender diversity of some gay and lesbian cultures the concept of transgender identity as it is used today had yet to develop. There were very few religious organizations that openly welcomed gay men and lesbians; all were local, and none were well-known. Those who opposed same-sex eroticism and gender variance generally defined such behaviors and self-concepts as symptoms of mental illness, and a few liberal religious commentators had attempted to argue that no sin was involved when the apparent "sinner" was instead sick.[39]

But it is not only LGBT history that makes the stories and communities in this book such a contemporary phenomenon; it is also the nature of identity and religion themselves. Fifty years ago, though the United States was already home to wide-ranging religious diversity, sociologist Will Herberg could still write a book entitled *Protestant, Catholic, Jew* and argue therein that the self-concept of the country was shifting from that of a Protestant nation to that of a "Judeo-Christian" one.[40] Fifty years ago, the dominant pattern of religious identity was what Wuthnow has called a "spirituality of dwelling": one was born into a religion, and one generally remained there for life.[41] Fifty years ago, as Anthony Giddens notes, tradition still had a strong influence on self-identity.[42]

In the early twenty-first century, on the other hand, one of the most popular areas of research for U.S. sociologists of religion is religion and immigration; while some of the immigrants who arrived after the 1965 liberalization of immigration law are Christian many others are not, and some whose families have been in the United States for generations are joining (or have long been a part of) such newly growing U.S. religions as Buddhism, Hinduism, Sikhism, and Islam. "Pluralism" is the word of the day in U.S. religious studies. Contemporary religious identity has shifted to a "spirituality of seeking,"[43] and self-identity in general has likewise become a "reflexive project."[44] Although still lacking federal anti-discrimination legislation and often at the center of national political firestorms, openly LGBT people are now elected officials, religious authorities, police officers, teachers, psychologists, and even the protagonists of television shows and Hollywood films. Though transgender identities remain associated officially with a psychological condition,[45] same-sex attraction was removed from classification as a mental disorder in 1974, and with the U.S. Supreme Court's 2003 decision in *Lawrence v. Texas,* private, consensual same-sex erotic activity is no longer a crime in any state. Separate as these changes may seem—*Lawrence v. Texas,* religious pluralism, the reflexive self—they are deeply intertwined causally as well as practically in the religious and spiritual lives of LGBT people. This is especially true of the lives of the women who shared their stories and their spiritual communities with me during the course of this study.

Overview

As this introductory chapter has noted, historical, cultural, and regional context all affect the negotiation of religious and sexual identities. Though ultimately I wish to argue that the women who contributed to this book are exemplary cases of patterns evident both in U.S. LGBT communities and in the country as a whole, in order to make this argument and in order to understand the individual identity negotiations of each of these women it is first necessary to examine the geographically and culturally specific contexts in which they have shaped and reshaped their identities. To this end, the book begins with an exploration of the historical and contemporary queer and religious contexts of Los Angeles before moving on to introduce the life stories of the women whose experiences form the backbone of the study. With these foundations in place, the second half of the book considers these women's stories as both exemplary case studies and extended case studies. Considering the women's stories of religious identity negotiation and their patterns of religious participation, these chapters move beyond the context of Los Angeles to, as Burawoy puts it, "extract the general from the unique, to move from the 'micro' to the 'macro,' . . . by building on existing theory."

Because of the importance of geographical and social location in gender and queer theory and in studies of religion in the United States, chapter 2 is devoted to Los Angeles history. This includes L.A.'s diverse, innovative, and quite unique religious history as well as the city's LGBT history and its LGBT religious history. Though San Francisco and New York are better known as early centers of LGBT activism and social activity, the earliest national gay rights group in the United States was founded in Los Angeles, and the city has also seen the founding of more long-lasting LGBT religious movements than any other city in the country. Chapter 2 discusses religious histories and queer histories separately, then brings them together to discuss the city's unique position as an apparent center of LGBT religious innovation.

Chapter 3 offers a sampling of that religious innovation, presenting some of the religious organizations that welcome and, increasingly, directly market to LGBT people in the greater Los Angeles area. During my interviews, I asked each core participant whether she was involved in any organizations as a part of her spiritual practice. Though only about half of the participants answered this question affirmatively, they attended or had recently attended twenty-one different organizations in all, and chapter 3 draws on brief fieldwork I conducted in these organizations. While LGBT niche congregations have some tendency to cluster geographically—and this tendency has important implications for their congregants—a growing number of religious organizations can be found across the city and throughout its environs that welcome LGBT people without focusing specifically on LGBT political or theological issues. This points to the increasingly complex nature of the connections between religion, LGBT identities, and social geography, especially in the notorious city of sprawl. Also interesting in this context is that the "expressive individualism" described earlier plays a role in shaping and sometimes even creating providers of spiritual sustenance: not all of the groups described in this chapter would identify themselves as primarily religious or even spiritual organizations.

One of the core participants in this study described herself as "a spiritual being having a human experience." This perspective fundamentally influenced this participant's understanding of herself as a bisexual, multiracial, female, sex-positive Religious Science practitioner. Using her story as a launching point, chapter 4 sets out to explore the relationships between belief, practice, and identity in the life stories of the core participants. The chapter's focus is on participants' complex patterns of religious belief, practice, affiliation, and disaffiliation, and the ways in which those patterns were profoundly influenced by developments such as coming out, going to college, discovering one's cultural heritage, the death of loved ones, and even homelessness. Readers who wish to follow particular women's stories from this chapter through the more analytically oriented final chapters will find an index of participants in the appendices.

Chapter 5 returns to the question of lesbian, bisexual, and transgendered women's participation in religious organizations, moving into more theoretical considerations of these women's roles as exemplars—in this case, of patterns that appear in a striking number of studies on LGBT religiosities from urban areas across the country. Consistent with previous research, the women in this study are far less frequent religious attendees than U.S. women are on average, and yet many of them do have some sort of involvement with religious groups. Chapter 5 draws on both sociological and psychological literature—the former on factors affecting religious attendance, the latter on LGBT identity formation—to explore the possible reasons for this discrepancy. It concludes that there is no simple answer; rather, a number of factors seem to interact in shaping these women's attendance patterns. Not surprisingly, though, sexism and homophobia, especially in combination, seem to be among the most powerful influences driving LBT women away from more traditional religions.

Chapter 6 moves to a broader consideration of exemplarity, and links the stories of the women in this study to contemporary studies of sexual, sacred, and social selves. Drawing on a wide variety of recent research on the nature and construction of the self, the chapter explores the self at the intersection of identities through the themes of "everyday sacralogies," narrative self-construction, queer intersections of identities and spaces, the search for a "true self," and the experience of what I call "enselved bodies." I argue that postmodern aspects of the self can be seen clearly in the stories of the women who participated in this project, through concepts of the sacred, concepts of the self, and most importantly, the intertwining of the two.

Chapter 7 pulls the varied themes raised throughout the book into a single space in order to explore their relationships in greater depth. It considers the uniqueness and, simultaneously, the broad applicability of these stories of spirituality and sex in one Southern California city, and considers the lessons these stories carry about queer identities and communities in a postmodern age. Finally, it returns to the question with which it opened: what can we learn about women, sexuality, and religion in the twenty-first-century United States by focusing on the exemplary/extended and perhaps somewhat counterintuitive case studies of these self-made spirits?

2 *Setting the Stage*

HISTORICAL CONTEXTS

"All the fruits and nuts are in California." So goes the saying, referring not only to the state's bounteous produce but also derisively to gay men (fruits) and followers of new religious movements (nuts). This saying was particularly apropos in the 1960s and 1970s; however, California has a long history of both religious and sexual diversity, and Los Angeles has played a prominent part in that history. Though many of the women who contributed to this book were born and raised elsewhere, at the time of our interviews all were negotiating their religious, sexual, and gender identities in this rich milieu. While I will argue that their reflexive and individualistic approach to identity negotiation is a product of a much larger postmodern context, the specific resources available to these women are directly tied to their geographical and historical location. In the interest of understanding this location and its impact on contemporary queer women in L.A., the present chapter provides a brief overview of religious history in the Los Angeles basin and LGBT history in the city and its environs, before turning to a discussion of L.A.'s LGBT religious history.

Religious History

The modern story of religious immigration and encounter in the Los Angeles area begins with the Gabrielino people, who before Spanish colonization were in contact with a variety of cultures through traders' visits to their homes. Though pre-invasion histories are difficult to come by and early European sources on Native Americans must always be treated with some suspicion, it appears that pre-invasion Gabrielino religious practices centered on a single creator deity, with respects paid as well to the sun, moon, and stars, and to Crow, Raven, Owl, and Eagle.[1] Spanish contact with the native peoples of coastal North America began with Juan Rodriguez Cabrillo's 1542 sea expedition, but active colonization began only when Portolá and Serra's 1769 land exploration led Spanish soldiers and missionaries to plan a settlement on Gabrielino lands. The resulting San Gabriel mission, founded in 1771, imposed its name on the people of the region (thus "Gabrielino"), along with the forced-labor conditions that characterized the missions' relationship with native people and the additional violence that came with the accompanying soldiers.[2]

Though (white) academic sources claim that most speakers of the Gabrielino language died in the nineteenth century and that there was little left of the Gabrielino population, culture, or identity by the beginning of the twentieth century, the later decades of the twentieth century saw the rise of a movement for government recognition of the Gabrielinos. In the 1990 census, 581 people identified as Gabrielino; in 2000, the number had increased to 1,775.[3] California recognized the tribe, now also called the Tongva, in 1994. There were efforts in the 1990s to restore a spring considered sacred to the Gabrielino people, and there is ongoing work to revive and strengthen cultural traditions and to attain federal tribal recognition.

The traditional cultural practices of the Gabrielinos characterized the Los Angeles basin until the late eighteenth century, but under Spanish and Mexican rule the area was by law Roman Catholic, and Catholicism has left a strong imprint there. Yet Catholicism has also changed with the times. Though the San Gabriel mission still stands, its literature is now published not only in Spanish but also in English and Vietnamese—two of the many languages represented in twenty-first-century Angeleno Catholicism. Mexican culture continues to influence the city in myriad ways, and over the decades of the twentieth century Mexican influence increasingly combined with that of various other Latin American cultures. Early arrivals brought *curanderas* (folk healers) and Mexican spiritualists into Los Angeles, and though many Latinos in the region remain affiliated with the Catholic Church, recently the Pentecostal movement has made major inroads in their communities just as it has in many Latin American countries.

The U.S. conquest of northern Mexico in 1848, and the subsequent California gold rush of 1849, altered Los Angeles significantly. To Anglo eyes, the predominantly Catholic Mexicans in the region became like the Gabrielinos and other native peoples: "perceived as a 'conquered race,'" in the words of historian

Antonio Ríos-Bustamante.[4] A powerful trend of anti-Catholicism in the United States as a whole during the nineteenth century also ensured that L.A.'s Catholics would receive a rough welcome from their new federal landlords. Protestant missionaries from many different denominations arrived in this new mission field in the 1850s; some of them left again, in despair at the violent culture of the post-annexation gold rush city. Others stayed, reaching converts as they did in other frontier towns: through camp meetings. In the first decades after annexation these were held solely in English and largely in areas on the outskirts of Los Angeles, which remained at its center a defiantly Mexican, Catholic, Spanish-speaking town. Over the course of the next seventy-five years, however, Los Angeles underwent enormous demographic and religious change.

Starting from a pre-annexation population that was predominantly of Spanish, West African, and indigenous descent, Los Angeles rapidly developed a wide variety of ethnic communities and religious organizations. In 1854, just six years after annexation, the city's Jewish residents founded the Hebrew Benevolent Society; in 1862 they founded Congregation B'nai Brith, known today as the Wilshire Boulevard Temple. The first Protestant church in the newly acquired U.S. city was a white Presbyterian one, founded in 1855. In 1872 the First African Methodist Episcopal Church, also known as First AME, took root. L.A.'s first black Baptist congregation also organized around this time, and by the 1880s an expansion of the black population in the city added Wesley Chapel Methodist Episcopal Church and a congregation of the African Methodist Episcopal Church–Zion. In 1875 L.A.'s Chinese community dedicated its first temple, and in 1884 the First Chinese Presbyterian Church received formal approval. By the 1880 census nearly five hundred L.A. residents identified as Jewish (though many of them may not have been attending the synagogue, which in 1876 had sixty members).[5]

The 1890s added another prominent black denomination, the Colored Methodist Episcopal Church (now Christian Methodist Episcopal), to the mix, and by 1916 Los Angeles had seventeen black churches. By 1936, the number was up to fifty-four. Judaism, too, developed in several directions during its earliest decades in L.A.: the social liberalism of this frontier "cow town" made it amenable to the growing Reform movement in Judaism, while the presence of recent immigrants from eastern Europe made it home as well to Orthodox Jews. By the late 1940s, the Jewish population of the city was extensive enough to support the newly founded University of Judaism, which today is also home to a Conservative rabbinical school.

In addition to bringing their traditional religions with them to L.A., most of these immigrant groups interacted with the religions that preceded them to the city. Though some Japanese immigrants brought Buddhism and Shinto with them, for instance, due to social changes in Japan many of the late-nineteenth-century arrivals were disaffected with both religions, and some of these people proved to be prime contacts for Protestant missionaries. By the early 1930s, eleven Protestant denominations in Los Angeles claimed Japanese members.[6] On the other hand, many early-twentieth-century Japanese immigrants, affected differently by Japan's recent social changes than were earlier immigrants, remained dedicated Buddhists. While the lives of Japanese Americans were severely disrupted by their internment and the seizure and resale of their property during World War II, many Buddhist priests and monks continued their practice and teaching at the internment camps and served as important sources of support and solace for the lay Buddhists living there.

Furthermore, just as mostly white Protestant missionaries were putting their best efforts into attracting the Chinese and Japanese residents of Los Angeles, some of the city's white residents were becoming interested in Asian religions. A series of 1889 lectures on Hinduism sparked this interest; they were offered by Swami Vivekananda, a participant in the World's Parliament of Religions at the 1893 World's Fair in Chicago and later the founder of the Vedanta Society. The Vedanta Society of Southern California began in 1929 under the guidance of Swami Prabhavananda, and continues to flourish today. It was preceded in 1920 by another Hindu-based movement for U.S. converts: the Self-Realization Fellowship, founded by Swami Paramahansa Yogananda. This movement, too, continues to thrive, presiding today over a recently constructed four-thousand-square-foot temple and a ten-acre, parklike "Lake Shrine" in Pacific Palisades, west of L.A. Theosophy, an offshoot of the nineteenth-century U.S. spiritualist movement, has also attracted Angelenos since the end of the nineteenth century and throughout the twentieth.

Middle Eastern religions have had a place in Los Angeles for a full century. The first Baha'i gathering met in 1909, and the first official Baha'i organization took shape in 1924. Several Middle Eastern branches of Christianity were added to the options available to Angelenos in the early decades of the twentieth century. Islam, however, arrived later; in fact, its first official representation in Los Angeles appeared under the auspices of the black nationalist organization the Nation of Islam in 1956.

Like many other religions, Christianity has experienced considerable innovation in the City of Angels. Most famous are the Azusa Street revivals, which are widely credited as the birthplace of the Pentecostal movement.[7] The leader of these revivals, a black preacher named William Seymour, came to Los Angeles in response to a preaching invitation from revivalist Julia W. Hutchins and began leading home prayer gatherings. When people spoke in tongues at such a gathering in April 1906, the news spread rapidly, and soon Seymour and his host had a genuine revival on their hands. Though the revivals drew widespread criticism, especially from whites who were horrified by the interracial nature of the booming congregation, they also initiated a movement that has since become a worldwide phenomenon.

Fifteen years later, another series of Protestant revivals drew attention not so much for their interracial congregation as for their female leadership and their unabashed use of show business production tactics. Revivalist Aimee Semple McPherson came to Los Angeles in her late twenties, and the city of show business soon came to know her for her scripted, choreographed, and even costumed presentations of Christian teachings. Historian Michael Engh relays two colorful tales of her ministry:

> On one occasion she rushed on-stage dressed as the quarterback for USC's football team, the Trojans. At another service she wore the uniform of a city police officer and rode a motorcycle onto the temple stage with light glaring and siren wailing. Holding up her hand, she shouted into the microphone, "Stop! You are speeding to ruin!"[8]

Interestingly, not only was McPherson taking advantage of the license to preach that the Pentecostal movement sometimes offered particularly "spirit-filled" women—thus taking on a role that was usually seen as masculine at the time—but she also embodied masculine roles through the pageantry of her sermons. McPherson's revivals led to the building of the 5,300-seat Angelus Temple in Echo Park, the founding of L.I.F.E. Bible College (now LIFE Pacific College) in San Dimas, and the organization of the International Church of the Foursquare Gospel.

Despite nationalism, restrictive immigration policies, racial tensions and violence, Japanese internment, and the cold war, the religious and ethnic diversity of Los Angeles continued to increase through the tumultuous twentieth century. In 1965, the United States removed restrictive immigration quotas that had strongly favored immigrants from western Europe, and the demographics of U.S. immigrants changed substantially over the course of the following decade. In addition to globalizing the immigrant population, who along with their children and grandchildren have altered the shape of the nation, this change also shifted the shape of religion in the United States, and the already multicultural city of Los Angeles found itself a center of these changes. The second-oldest and currently the largest mosque in Los Angeles, the Islamic Center of Southern California, was founded in 1961 to serve a primarily immigrant congregation, though it also serves African American Muslims. With the relaxation of immigration restrictions in 1965 the Muslim population of Los Angeles both grew and diversified; a 1994 study estimated that there were between thirty and forty mosques in the greater Los Angeles area, and that number is very likely to have grown since then.[9]

While some of the newer religions in Los Angeles have arrived in the hands and hearts of native practitioners, the 1960s and 1970s also brought in a bevy of religions aimed at converts. Some of these, like some of the early-twentieth-century conversion-oriented religions, are rooted in Hinduism. Others are Buddhist, Sikh (or Sikh-based), or Muslim (or Islam-based, including the Nation of Islam). Though many of these movements are national and often international in scope, they have found a particularly congenial home in Southern California, which for at least a century has been well-known as a site of religious innovation. The International Society for Krishna Consciousness, or ISKCON (more familiarly known as the Hare Krishnas), found a place there, as did the Siddha Yoga Foundation, Soka Gakkai International, and Transcendental Meditation, among others.

The 1960s and 1970s also saw the rise of the diffuse and individualistic New Age movement, which had several significant groups in Southern and Central California. The Esalen Institute in Big Sur was only a scenic five-hour drive from Los Angeles, and it exerted an influence over the New Age thinkers of the city. Theosophists remained active in Southern California during this period, and both UFO (unidentified flying object) groups awaiting salvation by advanced alien species and channels who relayed the teachings of otherworldly entities also found the region hospitable. Neopaganism settled comfortably among this mixture, with at least two branches of Wicca (Dianic Wicca and its close relative, the Re-formed Congregation of the Goddess) having roots in the L.A. area. As immigrants, emigrants, and lifelong residents interacted, some adhered to the religions of their childhood or even created religious organizations specific to their ethnicities as an affirmation of their identity and heritage. Others converted to one or more of the religions they found around them, and still others turned to interests of a more secular nature, leaving religion behind. In many ways, this broader picture changes little in the specific context of lesbians, gay men, bisexuals, and transgendered people—with the exception that, even more than heterosexual and cisgender Angelenos, they have had to choose their religions carefully or risk rejection and ejection.

LGBT History

As with any LGBT history, how one recounts the history of lesbians, gay men, bisexuals, and transgendered people in Los Angeles depends in part on whom one is willing to name with one or more of these terms. Yet even focusing specifically on people who viewed themselves as attracted to individuals of the same sex and on those who consciously identified and lived in a gender other than the one to which they were assigned at birth, one finds more than a century of rich and multiethnic history—or far more than that, if one considers the apparent existence of gender-variant roles in several pre-invasion native cultures of what is now Southern California.[10]

Though the overall trajectory of twentieth-century U.S. history demonstrates increasing acceptance and visibility for LGBT people, in most U.S. cities a more detailed examination of that history reveals a repeated waxing and waning of visibility, organization, community formation, integration, and activism. Gender-crossing was not uncommon for women on the frontier, and a fin de siècle annual party in L.A. called All Fools' Night seems to have been a prime opportunity for drag performance by both men and women. Then, in response to increasing prudishness on the part of L.A.'s conservatives, in 1898 the city council passed Ordinance 5022, banning cross-dressing.[11] Stage performers, including Aimee Semple McPherson, were able to cross-dress without much harassment for a few more decades, though men dressed as women drew more disapproval and condemnation than did women dressed as men.

Communities of same-sex-attracted people existed in the early decades of the twentieth century, and even before then certain parts of the city had become known as cruising spots for men. Historian Leila Rupp tells of a particularly high-profile police sting in 1914 in Long Beach, just southeast of Los Angeles, that netted fifty men charged with "social vagrancy," described by Rupp as "involv[ing] deviant sexual behavior." Lillian Faderman and Stuart Timmons clarify that the behavior in question was fellatio, which the recent invention of the zipper made much easier to commit in public. Subsequent media coverage claimed sensationally that the Los Angeles area was home to "a 'society of queers'" numbering in the thousands.[12] Out in the onion fields of West Hollywood, the permissiveness of early Hollywood film culture along Sunset Boulevard and the lack of city police jurisdiction in this as-yet-unincorporated area also provided ample space for members of the alleged "society of queers."

More substantial evidence of gay and lesbian community formation in Los Angeles comes, as in many U.S. cities, with the appearance in the 1940s of bars catering specifically to this clientele. As John D'Emilio argues, the social changes that accompanied U.S. involvement in World War II created numerous opportunities for same-sex-attracted people to meet and form subcultures.[13] For men during this period, such opportunities came primarily through the military, as they lived and socialized with other men and often traveled widely during their time in the service. Women, too, found a lesbian subculture in the military; as in more recent wars, the military prohibition of homoeroticism was relaxed or ignored in many cases, though in others same-sex-attracted women and men fell victim to military "witch hunts" that foreshadowed those of the 1980s and 1990s. Furthermore, the severe labor shortage that brought so many women into the workforce or into more lucrative positions than they had held before the war also brought many unmarried young women to the cities. Disrupting the expected pattern of marriage upon maturity, gathering large numbers of young men and women into homosocial environments away from traditional family and cultural influences, and placing in women's hands the financial resources to live independently, the war contributed to the formation of a subculture of same-sex-attracted men and women.

Los Angeles is perhaps best known in LGBT history as the birthplace of the first lasting gay rights group in the United States. Harry Hay, the group's main founder, had been pondering the idea of a homosexual rights organization for two years by the time he found four other men willing to be members and got the Mattachine Society off the ground.[14] These five, who would become the majority of the Mattachine's early leadership, first gathered at Hay's house in November 1950 to discuss their prospects for organizing. After several more meetings and the addition of two more leaders, they formalized the organization. Named after medieval French masked dancers, the Mattachine was represented by a front organization ostensibly run by the female relatives of two Mattachine leaders. Seeking positive representations of homosexuals above all, Hay and the other leaders invented the term "homophile" to describe themselves and their organization, and to counter the increasingly negative overtones of the term "homosexual."[15] As it grew during its early years, the Mattachine achieved two significant successes: the successful prosecution in 1952 of a landmark case against police entrapment,[16] and the founding of *One Magazine* in 1953.[17] Though suspicion about the founders' Communist sympathies led to a mutiny and change of leadership in the Mattachine in 1953, over the next two decades this historic group and its sister homophile organization, the Daughters of Bilitis,[18] would carefully lay part of the foundation for the gay and lesbian liberation movement of the 1970s, and for the powerfully influential decision by the American Psychiatric Association (APA) to remove homosexuality from the 1974 edition of its *Diagnostic and Statistical Manual.*[19]

Another part of the foundation for the gay and lesbian liberation movements was laid by a subculture often derided by the homophile organizations and especially by the Daughters of Bilitis: the bar culture. As they had since the early part of the twentieth century, gay and lesbian bars in the century's middle decades provided for many same-sex-attracted and gender-variant people a social outlet and a source of community. They also offered a comfortable home for working-class lesbians and gay men, and for butch lesbians and femme gay men—none of whom were generally accepted or comfortable in homophile organizations.[20] In Los Angeles, the bar scene that had taken shape in the 1920s and 1930s thrived and grew increasingly diverse in the following decades. Though some of the bars, especially those for men, stayed out of the reach of city police by operating in unincorporated West Hollywood,[21] police raids were still such a common occurrence that many bars had warning lights to allow patrons time to switch to opposite-sex dance partners. And in 1967, patrons and supporters of the Black Cat bar in L.A.'s Silverlake district staged a protest in response to a police raid.

This protest, termed by cultural geographer Moira Rachel Kenney "the most interesting omission in the national consciousness about Los Angeles's role in gay and lesbian history,"[22] was supported and promoted by L.A.'s leftist newspaper, and hailed by a homophile magazine as a turning point in the lives of lesbian and gay Angelenos. Why have the 1969 riots at New York's Stonewall Inn come to be seen as the watershed for gay liberation, while the earlier Black Cat protests have been consigned to relative oblivion? Perhaps because the police raid at Stonewall sparked immediate riots, while at the Black Cat the protests came nearly six weeks after the raid. Perhaps it was because, as Kenney notes, the Black Cat protesters refrained from using the words "homosexual" or "gay" on their placards.[23] Perhaps it was simply that no gay men or lesbians thought to use the police raid in Los Angeles as a catalyst for a new liberation movement; as Elizabeth Armstrong and Suzanna Crage argue, since the Black Cat protests failed to produce any meaningful change in police activities, they may not have seemed worthy of commemoration.[24] But whatever the differences between the two events, in June 1969, two and a half years after the Black Cat raid, the Gay Liberation Front (GLF) was born in the riots following a police raid at the Stonewall Inn on Christopher Street in New York's Greenwich Village.

Though founding credit for the new movement goes to New York, Los Angeles' LGBT communities were ready to record, celebrate, and join in the growing sea change. The *Advocate*, a news magazine for LGBT communities that now claims a circulation in the millions, began publication in early 1968 as what D'Emilio calls "a hard-hitting newspaper whose contents evinced an aggressive pride in being gay."[25] Los Angeles soon had a chapter of the new gay rights organization, the Gay Liberation Front, and that group was responsible for the city being among the first to hold a pride parade commemorating the Stonewall Riots: L.A.'s annual "Christopher Street West" parade began in June 1970.[26]

Since 1970, gay and lesbian—and more recently, bisexual and transgender—activism and visibility have grown fairly steadily. While the GLF in other cities remained a radical activist group, in Los Angeles it took a different form. Kenney notes the unique characteristics of this city that shape its LGBT organizations and movements differently from those in cities like New York and San Francisco:

> In Los Angeles gays and lesbians recognize a number of neighborhoods as "gay or lesbian friendly" that are not immediately apparent from the outside, neighborhoods like Venice that have few openly gay or lesbian establishments and no community centers. In addition, gay enclaves within

communities of color need to be understood on their own terms, as efforts to strengthen ties with ethnic neighborhoods.[27]

LGBT people in L.A. thus represent, again in Kenney's words, a "decentralized community living within an even more decentralized city."[28] Furthermore, because L.A.'s public transit is sorely underdeveloped, the city is so diffuse, and air quality is poor for much of the year, driving is the preferred method of transportation. With few people on the sidewalks and no neighborhood to target except the largely white, affluent, and male West Hollywood, street-based LGBT organizing is difficult in L.A. Finally, as Kenney again notes, "the drive for political visibility and separatist culture that typifies [gay or lesbian] enclave development in other cities runs directly counter to the desire, in Los Angeles, to find individual fulfillment within the safety and support of the community."[29]

For all of these reasons, LGBT organizing in L.A. has generally been focused away from marches and rallies, and on the creation of community. This was reflected in the efforts of L.A. GLF leaders to open a gay community center, a goal they achieved in 1972. Though the Gay Community Services Center, as it was first named, sought from the beginning to serve people from around the city and beyond, the difficulty of serving such a diverse and diffuse group in a single location has made the center a flashpoint for tensions within the community. As in other urban communities, in Los Angeles during the 1970s disagreements over sexism and unequal working relationships, as well as the basic ideology of the separatist feminist movement, led separatist lesbian and bisexual women (the latter often publicly identifying as lesbians in this period because of discrimination in lesbian communities) to form their own organizations. In L.A. this tendency also expanded the geographic diversity of the community. Three women's spaces that welcomed lesbians opened at the same time as the Gay Community Services Center: the Gay Women's Service Center, the Sisters' Liberation House, and the Westside Women's Center, home to the nationally distributed *Lesbian Tide* from 1971 to 1977 (the *Lesbian News* or "*LN*," which in 2006 claimed over 105,000 readers, began publication in 1975).

Though lesbian and bisexual women struggled with the sexism in the gay men's movement and the homophobia they faced among straight feminists, they managed to keep a hand in both movements in part through creating their own space, either literally or symbolically. At the Women's Building, open from 1973 to 1991 in downtown L.A., this insistence on being present and visible not only led to an important blending of lesbian and other feminist activism, but also enabled lesbians to create and showcase art to an unusual degree. A lesbian art show in 1980, for instance, included not only the work displayed at the Women's Building but also images of a number of other pieces on display elsewhere in the country.

As lesbian and bisexual women were working to create their own spaces within and beyond the gay liberation movement, so too were LGBT people of color. Some lived far from the main locations of gay and lesbian community building; others lived within accessible distances but felt intimidated or out of place in the neighborhoods they visited. Racism was, and still is, alive and well in LGBT communities, and some people of color preferred the "don't ask, don't tell" acceptance of their own neighborhoods to the more open but largely white gay and lesbian communities elsewhere in the city. Just as the efforts of the Gay Community Services Center (now the L.A. Gay and Lesbian Community Center) to include women often seemed too little, too late, so too the efforts of white-dominated gay and lesbian organizations to embrace and serve culturally diverse communities have often proved insufficient.

In response to these shortcomings, the 1970s, 1980s, and 1990s have seen the rise of a shifting constellation of organizations serving LGBT people of color in the L.A. area. These have brought with them their own tensions, such as the debate over the inclusion or exclusion of non-Asian/Pacific allies that eventually led to the formation of the Asian/Pacific-only group, Gay Asian Pacific Support Network (GAPSN) out of the Asian/Pacific and ally organization, Asian/Pacific Lesbians and Gays (A/PLG).[30] But they have also brought increasingly popular alternatives for LGBT people of color seeking a space free of both racism and homophobia. Since 1988, for example, L.A. Black Pride has been organizing events for black LGBT Angelenos (and many far-flung friends who come to the city for the group's famous Fourth of July beach party). The Centro de Mujeres in East Los Angeles (also known as Connexxus East, because it branched off from a West Hollywood lesbian organization) was the first public space for lesbians in this predominantly Latino neighborhood of the city. Smaller groups ebb and flow as the needs and makeup of L.A.'s widespread and culturally diverse LGBT communities continue to grow and change. And in the 1990s, as bisexual and transgender activism became more prominent and vocal, new organizations and support groups have sprung up to begin to address the needs of these constituencies. Though the L.A. community center is still tellingly named "gay and lesbian," its literature explicitly states that it serves bisexuals and transgendered people as well. As with women and people of color, this is another instance where the efforts of a single organization trying to serve the whole city catch up with a non-dominant group's needs only weakly and belatedly.

The arrival of AIDS sent L.A.'s LGBT communities, along with many other such communities around the country, into shock in the early 1980s. Unsure in the earliest years how the disease was transmitted, what caused it, or why it was striking gay men disproportionately, LGBT communities knew only that once someone showed visible signs of illness it could be only days or months before that person was dead. Communities responded with fear, uncertainty, grief—

and organizing. By 1983, AIDS Project Los Angeles (APLA) had come into being. Founded initially as a hotline project at the Gay Community Services Center, APLA soon obtained office space in West Hollywood and began providing services to people with AIDS.[31] As the epidemic spread, however, APLA faced the same challenges that other LGBT organizations in Los Angeles have faced: the diversity and diffusion of LGBT communities in the city made it difficult for a single organization to serve all who needed help. This was especially true in the case of AIDS services, as those most in need of the assistance APLA could provide were often too sick to transport themselves over long distances. Though APLA began outreach beyond West Hollywood as early as 1986, when it opened a food bank in Silverlake (a mixed gay, Central American, and Southeast Asian community), it nonetheless has long been perceived by communities of color as an organization serving white men. This is one of the reasons for the founding and long-term success of the Minority AIDS Project, which is housed across town from APLA in a largely black and Latino neighborhood. APLA, aware of these criticisms, has also continued to expand its boundaries and to work for the implementation of AIDS services, prevention, and education throughout the city.

AIDS brought street activism back to L.A.'s LGBT communities, which like other LGBT communities across the country had shifted to subtler forms of activism during the conservative turn of the late 1970s and the 1980s. Despite the persistent concentration of L.A.'s LGBT activism on community building rather than street protest, the first half of the 1990s witnessed a resurgence of guerrilla activist tactics in this city, as in others. The first new group to encourage insistently public, guerrilla-theater style protest was the AIDS Coalition to Unleash Power, or ACT UP; Los Angeles was home to the second-largest chapter of this organization. Founded, like its radical predecessor the Gay Liberation Front, in New York City (and adopted enthusiastically, if less confrontationally, in L.A. just as the GLF had been), ACT UP began in 1987 with the goal of bringing federal and local attention to the desperate need for AIDS health and welfare services, and for research on the disease. But it also encouraged community building and pride among LGBT people. As those involved in ACT UP became interested in applying their ideas and tactics to issues of LGBT concern beyond AIDS, and as ACT UP chapters around the country faced accusations of sexism and racism, another radical organization sprouted from its roots: Queer Nation. Both organizations were involved in the last major series of LGBT-specific street protests in Los Angeles: the 1993 protests in response to Governor Pete Wilson's veto of a bill outlawing job discrimination against lesbians and gay men.[32]

Despite the brief and somewhat limited resurgence of LGBT street activism in the early 1990s, Los Angeles remains a city where activism works best behind the scenes, and where many people are most interested in "find[ing] individual fulfillment within the safety and support of the community."[33] Already in the 1980s, Daughters of Bilitis founder and lifelong activist Phyllis Lyon was referring to women who followed this tendency as "lesbian yuppies," or "luppies."[34] In L.A., upper-middle- and upper-class (and mostly white) lesbians are frequently featured by name in the *Lesbian News* "Lesbians on Location" gossip section. They attend fundraising soirées, take cruises on the all-women Olivia cruise line, and attend the ritziest parties at the annual Dinah Shore golf tournament in Palm Springs. Though less well-heeled lesbians are also a presence at Dinah Shore and on Olivia's ships, the most high-profile lesbian destinations in Los Angeles at the turn of the twenty-first century were probably Dinah Shore weekend and a large and successful club called Girl Bar (complete with go-go dancers). Yet lesbians continue to be involved as well in social justice activism on a variety of fronts, and many would never be found at Girl Bar, at Dinah Shore, or on an Olivia ship. Though the "luppies" may be the most visible, they are far from representative of lesbian life in L.A.

On the other hand, even among some activists in L.A. there remains a sense of the importance of self-fulfillment; some aspects of the city's culture seem made for the "me generation" and never quite left that era. Perhaps this is an explanation for what remains one of L.A.'s entirely unsung claims to queer fame: while New York and San Francisco occupy the limelight as the centers of LGBT organizing despite the Mattachine Society's L.A. roots, over the past forty years Los Angeles has become the birthplace of the vast majority of LGBT religious movements in U.S. history.

L.A. LGBT/Religious History

The two earliest, long-lived religious groups to welcome LGBT people and to openly address the realities of LGBT lives in the context of religion were not in Los Angeles. The first, the Eucharistic Catholic Church, was founded in Atlanta in 1946 and eventually became part of the Orthodox Catholic Church of America.[35] Though ONE, Incorporated—an offshoot of the West Hollywood chapter of the Mattachine Society—briefly sponsored the Church of One Brotherhood in L.A. during the mid-1950s,[36] it was not until the mid-1960s that the second long-lived, LGBT-affirming religious organization came along: the Council on Religion and the Homosexual (CRH). CRH was more of an activist group than a religiously practicing one. It was founded in 1964 at a retreat for religious leaders and gay/lesbian leaders sponsored by San Francisco's famous social justice congregation, Glide Memorial Church. When San Francisco police raided a benefit New Year's Eve ball organized by the CRH at the end of 1964, many of the religious leaders on the council had their first direct experience of institutionalized homophobia. These heterosexual CRH members became ardent advocates for gay rights, and helped to start discussions about gay acceptance in a number of religious organizations during the late 1960s. A similar group, the Council on Religion and the Homophile, took shape in L.A. in 1965.[37]

Among religious organizations aimed specifically at LGBT people, however, many of the most prominent and still thriving movements have their roots in Los Angeles. The best known of these is the Metropolitan Community Church, or MCC.[38] Nine months before New York's Stonewall Riots, a defrocked minister from a small Pentecostal denomination placed an ad in L.A.'s brand-new gay news magazine, the *Advocate*. It notified readers that a church service for gays would be held on October 6, 1968, at the home of Troy Perry and Willie Smith. Perry, who had lost his ordination (along with his wife and children) when he came out to his bishop in 1963, had thought his call to the ministry was void until he sensed God telling him to start a church for gay people. Though Perry feared no one would respond to his ad, twelve people came to the service, and within a few months—still well before Stonewall—the small congregation could no longer fit in Perry's living room. It moved several times, renting a variety of facilities and meeting for a while in the Encore movie theater, where one of the members worked, before buying its first building in early 1971. During those first two and a half years MCC congregations had developed in four other U.S. cities, and the Universal Fellowship of Metropolitan Community Churches (UFMCC) had become a denomination.

Like any new religious movement, the UFMCC has had growing pains. One case involved dealing with sexism: in 1973 Freda Smith, the first woman to be ordained in MCC and at that time still the only woman minister, single-handedly convinced the denomination to change the pronouns in its bylaws from "he" to "he and she."[39] Another struggle involved tensions over the theological orientation of the church; these were resolved by creating an open and permissive doctrine that allows MCC congregations to range from metaphysical to conservative Pentecostal in orientation. As with most mainstream LGBT organizations, white predominance and a lack of sensitivity to or awareness of the differing experiences of LGBT people of color have also been long-standing issues within the UFMCC. And bisexuals and transgendered people have had to work particularly hard to gain their present level of acknowledgment within the denomination. Finally, throughout its history the UFMCC has dealt with homophobia. Less than two years after it was dedicated, the denomination's Los Angeles "mother church" burned to the ground; arson was suspected. As of the writing of Perry's 1990 autobiography, seventeen MCC worship sites had burned; in some cases church members died in the fires.[40] On a more institutional level, the UFMCC has repeatedly been denied membership in the National Council of Churches, and has been denied advancement from observer to full participant status in the World Council of Churches since 1991.

Yet MCC remains the largest and most visible of the LGBT religious movements worldwide. With over forty-three thousand members and close to three hundred congregations in twenty-two countries, the denomination has spread farther and faster than any other LGBT religious movement, but with its newest "mother church" building in West Hollywood and its denominational headquarters located there until 2006, it remains rooted in Los Angeles. It also maintains an active role in social protest, both within Christian circles and beyond them. Perry is known by many LGBT activists for his insistent presence, often in clerical garb, at LGBT rights marches and demonstrations; he was also one of the officiators at the mass same-sex wedding held in Washington, D.C., in 2000 to advocate for same-sex marriage rights. Though Perry retired as moderator of the denomination in 2005, the transition to new leadership seems to have been smooth, boding well for the future of this historic church.

MCC was just the first of the significant religious movements to emerge from within L.A.'s LGBT communities. Hard on its heels was Dignity.[41] Originally founded by Father Patrick Nidorf in San Diego, approximately two and a half hours south of L.A., Dignity soon followed its membership north to the larger city. Nidorf, a psychologist as well as a Catholic priest, had become concerned about the prevalence of shame among the gay and lesbian Catholics who came to him in confession. Dignity's official history quotes him as recalling that "it seemed obvious that the Church wasn't meeting the needs of the gay community."[42] After discussing with fellow priests the idea of a group for gay Catholics, Nidorf began such a group in 1969. He called it Dignity, after the trait that seemed to be lacking in the lives of so many of his gay and lesbian clients.

Nidorf soon began advertising Dignity meetings in the liberal *Los Angeles Free Press.* Because the majority of those responding to his ads lived in the L.A. area, he began alternating the meeting locations between San Diego and L.A. Within several months he had decided to focus the group in Los Angeles, where it met in members' homes. By 1970 Dignity had a rudimentary newsletter, was running ads in the *Advocate* as well as the *Free Press,* and had drafted a statement of purpose and principles. In June of that year, the same month as the inaugural Christopher Street West parade, Nidorf appointed one of the lay members of the group as its general chairman. In September Dignity met for the first time at a Catholic church (St. Brendan Church, in a neighborhood south of Hollywood and west of downtown L.A.).

With the Gay Liberation Front growing energetically and spreading through the nation's cities, with MCC steadily building and the Council on Religion and the Homophile in place in L.A., with the liberal reforms of the

Second Vatican Council fresh in their memories and Father John J. McNeill publishing articles supportive of homosexuals in mainstream Catholic publications, Dignity's members had much to hope for from their church. They began to work for formal recognition. In February 1971, against the advice of Nidorf, Dignity sent a request for recognition to the Los Angeles archbishop. The letter was not well received, and Nidorf was barred from having further contact with the group. While this news was a blow to the group initially, it would prove to be fortuitous in the long run. The most successful pro-LGBT groups in U.S. Catholicism have historically been lay-led, because although ordination can grant significant power, at least locally, it also places one strictly under the control of the church—a control exercised much less stringently over laypeople than over religious. Within its first six months of autonomy Dignity had launched a national newsletter, initiated a speaker series that was opened by noted psychologist and long-time homophile ally Evelyn Hooker, and held its first retreat. Within its first year of autonomy, the L.A. group had a sister chapter in Louisville, Kentucky.

At Dignity's first annual meeting in February 1972, it was reported that the organization had nearly two hundred members, of whom twenty-five were priests. Half of those members were from the greater Los Angeles area; the rest represented twenty states as well as seven countries outside the United States. By the end of the year the organization recognized ten chapters, and by 1977 an entire regional subdivision of Dignity was dedicated to Canadian chapters. This led to the formation of Dignity/Canada/Dignité, and the U.S. organization formally became Dignity/USA. In 1980 Dignity/USA moved its headquarters to Washington, D.C.

Having continued to call publicly for recognition of lesbians and gay men by the Catholic Church, Dignity increasingly ran afoul of church hierarchy. One by one, the religious who worked openly with Dignity were officially silenced—though more continued to appear, and many others worked more quietly behind the scenes. Jesuit John J. McNeill, a theologian and psychiatrist who eventually left the church, was the most prominent of the early silencing cases. The Vatican and the American church also began to issue doctrinal statements on homosexuality; the first was released in 1974 by the National Conference of Catholic Bishops, and the second in 1975 by the Congregation for the Doctrine of the Faith, the doctrinal office of the Vatican.[43] Neither of these statements was in any way positive about homosexuality, although the Catholic Church did differ from most Protestant churches at the time in suggesting that the inclination toward homosexual desire was innate. A decade later, the Vatican released another statement on homosexuality, reiterating its earlier opinion that same-sex sexual acts are intrinsically disordered and prohibiting parishes from providing meeting space for any group whose ideas contradicted church teachings.[44]

Within a month and a half of the statement's publication one Dignity chapter had lost its parish home, and many more were similarly evicted soon thereafter. Dignity persisted, however, meeting in Protestant churches and sometimes even sharing services with chapters of Integrity, the Episcopalian organization for LGBT people and their allies. Like many LGBT religious organizations, Dignity struggled to be inclusive of women through at least its first quarter-century of existence.[45] In its hometown of Los Angeles, Dignity also faces competition for members with the archdiocese's Ministry with Lesbian and Gay Catholics.[46] The national organization remains strong, however, and is an important participant in both national and international movements for LGBT rights.

While the development of Dignity added to the burgeoning diversity of L.A.'s long-established Catholic population and MCC represented yet another twist on the city's history of new Protestant formations, the next religious organization to take shape reflected the radicalism of the times as well as the contemporary interest in new religious movements. An avid proponent of radical feminism who was interested in women's culture, Zsuzsanna ("Z") Budapest felt that the women's movement needed a spiritual base. Unlike liberal feminists who worked to redefine traditional religions in gender-inclusive terms, Budapest was among those interested instead in developing a specifically feminist spirituality. Claiming to have descended from a long, matrilineal lineage of wise women and healers, Z Budapest argued that the most suitable religion for feminists was witchcraft.

Budapest was in good company in drawing on this negative and stereotypical image of women as a model for radical feminism. Arguing that patriarchal cultural systems had created such grotesque images as the witch and the harpy to denigrate women's power, radical feminists delighted in reclaiming and redefining these images.[47] But even before radical feminism took its place on the U.S. stage, witchcraft had already arrived—not in the form of the Salem trials, but in the Neopagan movement that began in the 1960s. This movement initially sprang from two books published in England by occultist Gerald Gardner, who claimed to have been initiated into a coven of "hereditary witches": people who had learned a religion called "witchcraft" or "the old religion" from their parents, and whose families had been covertly practicing that religion since it first went underground during the European witch trials.[48] The religion he described focused on an annual cycle of sacred stories about a goddess and a god that symbolically reflected the seasonal and agricultural changes of northern hemisphere temperate zones. Rituals, held on eight major holidays and each full moon, involved a coven with thirteen members including a high priest and priestess. Following steadily in the twentieth-century western occult tradition, rituals centered around symbolic practices and the use of "energy" to influence the outside world.

Gardner's ideas spread rapidly to the United States, where they fit well with the earth-centered, mystical, and experimental inclinations of the 1960s counterculture. Soon practitioners of witchcraft, or Wicca, appeared and organized across the country. As the movement grew, it sprouted branches almost immediately; one of the major divisions in Wicca, that between Gardner's followers and those of Alex Sanders, appeared almost before the movement left English shores.[49] And though Budapest claimed in her books and classes to be teaching the religion practiced by the women of ancient Europe and handed down to her by her foremothers, her version of Wicca bears close resemblance to the others that appeared around the country in the 1960s and 1970s.

Having decided to introduce modern U.S. feminists to witchcraft, Budapest gathered interested women together, and in 1971 they founded the Susan B. Anthony Coven No. 1 in Venice, a coastal suburb of Los Angeles. Naming their branch of Wicca "Dianic" after the Roman goddess Diana, who lived in the company of women (or, at least, wood nymphs) and was independent from men, Budapest and her co-religionists built their theology on equal parts of nineteenth-century matriarchy theory,[50] Wicca, feminism, and an amalgamation of female sacred figures borrowed from religions around the world. While most branches of Wicca were teaching the importance of balancing the sexes in the coven in order to combine male and female energies for the most effective magical work, Dianic Wicca defined its teachings as "women's mysteries" and refused to teach men or to open its rituals to any male over the age of three until the sexes had achieved equality.[51]

Though Dianic Wicca never sought to restrict itself to participants of a particular sexual orientation, the nature of radical feminism in the early 1970s was such that the new religion drew many lesbian and bisexual women. First of all, it was one of very few religious organizations that wholeheartedly embraced feminism and celebrated love between women. Second, because of its steadfast focus on women and on celebrating women's lives, early Dianic Wicca was especially attractive to those women who, for personal or political reasons (or, in proper feminist form, both), had chosen for the time being to focus their affections and sexual energies on women. Over the years, as feminism has changed and goddess religion has spread into the broader culture,[52] the demographics of the Dianic movement have shifted and lesbians are now less well represented than they once were. The Dianic movement continues, however, with covens across the United States and a small, closely related school in Wisconsin.

Back in the realm of more traditional religions, at the same time that Budapest was founding a coven, a handful of Jewish gay men and lesbians were, somewhat improbably, becoming part of a church.[53] Unwilling to join the Metropolitan Community Church because membership would entail religious conversion, these Jews nevertheless became involved with MCC because it served religious

LGBT people. Some even found the church a relatively comfortable place to worship. Yet when, one Wednesday evening in 1972, the four people attending a church rap group discovered they were all Jewish, they began to discuss the possibility of forming a synagogue. They met with Troy Perry, who encouraged them and offered MCC facilities as meeting and worship space. He also gave them the names of other Jewish participants in MCC, and a May 1972 meeting brought twelve people together to consider the idea of a lesbian and gay temple. Not only did the participants in this meeting agree to start such an organization, but they even named it: the Metropolitan Community Temple. Like the first MCC service, the first MCT Shabbat service on June 9, 1972, was advertised in the *Advocate*. Fifteen people attended. In July, an interfaith service celebrating the birth of the temple featured as one of its speakers a leading local Reform rabbi. Other Reform leaders soon lent their support to the temple, which began holding services on a weekly basis at MCC. The first High Holiday services drew 175 participants, and by early 1973 MCT had drawn up bylaws and elected officers. It had also selected a new name, more distinct from that of MCC: Beth Chayim Chadashim (BCC), the House of New Life.

The same night that BCC formalized its organization, MCC's first church building burned to the ground. The new president of Beth Chayim Chadashim managed to rescue the temple's borrowed Torah scroll from the burning building, but BCC had lost its worship space. A Reform synagogue in West Los Angeles stepped in; BCC members held Friday night services at the Leo Baeck Temple for over a year and dedicated their own Torah scroll there before relocating to MCC's new building in downtown L.A. and eventually buying their own space in the largely Jewish Fairfax district. Meanwhile, in 1973 BCC made the historic move of applying for membership in the Union of American Hebrew Congregations (UAHC), the U.S. organization of Reform synagogues. After some debate, the temple's membership was approved in 1974. UAHC membership brought both advantages and disadvantages for BCC, though from its members' perspectives the former clearly outweighed the latter. On the one hand, UAHC membership gave the temple legitimacy and access to resources it would not otherwise have had; on the other hand, BCC's commitment to Reform Judaism limited the outreach the synagogue could make to LGBT people from Conservative and especially Orthodox backgrounds. MCC had faced a similar dilemma, and in fact an LGBT synagogue founded in New York City less than a year after BCC addressed this challenge as MCC did: by remaining independent rather than affiliating with a denominational organization, and by offering a variety of services tailored to different worship styles.[54] Yet BCC's Reform focus has hardly hurt the synagogue, which continues to thrive and to serve members from across the different branches of Judaism. BCC has also continued to be a leader in Jewish LGBT organizing, as well as in LGBT communities as a whole. It was a participant in the first international conference of lesbian and gay Jewish organizations in 1976 and a founding member in 1980 of the World Congress of Gay and Lesbian Jews, which in 2001 became the World Congress of GLBT Jews. The synagogue has supported LGBT rabbinical students as well as laypeople, and remains a prominent part of L.A.'s LGBT religious scene.

While BCC had the unusual opportunity to join a mainstream religious organization as a group with a special outreach, other LGBT groups have existed as Dignity continues to do: affirming their members' identities as both LGBT and religious, but denied legitimacy by their "parent" religious body. This is true of a number of the groups that arose in the 1970s, 1980s, and 1990s to support LGBT members and former members of conservative Christian denominations; interestingly these groups, which generally do not offer religious services and thus are more like support groups than new religious movements in themselves, are the exception to the pattern of LGBT religious groups being founded in Los Angeles. This may be because L.A. in the 1970s was not exactly a stronghold of conservative Christianity. But one particularly active and early support group did gain its major impetus in L.A. and thus deserves mention here: Affirmation, the organization for LGBT Mormons.

Throughout most of the twentieth century, the Church of Jesus Christ of Latter-day Saints (LDS) has been a socially conservative organization. For this reason alone it is unsurprising that the LDS church teaches that same-sex sexual activity is sinful. However, the unique emphasis in Mormon doctrine on the eternal nature of the family (defined as a married, heterosexual couple and their children) adds force to the rejection of LGBT people by the official mainstream of the church and by many church members. The LDS church teaches that same-sex attraction and cross-gender identification (which the church generally conflates) are not innate, and the church's officially recognized outreach to LGBT people, Evergreen, is an "ex-gay" organization. Though LGBT people have long been an underground presence in Mormon culture,[55] save for a very few instances they have been isolated from each other by the need to stay hidden, by excommunication or voluntary resignation from the church, or by their own efforts to live as monogendered or heterosexual.

This situation began to change in 1977, when one member of a covert group of gay men at Brigham Young University (BYU) became interested in forming a national organization. Matthew Price founded groups in Denver and Dallas in addition to a group in Salt Lake City. He worked with others to write a constitution, and named the new organization "Affirmation: Gay Mormons United." Despite the great creative energy that went into Affirmation, it did not take off immediately. The Denver and Dallas groups soon faded, and the BYU group remained sporadic. In Los Angeles, however, a gay Mormon by the name of Paul Mortensen read an article about Affirmation in the *Advocate,* and decided to start a chapter. The founding of the L.A. chapter in January 1978 was the turning point for Affirmation. As the group's history (written by Mortensen) proclaims: "Although only six people attended the first meeting, the Los Angeles Chapter exploded and soon appeared as the leading chapter for Affirmation. Through its influence, chapters appeared in many cities around the country and, later in the year, a network was established to allow cooperation among the various branches."[56] Even if some authorial braggadocio is at work here, it does appear that L.A. was the first city to provide fertile ground in which the new movement could grow. Affirmation's first pride parade entry was in Los Angeles the following year; a few months later, in September 1979, members took part in the national LGBT protest in Washington, D.C. By December, Affirmation had held its first national conference (also in Los Angeles), and changed its name to Affirmation: Gay and Lesbian Mormons. Paul Mortensen was elected as the first director of the group, and Affirmation members drew up a charter and planned the launch of a national newsletter. Though its base has always remained in the United States, Affirmation has grown to include international chapter membership, including chapters in Hong Kong, South Korea, Australia, Canada, Italy, England, Nigeria, Spain, Mexico, Chile, Argentina, Peru, Uruguay, El Salvador, and Ecuador.

The L.A. chapter of Affirmation has seen shrinking participation in recent years, but it continues to staff the organization's international hot line for LGBT Mormons. Affirmation holds a national conference every year as well as offering occasional regional retreats and more regular chapter meetings in many urban locations. It also remains visible at both pride parades and protest marches. Perhaps most important for many of its members, though, is the staggering array of online resources available through its website, from a brief summary of "lesbian Mormon history" to online discussion groups and bulletin boards, from articles on same-sex parenting and the latest official statements on homosexuality from the LDS church to special pages for youth, women, fathers, families, transgendered people, and allies. The site also links to other LGBT Mormon organizations such as Gamofites (for gay Mormon fathers) and Gay LDS Young Adults.

As if to prove that even among LGBT people religious groups offer a wide spectrum of beliefs and practices, the next LGBT group to be founded in (or, in this case, through the auspices of) Los Angeles has little in common with Affirmation other than that it was founded by gay men. Even more interesting, at this point in the story a groundbreaking leader reappears, returning to the scene a quarter century after he was deposed from his leadership of the Mattachine Society. Ever the organizer, Harry Hay was the driving force behind the Radical Faeries until his death in 2002.[57]

Hay had mostly kept a low profile since the Mattachine mutiny. For nearly two decades he had focused on research, exploring academic resources that furthered his ideas on the innate uniqueness of what he came to call the gay consciousness. He explored gender variance in Native American traditions and in European folk cultures, and spent a great deal of time pondering what such traditions might mean to contemporary gay men and lesbians in the United States. After the Stonewall Riots he and his long-time partner, John Burnside, became involved briefly in the new wave of activism; Hay was even elected the first chair of the Southern California Gay Liberation Front. Several months later, though, the two men moved to San Juan Pueblo in northern New Mexico, and except for an increasing number of published articles, Hay withdrew again from high-profile activism. He continued to develop his ideas about the uniqueness and even the prophetic and salvific nature of gay men, whom he had begun to call "faeries" both as a reclamation of a previously derogatory term and as a reference to the "fairy folk" of Celtic lore.

While Hay and Burnside were living in New Mexico they maintained ties to L.A. and began to develop a close relationship with Don Kilhefner, first director of the L.A. Gay Community Services Center. Kilhefner and Mitch Walker, a fan of Hay's from Berkeley, began working with Hay in earnest to develop a retreat for gay men who were interested in alternative spiritualities. As their work became more intense and their ideas came closer to bearing fruit, Hay and Burnside decided to move back to Los Angeles. Before their move, they joined Kilhefner in a visit to the Sri Ram Ashram outside Benson, Arizona. The ashram had run an ad in the *Advocate* a few months earlier, and Kilhefner hoped that it might be the site they were seeking for their retreat. Though Hay needed some convincing, the three finally agreed to have their retreat at the ashram, and their plans went into motion. Hay and Burnside moved to east Hollywood in July 1979, and soon thereafter a flyer went out "to gay and leftist bookstores, schools, gay community centers, and health food stores."[58] Quoting Hay, New Age leader Mark Satin, and occultist Aleister Crowley,[59] the flyer announced "A Spiritual Conference for Radical Fairies" and declared:

> Many gay brothers are feeling the need to come together . . .
> To share new insights about ourselves;
> To dance in the moonlight;
> To renew our oaths against patriarchy/corporations/racism;
> To hold, protect, nurture, and caress one another;
> To talk about the politics of gay enspiritment/the enspiritment of gay politics;
> To find the healing place inside our hearts;
> To become Inspirer/Listener as we share new breakthroughs in how we perceive gay consciousness;

To soar like an eagle;
To re-discover/re-invent our myths;
To talk about gay living/loving alternatives;
To experience the groundedness of the calamus root;[60]
To share our gay visions;
To sing, sing, sing;
TO EVOKE A GREAT FAIRY CIRCLE[61]

The organizers had hoped to attract 25 participants in order to defray their expenses. They need not have worried, because 225 came to the ashram on Labor Day weekend in 1979. The next year, the Denver Faeries helped to organize the second annual gathering in the Rockies, and over three hundred attended.

Though power plays upended the leadership during the next year and AIDS added a sobering note to Faerie gatherings in the early 1980s, the movement's status as what Stuart Timmons calls a "not-movement" and some Faeries call a "dis-organization"[62] helped it to weather these strains in a very different way from the Mattachine—as did the very different perspectives of radical gay men in the 1980s, compared to homophile activists of the 1950s. Known in his later years as "the Duchess," Hay continued to play a central role in the Faeries until the end of his life.

Though the late Pastor Michael Cole had been known in his earlier years as Honey Carolina on the Long Beach drag circuit, his only link to Harry Hay was that he was the next Angeleno (or rather, L.A. transplant) to start a lasting LGBT religious movement.[63] Born and raised in southern Oregon in the 1940s and 1950s, Cole grew up attending churches in two Pentecostal denominations: the Assemblies of God and Aimee Semple McPherson's International Church of the Foursquare Gospel. Cole recalled knowing at a young age that he was called to the ministry, and that he was gay. As he came of age he turned away from the ministry and the church, moving to San Francisco in 1963 in search of gay community. He remembered with amusement his grandmother's warning to beware of the "Sodomites" in that city—a warning he failed to understand at the time. "I thought they were a religious cult. . . . So I figured I was OK. Later I found out that that was the reason I was going to San Francisco!"[64]

Though he felt distanced from God during this time, Cole nevertheless moved to Los Angeles to attend L.I.F.E. Bible College, the undergraduate institution of the Foursquare church. Having met an attractive man one Saturday night who planned to attend church on Sunday morning, Cole decided to go too—and discovered the Metropolitan Community Church of Los Angeles (MCCLA) during its earliest years. "MCC really saved my life," he told me.[65] Eventually, however, MCC's political stances began to grate on Cole. His main objection was to the use of gender-inclusive language in services, but he was also concerned with the ways in which the centrality of gay culture in MCC services might exclude heterosexuals. Cole's vision of an inclusive church was one in which no one—men, women, gays, or straights—worshipped or met separately from anyone else.

Beginning like many LGBT religious organizations with a small Bible study group in a living room, Christ Chapel outgrew Cole's house within a few weeks of its first meeting in December 1981. Three years later the church moved into its current building in Long Beach, southeast of Los Angeles, and about a decade after its founding, offshoots began to form in other cities. Christ Chapel now has six branches, in Long Beach, North Hollywood, Laguna Beach (at the southern tip of the Los Angeles sprawl), San Diego, Colorado Springs, and Denver. Cole also took credit for training Mark Elias, the pastor who later founded another LGBT-affirming church in the Los Angeles area, Calvary Open Door Worship Center.[66]

The final wave of this fourteen-year surge of large and lasting LGBT religious organizations in L.A. is the Unity Fellowship Church Movement (UFCM), which now has congregations in fourteen cities on the West Coast, on the East Coast, and in Detroit.[67] Unity Fellowship began and continues under the auspices of gospel singer and sometime recording artist Carl Bean. Like the founders of many other LGBT congregations and movements, Bean responded to his belief in divine affirmation of LGBT people by starting a home Bible study group. And as in so many other cases the home Bible study, which began in 1982, quickly became a house church. It outgrew its house and moved into a rented facility, then raised the money to buy its own church. This being Los Angeles, when Unity Fellowship expanded into rented space in 1985 it ended up, like the early MCCLA, in a theater. But there was one key difference: this was the historic Ebony Theater, a landmark for L.A.'s black community. Bean's church, unlike any other LGBT religious organization in Los Angeles at the time, was designed specifically to serve African American LGBT people.

Why a black LGBT church, when by 1985 Los Angeles already had two thriving LGBT Christian organizations, and several MCC congregations had people of color attending in small numbers? Reverend Elder Alfreda Lanoix, senior pastor of Unity Fellowship Church–Los Angeles, explains:

> *MCC is a wonderful organization, but it's not an organization that came from our roots, from our culture, you know. . . . And so that, to me, is the reason why a Unity Fellowship Church had to be created. Because it comes from who we are, our background, our culture, what we believe, how we worship—our emotional relief is done here. Because of the things that we have created for our own community. So MCC could not serve that need. And although it is, like I said, a great organization—but not for black people, honey.*[68]

As had happened so many other times in the brief history of L.A.'s LGBT organizations, the energies of even the most inclusive-minded white organizers went into groups whose focus and location reflected (albeit often unconsciously) white preferences, ideas, and priorities. MCCLA welcomed African Americans but offered no regular Sunday service that looked, sounded, and felt like an African Methodist Episcopal (AME), a black Baptist, or a Church of God in Christ (COGIC) service. Christ Chapel might please some LGBT people from a COGIC background, but could not provide affirmation of African and African American heritage; congregants would have to find that elsewhere. Derided from the pulpit in many historically black churches,[69] LGBT African Americans may have been inhabiting glass closets in their families' churches, but in LGBT churches they often felt (and some continue to feel) like the token minorities. The Unity Fellowship Church Movement offered an answer to that dilemma, and its nationwide success attests to fact that some find this a satisfying resolution.

When it incorporated as a nonprofit in 1985, Unity Fellowship Church also had its eye on another area where people of color were not benefiting equally from services organized mostly by white gay men. AIDS Project Los Angeles, though it tried to reach out to all people with AIDS, was generally not perceived by gay men of color and their allies as adequately serving their populations. Unity Fellowship addressed this need in 1985 by founding the Minority AIDS Project (MAP). This program, which is currently housed across the street from the church in a predominantly black and Latino neighborhood southwest of downtown L.A., claims to be "the first community based HIV/AIDS organization established and managed by people of color in the United States."[70] With close to fifty staff members and more than two hundred volunteers, MAP provides client services and education primarily to Central and South Central Los Angeles communities. It estimates that its clients are 75 percent African American, 21 percent Latina/o, and 4 percent Anglo and Asian.[71] Though the Minority AIDS Project is run separately from the church, the two are closely connected not only through history and geography but also through shared membership and resources.

Conclusion: The Forgotten Hub?

"The popular narrative of the gay and lesbian movement in the United States," asserts Moira Rachel Kenney at the opening of *Mapping Gay L.A.*, "tends to be a tale of two cities, centering on New York and San Francisco."[72] These two cities have prominent and popular books on their gay histories, published in 1994 and 1996, respectively, while L.A.'s history was not published until a decade after San Francisco's.[73] Yet the city has a long history of gay and lesbian culture, and is responsible for the founding of the earliest lasting gay rights organization in the country. Why, then, the neglect? Kenney suggests it is because, despite the existence of West Hollywood, L.A. does not have a "gay enclave" in the same way as the two other cities do. Indeed, given its massive case of urban sprawl (even on empty freeways, it can take as long as two hours to drive from one end of the greater Los Angeles metropolitan area to the other), L.A. has relatively few enclaves of any sort. Kenney also suggests that because LGBT people are so spread out in the city, activism has taken different, less high-profile forms. No Stonewall Riots here, just well-behaved protesters outside the Black Cat. No founding of the Gay Liberation Front, though L.A. was among the earliest cities to have a chapter of that organization—instead, the founding of the Metropolitan Community Churches, the world's first LGBT synagogue, Dignity, two Neopagan groups for lesbians and gay men, a church movement for LGBT conservative Christians, and another for African American LGBT people.

Is L.A. the forgotten hub of LGBT movements because, despite the importance of secular LGBT activism in the city, one of its main claims to fame is *religious* queer activism? Of all the religious developments discussed above, only MCC is mentioned in most LGBT history books, and it usually warrants no more than a sentence or two (though Faderman and Timmons's *Gay L.A.* is a welcome exception to that rule). With religion having been "the enemy" for so much of the twentieth century, but especially during the period after the APA's demedicalization of homosexuality in 1974, many LGBT activists and historians are uninterested in or even hostile toward religious groups. The time has come to take the "opium of the people" more seriously.

What made L.A. the largest center of LGBT religious movement building? This is an intriguing question, and one to which I can only offer speculative answers. Kenney's argument about L.A.'s lack of enclaves may be one clue: with many LGBT Angelenos living outside of West Hollywood, they may have needed a greater number of organizational spaces in which to gather and affirm their identities. This explanation does not account for the number of such spaces that were religious, though, nor does it take into account that West Hollywood is a recognizably gay space despite its ongoing diversity, or that many LGBT people in New York and San Francisco (especially women, people of color, and working-class people) live outside the Village (or Chelsea) and the Castro.

Faderman and Timmons suggest that the city's unconventional nature and its large LGBT population are responsible for many of its LGBT innovations. "Its location at the edge of the continent," they observe, "far from 'back home,' has sharpened its cutting edge and sanctioned experimentation such as would have been impossible elsewhere."[74] Yet they also note that L.A. is a city of power politics and is less prone to radical activism than a city like New York. Perhaps this too is a factor in the city's LGBT religious growth. Though religion generally does not drive power politics in the way that money does, its general ethos of respectability (except, perhaps, in the case of Dianic Wicca and the Radical Faeries) meshes nicely with L.A.'s lesbian and gay political groups like MECLA, the wealthy and influential Municipal Elections Committee of Los Angeles. Then again, perhaps the "City of Angels" was simply an irresistible location for LGBT religious organizing.

Another possibility is that the clue lies not in L.A.'s LGBT history but in its religious history. Early LGBT religious activism did not take place in L.A.; it took place first in Atlanta, during a period when L.A. was not in the throes of great religious ferment, and then in San Francisco, driven by a radical young pastor. L.A.'s LGBT religious activism began in earnest in 1968, when the city was in the midst of a period of great religious creativity. It was certainly not the only city to experience such creativity; indeed, L.A. has no district as historic in this respect as San Francisco's Haight-Ashbury. However, San Francisco had the radical left to serve its LGBT populations, in greater numbers and with greater organization than its neighbor to the south. And the radical left—Harry Hay and some members of the Faeries excepted—does not generally pay religion much heed. Furthermore, L.A. has a long and impressive history of religious revival, innovation, and change, rivaled in many ways only by upstate New York, the "burned-over district" of the early-nineteenth-century revivals. Perhaps it is fitting that this home of so many new religious movements should host yet another set of them, with yet another new, countercultural twist. California may indeed be home to the fruits and the nuts, but in L.A. more than anywhere else they seem to have come in the same package.

3 *Queering the Spiritual Marketplace*

The Reverend Susan Russell is a priest at All Saints Episcopal Church in Pasadena, just north of Los Angeles. Her main assignment there is to direct a project called Beyond Inclusion, a nationwide effort to convince the Episcopal Church to adopt a formal liturgy for blessing same-sex couples. The project is a ministry of All Saints, a large congregation long known for its social justice activism. Support for LGBT Episcopalians in the Los Angeles area, however, goes far beyond this one church. The Episcopal Diocese of Los Angeles, represented by the bishop himself, forms a contingent in the Los Angeles Pride Parade each June. "It's amazing how . . . healing that is, how sometimes unexpected it is," Russell reflects. "You know, between the Dykes on Bikes and the boom bar floats, and here comes 'The Episcopal Church Welcomes You.'" "And our bishop is there with us. . . . Big guy in purple, waving to the crowd."[1]

The religious landscape of queer Los Angeles has undergone massive change since the mid-1980s, when, as the Reverend Daniel Smith of West Hollywood Presbyterian Church recalls, "our church, MCC Los Angeles, and the one gay temple in the area, Beth Chayim Chadashim, . . . were the three primary spiritual care providers of the whole [LGBT] community."[2] When I began the research for this book in 2001, there were thirty-one listings under the heading "Religious and Spiritual Organizations" in the *Southern California Gay and Lesbian Community Yellow Pages.* All of them were in the greater Los Angeles area. Nine of these groups had ads in addition to their listings, and the Episcopal

Church had a full-page ad listing forty welcoming congregations within the Los Angeles diocese. Most of the listings (twenty-two) as well as the ads (seven) were identifiably Christian; they included LGBT-specific organizations such as Metropolitan Community Churches, Christ Chapel congregations, Evangelicals Concerned, and AXIOS, an organization for Orthodox Christian gays and lesbians. Also included were welcoming congregations of mainstream Christian denominations such as the United Church of Christ, the Presbyterian Church–USA, the Disciples of Christ, the Evangelical Lutheran Church in America, and of course the Episcopal Church. A 4½-inch by 2-inch spread at the top of one page asked, "Roman Catholic?" and advertised the Los Angeles archdiocese's Ministry with Lesbian and Gay Catholics, an officially sponsored ministry that emphasizes balancing Catholic doctrine with personal conscience. The Los Angeles chapter of Dignity was also represented. Three synagogues appeared in the listings, along with a Unitarian Universalist church, an "Emotional and Spiritual Healing Center," Gay and Lesbian Atheists and Humanists, and a chapter of the AIDS support organization Shanti. No ex-gay or otherwise non-affirming organizations were included in either the listings or the ads.[3]

The *Gay and Lesbian Community Yellow Pages* serves LGBT people of all genders, so there is no way of knowing whom exactly the organizations placing these ads and listings expect to attract or whom they actually draw. Yet a brief perusal of the June 2001 issue of Los Angeles' *Lesbian News* reveals similar results. Next to an ad for "go-go goddesses," for instance, and just inside the front page of the magazine, is a bold statement: "Even Jesus listened to Madonna (and no, not that Madonna)." This ad for Open Door Ministries, an Evangelical LGBT church southeast of Los Angeles, continues: "'There is no condemnation for those who are in Christ Jesus' . . . even if you're Gay or Lesbian!"[4] A few pages later, across from a story about Los Angeles' WNBA team, a half-page ad invites readers to "Kick-off Pride Weekend at BCC—The World's First LGBT Synagogue."[5] Also included is a Dignity ad that subtly challenges readers not to patronize the Ministry with Lesbian and Gay Catholics,[6] and the calendar lists over forty religion-related entries for the greater Los Angeles area alone—some of which specifically target women. Even at the Los Angeles Pride Festival in 2001, on the day of the women-focused Dyke March, I found booths representing several different religious organizations and was approached by members of a Buddhist movement known as Soka Gakkai, who asked whether I was interested in chanting "Nam-myoho-renge-kyo" for world peace. Apparently religion (or, as many Angelenos would say, "spirituality") has found a significant place within the LGBT communities of greater Los Angeles.

The twenty-one organizations that played, or recently had played, a role in the religious and spiritual lives of participants in this study are a well-rounded sample of those advertising in the community yellow pages and in the *Lesbian*

News—with a few surprises thrown in for good measure. In general terms, they fall into two religious categories, traditional and nontraditional, and two congregational categories, LGBT-focused and mixed (that is, welcoming to LGBT people but not directed primarily at them), resulting in four main types of congregation: LGBT-focused traditional religious groups; mixed traditional religious groups; mixed nontraditional groups; and LGBT-focused nontraditional groups. The pages that follow describe in some depth these four types and the groups that fall within them, offering a snapshot of the broad, dynamic patterns that make up the queer spiritual marketplace of Los Angeles.

LGBT-Focused Traditional Religious Groups

As chapter 2 made clear, Los Angeles is a prime location for LGBT-focused traditional religious groups. Heading most lists of religious organizations catering to LGBT communities is the Metropolitan Community Church (MCC), the only Christian denomination with a predominantly LGBT membership. Indeed, two prominent MCC congregations are among those utilized by participants in this study. Yet, before MCC even began, another church in the increasingly gay neighborhood of West Hollywood had already opened its doors to gay men: the West Hollywood Presbyterian Church (WHPC). Starting in 1964, claims longtime WHPC pastor Daniel Smith, "we had the first gay rap support group in Los Angeles here in the church. It was a remarkable place because it was one of the few places where gay men had ever met in the daytime, lights-on, face-to-face environment without the threat of the police."[7] Smith's predecessor, who pastored the church during this period, soon added an afternoon worship service specifically for LGBT people, and Smith estimates that by 1975 the congregation comprised predominantly gay men.

West Hollywood Presbyterian Church

Like many traditional religious organizations serving LGBT people, WHPC was painfully aware that its congregation was, as Daniel Smith related, made up of gay men—*not* gay men and lesbians, at least not in relatively equal proportions. When Smith became pastor in 1984, the church was approximately 80 percent male; it was also, despite the ethnic diversity of the surrounding community, almost entirely white. Both of these facts have been cause for concern in the congregation over the past two decades. Smith implemented an "education and transformation program"[8] on cultural diversity and white racism in gay communities, and the church worked especially hard on outreach to gay and lesbian communities of color; he reported in 2003 that his congregation was currently 25 to 30 percent Latino and African American. The church also implemented inclusive language throughout its services, attempted to incorporate feminist ideas into its ritual planning, and hired women as associate pastors and interns whenever funding was available. Yet, Smith says, although such measures are "a great plus, I don't think that's been the draw"[9] for women to join the congregation. Instead, he believes that the reason his congregation has approached gender parity in the early twenty-first century has to do with changes in the broader LGBT community: an increasing trust between lesbian and gay male communities, and the phenomenon sometimes referred to as the "lesbian baby boom." "We had done everything under the sun to try to attract women," he recalls. "But it was the children that brought about that transformation."[10]

Though its parent denomination continues to struggle mightily with even the question of ordaining lesbians and gay men,[11] West Hollywood Presbyterian has a long history of working quite forthrightly for the equal inclusion of LGBT people within the church. Daniel Smith was openly gay when he was hired by WHPC, and the church claims that he is still "the only openly Gay minister serving a congregation in the Presbyterian Church."[12] West Hollywood Presbyterian is also home to the Lazarus Project, launched by prominent gay Christian author Chris Glaser to work for LGBT rights in Christianity. From 1988 to 1991, Smith served on the national committee convened by the Presbyterian Church (USA) to study human sexuality. After the committee's report was shelved by the church leadership, Smith decided to focus his efforts more locally.

Today, WHPC stands out prominently as an openly accepting congregation. Approaching the church's small campus on Sunset Boulevard, one of the main streets through West Hollywood, one sees a large billboard whose left half sports a drawing of a green freeway sign. On the sign are a cross, a rainbow flag, a red AIDS ribbon, and the words "THIS EXIT," with a white arrow pointing down at the unassuming white building below. The top of the sign bears the church's name, and across the right half is emblazoned, in brilliant pink, the words "Wildly Inclusive!" Should anyone miss the billboard, rainbow banners frame the church's name on the side of the building.

Most of those attracted to WHPC today, says Smith, are drawn to its progressive values, its inclusive liturgy, and its outreach ministries for LGBT justice, AIDS support, interfaith work (its work in this area includes sharing its worship space with Congregation Kol Ami, an LGBT-affirming Reform synagogue), food programs for the homeless, and social justice advocacy. Some members of the congregation are from Presbyterian backgrounds, but "there's very little denominational identity anymore."[13] The membership of approximately seventy-five is generally upper middle class and progressive; few people now come to this church who are struggling with tensions between their Christian identity and homosexuality. "The younger generation that's coming," Smith reflects, "just doesn't even have the biblical hang-ups . . . it's become pretty much a non-issue."

St. Thomas the Apostle

A similar pattern holds for the other church in this study that, while belonging to a larger denomination that does not specifically serve LGBT people, has become an LGBT church by default. St. Thomas the Apostle Episcopal Church, named after the apostle who doubted Jesus because the bishop of Los Angeles "doubted" its viability when the church was first proposed in 1913,[14] is located at the edge of West Hollywood, in a heavily gay male area of Los Angeles. St. Thomas developed its gay outreach somewhat later than West Hollywood Presbyterian; the parish history recounts that in a 1985 survey of parishioners' priorities for the church, "'address[ing] the needs of the Gay Community in Hollywood' came in dead last (52nd)."[15] Yet, that history adds, with the hiring of a new rector the following year came "new openness especially to the gay community"[16] and (perhaps not coincidentally) significant parish growth. Since that time, the church has come increasingly to reflect its gay male constituency; like other churches serving this community over the past twenty years, this has especially meant dealing with the AIDS crisis.

St. Thomas has had several assistant priests who were gay; in 1989 one of them, Robert Kettelhack, died of AIDS. Shortly thereafter, a chapel adjoining the main sanctuary was designated as the AIDS memorial chapel for the entire Episcopal Diocese of Los Angeles. With a painting of Father Damien, the priest who worked at the Molokai leper colony, presiding over the small room, the chapel held an altar and "a specially-designed AIDS memorial book listing persons who have succumbed to the disease."[17] Though the diocesan AIDS memorial has since been moved to a more central location within the diocese, the chapel at St. Thomas continued in 2002 to hold a copy of the AIDS memorial book, which at the time contained over twelve thousand names, and an AIDS memorial service took place every Thursday.[18] Like West Hollywood Presbyterian, St. Thomas has seen an influx of children in recent years; the Sunday school reopened in 1994. How many are the children of same-sex couples is not clear but it is possible that a number of them are, as the current rector has expressed a concern with making the church more welcoming to heterosexuals (implying that most of his congregation is not heterosexual).

Though the gay culture of St. Thomas is far more subtle than that of the billboard-toting West Hollywood Presbyterian, it is nevertheless quite discernible—even aside from the prominent presence of the AIDS memorial. One clear example is that the church hired an openly gay rector at the end of 2001. When I spoke with him just a few months later, Father Ian Davies related a rather remarkable story about his job interview. The bishop, he recalled, "was very affirming and in fact sat me down and said, 'We'll talk about you in a moment, Father, but tell me about Paul first, your partner, and how I can make him feel part of the family.'"[19] This was no empty promise, either; Father Davies and his partner are British, and the diocese had to arrange visas for both men in the absence of domestic partner immigration rights.

When I visited St. Thomas Episcopal in March 2002, I was struck by the number of single men and male couples present. One man jokingly asked Father Davies after the service to tell "that blond who was sitting next to me to wear loose clothing—he's so distracting!" Though the services themselves, especially the late morning service, are quite High Church and formal, occasional subtle references to the gay male culture of the church snuck in nonetheless. In the midst of his sermon, for instance, Father Davies related a story from a novel. Mentioning that a handsome man was involved in the story, he joked that he knew this aspect of the sermon "would bring smiles to at least a few of the faces out there." The chuckling of male voices around me confirmed that at least some in the congregation did not believe Father Davies's comment referred to heterosexual women.

There appeared to be few women at the services I attended, and indeed, Father Davies noted in an interview that the congregation was predominantly male and that he wanted to bring more women into the congregation and to introduce a women's ministry.[20] Two and a half years later, he told me that St. Thomas had added a woman to its pastoral staff.[21]

MCC Los Angeles

Gender dynamics have become an issue in an entirely different way in the oldest LGBT-focused congregation in the Los Angeles area, the Metropolitan Community Church of Los Angeles (MCCLA). This congregation, known also as the "mother church" or founding church of the forty-three-thousand-member Universal Fellowship of Metropolitan Community Churches, underwent a change of leadership in 2000 when the Reverend Elder Nancy Wilson, who had served as the church's senior pastor since 1986, left to serve a congregation in Sarasota, Florida. An MCCLA associate pastor, Reverend Lori, recalls that the congregation averaged at least 50 percent women and sometimes even more during Wilson's tenure. Since her departure, however, although the rest of the (predominantly female) pastoral staff has not changed, both the interim senior pastor and the permanent senior pastor who was installed in 2002 have been male. Reverend Lori sees this as appropriate: "After Nancy Wilson being here for fifteen years, I think it's probably necessary for a man to lead right now. And we are in the middle of Boystown. You know, this is not really a lesbian neighborhood."[22] With this change in leadership, though, came a shift in the gender balance of the congregation. Many women, Reverend Lori says, left the church following Wilson's departure, while more men have been joining recently.

As the oldest extant LGBT-specific religious organization in Los Angeles, and as the mother church of a small but international denomination, MCCLA is well known in many Los Angeles LGBT communities. Since its move to the heart of West Hollywood in the late 1990s, the church is also prominently located in the largely white and male "gay neighborhood" of Los Angeles. From the vantage point of the coffeehouse across the street from the church one can simultaneously watch muscled and well-dressed gay men—clearly out to be seen—strolling down the sidewalk with their dogs, see people arriving for church, and scan the goods displayed in the window of MCCLA's immediate neighbor, a leather/fetish supply store called 665: One Number Short of Hell. Incongruous though this may seem, these institutions (not to mention the gym down the block) are an integral part of gay life in West Hollywood. At one of my visits to MCCLA, I encountered a special "leathers and feathers" service designed by the new senior pastor to reach out to the leather and drag (queen) communities, whose members might feel less than welcome at a more conventional church—even one with a mission to serve LGBT communities.

MCCLA is known for its long history of activism. Its founder and first pastor, Troy Perry, has been involved in gay rights protests nearly since the church's beginning in 1968. Under Wilson's leadership that legacy continued. Reverend Lori described the church's values as "diversity . . . socioeconomic breadth . . . space for the penniless and the homeless . . . and space for the millionaire. And racial acceptance and breadth of rainbow peoples."[23] Though she felt that the move to the fairly well-off and white city of West Hollywood made it difficult for the church to continue to act upon such values, she also noted that the new senior pastor came to the church with a well-established record of outreach and with plans for implementing such programs in West Hollywood. "Usually," she added, "our church does its best outreach by controversy. . . . I think this church leads by doing."[24]

Though MCCLA, and subsequently the denominational body itself, was founded by an evangelical Protestant, the West Hollywood church now espouses a broad and fairly liberal theology and serves members from a wide variety of Christian backgrounds. In 2002 it offered three services each Sunday to accommodate this diversity: a more formal, "liturgical" service at 9:00 AM, alternating "traditional" (i.e., mainline Protestant) and "contemporary" (i.e., evangelical) services at 11:00 AM, and a Spanish-language service described as "contemporary/Catholic" at 1:00 PM. Though the church still speaks of healing wounds and still distributes pamphlets countering homophobic interpretations of biblical texts,[25] there is far less emphasis than there once was—and still is at more theologically conservative LGBT churches—on countering Christian homophobia, and far more emphasis on the predictable aspects of the life of a church. Young adult meetings, potlucks, weekly Bible study, and a bereavement group dominated the weekly schedule each time I visited this congregation.

Glory Tabernacle MCC

At the MCC congregation in Long Beach, southeast of Los Angeles, the picture is quite different from that at MCCLA. Like several other California MCCs, Glory Tabernacle Metropolitan Community Church has a long history within the denomination; it was founded in 1972, just four years after MCCLA. The Long Beach congregation is best known, however, as the leader of the charismatic movement within the denomination, and as a result both of this fact and of its location, it attracts a very different crowd from that found at the church in West Hollywood. Every January, Glory Tabernacle hosts the Charismatic Conference, which draws both national and international participants from within and beyond the denomination. The church's commitment to charismatic forms of worship, moreover, is year-round. Much of the church's literature contains a section on "celebratory worship" that lists common worship practices at Glory Tabernacle, such as standing, clapping, dancing, lifting hands, and speaking in tongues, with accompanying biblical references offering evidence that these practices are legitimate forms of worship.[26]

In keeping with its charismatic tenor, Glory Tabernacle takes evangelism very seriously. As the UFMCC as a whole considers itself to have a special calling to serve LGBT Christians, so Glory Tabernacle sees itself as having a conservative, evangelical version of that call: to spread the teachings of Christianity to all gay men, lesbians, bisexuals, and transgendered people. While many MCC congregations focus on outreach to LGBT people who were raised Christian but left the church because of rejection, Glory Tabernacle goes farther, seeking to reach all LGBT people with the teachings of Christianity and specifically of MCC. "The Gospel in every nation, the Glory in all the earth," declares the church's internet home page.[27]

Differences in staff and theology make MCCLA and Glory Tabernacle very distinct churches, despite their shared denominational membership and similar roots. Glory Tabernacle, says senior pastor Sandra Turnbull, "tend[s] to attract people that are kind of hidden within their particular families and congregations. . . . [W]e do have people here that are just coming out."[28] What such people find most striking about Glory Tabernacle, she says, is its similarity to their own churches—perhaps "a mainline church, or their family's church, or . . . a Vineyard Church, or a Calvary Chapel, maybe a nondenominational church"—but with one key difference: Glory Tabernacle is "filled with gay and lesbian, bisexual, transgender people and their friends and families, daughters and sons, and everybody else. So it really is mind-blowing"[29] for new visitors. Serving congregants who are more likely to be from theologically conservative backgrounds than those at MCCLA, St. Thomas, or West Hollywood Presbyterian, Glory Tabernacle is still keenly aware of the struggles that may be involved in integrating Christian belief and practice with a nondominant sexual or gender identity. The church offers a quarterly class on the Bible and homosexuality, as well as structured "life-cell group" communities to foster interpersonal relationships among newer and more established congregants.

True to the pattern evident in the other churches discussed so far, Glory Tabernacle's female leadership has led to a strong female presence in the congregation. Reverend Turnbull estimates that women constitute 70 percent of the congregation, which has a total attendance of between a hundred and two hundred people at its two services each Sunday. She attributes this gender disparity not only to her own presence as a female senior pastor, but to the fact that the church has more than a twenty-year history of female leadership.[30] The congregation is also quite young, ranging generally from twenty to forty years of age, with an average age of around thirty.[31] As in most MCC churches the congregation is also primarily white; approximately 15 percent of those present when I attended were people of color.

Christ Chapel of Long Beach

Just a few blocks from Glory Tabernacle, equally theologically conservative and equally inclusive of LGBT people, stands a church that is otherwise quite different from the Long Beach MCC congregation. Decorated almost entirely in pink, it was pastored during the time of this study by the late Reverend Michael Cole, a man with the face of actor Wilford Brimley, the voice and rhetoric of a fire-and-brimstone preacher, and a previous career as Honey Carolina on the Long Beach drag circuit. Like its pastor, Christ Chapel of Long Beach was straightforward with few frills: it had no website at the time, did little advertising, and focused instead on serving its congregation and the many people in the Long Beach area who benefit from the church's AIDS food bank. Despite his low profile, however, Cole was an important figure in the queer religious landscape of Los Angeles because his church had spun off six other congregations—four of them in Southern California—in its quarter century of existence.

As was discussed in chapter 2, Christ Chapel is in essence an offshoot of MCC. Cole began attending MCCLA in 1970, while the church was still meeting in the Encore Theater, but within about a decade he became distressed by a number of newer developments. One of these was inclusive language, which grated against his Foursquare Gospel church upbringing; another was the focus on gay culture within MCC services, which he feared might work to exclude heterosexuals who wished to join. In 1981, Cole held a Bible study that steadily grew into a church of its own—Christ Chapel. In the early 2000s, the church attracted roughly equal proportions of men and women, despite its all-male leadership and Cole's aversion to inclusive language. Like Glory Tabernacle, Christ Chapel drew new congregants who came from conservative backgrounds and are struggling with their identities. "I can sit here on a Sunday morning," Cole said, "look out over the congregation, and I'll see a few new people. And I'll see some poor little guy there . . . or a little girl, just the tears running down their face, and they cry through the whole service. I can almost guarantee you they come from a fundamentalist church." He continued: "I have to say that through the media, through documentaries, through teaching, I see a lot more healthier young gays and lesbians than I've ever seen before."[32] The church drew a small number of ethnic minorities and a small number of heterosexuals, all of whom Pastor Cole tried to encourage to feel welcome and included. Though the church's charismatic leanings were downplayed far more than those of nearby Glory Tabernacle, there was little question about Cole's religious roots when he hit his stride in a sermon; Christ Chapel is clearly another of Long Beach's queer, conservative churches.

Beth Chayim Chadashim

Two years after Michael Cole discovered MCC, that fledgling denomination saw a striking development: the founding of MCC's first temple, which became Congregation Beth Chayim Chadashim (BCC).[33] In 1994, BCC hired its first openly lesbian rabbi, Lisa Edwards. Rabbi Lisa, as she is known, still serves the congregation, and together with the temple's lay leadership she offers a packed schedule of events. In addition to Friday night Shabbat services and holiday celebrations, BCC offers a monthly "traditional egalitarian minyan" (traditional prayer services open to both men and women), a monthly children's Shabbat, "Queer Talmud" classes, weekly Torah and Bible study, frequent visiting speakers, and a variety of social events. The temple uses a feminist siddur, or prayer book, and holds a special Shabbat service for Pride Weekend ("BCC's other High Holy Day,")[34] in June.

Like MCCLA, BCC draws participants from a wide variety of backgrounds, and has become somewhat ritually creative as a result. Though the synagogue belongs to an established branch of Judaism and therefore has fairly standardized doctrines and practices, its focus on feminism and its predominantly LGBT congregation make it markedly different from many Reform congregations. Furthermore, Rabbi Edwards feels that the presence of people from Conservative and Orthodox backgrounds at BCC "calls for lots of conversation and lots of openness." She describes this as a challenging and simultaneously exciting aspect of her work, and adds, "I always laugh when Reform Jews come [to BCC] for the first time and say, 'That service seemed more traditional than I'm used to,' and then a traditional Jew will come for the first time and say, 'It's not as traditional as I'm used to.'"[35] To further complicate matters, BCC also has a number of members who are converts, or what Rabbi Edwards calls "Jews by choice." All of this diversity in background is one of the reasons for the temple's wide range of activities.

With both the rabbi and the cantor being women, and with the importance of feminist values in the congregation, it is perhaps unsurprising that roughly half of BCC's more than 250 members are women. Like West Hollywood Presbyterian Church's Daniel Smith, Rabbi Edwards has noted an increase in the number of children in her congregation in recent years—and she remarks with evident delight that several children have already grown up and become bat or bar mitzvah in the congregation. Weddings, too, are on the rise, perhaps in response to the growth since the mid-1990s of the same-sex marriage movement. At the same time, though some people still seek out BCC in the midst of a struggle to reconcile being LGBT with being Jewish, Rabbi Edwards sees far fewer such cases than she once did. It is hard to say how many of these people never make it to BCC because the synagogue's liberal religious affiliation keeps them away, but given the efforts made to accommodate those from more traditional backgrounds, it seems likely that this reflects a real drop in people struggling with coming out within Judaism—at least in Los Angeles.

Affirmation: Gay and Lesbian Mormons

Somewhat surprisingly—especially given the number of people in crisis who still arrive on the steps of theologically conservative Glory Tabernacle—among Mormon youth in L.A. there also seems to be a decline in crises related to sexual or gender identity, if the perceptions of the leaders of Affirmation's Los Angeles chapter are correct. Affirmation differs from the other explicitly religious organizations discussed in this chapter in that it does not hold services. In fact, some of the people it serves, including one of the L.A. chapter leaders, no longer identify as religious at all. Jacki Riedeman, another chapter leader, explained this to me. "[W]hen you're Mormon it's not so much just a religion. It really is a cultural identity. . . . We have our own vocabulary, basically. We have our own way of looking at things. And so you can't give up all that along with the religion."[36]

There are currently several options for someone coming out as LGBT within the Church of Jesus Christ of Latter-day Saints, or LDS church.[37] One can stay tightly closeted and remain within one's local ward (congregation); one can leave one's local ward, come out quietly in secular settings, but keep quiet about one's identity in Mormon circles and remain on the rolls of the LDS church; one can join Evergreen, the Mormon ex-gay organization; or one can choose to leave the church and ask to have one's name removed from the rolls. Those who come out publicly, or are outed by others, face an often painful process of excommunication. In tight-knit Mormon communities, this can mean an almost complete loss of social networks and cultural ties, often rejection by one's family, and even loss of one's job. The Reorganized LDS Church (now called the Community of Christ) is increasingly open to gay men and lesbians, and allows the ordination of women; thus, it may be on its way to becoming a significant resource for LGBT Mormons and their families. A smaller group, LDS Reconciliation, also offers a more religious approach to LGBT Mormon life. And, in the Los Angeles area, an LDS ward hosted a gay and lesbian outreach group from 1993 through 1998. "The church [headquarters in Salt Lake City] canceled that meeting," Ben Jarvis recalls sadly, "in preparation for the Prop 22 campaign."[38] Since 1977, however, Affirmation has been supporting LGBT Mormons (cultural or religious) in a nonliturgical context.[39]

Affirmation chapters are relatively autonomous, and therefore tend to focus on different activities depending on the needs of their members. In the Los Angeles chapter there once were regular meetings with invited speakers and packed audiences. Since the mid-1990s, however, attendance at L.A. chapter meetings has dropped steadily. The group now holds a monthly dinner in the Santa Clarita Valley north of Los Angeles, where its current leaders reside, and hosts an annual pool party. The dinners are casual social affairs at local restaurants and draw a small handful of people—perhaps unsurprisingly, given the wide geographic area the chapter covers, the scheduling of the dinners on weeknights, the ubiquity of snarled commute traffic in the greater L.A. area, and the inadequacy of public transit between L.A.'s outlying areas. The pool party, on the other hand, is the chapter's most popular event, drawing thirty to forty people each year. Traditional Mormon recipes and songs are an important aspect of the party for many.

Affirmation seems to be a predominantly male organization. Jacki Riedeman and Tere La Giusa, a couple who are part of the L.A. chapter leadership, recall attending their first annual conference with Affirmation in 1992. Despite the conference location in Santa Cruz, a city popular with lesbians, they counted only six other women among the roughly two hundred attendees. The peak of women's attendance, they say, was the Seattle conference in 1995, which took place when women served on the national board of directors. That year, they estimate that forty women attended. A similar scarcity holds for bisexual and transgendered members of Affirmation, although in 2003 one of the national directors was a transgendered woman. Like many LGBT organizations, both religious and secular, Affirmation seems to have a primarily gay male culture that is struggling to reach out to lesbians, bisexuals, and transgendered people. Furthermore, Riedeman and La Giusa believe that women who leave the LDS church are less interested in Affirmation because they find both the sexual politics and the gender politics of the church offensive. "'cause, you know," says

Riedeman, "if it says Mormonism and it's got men in it, then definitely men are going to be running it. And that's what they [former LDS women] think, be that true or not. And so I think that they just throw everything out, and say, 'I'm not dealing with that.'"[40]

The leaders of the L.A. chapter hypothesize that much of Affirmation's former role as a support group for LGBT Mormons has been taken over by the organization's extensive and detailed website.[41] This site, accessible worldwide to anyone with a computer and internet capability, offers personal messages from the national leaders, access to local chapters, history, membership information, e-lists, online chat forums, news bulletins, and a large online library of fully downloadable reading materials on LGBT (mostly gay and lesbian) issues in the LDS church. There is also a long-standing helpline, staffed by two of the current L.A. leaders, that continues to receive phone calls regularly from LGBT Mormons who are in the process of coming out. Affirmation's annual weekend-long national conference remains popular as well, but the local leaders in L.A. believe that the organization is unlikely to remain intact for another quarter century.

Unity Fellowship Church—Los Angeles

Seeking directions to the Unity Fellowship Church of Los Angeles in 2002, I pointed my browser to the church movement's website, and was startled to see an error message pop up.[42] Inspecting the small window that had opened on my screen, I read: "WARNING: God is love and love is for everyone!" I had to click on a button labeled "OK" before I could enter the site itself. This, in a nutshell, is the ethos of the Unity Fellowship Church Movement (UFCM). UFCM's brief official history states that its founder, gospel singer Carl Bean, came to his ministry through "experiences, visions, and years of study which compelled him to seek spiritual truths, both liberating and inclusive of all. This was what was constantly revealed to him: 'Nothing compare[s] with, equals, or surpasses Love. For God is Love and Love has no respect of person.'"[43]

This message of unconditional love and acceptance, combined with the emphasis on affirming the African heritage of most congregants, is a powerful draw for some LGBT African Americans. Larger MCC churches, like MCCLA, are sharply aware of the cultural differences between their congregants, and they make great efforts to address those differences by offering a variety of worship styles in their Sunday services. Yet only rarely do MCC services have the feel of services in historically black denominations. I have heard white MCC members suggest that their evangelical "contemporary services" or "praise services" ought to be familiar and comfortable to those from traditional black churches, yet white evangelical church culture is not the same as that found in the historical black denominations. People may shout in both services, but the music is often different, the social norms for worship vary, and black lives and cultures are rarely if ever addressed from the white evangelical pulpit. Furthermore, people of color have often faced racism and ethnocentrism within LGBT communities, and there is no reason to expect LGBT religious organizations to be different from other community institutions in this respect. For the same reasons that black Methodists separated from white Methodists in the eighteenth century (thus creating the African Methodist Episcopal (AME) Church), for the same reasons that congregations like MCCLA and Beth Chayim Chadashim were founded, the Unity Fellowship Church has grown and thrived in its service to a community insufficiently served by other religious organizations.

Carl Bean now serves as archbishop of the Unity Fellowship Church Movement, which in 2008 had fourteen congregations in eight states and the District of Columbia. He spends half of the year in Los Angeles and the other half as a circuit preacher, visiting every one of the movement's congregations. While the L.A. church is firmly Afrocentric and hosts worship services that feel very much like those at a typical AME church, Bean's theology borders at times on the metaphysical and is clearly universalist. The L.A. church's home page stresses that the UFCM "is rooted in spirituality and not in religion," and adds that "whether your background is Baptist, COGIC, Apostolic, Catholic, AME, Buddhist, Agnostic, Atheist, etc., you are welcome!"[44] A church pamphlet describing "What We Believe" declares in capital letters, "God is greater than any religion, denomination, or school of thought," and "Enlightenment and revelation are continuous and did not stop with the Bible writers."[45] These assertions apparently do not fall on deaf ears: though the majority of the congregation is Christian, assistant pastor Gerald Green notes that some who have attended the church hail from backgrounds in Religious Science, agnosticism, and even Islam and Hinduism.[46]

In addition to religious services, social services are high on the agenda of this five-hundred-member church. Its Minority AIDS Project began, like the church itself, in 1985, and has since then provided AIDS education, counseling, and support services for communities of color that have often been underserved by other AIDS organizations. The church houses an alternative high school for LGBT students within the Los Angeles school district, as well as a youth group, an adult Sunday school, and a special outreach for women called Say, Sistah! The Reverend Elder Alfreda Lanoix spoke passionately and at some length about the need for the latter program:

> *Women of color, we're number one in breast cancer, we're number one in heart disease, we're number one in diabetes, we're number one in our children being killed and put in prison, we're number one in heart attacks and* strokes! *I'm having women now that are thirty-five, having strokes! . . . It's like we're beaching ourselves. It's*

like the dolphins, it's just like, we're so tired now, we're just really tired. Because we've tried everything that society says we should do, in order to be accepted, and we're still not accepted. So now, here we are, women of color, and now I discover I'm a lesbian. And then I discover—sometimes it can just be too much. And so what I've found out is that we are not making those choices for our highest good.[47]

By providing a wide range of social services, networking, and support, Say, Sistah! offers an integrated approach to addressing this complex and interwoven set of needs—in addition to the LGBT-affirming and politically outspoken community that gathers at this church every Sunday morning.

Mixed Traditional Religious Groups

Though like all metropolitan areas Los Angeles has its conservative pockets, as the home of decades of religious innovation and LGBT activism it also has a large number of welcoming congregations among its mainstream and predominantly heterosexual religious organizations. These mixed traditional religious groups span a wide range of Jewish and Christian congregations, from Reform and Reconstructionist synagogues (and the occasional Conservative congregation) to Catholic parishes, from More Light Presbyterian churches to Disciples of Christ congregations. Participants in this study were drawn to two Unitarian Universalist churches, two Episcopal parishes, and a large, active Catholic parish.[48]

Unitarian Universalist Churches: Throop and Neighborhood

The Unitarian Universalist Association (UUA) was formed in 1961 from the union of Unitarians, a movement opposing the Christian doctrine of the trinity, and Universalists, a movement believing in universal salvation. Though both movements were Christian in origin, by the time of their merger they had changed course, embracing above all the value of the individual search for truth. A brochure about the denomination includes a "We Believe" section, which ironically but fittingly declares: "We will not be bound by a statement of belief." Unitarian Universalism, rather, "is a noncreedal religion."[49] Though services retain the feel of liberal Protestantism, they include readings from a wide variety of sacred and secular texts, and UU members come from a range of religious backgrounds. This doctrinal openness led the UUA in 1970 to become one of the first religious organizations in the United States to issue a formal statement affirming the rights of lesbians, gay men, and bisexuals.[50] Though transgendered people were not included in the statement at the time, few other religious organizations noticed the existence of either bisexuals or transgendered people for a number of years thereafter, and the UUA now explicitly includes (and affirms) transgendered people in its literature.

Both of the Unitarian Universalist churches that have played a role in the lives of study participants are located slightly north of Los Angeles, in Pasadena. Both were founded in 1885, one as a Unitarian congregation, the other as Universalist. When the movements merged in 1961, these churches became members of the same denomination.

Throop Memorial Church, founded as the First Universalist Church of Pasadena and later renamed after its founder (who also founded the California Institute of Technology), claims to be "the oldest liberal religious congregation in Pasadena."[51] It has an august past, having been led by an organizer of the 1893 World's Parliament of Religions as well as by a pastor who went on to head the national Universalist organization. The church assisted interned Japanese Americans during the Second World War and was involved in the civil rights and peace movements of the 1950s and 1960s. Never an enormous congregation—the sanctuary seats approximately 250 people—the church was quite small at the time of this study. Beth Leehy, a longtime member whom the church sponsored for ministerial training, noted in 2003 that membership had recently been as low as seventy, and that most of the congregants were elderly. She also suggested, though, that the congregation was beginning to grow again, especially because it was proving attractive for families with children.[52]

One of Throop's challenges is that the denominational merger in 1961 placed it into direct competition with a much larger church nearby. Yet although Leehy acknowledged that this was a possible contributor to Throop's growth struggles, she also claimed that the two churches "fulfill different niches." Throop's niche, she suggested, was as "a warm, friendly, ideal place for families. . . . I think because it has been small for many years at this point, that for that reason it's pretty accepting of differences, and honoring of individual gifts. It's a friendly place. And that's one of its big strengths."[53]

For LGBT people, a small congregation can be a mixed blessing. On the one hand, members may feel accepted as individuals, rather than being anonymous or being treated as token members of a target group, and small congregations can excel at welcoming newcomers and making them feel at home. On the other hand, a small congregation can also feel exclusionary to a newcomer, and such congregations often cannot muster the resources or the congregants to host interest groups such as a chapter of Interweave, the national UU group focusing on LGBT concerns. Nonetheless, in the early 1990s Throop underwent the process of becoming a "Welcoming Congregation,"[54] and for several years it hosted a Valentine's Day dance for same-sex couples. Leehy recalls that the congregation had no openly LGBT members when it underwent the welcoming process; the director of religious education who led the welcoming program came out as a lesbian during the process, and faced controversy that eventually led to her departure from the church. However, after the church voted to become a Welcoming Congregation, and as it became known as such through the dances it held, a small number of gay men and lesbians—mostly lesbians—began to join.[55] Despite the fact that its sole pastor is male, the church may be attractive to women in part because its lay leadership is predominantly female and it has a strong history of female pastors and a commitment to inclusive language within and outside its services.

Like Neighborhood Unitarian Universalist Church, its larger neighbor less than two miles away, Throop is located in a city with significant African American and Latino populations. Both churches have an interest in increasing the ethnic diversity of their congregations, but for a variety of reasons—many having to do with the staid nature of Unitarian Universalist services and the upper-middle-class white history of the denomination—they remain largely white.

Aside from racial demographics, Neighborhood Church is in many ways Throop's opposite. It has a large and thriving congregation (well over six hundred in 2003, by the senior minister's estimate),[56] a large staff, and a busy schedule of events and groups. Though sharing Throop's history of social activism, especially in the peace and civil rights movements, Neighborhood's current congregation has the numbers to put these commitments more obviously into action through its own numerous groups as well as its affiliations with local outreach organizations. A 2003 list of "Neighborhood Church Justice/Outreach Projects" included fourteen separate entries,[57] and the church's outgoing minister at the time called Neighborhood "one of the more socially active [Unitarian Universalist churches] in the whole nation."[58] Unlike Throop, Neighborhood has a group—the Neighborhood Alliance—specifically for LGBT church members and their allies, and it also hosts the Rainbow Youth Alliance, a local group for LGBT and ally youth. Neighborhood underwent the welcoming process later than Throop, voting in 1996 to become a Welcoming Congregation, but in 1999 it conducted a high-profile, public "rainbow marriage service" for its director of religious education and his partner.[59]

Though LGBT inclusion at Neighborhood is clearly visible in the rainbow stickers marking the name tags of some members and at the table bearing information on Neighborhood Alliance and LGBT Unitarian Universalists, individual LGBT members appear to blend in with the rest of the congregation. Senior minister Lee Barker sees this integration, and the fact that Neighborhood has no women's groups, as part of the church's theme of "oneness." "And that doesn't mean," he adds, "that those kinds of identity-based programs don't offer people a new way to be empowered. It just means that . . . what people are looking [for] here is for those separate strings to come together."[60] Contrasting Neighborhood to two other churches in this study, Barker explained:

> *The kind of people that come here, as opposed to . . . the Metropolitan Community Church, are people who are looking to have a feeling of being integrated into the whole of society. That's their refuge. . . . The other kind of place that you'll find a difference is All Saints [Episcopal Church of Pasadena]. All Saints, which is incredibly hospitable to gay and lesbian people, is also fighting the denomination on . . . performing union and marriage ceremonies, which is not what we're doing. And so people come here from there because they just get tired of fighting. They want to live their lives. The fight's over [in the UUA], you know? It's been over for years and years and years.*[61]

Episcopalian Churches: All Saints and the Chapel of St. Francis

In mid-August 2002, All Saints Episcopal Church in Pasadena received a fax—a "calling card," as church member and LGBT organizer Mary Mitchell wryly put it, from infamous anti-gay activist Fred Phelps. The fax informed All Saints that Phelps and members of his Westboro Baptist Church would be picketing outside the church on September 8 to protest All Saints' affirmation of LGBT people. The rector, the Reverend Ed Bacon, was out of the country, due to return from a five-month sabbatical on September 10, and according to Mitchell, associate rector Scott Richardson decided that the best response to such a vituperative attack was to ignore it. With three weeks' advance notice the church warned its members of the likely explicit and offensive nature of the protest, and Mitchell expected many church members to stay at home that weekend. Instead, "we had almost the [whole] Easter crowd show up." Many members brought their children with them, "and [the church] did youth group programs . . . and told the kids, and even the little ones, that these weird people across the street were saying that God hates people. And that's what we tell the kids not to do, you know, you don't hate anybody."[62]

Although a visit from the Westboro Baptist Church is rarely if ever a welcome event, it is often an indication of an organization's commitment to combating homophobia.[63] Indeed, the day before All Saints was picketed, members of the group Mitchell chairs, Gays and Lesbians/All Saints (GALAS), joined with the Pasadena chapter of Parents, Families, and Friends of Lesbians and Gays (PFLAG, also supported by All Saints) to picket a meeting of the ex-gay organization Love Won Out. Their message was much different from Phelps's:

the All Saints picket signs read, among other things, "God loves you anyway."[64] However, picketing is far from the full extent of All Saints' activism on behalf of gays and lesbians (and sometimes bisexuals and transgendered people as well). As was mentioned at the beginning of this chapter, All Saints priest Susan Russell directs a national project aimed at developing an officially sanctioned liturgy for blessing same-sex marriages in the Episcopal Church. Beyond Inclusion, as the project is called, has a membership that is approximately three-quarters LGBT and one-quarter ally, and is a ministry of All Saints. Russell notes that most of the LGBT members of the church, when they are involved in LGBT-specific organizations at all, choose the primarily social outlet of GALAS over the activism of Beyond Inclusion. However, few mixed churches can even offer their LGBT members this range of options.

Like Neighborhood Church, All Saints can be as activist as it is in part because of its size. Russell explains that the church "is counted as the largest Episcopal church west of the Mississippi," with "over six thousand congregants." While that number includes sporadic attendees as well as regulars, she estimates that total attendance at the three Sunday services averages around two thousand each week.[65] The church practices open communion, not restricting access to communion on the basis of denomination, baptismal status, belief, or any other criterion, and its greeting to newcomers states: "We believe that the spirit of God resides in every human being and that we are called to inclusively seek out that which unites us while at the same time celebrating the glorious diversity of God's creations."[66]

In part because of the opportunities afforded by the congregation's size, All Saints has a number of services and groups directed at LGBT people and a number directed at women. In 2002 the former included GALAS, PFLAG, and Beyond Inclusion as well as an AIDS service center and same-sex blessings performed by All Saints clergy. Among the latter were Ad Lib, "a feminist study group"; a parenting support group for mothers and their partners; a "women's issues committee"; and a women's spirituality group.[67] Interestingly, the church does not have a chapter of Integrity, the national organization for LGBT Episcopalians and their allies; in fact, according to Russell, there is no longer an Integrity chapter in the Los Angeles diocese, though many churchgoers in the diocese are "members-at-large" of Integrity. In such an accepting diocese, she says, "there's a certain ennui that 'we don't need that any more; we're past that.'"[68] On the other hand, there is less support for bisexual, and certainly for transgendered, members of the church. Susan Russell notes that, as in many gay and lesbian communities, full inclusion and celebration of bisexuals and transgendered people is "still a struggle for us."[69] Mary Mitchell adds that GALAS has "done a couple speakers' programs on bi issues. We really haven't done anything on trans. And I think it's going to take somebody that's got the interest and the time to make it happen."[70] As of 2003, apparently, no one had volunteered.

Like its Unitarian Universalist neighbors, All Saints struggles to reflect the ethnic diversity of Pasadena in its congregation. While some members come from more than an hour and a half away to attend services, the congregation's geographic diversity far outweighs its ethnic diversity. Though the church, says Russell, has "a real core of second- and third-generation African American Pasadena folk," it remains predominantly white. Among the efforts to change that situation is the hiring of three new clergy, two of whom are African American and a third a white South African who is assigned specifically to "multicultural outreach."[71]

Ironically, multicultural outreach is much less of a problem for the comparatively tiny Episcopal Chapel of St. Francis, which is located in the mostly Latino neighborhood of Atwater Village. The church recently hired a bilingual priest, Father Juan Barragan, and it holds services in both Spanish and English each Sunday. Split across three services, the congregation of approximately one hundred twenty people lends itself to an intimate church experience and leaves little opportunity for the kinds of specialty groups offered just over ten miles away at All Saints. It also offers a very different church experience, in some ways, from its Episcopal neighbor six miles to the west, St. Thomas the Apostle. The smallest of the three Episcopal churches in this study, St. Francis has neither a broad social justice orientation nor a predominantly gay congregation. Yet, says Father Barragan, "we are opening the doors to everyone."[72] Like the staff at Christ Chapel and Throop Church, Father Barragan claims that at St. Francis "we don't see when [people] come in if they are gay or lesbian or transsexual. We can only see human beings coming inside the chapel."[73]

Though he welcomes all LGBT people to his church, which is listed within the diocese as a welcoming congregation, and though he believes the church has a few lesbian, gay, and/or bisexual members, Father Barragan is especially concerned with ministering to transgendered women. "I want to work with them by prayer," he explains, to encourage them to "have confidence in themselves." He also emphasizes ministry with women in general, confiding that "I think sometimes women are superior to men." Though most of the ministries to which Father Barragan can refer his female and LGBT parishioners are diocesan rather than in his own parish, he is clearly aware of those diocesan organizations and able to direct people to them. He is also working to develop within his own church a computer training program for "abused women, women coming out of welfare, and Hispanic women."[74]

St. Monica Parish Community

Some readers may be surprised that one of the traditional congregations in this study that is mixed in sexual orientation yet welcoming to gays and lesbians is St. Monica Catholic Church. "According to legend," claims a history of the parish, the coastal area west of Los Angeles received its current name of Santa Monica when "Spanish soldiers with [Padre Junipero] Serra's party discovered two springs on the site which they likened to 'the tears of Saint Monica,' mother of the once wayward Saint Augustine. . . . Serra apparently named the region in honor of her feast day," which he celebrated there before continuing up the coast to Monterey.[75] Though a parish was not established in Santa Monica until 1886—a year after both Throop and Neighborhood churches were founded, and the same year in which All Saints was incorporated as a parish—the church quickly developed a school and hired a second priest. At the beginning of the twenty-first century the St. Monica parish community had five priests and a staff of three, a sizable school, and an entire block of prime Southern California real estate. It was holding several masses every day of the week, including six masses on Sunday, in its cathedral, which could hold about eight hundred people.

Setting St. Monica apart from most other sizable and thriving Catholic churches is the open presence of GLO—Gay and Lesbian Outreach. This ministry of the parish, clearly featured in both print material and online information about the church, is part of an archdiocesan project begun in 1986, called the Ministry with Lesbian and Gay Catholics (MLGC). Publicity material for this project is powerful and direct. One large glossy brochure has the following on its cover:

> I miss my community of faith.
> I wish there was a place for lesbian and gay Catholics within the Roman Catholic Church.
> I wish there was a way for gay and lesbian Catholics to come home.
> I wish there was somewhere I could share my journey of being both Catholic and gay.
> *There is.*[76]

One of the striking aspects of this narrative is the prominence of the words "gay" and "lesbian"—identity terms—rather than "homosexuality," the term more commonly used by the Vatican to describe what it views as an innate but unfortunate "condition." The ministry is extremely cautious in its presentation of gay and lesbian lives within the Roman Catholic Church, and clearly states that official Catholic teachings enjoin celibacy on lesbians and gay men. Yet it emphasizes the more inclusive statements the church has made,[77] and places clear stress on the primacy of individual conscience over church doctrine. This is in keeping with the archdiocese's—and St. Monica's—emphasis on reaching out to those who have felt alienated by strict Catholic teachings that seem to some to be out of step with the realities of contemporary life. Part of the mission statement of the Ministry with Lesbian and Gay Catholics reads: "MLGC takes its inspiration from the Gospel;[78] is shaped by Church teachings and pastoral practice; borrows appropriately from the insights of the social and biological sciences; and listens, ponders, and prays over the lived experience of those to whom it ministers."[79] While the archdiocese and the parish gingerly toe the party line on this issue, there is clearly a great deal of space for individual Catholics within the Los Angeles diocese to come to their own conclusions about the propriety of their personal relationships.

This balance is exemplified by the director of the ministry until 2003, Fran Ruth, a lay Catholic who is herself in a same-sex relationship.[80] "What you have to do," she explains,

> *is you have to take an issue . . . such as homosexuality, you have to read up on what the church teaches, why the church teaches, discern it, pray over it, and then if you can honestly say to yourself, 'I can't go along with this teaching. I have to follow my conscience,' then the church says by all means that's what you need to do. And that kind of brings us to where I am, as far as being Catholic and gay. I don't see a problem with it because it would be against my conscience, it would be against my humanness, to be in a straight relationship, have a husband, have children, because it's totally against my nature.*[81]

Such naturalistic arguments seem to work well, at least within this diocese, for gay men and lesbians, because St. Monica's is clearly home to a thriving, albeit relatively small, gay and lesbian community. Several of the people with whom I spoke before mass were obviously part of same-sex couples, and none were reticent about their identities. On the other hand, clear exclusions are also introduced by this rhetoric. One woman with whom I spoke had just begun attending St. Monica's. Though she felt warmly welcomed, she also was distinctly uncomfortable with the way in which people—both gay and straight—regarded her bisexuality. Her perception, she said, was that some members of the congregation believed that since she *could* conceivably be in an opposite-sex relationship, that was what she *should* do. In other words, the naturalistic argument put forward by Fran Ruth above serves to efface the lived reality of bisexuals in the church. Neither the GLO nor the MLGC offers resources for transgendered people; indeed, though Ruth was widely knowledgeable about lesbians and gay men, she admitted to not knowing much about transgender communities.

St. Monica's GLO is predominantly male, and although Fran Ruth mentioned one GLO group that had slightly more women than men, as far as she could recall most were male-dominated. Though St. Monica's bookstore carries feminist theology (and not, it may be worth noting, queer theology) and has women actively participating in mass and even serving communion, the fact that even in this liberal Catholic church it is still only men who have access to ordination may be too much for many Catholic lesbians. On the other hand, this is a more ethnically diverse ministry overall than many in this study, though St. Monica's itself, reflecting the immediate area, is predominantly white. The MLGC produces most of its written material (including its online material) in both Spanish and English, and Fran Ruth estimated that roughly half of the phone calls she receives about the ministry are from Latino Catholics. Few calls come from Filipino or Vietnamese Catholics, despite the significant representation of these groups in the L.A. area; most of the other 50 percent of callers are white.[82]

Mixed Nontraditional Groups

Just as the history of religion in Los Angeles is extraordinarily complex and diverse, so too is the queer spiritual marketplace today. While offering a wide variety of options—sampled above—for LGBT people wishing to retain their affiliation to childhood traditions or even to convert to traditional western religious organizations, this marketplace also offers a broad palette of nontraditional religions, new religious movements, and nonreligious organizations on which some people draw for their spiritual fulfillment. Many of these, as discussed below, cater equally to LGB and straight, trans- and cisgendered; they are mixed but nontraditional groups. Others, discussed in the final section of the chapter, serve primarily (but not exclusively) LGBT communities.

Agape International Spiritual Center

In Culver City, west of downtown L.A., in the midst of a sprawling business park made up of nondescript, rectangular buildings that house corporate headquarters and research-and-development facilities, stands an unusual megachurch. It is not evangelical; it is not theologically or politically conservative; in fact, it is not even Christian. The Agape International Spiritual Center prints the following statement in its bulletin for Sunday services:

> Our purpose is to create an environment where we realize that we are special and unique emanations of God, the Love-Intelligence that governs the universe. We are committed not only to the theoretical understanding of our oneness and union in God, but also to the active practice of this spiritual truth in our everyday lives. Through the teachings of the Science of

Mind and Spirit and the energy of unconditional love, our aim is nothing short of spiritual transformation.

SIMPLY—WE ARE HERE FOR GOD.

Agape is a New Thought megachurch.

Founded and administered by the young and extraordinarily energetic Reverend Michael Beckwith, Agape grew from a twenty-person gathering in the mid-1980s to claim in 2002 "more than 4,000 active members and over 12,000 friends throughout the world."[83] With its prominent African American leadership, the church is unusually ethnically diverse, especially for a New Thought congregation. When I attended in 2002, for instance, I estimated that 45 percent of those at the service were white, 45 percent African American, and approximately 10 percent Asian American, Latino, and Native American. Having only two services each Sunday to accommodate its considerable membership, the church draws between one and two thousand people at a time to its capacious sanctuary, and sends them out again after services to browse the bookstore for a new "all religions" charm bracelet or a copy of the I Ching, to enjoy the organic, vegetarian/vegan sandwiches and cookies for sale outside, or to contemplate the curly bamboo plant and gold-plated "OM" carvings in the ladies' room.

Services begin with half an hour of meditation, followed by music, self-affirmations, and a reading of the church's purpose statement. Though the subsequent structure follows that of many Christian worship services, with readings, a sermon, music performances, and congregational singing—not to mention the collection of an offering, for which two envelopes are provided in every bulletin—the content is far from Christian. Focusing on the New Thought doctrine that one's own thoughts help to manifest one's lived reality, the service stresses affirmations and positive thinking. "I am here to be a dynamic, creative expression of the most high God!" the congregation recites together. "My life is filled to overflowing with divine spiritual insights! God's blessings are multiplied all around me! All of the qualities of spirit are always expressing as me! Gratitude, appreciation, and high praise are my calling cards! I let go, I let God, and I let it be! And so it is! Amen!"[84] In February 2002, the monthly sermon theme was "Don't Miss Your Mission." Sounding with his intense, rapid-fire delivery style like an unlikely combination of traditional black preacher, New Thought teacher, and auctioneer, Beckwith described the goal of "downloading the kingdom of God" into one's own life and cautioned listeners not to "miss your mission" of revealing a "new order" of peace and love. "Practice the presence of God," he urged the congregation, and remember that "the potential is the eventual"—what one sees as possible is what will happen. "Attitude determines destiny."[85] After the service ended, Religious Science practitioners were available around the sanctuary for "spiritual mind treatment."

Reverend Sage Bennet, one of six assistant clergy at the church and the one-time organizer of TLC, Agape's group for lesbian and bisexual women, says that despite the wide range of ministries offered by the church, women attending her group tend to start with and remain a part of the larger church community rather than focusing their practice on the far more intimate experiences available through such small groups.[86] LGB ministries[87] at Agape include TLC, called by Reverend Bennet and study participants "The Lesbian Connection" but referred to as "The Love Connection" in church materials; "The Circle," which serves lesbian, bisexual, and gay members of the Agape community; and "The Relationship Group." Each meets monthly. The forty-odd other opportunities to be involved in small groups at Agape range from Toastmasters to yoga classes to a women's spirituality group, from dance and acting classes to recovery groups (explicitly *not* 12-step, interestingly) to adoption support, and from elders' spirituality to Jewish New Thought to the church choirs. Agape also offers a range of fee-based classes on New Thought, Science of Mind, and Religious Science, and runs a master of divinity program in "consciousness studies."

Asian "Export" Religions: The International Buddhist Meditation Center and the Siddha Yoga Meditation Center of Los Angeles

While Buddhism and Hinduism are traditional religions—that is, the religions of one's parents or forebears—for a sizable percentage of the U.S. population, branches of those religions have also been "exported" and "imported"[88] to the United States and marketed to potential converts. Though export and import forms of Buddhism and Hinduism have found converts in the United States since the nineteenth century, immigration reform and cultural changes in the 1960s drove rising interest in these religions through the latter part of the twentieth century and on into the twenty-first. In addition to its Buddhist and Hindu temples serving recent immigrants and their children, and occasionally third-, fourth-, and even fifth-generation Americans of Asian descent, Los Angeles is also home to a variety of convert-focused branches of these two religions. Study participants were attracted to two of these, the International Buddhist Meditation Center and the Siddha Yoga Meditation Center of Los Angeles.

Founded in 1970 by the Venerable Dr. Thich Thien-An, a visiting professor from Vietnam who was also a Zen master, the International Buddhist Meditation Center (IBMC) claims to be "one of four original Zen centers founded in the United States to cater specifically to the needs of Western-born Americans." It also names itself as "the first American temple to ordain Westerners as bhikkus and bhikkunis (fully ordained monks and nuns) . . . , the first to have a full ordination ceremony presided over by a woman and the first to have Western disciples of Asian masters fully ordain their own disciples."[89] The center occupies a small house in a predominantly Latino neighborhood slightly northwest of downtown Los Angeles. It features a quiet meditation garden in its backyard, a public meditation room on the ground floor, and housing (in the main temple and across the street) for the forty monks, nuns, and lay practitioners who live in the community. Services draw on Buddhist texts in a variety of languages, including Sanskrit, Pali, Vietnamese, Japanese, and English.

Abbess Karuna Dharma, an older white woman who helped to found the center and took over its leadership upon the death of her teacher in 1980, recalls that in L.A. "when [the center] was set up in 1970, there were basically no places where American folk could go to learn Buddhism." There was clearly interest in what the center had to offer, as it has in the past housed as many as sixty people at a time. Not all who live in the center are Buddhist, but they are required "to be following some sort of spiritual path which is not inconsistent with Buddhist ideals."[90] Some are Hindu, some Christian, some Jewish, and some from other religious backgrounds entirely. Most work outside the center, so after the communal meditation and meal in the morning they disperse, leaving the center relatively uninhabited throughout the day. Services on Sundays, says Dharma, draw around twenty people; many who live in the community do not come to the Sunday meditation service. Thus, while the temple serves a relatively large number of people and has a fairly full calendar of services, ceremonies, and classes, it nonetheless manages to retain a quiet, introspective feel.

The vast majority of the center's patrons are white, though Dharma notes that several Asian Americans and African Americans are also regular attendees. She tends to have more male students than female students, whereas when her predecessor ran the temple the gender balance was reversed. "A lot of people have identified me as being a role model for women," she said. "I never thought of myself in that way at all. Probably that's because I never needed a role model myself, because my teacher was remarkably anti-sexist."[91] If the theme of anti-sexism continues at the center, so too does a clear opposition to homophobia. "As long as you're involved in a committed relationship, that is proper sexual behavior," she asserts, referring to the Buddhist prohibition on sexual misconduct among lay practitioners. "That's probably the American in me speaking to those issues."[92] Regardless of the source of this sentiment, it has led the IBMC to attract a community that Dharma estimates to be approximately one-third gay and lesbian.

Across town in West Los Angeles, the Siddha Yoga Meditation Center offers a blend of Shaivism, a branch of Hinduism focused on the god Shiva, with Vedanta, a meditative branch of Hinduism first popularized in the United States in the late nineteenth century by Swami Vivekananda, a student of Indian mystic Ramakrishna. First brought to the United States in the 1970s by Swami ("Baba") Muktananda, Siddha Yoga is administered in this country by the SYDA Foundation, housed at the group's ashram in upstate New York. It has fifty centers in the United States today, including four ashrams or retreat centers, and also has a presence in thirty-two other countries around the globe. Under the guidance of Muktananda's successor, Gurumayi Chidvilasananda, the movement has strengthened its ties to its home country, initiating programs to support development projects and scriptural research in India despite the location of its headquarters in the United States. However, the L.A. center, at least, draws mostly converts rather than people who grew up as Hindus.

A brochure produced by the SYDA Foundation and available at the Los Angeles center explains that "Siddha Yoga meditation belongs to everyone and is rooted in a universal philosophy that embraces all religions, all nationalities, and all races. . . . [T]he purpose of every activity and practice is to allow a seeker to have an experience of God, the divine consciousness that permeates the universe." This experience is heightened, the brochure says, through "*shaktipat* initiation," which the brochure defines as both "the awakening of the inner meditation energy" and "the transmission of spiritual power (shakti) from the Guru to the disciple; spiritual awakening by grace."[93] Readers are assured that Siddha Yoga is compatible with a wide range of belief systems, and can be practiced alongside many religions. Indeed, experience rather than belief seems to be most central here; though the center offers a fifteen-minute "Orientation to Siddha Yoga Meditation" before its Tuesday and Saturday evening public chanting and meditation services, and though classes and other forms of instruction are available, the vast majority of events taking place at the center are practice-oriented. In fact, even the instructional programs seem aimed not at increasing one's knowledge of Hinduism or even of Siddha Yoga per se, but rather at improving one's practice in order to approach enlightenment.

Tuesday and Saturday public services, which draw anywhere from fifty to several hundred people, are a one-hour combination of chanting and silent meditation. True to SYDA's Shaivite roots, the chanting honors the god Shiva, yet with an interesting twist: Shiva is said to represent not an external deity but divine consciousness or the divine within.[94] The meditation may be introduced by a recording of SYDA's guru, often available at the center's bookstore following each service. Daryl Glowa, a practitioner for several decades who volunteers as a public relations specialist for the center, notes that women tend to predominate at the evening services, though there are often more men at the smaller morning chanting services. While there is a wide age range and some representation of ethnic minorities at the center, attendees are predominantly white. Glowa also believes, based on her own experiences, that many of those attending services are gay or lesbian. Occasionally transgendered people attend the services; though men and women sit on opposite sides of the meditation hall, creating a potentially problematic setting for some transgendered people, there is also a back section where seating is mixed, and Glowa notes that seating is self-selected.[95]

Of great importance to Glowa is the centrality of women in the movement and the respect with which they are treated. "[I]t was so beautiful to see Gurumayi, as a woman, being successful," she says. "Because we, as American women who came out of the sixties, suddenly had a female role model that we could look up to. . . . I find that there are a lot of women who do like to come because our path does offer a woman as a teacher." Glowa feels that the inner, personal focus of Siddha Yoga, as well as the local leadership opportunities, help women to be more empowered in other areas of their lives. She credits the movement with giving her the skills and the self-confidence to land her current position in production with a major film and television company. "Underneath it all," though, "we just want everybody to have a great experience of the self. . . . We want them to be happy in life."[96] Some would say there is no better fit for the cultures of Los Angeles and the entertainment industry.

Feminist Wicca: The Circle of Aradia and ReWeaving

In 1971, radical feminist Zsuzsanna Budapest (known as "Z") decided that the burgeoning feminist movement needed a spirituality of its own, and she knew what form that spirituality should take. She was not alone in her convictions; throughout the 1970s the branch of the feminist movement known as cultural feminism would experiment with spirituality as one way of exploring and celebrating women's cultures. She was, however, one of the few leaders in the feminist spirituality movement to start her own religion. With the founding of the Susan B. Anthony Coven No. 1 in Venice, west of Los Angeles, in 1971, feminist Dianic Wicca was born. It would grow over the next thirty years across the United States and into other countries where Wicca attracted followers, especially the United Kingdom and Australia.[97]

The Susan B. Anthony Coven No. 1 passed into the hands of priestess Ruth Barrett ten years after its founding, when Budapest moved to Northern California. Barrett brought with her not only five years of work with Budapest but also the influence of feminist spirituality leader Shekhinah Mountainwater; the coven came to reflect both influences. The Susan B. Anthony Coven split in the 1980s, and after leading one of the offshoot covens for several years, Barrett founded the Circle of Aradia in 1988. Five years later the Circle of Aradia became the first coven to be consecrated in the loosely Dianic organization known as the Re-formed Congregation of the Goddess.[98] In 2000 Barrett handed the coven over to the leadership of its current high priestess, Letecia Layson.

Like all branches of the acephalous, loosely organized Wiccan movement, Dianic Wicca focuses its practice on a goddess and—very secondarily and strictly in the background for Dianic witches—a god. Dianic Wicca conceives of these deities as unitary, but believes them to embody all of the world's deities as different facets of their own being. Layson explains the focus on the Goddess: "What we're doing at Circle of Aradia is to have women be women-identified. So we want women to see their own faces [in the Goddess], and to see that image as woman. That's one of the reasons why we don't allow males. There's a lot of undoing [of internalized sexism] that needs to be done."[99] Rituals follow the agricultural year, with the equinoxes and solstices making up half of the religion's annual celebrations. Smaller rituals follow the cycles of the moon, and are often held at either the full moon or the new moon. Where Dianic Wicca differs from most branches of Wicca is in its focus specifically on the Goddess and on women. True to the movement's second-wave, separatist feminist roots, Dianic Wiccan rituals and classes are open only to those whom Dianics term "women-born women"[100]—people identified as females at birth, raised as females, and currently identifying as females. The only males allowed are children three years old and younger.[101]

Like much of separatist feminism, Dianic Wicca initially appealed largely to lesbians. During the 1970s, some feminists saw lesbianism as a political identity and not simply a sexual one: if foundational French feminist Simone de Beauvoir could argue that women were the only oppressed class who lived intertwined with the oppressor class,[102] then it only made sense for women to separate from men during the battle to put down patriarchy. To some women this meant social separation, but for others it meant avoiding intimate relationships with men as well. Dianic Wicca, taking shape during these debates, thus appealed not only to women with a long-standing lesbian identity, but also to women who were electing to be intimate solely with other women until the battle with patriarchy was won.[103] As the decades went by, however, this dynamic shifted, and more women who identified as heterosexual began to be involved in Dianic Wicca. Layson explains: "I would say . . . between 60 and 80 percent in the early days of the Dianic tradition were probably lesbian and bisexual. Now it's probably flipped. It's probably more like 75 percent heterosexual women, and maybe 25 percent lesbian."[104] Perhaps fittingly, since Layson's ordination in 2000 the Circle of Aradia has had, for the first time in its existence, a heterosexual high priestess.

Layson is also one of the first high priestesses in the Dianic tradition to be a woman of color. She admits that this has brought its challenges: "The issues of race and class come into play. Because most of the women in my community [the Circle of Aradia] are pretty much white, middle-class women. And I was raised by a mother who swept dirt floors in the Philippines, so I come from a really different perspective." She tries to use this difference to educate the women around her, but has often found this to be difficult:

> *There's an assumption in the class work, . . . even in the dialogue*

> *and training, where women are wanting to be inclusive, they assume that you come from a European background. So I've actually had to speak up, and it was painful to say, because I'm making myself* other, *and then people would say, "Oh! I don't ever think of you as a woman of color!" And then I ask the question, "Are you color blind?!" So it becomes, then, an opening, and it's a challenge.*[105]

Since the goddess movement, and Wicca itself, continue to appeal primarily to whites, Layson likely has her work cut out for her when it comes to educating her community about race and racism.

In the 1970s, a University of California–Los Angeles undergraduate named Miriam Simos discovered Z Budapest and studied Dianic Wicca with her. Moving to the San Francisco area after college, Simos studied another branch of Wicca known as the Feri tradition, and became involved in the anarchist movement. She and a circle of friends began gathering for Wiccan rituals that reflected all of these influences, and the movement that developed out of these gatherings in 1980 came to be known as the Reclaiming Collective. Simos, who had a vision of a hawk and a star early in her Wiccan studies, is better known today as Starhawk—outspoken witch, feminist theologian, environmental and political activist, and author of the widely read introduction to Wicca *The Spiral Dance,* which is now in its third edition.[106]

Dissatisfied with Dianic Wicca's separatism, yet persuaded by its feminism, Starhawk initially taught a more orthodox Wiccan theology of complementary male and female energies, reflected in a paired god and goddess. As a student of Jungian psychology, she wrote a great deal about aspects of the God and the Goddess in all people. Her involvement with the gay, lesbian, bisexual, and later transgender and queer movements in San Francisco eventually led her to repudiate this model as both binary and heterosexist, and Reclaiming today is one of the most fluid branches of Wicca when it comes to concepts of gender and sexuality.[107]

As Reclaiming grew and Starhawk's writings became well-known, a number of individuals and covens within and beyond the United States began to identify with Reclaiming. Though the Reclaiming Collective initially resisted becoming a movement, in 1997 it agreed on a set of principles that would govern any organization wishing to call itself a Reclaiming group. These "Reclaiming Principles of Unity" are too extensive to reproduce here, but they include a commitment to the earth, the Goddess, and political action; an understanding of humans as the embodiment of the divine; a commitment to "intellectual, spiritual, and creative freedom" and to an evolving tradition; an emphasis on personal empowerment, consensus, and "social responsibility," including "service to the earth and the community" and nonviolence; and an honoring of diversity in gender, race, age, sexual orientation, and "differences of life situation, background, and ability" as well as a commitment to feminism and social justice activism. The final principle sums up the other six: "All living beings are worthy of respect."[108]

A few years before Reclaiming underwent its reorganization, several people from the Los Angeles area attended a "Witch Camp"—essentially, a retreat—held by Reclaiming. They returned from that camp committed to forming a Reclaiming-style group in Los Angeles. After advertising and starting a newsletter, they held their first ritual on Samhain (Halloween) 1996. The new circle was called ReWeaving Southern California.[109]

Reclaiming reorganized shortly after ReWeaving began. In the late 1990s, ReWeaving decided to go through the process of formally affiliating with the San Francisco movement. This led to some confusion, as not everyone who had initially joined ReWeaving agreed with all of the Reclaiming Principles of Unity. Since ReWeaving was still quite new, there were likely few social bonds holding members together, and as a result the group splintered in 2000. A smaller group retained the name ReWeaving and continued to organize public rituals and offer classes; the rituals I attended in the course of this project drew twenty to twenty-five people. Nearly all were white, and ReWeaving's rituals (like most Wiccan rituals) reflected this in the choice of deities from European pantheons—primarily Greco-Roman and Celtic.

ReWeaving rituals are strikingly informal, with participants arriving in a variety of clothes ranging from jeans and T-shirts to loose dresses and skirts (on men as well as women). Held outdoors at the Paramount Ranch northwest of Los Angeles, the rituals generally started half an hour or forty-five minutes after the appointed time and were conducted with a great deal of sudden innovation and flexibility (such as when the magical procedure of "casting the circle" was extended across a hiking path to the bathrooms, so that no one would have to formally "open a door in the circle"—the usual Wiccan procedure—if someone needed to use the facilities). The obvious fluidity of gender norms makes this one of the few organizations in this study that is explicitly welcoming of transgendered people, rather than implicitly welcoming, tolerant, or, as with the Circle of Aradia, actively unwelcoming of them. Some founders and leaders of the group identify as bisexual or lesbian; gay men were less well represented in ReWeaving at the time of this study, but there was little question that they were welcome. An exchange that took place during my interview with ReWeaving's leadership is telling in this regard. As we were discussing the place of LGBT people in ReWeaving, Firewalker observed with a grin, "I think I may be the token straight person." Kerry responded, "Wait, wait, wait! Over here," and through the ensuing laughter Flame added, "Actually, it's really funny because at camp [Witch Camp] I heard someone describe it as, like, 'The cool people are queer.' In the [Reclaiming] tradition."[110]

Santería

Paralleling the rising interest in Neopagan reconstructions of European pre-Christian traditions has been an upsurge of interest among Latinos and African Americans in a family of religions sometimes termed the African diasporic traditions. The best known of these in the United States today are Santería and Vodou, although a number of other forms are present as well.[111] All of these traditions are rooted in the encounter between West African indigenous religions and Catholicism in the Americas during the African slave trade. Forced by slave owners and priests to attend Catholic services, African slaves in Catholic-colonized parts of the Americas recognized their own deities in the Catholic saints and proceeded to blend the two pantheons (or, some would say, to Christianize their iconography in order to continue practicing their own religion), matching deities with saints based on the specialties or iconography of each. The resulting blended traditions developed differently in different countries, based on the region of West Africa from which those in each country originated, the language and culture of the new country, and local variation. The earliest branch of these diasporic religions in the United States is Vodou, which developed under French Catholicism in Haiti and established a presence in Louisiana as well. However, as immigration from Latin America to the United States has grown in the latter half of the twentieth century and into the twenty-first, so too has the representation of the African diasporic religions in this country.

The main form of the diasporic religions in Southern California is Santería. Originating in Puerto Rico and Cuba, Santería shares with Vodou an unearned reputation for evildoing, in part because of the eager interest of U.S. media in Fidel Castro's associations with the religion. True to its West African indigenous roots and in company with the other diasporic religions, Santería does practice animal sacrifice on certain occasions, a practice that brought it high-profile attention in a 1993 Supreme Court case.[112]

Attitudes of the diasporic religions toward LGBT people range widely.[113] In some branches, the lack of acceptance is clear and final. In others, acceptance is common. Since these traditions are largely acephalous, LGBT inclusion or exclusion is often determined by the opinion of an individual priest or priestess—some of whom are themselves same-sex-attracted or gender-variant, some of whom may themselves identify as LGBT. Unfortunately, this is the only case in this study in which I know of a participant's involvement in a religious organization but was unable to conduct fieldwork there. Corinne Garcia told me with great pleasure that she had found a *santero* (a priest) who was open to working with people of all sexual orientations and genders, and promised to introduce me to him and to obtain permission for me to attend a ritual with her. However, I lost contact with her shortly after the interview. All I can report in this case is that there is at least one *santero* in the Los Angeles area—and I suspect there are significantly more than that—who accepts LGBT people into his spiritual household.

LGBT-Focused Nontraditional Groups

One of the advantages of focusing a study on individual "spirituality" rather than on organized religion, and of taking individual practices rather than organized communities as one's starting point, is the ability to spot the unexpected among the resources on which people draw for their sense of the spiritual. The final two organizations covered in this chapter, both LGBT-focused but distinctly nontraditional as religious organizations, fall squarely within this category of the unexpected. Neither is generally regarded as a religious organization at all, and yet each serves as an important site of spiritual practice for a core participant in this study.

The Gay and Lesbian Sierrans

In 1986, a new "activities section" formed within the San Francisco Bay Area chapter of the Sierra Club: the Gay and Lesbian Sierrans (GLS). Passionate about the outdoors and committed to conservation, the members of the Bay Chapter GLS wanted an organization in which they could live out these commitments without worrying about homophobia. The idea quickly spread to Southern California, where a Gay and Lesbian Committee was formed by interested members of the Angeles Chapter. By September 1986, the Gay and Lesbian Committee had submitted a proposal to form a GLS activities section in the Angeles Chapter. As the section's history notes: "The proposal was rejected by a vote of 12 to 3. Reasons for rejection were unclear, but appeared to generate from a fear of 'promoting' gay and lesbian lifestyles, and involving the [Sierra] Club in 'gay politics.'"[114] The rejection itself, it seems, was a clear indication of the need for a separate section if gay and lesbian members of the Angeles Chapter wished to avoid homophobia in their involvement with the Sierra Club.

In the following two years the Gay and Lesbian Committee worked to raise awareness about its proposal and to gather supporters within the chapter, and it began hosting its own hikes. Approximately fifty people attended the first outing, providing evidence that the proposed new section had a good chance of success. In 1988, when supporters brought the proposal to the chapter council for the third time, it passed, and the Angeles Chapter of the Sierra Club officially recognized the Gay and Lesbian Sierrans. The section history notes that as of 1997 the Angeles GLS had 450 members. As of the June 2003 newsletter there were six other GLS chapters in the country, five of them in California and the sixth in Colorado. The Angeles GLS continues to use only the terms "gay" and "lesbian" to describe its constituency; whether it would be supportive and welcoming of bisexual and transgendered Sierrans is as much open to question as the inclusiveness of any gay/lesbian-specific organization. When I attended a weekly hike, the chapter membership also appeared to be predominantly white.

As in most Sierra Club chapters, the primary activity of the Angeles GLS is organizing outings. A weekly hike takes place in Griffith Park, the municipal park and hilly open space of more than 4,107 acres northwest of downtown L.A. that is home to the famous "Hollywood" sign. Other outings take place mostly on weekends, and range from tide pool strolls to thirty-mile day hikes, from camping and backpacking trips to kayaking. GLS outings are open to people of all sexual orientations, and Sierra Club activities beyond those hosted by GLS are advertised in the section's bimonthly newsletter. Some of these are for women only; one notice specifically notes, "Women of all orientations are invited to join us."[115] While activities such as meetings or social events can be hosted by any member of the chapter, under Sierra Club policy members must undergo special training in order to become approved leaders for hikes and outings. Of the thirty-six people listed as approved leaders for the Angeles GLS section in 2003, twenty had identifiably female names, and of the twenty-eight outings listed in the May/June 2003 issue of the Angeles GLS newsletter, only two had solely male leadership. Women seem to be well represented and highly active in this section.

The Sisters of Perpetual Indulgence

"A long, long time ago," begins the official "sistory":

> Let's say 1976—in a place very far away (Cedar Rapids, Iowa), a convent of Roman Catholic nuns lent some retired habits to a group of men performing their version of the Sound of Music. Three years later, those habits resurfaced in the streets of San Francisco's Castro District . . . [T]hree men . . . went in full, traditional habits through the streets of our city and down to the nude beach. One even carried a machine gun and smoked a cigar. They were met with shock and amazement, but captured everyone's interest.[116]

Thus were born the Sisters of Perpetual Indulgence. In their whiteface decorated with ornate makeup, their bulky wimples, and their often outrageous outfits, the Sisters have become well-known in urban LGBT communities, especially on the west coast of the United States. Because they combine Catholic imagery with drag and leather cultures, and because their founding, as described above, took place and is regularly commemorated on Easter Sunday, the Sisters are often castigated as a spiteful and sacrilegious parody of Catholic nuns. In fact, the organization is much more complex than such simplistic characterizations suggest—despite the fact that they claim to have been placed on the papal list of heretics in 1987.[117]

The Los Angeles "house"[118] of the Sisters of Perpetual Indulgence, which began in 1995, explains that it is

> an order of gay male, lesbian, bisexual, transgender, and non-gay nuns whose mission is the expiation of stigmatic guilt and the promulgation of universal joy. The same way the Catholic Church sold indulgences in the Middle Ages to forgive people their sins, the Sisters have granted the lesbian and gay community a perpetual indulgence, forgiving them of all sin and guilt often placed upon them by right-wing religious and political organizations.

The Sisters' main goals, says the Los Angeles chapter, are "to strengthen [their] community through drag activism, by raising much-needed funds for community charities, and by bringing about a better understanding of gay spirituality."[119]

While outsiders have often cast the Sisters as not only unreligious but actively *anti*-religious, the Sisters see themselves as serving a highly traditional religious function in a nonreligious or even postmodern-religious setting—they see themselves as "21st Century nuns."[120] They perform many of the community service roles often taken on by Catholic nuns, but do so in communities where Catholic nuns generally are not willing or not permitted to work. They appear in pride parades, at benefit dinners, in street protests, and at health care centers. Though much of their charity work in the past has focused on AIDS fundraising and sex-positive safer-sex education, their scope has broadened in recent years.

The L.A. house has raised funds for breast-cancer-related causes, and in 2001 and 2002 its members staged performance pieces to benefit a women's performance space that had lost its federal funding. Interestingly, both of these original works, written by a Sister who teaches at a local acting school, focused on religion. The 2001 performance, "The History of Religion Presented by the Sisters of Perpetual Indulgence," was a spoofy and yet simultaneously serious exploration of the major religions of the world. Since its author was Sister Unity Divine, it is perhaps unsurprising that a central theme of the piece was the underlying unity of religion. The 2002 work, titled simply "Sin," was a spoof on a catechism class dealing with the seven deadly sins. Though the "class" came complete with a prurient and severe nun as its teacher (Sister Unity herself) and a great deal of playfulness, it also offered a critical commentary both on the complexity of sin in individual lives (one Sister spoke of lying about being HIV-positive to Southern Baptist parents who refuse to believe that s/he is gay) and on the damaging nature of the concepts of sin and damnation. Thus, the Los Angeles house seems to have a particular concern with religion and spirituality. Indeed, the house's self-description notes that "much of the group's ritual has roots in faerie paganism and eastern philosophy."[121]

Conclusions: L.A.'s Queer Spiritual Marketplace

Describing the prominent mood of baby boomer spirituality as "questing," Wade Clark Roof has turned to the metaphor of the marketplace to understand the interactions between religious individualism and religious communities.[122] Rather than locating themselves firmly within the religious traditions of their youth, the participants in Roof's long-term study "shopped" for the right congregation, denomination, or even religion. Ultimately, they shopped for the truth, and for the religious institution whose truth agreed with theirs and was accompanied by rituals and resources that fit their needs, tastes, and schedules. In a capitalist economy and a religiously pluralistic culture even religion can become a commodity, hawked from market stalls or displayed on the tenth shelf of a supersize grocery store.

In a city such as Los Angeles, with its long history of religious innovation and LGBT organizing, it is logical (if perhaps at first surprising) that LGBT communities in the twenty-first century should have their own spiritual marketplaces. As with other aspects of commerce in the United States, this queer spiritual marketplace overlaps but is not coterminous with the broader spiritual marketplace. LGBT people are welcome and even actively supported in an increasing number of heterosexual-dominated religious organizations, ranging from Episcopal churches and Reform synagogues to Buddhist meditation centers and Santería houses. Also in the market, however, are "niche" businesses: religious (and not-so-religious) organizations that, while welcoming monogendered heterosexuals, serve primarily LGBT people. Furthermore, even this subset of the queer spiritual marketplace grew ever more diverse over the final three decades of the twentieth century: it now encompasses a wide range of Christian perspectives, welcomes Jews from many different traditions, provides ample space for queer-identified Neopagans, and even offers unexpected spiritual resources in such groups as the Sisters of Perpetual Indulgence.

I have been asked many times during the course of this project whether I find L.A.'s queer spiritual marketplace to be unique or commonplace. Long at a loss to answer this question, I finally realized that I struggled to answer because

I could not choose between these two options: Los Angeles is both. It is unique because of the central role it has played in the formation of national and international religious movements serving LGBT people: MCC, Dignity, BCC, Dianic Wicca, Affirmation, the Radical Faeries, Christ Chapel, the Unity Fellowship Church Movement. It is unique because of L.A.'s important role in the religious creativity of the 1960s and 1970s, combined with its more moderate approach to LGBT activism. In bringing together a penchant for religious innovation with the queer undercurrents of Hollywood and the political savvy of a bevy of wealthy whites, L.A. offered particularly fertile soil for the paradoxically radical and assimilative development of "queered" versions of traditional religions, and in its wilder moments it offered opportunities for more radical religious developments that might not have taken root in the more secular gay liberation and lesbian feminist movements in other U.S. cities. Though I conducted this study several decades after the spiritual and political innovations of the 1960s and 1970s, the effects of those innovations remained strongly evident—most clearly in the many religious organizations that had been founded in earlier decades but that remained a vibrant part of L.A.'s queer spiritual resources at the beginning of the twenty-first century. For all of these reasons, L.A. is a unique location in which to conduct a study such as this.

Los Angeles is also commonplace, at least among metropolitan areas of the United States. Like other metropolitan areas, it has a long history of LGBT presence—more or less closeted depending on the era and the particular city. Like other metropolitan areas, it has seen the growth of LGBT activism since the 1960s or 1970s, and that activism has stemmed from and fed back into a variety of LGBT communities—some of which were and are religious. Like other metropolitan areas, it has LGBT religious organizations, including several LGBT-specific churches and at least one synagogue. It also has less mainstream religious organizations that serve LGBT people, and it has a significant number of LGBT people who are completely uninterested in organized religion. Like other metropolitan areas, L.A. is home to a spiritual marketplace whose wares range from Southern Baptist and Pentecostal churches to Hindu temples, from Wiccan circles to Orthodox shuls. Like other metropolitan areas, L.A. draws from and feeds into a broad pattern that appears to characterize even rural areas of the United States: religious individualism. In this way, L.A. is commonplace.

Being simultaneously unique and unremarkable makes L.A. an excellent setting for what I have called an exemplary case study of religious individualism. On the one hand, its relatively long queer religious history ensures a large and widely varied set of spiritual options from which LGBT Angelenos can choose. On the other, because other cities have similar (if newer) options—even if in somewhat different proportions, as we might expect from the varying religious demographics across the country—insights drawn from L.A. are clearly relevant in a larger, national context. The rest of the book develops such insights, beginning in the next chapter with a discussion of the spiritual life stories of twenty-nine lesbian, bisexual, and transgendered women in Los Angeles.

4 *Negotiating Religion*

CONTINUITY, CONVERSION, INNOVATION

Asked how she would introduce herself to people interested in this research project, Christine Peña said simply, "My name is Christine. I am a spiritual being having a human experience, here on this planet. Hello."[1] Though each participant answered this question in different ways—and some found it awkward and had trouble answering at all—their experiences and beliefs reveal a similar breadth and interconnectedness in the roles played by religion in their lives. Certainly not all would describe themselves as "a spiritual being having a human experience," but the human experiences of childhood, parenting, family tensions, daily stresses, sexual awareness and exploration, moments of great beauty and utter despair, are all intertwined with and sometimes read through their religious beliefs (or lack thereof), their beliefs *about* religion, their religious and spiritual practices, and their past experiences with religions and religious people.

Although all but one of the core participants were raised within traditional religions—two in Judaism and twenty-six in various branches of Christianity—only six remain active participants in those religions, and only one of those reported no significant period of non-attendance or unbelief during her life. Four others have retained their identification with the religion of their childhood, but have enough disagreements with the institutional forms of that religion that they have elected not to attend services. Eleven participants, on the other hand, regularly include organizations outside of Christianity and Judaism in their spiritual repertoire, and while some of these organizations are explicitly religious, others are not—as the final section of chapter 3 demonstrated. The latter groups serve as religious resources less through design than through the individual innovations of their members.

In relating the history and the present state of their relationships with religion, the women in this study told me stories of ardent commitment and deep disagreement, of intensive spiritual searches, indifference, and even revulsion. Tradition is important to some as a source of continuity in their lives; it has brought only rejection to others, and for a third group it has provided a theme upon which to base improvisations. Each of these stories is different, sometimes to a surprising extent. What holds them together is not a similar pattern of growth or development, but rather a similar complexity: what these women believe now and what they practice now are inseparable from their past experiences with religion, their cultural backgrounds, their journeys of sexual and gender identity and sometimes equally complex journeys involving other identities, their experiences as women, their experiences as lesbians, bisexuals, and polysexuals, their theology, their economic status, their parents, siblings, children, and extended families. To tell the stories of religious change and continuity in these women's lives *is,* in some ways, to tell the stories of their lives. Consequently, this chapter begins at the beginning, as it were, by discussing the religious upbringings of the participants. It then moves to a consideration of participants' experiences with developing and claiming sexual and gender identities—experiences that are deeply intertwined with family dynamics and aspirations and, to a lesser extent, with religious identity.

Religious histories, familial relationships, and coming-out experiences all provide a grounding for participants' more recent negotiations with religion, and it is such negotiations that are the heart of this chapter. The development and current forms of participants' religious beliefs and practices fall along a spectrum that ranges from continuity through conversion to innovation; participants also frequently weave together aspects of these three main patterns, both over time (for instance, someone who followed one pattern in young adulthood but another in middle age) and simultaneously (perhaps by emphasizing conversion but retaining a strongly innovative aspect to their religious practice). Thus, although I discuss these patterns separately below, like all ideal types they become far more complex when applied to real human lives.

Within the three overarching rubrics of continuity, conversion, and innovation are several subtler distinctions. Those whose religious pathways show primarily patterns of continuity have chosen either what I call a "stay the course" path, remaining within traditional congregations of the denomination or religion in which they were raised, or a "tradition with a twist" approach, drawing on innovations within their religious traditions to find or create a comfortable space for themselves. Those I class loosely under the rubric of "conversion" include women whose primary religious move as adults has been to reject religion altogether as well as those who have rejected one religion in favor of another. Finally, it should come as no surprise that among the participants in this study are a sizable number of religious innovators. One group of innovators I class under the rubric of "seeking." This term has been used with some variation by sociologists of religion;[2] I define it here as encompassing those who are aware of some sense of the divine or the sacred and who desire some sort of spiritual practice, but who are still searching for the beliefs, the practices, and maybe even the religious or spiritual organization that feels "right" to them. The second form of innovation I call "bricolage." This term, borrowed from anthropologist Claude Lévi-Strauss,[3] has gained increasing currency in the sociology of religion as a way of describing the cobbled-together nature of religious beliefs and practices in a time and place of widespread religious individualism.

While Vassilis Saroglou and Danièle Hervieu-Léger caution against the indiscriminate use of "bricolage" to refer to what the latter terms "la vision post-moderne d'une pure et simple dispersion atomisée des productions symboliques contemporaines [the postmodern vision of a pure and simple atomized dispersal of contemporary symbolic productions]," the fluidity and multiplicity of bricolage make the concept uniquely suited to address postmodern identities and religious practices, especially those that fall explicitly outside of many traditional religions and therefore require their bearers to break new ground.[4] Furthermore, Hervieu-Léger's recent work on bricolage stresses very similar points to those at the center of contemporary identity scholarship. Rather than simply a "postmodern . . . atomized dispersal," bricolage in Hervieu-Léger's formulation is externally constrained both by the sociocultural environment and by unequal access to symbolic resources. As she notes:

> On ne bricole pas de la même façon si on est un homme de 40 ans vivant dans le centre d'une métropole européene, issu d'une grande université et passant un tiers de son temps en voyages d'affaires, et si l'on est une femme de 30 ans, fraîchement arrivée des Caraïbes et travaillent comme femme de ménage dans des immeubles de bureaux à la périphérie urbaine. [One does not do bricolage in the same way if one is a forty-year-old man living in the center of a European metropolis, the product of a large university who spends a third of his time traveling on business, and if one is a thirty-year-old woman, recently arrived from the Caribbean and working as a janitor in office buildings on the edge of the city.][5]

Remaining in or transforming their traditions, converting to irreligion or to another religion, seeking the perfect religious match or creating that match through bricolage, the women in this study take part in much broader, widely recognized trends in twenty-first-century U.S. spirituality. At the same time, as transgendered people, bisexuals, and lesbians, as Latinas, Native Americans, African Americans, and multiracial women, and in their many other nondominant identities, they also add their own unique twists to each of these otherwise familiar patterns.

Religious Upbringing

Although almost all of the study participants grew up having some association with traditional forms of religion, the strength and nature of those associations varied enormously. Thirteen of the women in the study recalled that their families were regularly or even highly involved with a particular religion, and that their own personal commitment as children and teenagers was similarly high. Another ten participants remembered high religious commitment among their families but low commitment on their own part. Four experienced both low family commitment and low personal commitment, and only two were raised in families with low or no religious commitment but sought out religious activities on their own.

Low Family Involvement, High Personal Involvement

Christine Peña, whose self-introduction opened this chapter, is one of the latter cases—her family was not particularly religious, but she remembered being very religiously curious as a child. Her father took his children to a variety of Christian services in order to expose them to many aspects of the religion, but he passed away when Christine was only nine years old. After that, Christine recalled, she asked her mother what religion the family was. "I said, 'Well, you know, like they're Baptist, and they're Catholic, and what are we?' And she said, 'Well, you're Christian.' So I said, 'Oh, okay, I'm Christian.' . . . It didn't mean anything to me, really, except we celebrated Christmas."[6] Dissatisfied with this state of affairs, Christine began attending a Baptist church with her best friends, who lived nearby. "I grew up, kind of, in the Baptist church by default," she explained. Besides, "I thought Jesus was a fox. . . . You know, all those pictures they have of Jesus, the long hair, and it was the seventies, so he was a good-looking guy to me. So I fell in love with Jesus." She enjoyed studying the Bible on her own, and was baptized in her friends' church when she was around twelve or thirteen.

Within two years, though, Christine's newfound religious commitment hit a roadblock: sexual awareness. "I remember that I was going through the Bible one day, and it said something like, 'It is better to marry than to burn with lust.' And I thought, 'Oh no, I'm going to have to get married. I'm fifteen years old!"[7]

Christine was discovering attractions to both men and women at this age, and reacted more to what she saw as a general condemnation of sexual desire than to a concern with her desires for women. Unable to fathom marriage at that age, and unable to reconcile her growing sexual awareness with the idea that sexuality might be sinful, Christine started drifting away from church. "I was also starting to drink," she added with a laugh. "I'm not anonymous, okay? I'm a recovering alcoholic too. So I was drinking and partying and carrying on . . . as a teenager I was really just a little hell-raiser." She offered a particularly colorful explanation for why this developing personality failed to fit in with her chosen church community:

> *I grew up in a Baptist church that was . . . it was, like, in the days when they all wore white buck shoes and white plastic belts and wire-framed glasses and, and . . . no offense, Schuller, I love you, but, um, everyone looked like Robert Schuller. I mean, they all did. They had white hair and, you know, and steel glasses and all that stuff, and they were just really strait-laced people. And the women were all in little polyester dresses . . . and it was like, I'm never going to fit in here.*

Though she expected never to fit into a church environment again, and in fact recalled having little desire to do so, Christine's ongoing involvement in the realm of the spiritual during this time of her life was evident in her growing tendency to have what she calls "profound spiritual experiences" through dreams.

Low Family Involvement, Low Personal Involvement

All four of the participants who recalled both low family commitment and low personal commitment to religion during their childhood and teenage years cited their mothers as the main reason for that low commitment. These mothers were skeptical of organized religion or of their own religious traditions; consequently, they encouraged their children to explore religious options and often to think critically about religious teachings. All four mothers were also from fairly socially conservative religions: two were Catholic, one Pentecostal, and one Southern Baptist.

Ruth Tittle's mother was one of these independent thinkers; she grew up attending a one-room Pentecostal church in southern Illinois. She had moved to Chicago by the time Ruth was a child, and Ruth recalled that "there was a lot of superstition in my life, in my family history," but "I wasn't raised in a spiritual or religious home."[8] Her father, she explained, grew up in an orphanage but knew that his family had been Baptist. Neither of Ruth's parents was particularly religious, and their children grew up with minimal religious involvement: "I think the only time . . . there was ritual it was maybe Thanksgiving or Christmas, you know, that we said grace at the table." Only when they visited her mother's family did Ruth and her siblings attend church. "And I would sort of stay in the back," Ruth recalled, "because I had slacks on, and at the time all women had to wear dresses. And so I would sort of just sneak in and stay in the back part and watch what everyone was doing. And I heard people speaking in tongues. . . . It was kind of frightening to me, as a kid."

Equally daunting may have been her mother's folk practices and beliefs, which Ruth remembered as being based on fear. She described her mother as "a rebel" who "would always say something to me like 'I can't go into a church; it would fall in on me.'" She also remembered her mother fearing bad spirits and refusing to go into water past her knees. "I don't know exactly what that [the fear of water] was about," Ruth acknowledged, but she did classify it among her mother's "superstitions." In addition to a number of folk beliefs about the significance of daily occurrences such as spilled salt (bad luck unless one then threw some over one's left shoulder) and itchy noses (indicating different impending visitors depending on the location of the itch), Ruth also remembered her mother believing in séances and her uncle making tables rise from the floor.

Tragedy hit Ruth's family when she was twelve. In the same year, both her father and her sister died. Ruth's mother turned to alcohol in her grief; Ruth, at first, turned to prayer. "I cried and prayed so much during that time," she told me, "and both of those people still died. . . . At that time I remember saying to myself that I had no more tears and that I did not believe in God, that there could not be a God, because they told me to pray and God would answer my prayers. . . . And my prayers weren't answered. And I think I buried God at that time." Through high school and college, Ruth remembered with a chuckle, this fit in well with the culture around her anyway. "It seemed fashionable . . . to be atheist. . . . So I went around, you know, and I said, 'Well, I think I'm an atheist. I think I'm an atheist.'"

Shortly after finishing college and beginning a career in undercover law enforcement, Ruth succumbed to what she describes as a family allergy to alcohol; her mother and one brother also struggled with alcoholism. Her brother, who joined Alcoholics Anonymous, began encouraging Ruth—forcefully—to join the program too. "In fact," she laughed, "he was the one who kept telling me, you know, that he wasn't going to talk to me ever again unless I went to a program. You know, he would just say, 'Go to AA,' and hang up the phone." Ruth went.

Involvement in AA was a challenge for a self-declared atheist; the centrality of "a God of your understanding" becomes difficult when one's understanding is that there *is* no God. About six months after joining the organization, Ruth found God in a most unlikely place: an Ann Landers column. A letter in the column described the writer's rediscovery of God after having discarded belief in the divine because of a childhood experience. "And it clicked with me. I thought, *That's* what I did. And then I remembered when I decided there wasn't a God. And it was when I decided I wasn't going to cry ever again." The awareness that she gained through this Ann Landers column, Ruth explained, helped her to work through the early steps of AA.

High Family Involvement, Low Personal Involvement

While Christine and Ruth grew up in families with little religious involvement, Mary Jane and Betty are among the ten participants who belonged to religious families but remember being or becoming disaffected with religion in their youth. Mary Jane began her interview by telling me that she was "brought up in Catholic school." "Twelve years of religious school," she emphasized. "But the church doesn't interest me."[9] "Was there a turning point?" I asked. Indeed there was. Like several other participants, Mary Jane remembered a specific event that triggered her loss of faith in the religious institution of her childhood—though it was not accompanied, she told me, by a loss of faith in God. She remembered thinking as a child that her parish "was a close-knit parish, you know, all these big families, always having a fiesta, or all the things and events that went on in this church, and we knew all these people." Her parents were active as volunteers in the church, and she had attended school there for eight years. During her sophomore year in high school, however, a child abuse accusation rocked the parish. "And once that event happened," she recalled, "to see two sides come about, two factions come out of the parish . . . It was, you know, an us-against-them thing."

Soon thereafter, Mary Jane's mother began bringing her children to other area churches, not settling at one but rotating. This, too, disturbed the young Mary Jane, who wondered, "If church is supposed to be a family, then how come we can't go to our regular church?" As the infighting in the parish turned priests, nuns, and parishioners against each other, Mary Jane concluded that her church had been overrun by hypocrisy. "And after that," she added, "I noticed little things about things that were said versus the actions that were taken, and that really turned me against what was going on. So my last two years of Catholic school were always questioning and always bugging the nuns." She felt that her teachers evaded many of her questions, "so that just left me with a big hole, you know? If they can't answer it, . . . if this is not true, then why am I going to church? Why am I following a religion?" She also tried attending Bible study on her own during this time, but felt that she faced the same problem: her questions were unwelcome and went unanswered.

"I was religious," Mary Jane recalled of that time in her life. "I wanted to believe in something, I wanted to see if there was anything else out there." She knew she was not attracted to the life of a nun, but one nun with whom she discussed such issues suggested that she might instead become the first woman priest. "Then I figured if I became the first woman priest, then I could kind of change things. But that didn't happen." Between the hypocrisy she saw in her parish, the inability of her teachers to answer her questions, and the sexism that kept her from having access to the priesthood, Mary Jane had had enough. She left the church.

She did not go far, though. She taught at a Catholic school for seven years, and served regularly as a volunteer counselor at YMCA camps. Describing a goal-setting exercise for the children at her camp, Mary Jane reflected on its impact on her as a young adult: "That was the first time I ever actually had a chance to sit down and say, 'What do I want to do with my life?' or 'What do I want to do here?' . . . And that changed my life as far as being virtuous and moralistic." Though she avoided the chapel at YMCA camps and hated going to church even while she was teaching at a Catholic school, Mary Jane admitted that her current beliefs were powerfully shaped by her Catholic upbringing, and that background remained a part of her life on a cultural level.

Like Mary Jane, Betty Walker retained a belief in God throughout her life, and was fairly involved in church activities as a child. "Our church, growing up from ever since I could remember, actually until I had my first child, was New Shiloh Baptist Church. . . . They made three different moves to three different buildings, and we stayed with them every move they made."[10] Her family attended church every Sunday, and Betty attended a Baptist elementary school and, later, a nondenominational Christian school. She added, however, that religion had only recently become important to her. Once she was eighteen and was allowed to make her own decisions about going to church, Betty stopped, "'cause I had been, I guess, told to go so much." Another problem was the Bible, or at least the challenging translation her church used. "The King James version," she remembered, "that was a problem right there for me. All through growing up, that was an issue for me. But I always felt like, okay, it was me, that I was the only person that needed to have something different, so I could understand what's being said here."

Throughout her late teens and most of her twenties, Betty lived with a man who was agnostic. Even when she was interested in going to church, it was difficult for her to attend during this time because of the conversations that ensued at home when she returned. "I just didn't want to hear all the confusion that it [going to church] caused, so I didn't go. And that was for probably—ten years." When that relationship ended and she came out as a lesbian, Betty remembers that she "really wanted to start getting a little more spiritual." She became interested again in reading the Bible, and discovered a translation written in more contemporary language. "When I got the New International Version I was really able to break it down and read it and understand it." There was only one problem: "I didn't like what was there."

Christian co-workers who saw Betty's coming out as an indication of sin shared their views with her and referred her to particular verses in the Bible; in the translation she had chosen, the condemnation of homosexuality seemed all too clear.[11] Though Betty had continued to see herself as a Christian throughout her years of living with an agnostic, and though she had begun attending Unity Fellowship Church as soon as she came out, she found that she could no longer open the Bible at all, because she could not see the positive message of Unity reflected in the condemnation her co-workers had shown her in the Bible. For Betty, the Christian condemnation of homosexuality was the final straw. She did not remember hearing such condemnation in her childhood church. However, "when I finally did hear people talk about, that were Christian, . . . that being a homosexual was bad, I think that's when I really considered right there that I was no longer a Christian." Betty's family remains Baptist, but she is long gone from this religion, which never drew her all that strongly in the first place.

High Family Involvement, High Personal Involvement

In contrast to Betty and Mary Jane, Coco Gallegos is among the thirteen participants whose strong religious involvement as children echoed that of their families. Coco, who was raised in Mexico, grew up as and remains a devout Catholic. "My mother," she told me, "is the one that has influenced me the most. . . . She did not insist on . . . me going to church or anything. But to just see her, how devoted she was to mass, and to pray."[12] She described her mother as "not a very loving provider, but she prayed a lot. And . . . that's like the biggest gift that I ever got, that my mother would pray for us." Sitting out on the patio under the stars, Coco's mother would ask the moon and the Virgin Mary to watch over her children up north in the United States. Coco believed that those prayers had protected her from many ills, including homophobia and racism.

"I was a troublemaker in Mexico," Coco confessed. "To my mother, anyway." For that reason, when Coco was sixteen her mother sent her to California to live with an older sister. Coco remembered that there were few Spanish-language masses near where she and her sister lived; for a while, they sought out the churches offering such masses, because Coco was still learning English. "Then I discovered the English masses," she recalled. "Just to hear it [the mass] in a different language, it was very powerful for me." "In what way?" I asked. She offered an example: "The rosary, when I prayed it in Mexico, it was very fast, you know? You just pray it and don't even know what the words are saying. The Our

Father is the same. And then, when I had to say it slowly in English, *Oh, my God!* It *is* a beautiful prayer." Today, Coco believes that praying and attending church together are two activities that help to maintain the strength of her relationship with her partner, whom she met and began dating soon after her arrival in the United States over thirty years ago.

Ronni Sanlo had a similarly devout upbringing in a Jewish family. "I grew up in an Orthodox household," she explained. "My family was kosher, my grandfather was a rabbi. And my family pretty much subscribed to all of the rules and those sorts of things, and I always thought when I was a child that I would be a rabbi. And it never occurred to me that I wouldn't be."[13] Others in her synagogue corrected her. "People would say to me, basically, 'Well, that's good, that's fine, that's very nice, but you're a girl. You don't want to *be* a rabbi; you want to *marry* a rabbi.' And I remember thinking that no, I don't. I *want* to be a rabbi." Though Ronni was "absolutely devastated" when she realized as a teenager that she could not in fact be a rabbi (this was before even Reform Judaism had begun ordaining women; Orthodox Judaism still does not), she remained heavily involved in the religion. "It was just very much a part of my family," she recalled. "I never thought about it, I didn't think about *not* having religion in my life; it simply was part of who my family was. . . . It permeated every aspect of my life and my family's life, in my adolescence." Ronni attended Hebrew school and Jewish youth groups through her high school years, and she remembered that her entire social circle in her hometown of Miami revolved around her family's synagogue.

When she turned twelve, Ronni decided that she wanted to have a bas mitzvah. "Boys had bar mitzvahs, girls didn't. Except that I did, because I wanted one. And I thought if the boys had one, why *wouldn't* I have one?" She also noticed that boys received bar mitzvah rings to commemorate this important stepping-stone in their lives. But "I didn't even ask for it. I knew nobody would get me a bar mitzvah ring. What they would get me is a stupid-looking little gold necklace with my name on it, which they did, which I still have. And I even sometimes wear." Showing an impressive level of foresight for a preteen, Ronni put a bar mitzvah ring on layaway at the jewelry store when she turned twelve. By her thirteenth birthday and her bas mitzvah she had paid the bill in full, using her allowance every week for a year. She has worn the ring ever since.

When Ronni started college in the mid-1960s no branch of Judaism was yet ordaining women. She became increasingly disillusioned with women's roles in Judaism:

> *I just so much questioned my role in the synagogue as wanting to be something really important that I thought would be helpful and useful, and wasn't being valued. And that's probably pretty much when*

> *I realized also that women weren't particularly valued in Judaism, certainly not in the Conservative-to-Orthodox brand that my family practiced. So, in much dismay and much disillusionment I left the synagogue. I left the synagogue for thirty years.*

At the time, Ronni recalled, "I felt like God had left me for a while. It took me a while to figure out that I had left God." Yet, although what she terms the "religious part" of Judaism was no longer a part of her life, she retained many of the other aspects of the religion. "I still had the cultural part," she explained. "I still had the traditional part. I think the spiritual part waxed and waned throughout my life." Though she avoided the synagogue and paid little attention to God, Ronni "always celebrated the major holidays." And although she lit no candles, "every Friday night I would know that it was Shabbos." Looking back at this period of her life, Ronni now believes that these traditional observances were "a way that I could stay connected to my family," who had moved to California while she remained in Florida.

Coming Out: Religion and Family

Twenty-four of the twenty-nine participants recall being aware before their midtwenties, and often quite a bit earlier, of an attraction to women or a sense that they had been socially assigned to an inappropriate gender.[14] Of these, nine—about a third of the participants in the study—spent a number of years fighting that identification by marrying, having children, or both. Four struggled for no more than a few years to fit their new identity into their social or religious understanding of the world around them, and eleven recall few, if any, struggles with coming out. Interestingly, at least among the participants in this study, these patterns do not seem to be strongly associated with particular religious affiliations or levels of attendance.[15] Coco, for instance, the devout Catholic discussed above, remembered having no personal struggles with coming out when, at the age of sixteen, she first met the woman who was to become her life partner. And Betty, who left her family's Baptist church as soon as she turned eighteen, married a man and had children not because of church doctrine but because she "just pretty much went along with what society said."[16] On the other hand, there is some indication that ethnicity may play a role in coming-out histories, since all three of the African American women in the study—including Betty—married and bore children before claiming lesbian identities, and two of the three also spoke explicitly about the lack of communal support available to them because of racism in LGBT communities and homophobia in black communities.

Pursuit of Social Norms

For those who were aware of a nondominant sexual or gender identity in their youth but attempted to suppress it for a number of years in the interest of adhering to social norms, religious and secular influences are often difficult to disentangle. For Danielle, who remembered being the only member of her Mormon family who was deeply involved in the church when she was growing up, both factors probably played a role. Danielle, who was assigned male at birth, remembers already "wanting to be more of a girl" by the age of two or three.[17] This desire manifested mostly in clothing and toy preferences at the time: "I didn't feel that I should be wearing this, I wanted to wear *this*. I liked the dolls instead of *this* and yet, I did both, because I was versatile." As Danielle became older she joined a Scout troop affiliated with her local ward, and eventually earned the rank of Eagle Scout. At the same time, though, "I also had the secret side of me in which I dressed at home, because I felt like I was really not what I was physically looking like. [I was] a girl." Telling the story of her childhood in the 1950s and 1960s, Danielle wove together its Mormon and transgendered aspects in a way that spoke of their simultaneous importance and irreconcilability:

> *Growing up in the church, I went to church every Sunday. I became involved with the priesthood and the scouting. But I also had a secret desire, wanting to be a girl. I became a pianist and organ[ist] for the church later on, when I became sixteen and seventeen. But again, I also didn't know that there were people out there that were like me, that you could get help, or any of that stuff, because in the Mormon Church you're really not exposed to the world out there. You're more or less constantly in church, scouting, or whatever.*

Danielle eventually found two biographies of transgendered people that showed her that others like her existed and that she really could live as a woman. Further information, however, was difficult to come by. "I went to the underground magazines to try to find out and try to meet other transgender people. Well, they [the women she met through the underground culture, who were mostly prostitutes] didn't want to talk. They just want you to pay the money for sex, which I didn't really want. . . . I just want[ed] the information." Finally she found more resources in the library, and discovered to her dismay that a medical condition made her a poor candidate for sex reassignment surgery under the guidelines of the time. "So I put it away and went on, and became involved . . . in the Marine Corps, trying to do that, and I tried to be a paramedic, got married, tried all these things, and put away that other element." Ironically, the Marine Corps, to which Danielle turned in an effort to block out her feminine identity, only strengthened it. "See," she told me, laughing, "men believe calling guys 'girls' or 'women' or something is bad, but I liked that, see. But they didn't know that." Danielle was discharged after an irreparable injury to her inner ear left her partially deaf. She still has a Marine Corps uniform, but with one small twist: she has exchanged her man's uniform for a woman's.

Danielle retained close ties to the church throughout her time as a marine, and even considered evangelizing to and baptizing fellow marines to be an extension of her Mormon mission work, which had been truncated by her entrance into the military during the Vietnam War. Though her Catholic wife would not convert to the LDS Church, Danielle maintained her own affiliation. Then she decided to begin transitioning, to begin living as the woman she had long felt herself to be, and everything changed. "The church didn't want me, my ex-wife didn't want me, my family didn't want me. So I became very battered out of character. So I did a lot of stupid things. But nothing really serious, just lost a job and all that stuff." Like many transgendered people, Danielle has experienced repeated employment discrimination; she has been unable to keep a steady job since she transitioned.

Her religious experiences have also been trying. "My own church," she told me, "obviously, they don't even know what to do with people like me . . . they don't understand it. 'How can you want to be what you are? And you were an elder in the Mormon church'—which is supposed to be a higher rank [and is open only to men]—and I want to go to Relief Society [a women's organization] and they don't understand that." In 1985, Danielle convinced an elder of the church to rebaptize her as a woman. She has also had some involvement with the Los Angeles chapter of Affirmation. Although she found the members friendly and the group welcoming, she also felt that she did not fit in. At the time I interviewed her, however, Danielle had plans for the future. Newer medical knowledge makes it possible for those with her medical condition to undergo sex reassignment surgery, she said, and she had scheduled that surgery for a date close to her birthday the following year. After the surgery she planned to move, in order to start afresh as a woman in a new ward.[18]

Emile's story is similar to Danielle's in many ways. She has a strongly religious and highly conservative background—she was raised in the Church of God in Christ, a historically black Pentecostal denomination—and resisted coming out for a number of years. Like Danielle, Emile married in an effort to stave off feelings that she thought could not be allowed expression. Unlike Danielle, Emile had children. Again, though, it is difficult if not impossible to disentangle religious and cultural influences on Emile's decision to follow social norms.

"When I was, like, four," Emile recalled, "I knew there was something different about me . . . because I found myself looking at little girls. And I'm like, 'what is this?' I didn't know."[19] As it was the mid-1960s, she added, "no one really talked about homosexuality." The feeling of difference persisted, along with Emile's inability to define it, until one day she heard her mother and her older sisters "gossiping about these two ladies at my church."

> *You know, and they're saying, "Ooh, they're funny," you know? I'm like, "What's 'funny'?" . . . And I finally caught on. . . . I knew I couldn't tell them. You know, I was like, "If they talking about these people, they're going to talk about me." So I just closed down, shut up, didn't say anything to nobody, just kind of went on my merry life, you know, in the church, accepted Christ into my life when I was sixteen, and kind of push all of that back into my mind.*

Despite the fact that she was "a little tomboy" even after this experience, Emile tried to live by what she perceived as both social and religious norms: "I was trying to follow society and do the normal things. You know, if you love God, you're not supposed to be gay." She married at twenty-two and had two sons shortly thereafter.

When Emile was twenty-five, her mother passed away. Though her father had been a deacon in their church, Emile associated churchgoing especially strongly with her mother's memory, and she found it too painful to attend church for many years thereafter. Three years later, having divorced, she describes herself as "so busy suppressing things" that she "was celibate." A friendship with a female co-worker turned into a relationship, however, "and that kind of blew me away." Frightened, Emile entered a series of short-term relationships with men, "still trying to just, you know, run from it and kind of do still what society says you should do." She even asked God to take away her desire for women.

That period in her life, Emile remembered, lasted another two years, bringing her to the age of thirty. At that point, her niece invited her to go to a gay club. "When I first went into the club," Emile recalled with a smile, "it was like, 'Wow!' It's like my soul was just set free, that I can actually be in a place where I am comfortable. . . . And I felt like I wasn't an outsider anymore." A few years later, she began a long-term relationship with a woman. "And everything was hunky-dory and everything, and, you know, then you've got this tap-tap-tap at your heart. Especially, you know, I already accepted Christ into my heart when I was sixteen." Emile told her girlfriend that she needed to go to church, but her girlfriend responded, "I can't be gay and go to church." The relationship ended soon afterward and, Emile told me, God began directing her church attendance. "The Lord spoke to me one day, and he was like, 'I want you to go to Unity [Fellowship Church], . . . but I don't want you to join.'" Emile followed these directions, enjoyed Unity, but found it too political for her taste. After asking around in a nightclub she learned of Christ Chapel of Long Beach, and began attending there. Though she prefers the upbeat music of the largely African American congregation at Unity Fellowship Church, Emile found the message of the Christ Chapel services more appealing. Over the next several years she rotated her attendance between Christ Chapel congregations in Long Beach and Denver, and Glory Tabernacle MCC. In an online article written shortly before our interview, Emile summarized her struggle with coming out: "I did want to be 'normal' and live a 'good' Christian life. But now I know that I am normal. To be a lesbian is who I am. And I'm a believer who lives to exalt the name of Jesus Christ."[20]

Extended Questioning

While nine of the study participants, including Danielle and Emile, were aware early on of same-sex attraction or cross-gender identification but spent many years refusing those desires and pursuing more socially normative lifestyles, four others pursued a more truncated version of this path. Concerned at first by their apparent lesbian, bisexual, or transgender proclivities, they hesitated to identify as such. However, within a few years of concretely considering their sexual or gender identities, they had come out. Sue Field, for example, was strongly involved in religion as a child. She also knew fairly early on that she was attracted to women. Though she struggled to understand this part of her in the context of her faith and her social norms, she came to a point of acceptance much earlier than did Danielle or Emile. Part of the explanation for this difference may lie in Sue's questioning of her religious beliefs during her high school years.

Sue attended Catholic school all the way through the twelfth grade. It was a positive experience for her, and she recalled that in her earlier years there "it was easy to accept all these things these wonderful people were telling me." In high school, though, the situation became more complicated. "There were things I didn't quite agree with that I was taught in Catholic high school, that made me go, 'Well, really? Maybe, maybe not.' Women's issues, family issues, a little bit birth control, although I didn't know too much about it to really understand the issues."[21]

When she started college Sue greatly expanded her social circle, which had previously been almost exclusively Catholic. She discussed religion with friends who were Protestant and Jewish, and brought questions to the priest who led her campus's Newman Club (a Catholic organization for college students). "One time," she remembered of this priest, "he kind of got mad at a group, and he says, 'Why do you always ask me these questions? Do you think I have all the answers?' And you know, we thought he did. We thought priests were God's word on earth." This incident further disillusioned her.

Meanwhile, Sue was also exploring the possibility that she might be a lesbian. She remembered having crushes on her female friends in high school, and she recounted an especially powerful incident that took place during her senior year. *Life* magazine had published a photograph of lesbians.[22] Sue's mother found the picture, and surprised by the unusual subject matter, showed it to her daughter, who can't recall ever having heard the word "lesbian" before that moment. Sue remembered the picture portraying "two women by this bar, at night, with some kind of neon sign in the background. And they're kind of in black leather, a little bit sleazy, and in dim light." Sue told me, "I was drawn into it [the picture], jumped up from the kitchen table, ran into the bedroom as fast as I could, [and] slammed the door, screaming, 'I'm not one of those! I'm not one of those! I'm not one of those!'" Her startled mother hastened to reassure her that she had thought nothing of the sort, but, Sue says now, "I can look back and say, 'There was something funny about that.'"

In her first year of college, Sue had a classics professor who discussed homosexuality with a nonchalance unusual for the mid-1960s. He also told his class that contemporary homosexuals had their own communities in larger cities around the country. Previously, Sue remembered, the *Life* picture had led her to believe that lesbians "were sort of like the Hell's Angels." She still thought about moving to a city and joining such a community, but was afraid that, with her college education and her aspirations to be a teacher, she would not fit in.

> *[I thought] they probably didn't like to go hiking. They probably just sleazed around in bars and stuff. . . . But when Mr. Bell said that people were from all walks of life, they just had an attraction toward people of their own sex, and they had deep friendships like the Roman soldiers . . . it's like a lightbulb went on. . . . It just opened up a world of possibilities.*

Sue began researching homosexuality in her college library—a project that would span all four years of her college career. She found books written by therapists, but they relied on such abnormal cases that Sue knew they had little to do with her own experience. However, the library also had a collection of contemporary pamphlets, and these connected Sue with what are now landmark organizations in the history of LGBT movements. She found a pamphlet from the Council on Religion and the Homosexual in San Francisco, and decided to write to that organization because the word "religion" in its name connoted safety to her. The person who responded gave her information on the Daughters of Bilitis, a homophile organization for women that was a little over fifteen years old at the time, as well as two religious organizations that had just started in Southern California: Dignity and the Metropolitan Community Church.

Then Sue's parents found a copy of *The Ladder,* the Daughters of Bilitis newsletter, among her belongings. "They found it, opened it, and were shocked. 'Where did you get this stuff?' I could have lied and said, 'Well, I'm doing a research project on lesbians.' But I didn't want to lie to them. I said, 'No, I'm just curious.'" She was telling the truth—as she recalls it, Sue had not at that point decided for sure whether she was a lesbian, but she felt she owed it to herself to find out. In 1969, she believed that the only way to do that was to move to a city. She arrived in Los Angeles in 1970. "I came to California," she told me, "and my hunch was correct. I was gay. . . . And I found other people of my same kind, my age group, my caliber, . . . my interests. . . . So that was very healthy and wholesome." After she moved in with a lover, Sue decided to return to her small Colorado hometown and tell her parents. They responded by affirming their love for her.

While she was exploring what it meant to be a lesbian and whether she might be one, Sue was also exploring the reactions of Christian leaders to homosexuality. She received mixed messages:

> *I'd go to confession or whatever, and talk to priests about it, and I heard different things. . . . One guy in one church was really negative. . . . Then I'd go to another Catholic church . . . that was considered more liberal and loving, and they'd say, "Well, you know, at this time the church says you can be a gay person or a homosexual, but we don't want you to practice."*

Sue, who had been questioning Catholic teachings since her high school years, found both answers "ludicrous. One was totally negative and rejecting. The other one was like, 'Well, it's all right to have eyes, but you shouldn't open them and look at the flowers.'" She and her Presbyterian girlfriend received a similarly unclear answer from a Presbyterian minister they visited, and Sue stopped going to mass. She did attend MCC with her girlfriend for several years, and maintained an involvement with Dignity as well. Later on, in the late 1980s, she joined a group for women in Dignity. Overall, however, by the late 1970s Sue had ceased attending religious organizations, preferring to define herself as an ex-Catholic and find her personal spirituality in nature.

In contrast to Sue, Vanessa had not yet resolved her struggles with her sexual orientation and her religion when I first interviewed her in 2001. Like Ronni, Vanessa was raised in an observant Jewish home. Her parents are Conservative, and she attended an Orthodox school until the fourth grade, when she transferred to a public school. Though she struggled as Ronni did with gender roles, especially at the Orthodox school, Vanessa also remembered hearing from her parents that she could do anything she wished with her future and her career. She never wanted to be a rabbi, though being several decades younger than Ronni, she could have attended a Conservative rabbinical school and been ordained after college. Also unlike Ronni, Vanessa was still involved with Judaism when she began to be aware of her attraction to other women.

Throughout her time in college Vanessa participated in Hillel, a Jewish student organization. Though she was bothered by the rumors about her sexual orientation that traveled through the organization—rumors she also remembered as being inconsistent, classing her alternately as straight, bisexual, lesbian, and asexual over the course of five years—she also appreciated the fact that her school's Hillel group was generally accepting of all sexual orientations. In her last term of college Vanessa began dating a woman, and was equally disturbed by the sudden attention from the LGBT community at her school. With some of her straight friends rejecting her, and the LGBT community overwhelming her with its welcome, Vanessa found herself struggling to negotiate a way between her actions and her identity. Her friends on both sides made the assumption that dating a woman meant she was a lesbian; Vanessa was not so sure. "I was so internally homophobic that I was like, 'Oh my God! No, no, no, I'm straight. This is just situationally.'"[23] She was still in the process of this negotiation when I interviewed her. "If somebody asked me right now what I am," she told me, "I would say 'open.' But you know what? I am *so lesbian*." She laughed. "I don't see anything in men that I want. I mean, it's women. But if somebody asked me, . . . I would say 'open' because 'open' sounds easier. It just sounds easier for me to say. . . . I know what sex I like. And I can just say 'open,' and that one-in-a-million chance I can maybe find a guy, but, you know, right now it's not going to happen."

In the course of our interview it became clear that Vanessa was fairly certain she was attracted to women exclusively. What that meant for her identity was much less certain. At times she told me that she dislikes all labels, and resists being put in boxes. "You know, whatever I do in the bedroom, whoever I go out with, that's *my* business. I mean, even if people want to label you—and they will, they'll label you hard—I will never put that, quote, 'label' in my head. It's not me." She was willing to identify as someone who "date[s] chicks," but added, "Lesbian is such a hard word. It's so hard for me to accept." Yet she also used the word "lesbian" repeatedly when talking in general about her experiences or about other women who are attracted to women, and occasionally used it to describe herself.

A significant part of Vanessa's struggle was the fact that she could not see a way of connecting being Jewish with having a girlfriend. "It's not in the Jewish tradition to be lesbian," she told me. "It doesn't seem kosher to be a Jewish female and a lesbian, or a Jewish male and gay. . . . It's contradicting the whole Jewish tradition. That's my feeling." The first time she went to a synagogue after she started dating women, Vanessa remembered, "I didn't know how to pray . . . I was going, 'Well, am I a Jewish woman? Am I not a Jewish woman? Am I a sinner? Am I going to hell? . . . I mean, the sinner factor, I don't think it was right for me to pray. When I first came out, I didn't feel that I was Jewish anymore." She added that her entire identity is Jewish, but once she came out, her entire identity also was dating women—and the two were fundamentally incompatible.

Vanessa did not believe that gay men and lesbians were part of God's plan, but she also did not believe that God could control their existence. "I don't think he would understand them if he actually was here on earth. He would be like, 'Well, why are these men together? And why are these women together? That's not how I set out the world.'" And yet, Vanessa also was not entirely convinced that God disapproved. She thought that he might, but felt that she did not have proof of her suspicions. At the same time, she said, "It's my life. And . . . you're supposed to do the best in your life that you can, and this is what makes me happy. So if this makes me happy, you know, I think I should go for it."

At times, Vanessa's struggle focused specifically on community, and this is where the importance of background for her becomes clear. Vanessa had attended both of the LGBT-focused synagogues in Los Angeles, but felt that the services there were "not like a real service for me." I asked why that was, and she responded, "It's, like, way Reform. It's way Reform prayer. I mean, they clap, they snap, . . . and I'm like, 'Oh, my gosh.' It's not the way I'm used to." Later she added, "Most of the gay and lesbian synagogues are just *so* gay and lesbian. I mean, it's not tradition, it's not what I'm used to. And the Conservative [synagogues] are so—it's like *man, woman.* And if I brought my girlfriend over there, they would look at me like I was crazy." With the LGBT synagogues not traditional enough for her, and the Conservative synagogues alienating her, Vanessa generally avoided services entirely. She sometimes went to a synagogue to pray by herself, and occasionally she brought a male friend to services to pass as her boyfriend. During the interview she even toyed half-seriously with the idea of marrying a gay Jewish man in order to pass as a heterosexual. Tellingly, toward the end of the interview, when I asked Vanessa whether she had anything she would like to say to the religious leaders whom she knew when she was coming out, she responded, "I would tell them, 'You know what, don't look at the outer shell. Look inside and see, that's a human being and not a sinner, who wants to pray, who wants to just be in the Jewish community without negative stereotypes, without negative feelings towards them.'"

The epilogue to this story is that two years and some months later, when I mailed Vanessa the transcript of her interview, she e-mailed me in response. "I can't believe some of the stuff I said in that interview," she wrote. "I am older and more mature now. I have met some Jewish lesbian[s], which back then [I] thought . . . didn't exist." She added a few days later, "I have been reading a lot on Buddhism and I really like it a lot. I think it is a more energizing religion. . . . I have not been to temple in a long time, except for the holidays with my parents."[24]

Acceptance

In contrast to those who pursued socially normative lives for extended periods of time and those who went through several years of questioning their sexual or gender identities, one-third of the participants in this study not only were aware before their midtwenties of an attraction to women or an identification with the opposite sex, but also remembered having little or no difficulty with accepting that aspect of themselves and incorporating it into their identities when useful language and concepts became available to them. Corrine Garcia offers one example of this pattern.

"I think, for me," Corrine said, "I've always been queer. I never identified as anything else, even when I couldn't speak. But I thought I was a boy."[25] She remembered being confused as a small child by the clothes her mother chose for her: "I wondered why my mother kept putting me in these little dresses, you know? . . . She would send me outside to play with my brother, and I would take my shoes off, and put my socks in my shoes, and take my dress off . . . and fold it on top of my shoes, and then I would be playing naked." When her mother scolded her, Corrine recalls, she put her clothes back on—but only until her mother's back was turned again. Corrine remembered these incidents as her childhood response to feeling like a boy yet being treated like a girl.

Corrine, who is of Laguna Pueblo, Spanish, Blackfoot, and African descent, was raised as a Catholic in the strongly Latino culture of East Los Angeles. A self-identified "city Indian," she was teased by her childhood friends when she told them her family was from New Mexico. "There's no such thing as New Mexico!" she was told. "You mean Mexico." At the same time, after visiting her Pueblo relatives for the first time when she was sixteen, she has discovered a lack of acceptance in Native communities as well, especially in the context of religious practices. "I couldn't really go into the Native community and be able to practice their religion without everybody always saying, you know, 'She's from the city.' . . . I was always an outcast because I wasn't part of my culture."

I wondered whether her strong involvement with Catholicism as a child had influenced her sense of self, given her confusion over wearing a dress when she identified as a boy. "I could go back to being in a dress," she told me, laughing, "because the priests were in dresses too. You know? I was like, 'Okay.' I could dig it." One early experience, which today Corrine also connects to religion, stands out in her memory for the effect it had on her comfort with her sense of gender incongruity. "When I was three," she recalled,

> *I met a little boy who lived in back of us. . . . He was bald, and he wore a dress. And he wore red lipstick and red fingernail polish. . . . And he wore this same little dress, it had little checkers on it, every day. And, you know, it went at the waist like this [indicating a flared skirt], and it had a little tie in the back . . . and it was red checkers.*

Corrine's brother, she remembered, was puzzled by this neighbor and repeatedly asked him why he wore a dress, to which the boy simply responded that he liked it. As Corrine remembered it,

> *That was my first experience with a boy who dressed like a girl, so I thought it was normal, you know, for people to be dressed in the wrong clothing. So it was okay now for my mother to dress me in dresses. I could be like my friend. . . . And I accepted that my mother dressed me like a girl, and I just enjoyed it. So, you know, I was a sissy-boy.*

During our interview, Corrine insisted on a fluid self-definition. At times she used the term "transgendered," at other times the term "butch dyke." In a preliminary screening interview, she told me that she identifies as female but lives as a man. Basically, she sees herself as having both masculine and feminine sides, and she gives expression to each in different settings. Because she identifies with both genders she is not inclined toward sex reassignment surgery, preferring instead the challenge of living in the ambiguous space between genders and consequently also the ambiguous space between sexualities.

In exploring ways to express her ethnic heritage religiously, Corrine discovered Santería, and liked it both because it connected her to her African heritage and because it developed out of a form of Spanish colonial oppression that she feels is similar to that visited upon the Pueblo people. Corrine first came in contact with the religion when, on a whim, she walked into a *botánica,* an herbal and magical supply store, in New York City's Spanish Harlem. The store owner told her, "You were pulled in here for a reason." He laid before her images of the saints of Santería and said, "Pick out three that belong to you." She selected Changó, San Lázaro, and Yemayá. San Lázaro represents to her the work she does in AIDS education, Yemayá represents her bond with the ocean, and Changó represents her dual-gendered nature. A warrior saint, Changó has some hints of gender fluidity in his African form but is generally considered to be strongly masculine. His Catholic form, however, is the female Santa Bárbara. Because of this, Corrine sees him as an especially powerful saint for transgendered people like herself. Interestingly, Changó's colors are red and white—the same colors Corrine remembered seeing on the dress worn by the little boy who convinced her that it was "normal . . . to be dressed in the wrong clothing." Corrine commented on that parallel when telling me about the little boy. When I asked later on whether saints like Changó might appear to people in human form, she responded by pointing out the importance of spirit possession in the religion, and added, "Yeah, that could have been the first point where I was pointed in the direction of Santerismo [Santería]."

As an adult, Corrine says, "I don't have a problem with my anatomy because I don't have issues about my body, because of my spirituality. My spirituality says that I can accept myself for who I am, and I can be who I am through my religion, and be accepted within my religion." After much searching, she has found a *padrino* (a religious leader) who also identifies with both genders, and who is comfortable working with her. Most recently she has been paying a debt to San Lázaro by refurbishing her statue of him and buying jewelry dedicated to him ("This is an expensive religion," she adds wryly), but she remains closely tied to Changó as an expression of her own gender fluidity.

Though their stories are in many respects quite different, Corrine and Carmen share a consistent, lifelong sense of self-acceptance. Carmen remembered no struggle, religious or otherwise, with any sense that her attraction to other women was wrong or abnormal. Raised in the Caribbean, Canada, and England, Carmen was and still is a dedicated Presbyterian. "I grew up in a religious home," she told me right at the outset of our interview, "in a religious family, and it [religion] defines everything I do."[26] Her grandfather was a senior elder in the church, and she remembered attending both Sunday school and church services every Sunday morning throughout her childhood in the 1960s and 1970s. She attended a Presbyterian elementary school, then switched to a Catholic high school because her closest friends were Catholic.

Given the long history of struggle within the Presbyterian Church (USA) over the rights of gay men and lesbians, it would be reasonable to expect that someone from such a devout Presbyterian background might experience some self-doubt about same-sex attraction. But, Carmen said, "I cannot go back to any time in my life, even as a child, when I actually believed that [that gay men and lesbians are eternally damned]. . . . I can't say I've questioned my religious conviction about my sexuality." She speculated that this confidence might relate to her family's habit of holding lengthy political and religious discussions at the dinner table. "We had our own opinions as kids, and we would be asked, 'What's your opinion?' . . . So I kind of had a lot of—sort of building my own thoughts and my own ideas and my own belief, and that's what sustains me and carries me through."

Perhaps another source of sustenance is Carmen's family. With the exception of a Pentecostal uncle, with whom Carmen has an unspoken agreement not to discuss homosexuality, her family has been supportive; in fact, they seem to have seen her attraction to women as inconsequential. For instance, she remembered that one evening another uncle (not the Pentecostal one) asked her "if I was interested in this particular girl. And [I] said, 'Yes, and what's for dinner?' And that was the next story. That was it. 'Well,' he says, 'what's for dinner?' Yeah, kind of carried on."

Coming Out Later in Life

The final pattern in the coming-out narratives in this study is that of five participants who were not consciously aware of their sexual attraction to other women until after their midtwenties. Christine Logan and Cassandra Christenson, both of whom married and had children as self-identified heterosexuals before deciding that they were in fact lesbians, offer two different perspectives on this experience.

Christine was a lifelong, third-generation Christian Scientist before coming out, and she still identifies as a Christian Science practitioner. An upper-middle-class homemaker with two children, she was deeply involved and highly respected in her church. However, she had "a huge secret. Here I was in the church, I was a reader, I was a Sunday school teacher. . . . I couldn't stop drinking. I even got the courage to go to [Christian Science] practitioners and have them pray for me." Then, one year, "I ended up in West Hollywood helping a friend die of AIDS. And he was five years sober."[27] Her friend was a member of Alcoholics Anonymous (AA); when his illness became too severe for her to manage alone, he called on his friends from AA. Christine came to know these friends, and was impressed by conversations she had with them about God. She joined the West Hollywood gay AA group, and says, "I went from religion to spirituality." She told me that "it was as if God had said, 'Okay, you've had enough of this religion [Christian Science]. You need to be more open; you're getting very closed-minded and rigid here. . . . So he just plucked me out and put me in a community where there's no room for that."

When she had been sober for eleven months, Christine fell in love with another woman. She was forty-seven. She went into therapy, unwittingly selecting a therapist who was gay himself, although she had chosen him because he too was a recovering alcoholic. "I think, at that moment," Christine reflected, "being newly sober, coming out, I was just, like, blind. I was just like, 'Take my hand and tell me what to do.'" Christine believes that her first relationship with a woman "was the first time I'd ever fallen in love. . . . I knew I wasn't in love with my husband. I knew it all along. But I didn't know why. And I *loved* him. . . . But I didn't realize till I fell in love with her that I wasn't ever *in* love with him. It was a whole different thing." She began divorce proceedings.

In what she describes as "part of the coming-out process," Christine was in a relationship with her first girlfriend before she actually identified as a lesbian. Laughing, she told me, "my therapist said to me, 'Well, have you ever considered you might be a lesbian?' I mean, here I was sleeping with her, you know, and . . . I went, 'Oh, my God! No! . . . Is that what this is?' And then I was perfectly comfortable with it. There was no problem." In fact, she believes that God led her to the experiences that resulted in her coming out. "I wasn't ever saying, you know, 'Ooh, I wonder if God loves me?' I knew that. I had that solid foundation. . . . There was no doubt for me that there was nothing wrong with homosexuality. . . . It's been faith all the way along, trusting in God." On the other hand, she was unable to get an answer from the Christian Science Mother Church in Boston about acceptance of homosexuals within the religion. Having backed off from her involvement in the church once she joined AA, and struggling as well with her divorce, Christine decided to leave Christian Science. She did not go far, though: except for occasional forays to MCC with a girlfriend, Christine has found herself most drawn to Religious Science, a universalist offshoot of Christian Science. A few months before our interview, she had acted on the advice of friends and had attended the Agape International Spiritual Center for the first time, "and *just* loved it."

Cassandra, too, believed that God led her to come out, and she too remembered feeling completely comfortable—religiously, at least—with identifying as a lesbian as soon as she realized that she was one. She gives much of the credit for her coming out, though, to a most unlikely source: Mother Teresa.

Cassandra now believes she had a crush on a girl when she was young, but she identified as heterosexual until she was fifty-five. Though raised a very devout member of the Disciples of Christ—so devout that having to work on Sundays at her cinema job caused a serious ethical crisis—by the time she finished her education in nursing she had become an atheist. In her late thirties she returned to school for a bachelor's degree in psychology and social relations, and she attended a Catholic college. "I took all kinds of spiritual [courses]," she recounted, "and stuff that really revved up my inner thinking and exploring, and then I realized I was profoundly spiritual. And I had to know that my life made a difference."

In her midforties, Cassandra recalled, "after I got my second divorce, . . . I had failed at so many things, and I told God, I said, 'You give me a mission! . . . I want to make my life count.' . . . And then this woman who was dying asked me to talk her through her death. And I did that, and it was *incredible*." Cassandra would spend the rest of her career using her nursing training and her interest in spirituality to work with the dying. A few years later, serving as a volunteer chaperone for *The Dating Game,* Cassandra was changing planes in Miami when she saw Mother Teresa making her way through the airport. "And I went up, and I acted just like a groupie, and grabbed her hand and shook it. . . . And I said, 'Oh, Mother Teresa, I'm just like you. I work with the dying.'" The nun asked Cassandra, "Do you work with AIDS?" Cassandra answered, "Not really." But, she told me, the real answer should have been "'Not at all.' In fact, I was homophobic! . . . So [Mother Teresa] took this little, skinny finger, and she said [shaking her finger emphatically], 'You—work—with—AIDS!' Like this divine directive. So I came back, and that's when I met my lover, my partner, through the AIDS organizations." Later in the interview, I asked Cassandra what it was that changed her earlier homophobia. "Mother Teresa," she answered simply, and then laughed.

Cassandra returned to Los Angeles to start Project Night Light,[28] a now-defunct organization that trained volunteers to care for people dying of AIDS and for patients' partners and families. Through her contacts with the gay men she served and worked with, Cassandra recalled, she quickly lost the homophobia that she calls her "baggage from the fifties." "It was like a process," she told me, "to be embraced by the gay community, the guys, and then when I fell in love. And . . . I just started writing poetry. So when I started writing this incredibly sexual poetry, I went, 'Whoa! That's who I am! Of course! Makes sense.'" God, she feels, was closely involved in this process. "It was a deeply spiritual experience to be guided through this process, that helped me to work with the dying, and to teach others, and to start a nonprofit, and to get in touch with my own lesbian self."

Since her partner's death four years ago, Cassandra has been struggling through a process that she says never took place when she was an adolescent: learning how to express attraction to another person in socially acceptable ways. This, combined with a shyness that she attributes to persistent traces of internalized homophobia, has made socializing with other lesbians very difficult. The problems have been exacerbated by financial troubles, including a period of homelessness after she nursed her dying mother. Having been diagnosed with depression and anxiety while she was homeless, at the time of our interview Cassandra lived in state-sponsored housing for the mentally ill. Yet she continued to try to see the spiritual benefits in everything she experienced, even as she acknowledged the traumatic aspects. "I felt I had a mission. . . . And then all of a sudden I had nothing. And it was a spiritual journey, an important one. I'm grateful for it. . . . I think it's quite wonderful, but I still haven't totally recuperated. I still kind of identify with being a bag lady." A spiritual seeker since her return to religion during her bachelor's degree program, Cassandra continued at the time of our interview to believe in God and to have deep respect for a wide variety of religions. She was most drawn to Buddhism and to Siddha Yoga, and selected the International Buddhist Meditation Center as our interview location.

Religious Pathways: Continuity

Like many people in the United States, regardless of gender or sexuality, the women in this study often have lengthy and complicated stories to tell about the religious and spiritual directions their lives have taken. While I have framed my discussion of these directions in terms of continuity and innovation, this does not imply that there are only two possible paths or that they are mutually exclusive. Rather, as with other aspects of these women's lives, each story has its own quirks that are affected not only by factors such as religious background, ethnic identity and cultural heritage, gender identity, and sexual orientation, but also by individual factors such as unusual experiences, chance occurrences, specific religious settings, and particular family dynamics. Thus, while the following discussion turns at the largest level on a distinction between tradition and innovation, each of these categories has subsets and each contains within it at least some aspects of the other.

Staying the Course

In the entire study, only two participants remained within the religion of their childhood and continued to attend mixed churches. Nevertheless, both of these women spent some time away from their childhood religions before returning. One of these is Coco, whose Catholic background was discussed above. Though Coco had been consistently and deeply involved in Catholicism for over fifteen years when I interviewed her, she told me that there was a period between her midtwenties and her early thirties when she explored other religions. She remembers having out-of-body experiences—what she calls "astral projection"[29]—when she was asleep, and wanting to learn how to control those experiences and how to have them at will. She also wanted "to know the future"; she described this period in her life as "wanting to be in control and wanting to know it all." These desires, she told me, turned her interests toward the New Age movement, because she felt that she could not have such control and independence within Catholicism. In 1985, however, her partner's brother was diagnosed with AIDS, and someone told Coco and her partner about the charismatic movement within Catholicism. Interested in charismatic healing, and feeling that it offered many of the same experiences and benefits as the New Age movement, Coco and her partner began attending healing services with their ill relative. Though her partner's brother passed away soon afterward, Coco now sees a larger meaning in her attraction to charismatic Catholicism. "What I didn't know," she reflected, "is that God was using that to bring us back to the Catholic Church."

Margaret Jensen's childhood commitment to religion was just as strong as Coco's, as was her commitment upon her return to the religion. Moreover, although she left that religion for longer than Coco did, she did not go as far, merely switching Protestant denominations for a number of years. Margaret was baptized in a Presbyterian church, and she believes that her family briefly attended a Congregational church. By the age of seven, though, Margaret was a part of the denomination that would become the mainstay of her religious practice. "I've been away from the Episcopal Church at times in my life, for a variety of reasons," she told me, "but always come back, and consider myself a lifelong Episcopalian."[30] Margaret speaks passionately of the presence of God in her life, and believes that her faith is responsible for her emerging in relative spiritual and mental health from what could have been a very damaging childhood. "I knew that the church was a safe place, and that God was a safe person, or entity or being, and so that was what I fell back on." Margaret remained in the Episcopal Church until it modernized its prayer book. Disliking the changes, and also needing a church that offered Sunday school for her young children, Margaret found a local Methodist church to be more to her taste. When her family moved, the Methodist church closest to their new home did not interest her, but the local Presbyterian church did. Margaret stayed with that church until her children were grown and she was divorced.

At that point, "I really wasn't quite ready to give up looking to find something that resonated with what I believed in. . . . I think I was looking for a flexible format, I guess, for religious expression." She tried a Unitarian Universalist church, and greatly enjoyed it until Christmas came around. "And then they didn't talk about Jesus. And I thought, how can you have a candlelight Christmas Eve service and not talk about Jesus? And then I finally realized that this wasn't the answer." She returned to the Episcopal Church, eventually rejoining the congregation of her childhood.

In hindsight, Margaret thinks that her "journeys away from the Episcopal Church . . . were a search for relevance in my religious expression." She found that relevance in full force when she began to feel a call to greater service in the church. Though two bishops in succession refused to sponsor her for ordination, she continued with her ministerial training, completed a master of divinity degree, and spent three years as assistant professor of theological education in the Diocese of Panama. When she returned, she found that her childhood church had a new priest and the services were no longer conducted in a style that she liked. Furthermore, she felt that the church was not interested in much lay involvement, and although her missionary service was over, she wanted to be able to continue contributing. She transferred her membership to the Chapel of St. Francis, where a former seminary classmate of hers was the priest.

It was at this church that Margaret met her partner and came out as a lesbian. "My priest knew, immediately," that she and her partner were together, Margaret recalled. "And I don't know how she knew. . . . But she counts us as one of her success stories. We found each other in her congregation." By the time of my interview with Margaret, her classmate had left St. Francis and a new priest had been hired. Margaret was unsure whether she and her partner would be staying in the church. During a follow-up phone call nine months later, Margaret's partner told me that they had left and were looking for a new church—maybe Episcopal, she said, maybe Methodist—but they had not yet found one.

Tradition with a Twist

In addition to Coco and Margaret, eight other participants in the study currently identify with the religions of their childhood. Four of these have found LGBT-focused congregations, and four have chosen not to join a congregation. Of those in LGBT-focused congregations, Carmen is the only one—in fact, the only person in the entire study—who has never left her religion for any significant period of time. A lifelong Presbyterian, she is delighted to have found West Hollywood Presbyterian Church (WHPC), and she says that this congregation is one of the reasons she has remained in the Los Angeles area for as long as she has. Though she also likes to honor her South Asian heritage by visiting the Lake Shrine at the Self-Realization Temple west of Los Angeles—a sort of spiritual park that is Hinduism-based but universalist—and she enhances her "own spiritual growth" by attending Torah study classes with friends at Congregation Kol Ami, which meets at her church, Carmen is still a dedicated member of WHPC. Until she began attending this church, Carmen says, "even though I may not have intended or even realized I was doing it before, I made compromises for myself . . . I was always . . . somewhat on edge or somewhat conformist [at church]."[31] She went on to explain that she had always been circumspect, if not closeted, about her sexual identity in other Presbyterian churches, and that she appreciates the opportunity to be more open at WHPC.

The contemporary religious aspects of Ruth Tittle's story are worth dwelling on at some length. Having been raised with some exposure to Pentecostal Christianity through her mother's childhood church in southern Illinois, Ruth decided in high school that she was an atheist. She had relatively little contact with religion during her early adult years, except for an attempt to take her daughter to a Baptist church when she lived in Lexington, Kentucky. "I would hear the minister start saying terrible things about homosexuals. And I was always out, I was out to my daughter from the time she was two or three years old. And—how could I take her to church and have the minister—saying terrible things about who I am?"[32]

About ten years after Ruth found God through Alcoholics Anonymous and an Ann Landers column, she found out that the brother who had encouraged her to join AA was HIV-positive and that he was becoming very ill. She took a leave of absence from her job and came to West Hollywood to take care of him. When he went into the hospital for his first surgical treatment, "he was very frightened. . . . He would ask me questions: what did I think it would be like on the other side?" As Ruth waited in a lobby for her brother to come out of surgery,

> *the elevator opened and there was a clergy that came walking out of the elevator, and I could tell by looking at her—seemed to me my gaydar was on, you know? It was on. And it was like, 'This looks*

> *like a lesbian minister to me.' And so she was briskly walking by me, and I reached out and grabbed her arm and I said, 'Wait a minute. What church are you with?' And she stopped, and she said, 'MCC.' I said, 'Oh, I thought so. Can I talk to you for a minute?' And then I quickly told her who I am, why I was standing there, what was going on with my brother, and can she help us? You know, could she come back and talk to him? And . . . it was Nancy Wilson.*

The Reverend Nancy Wilson, senior pastor at MCC Los Angeles at the time, was one of the main providers of pastoral care for people with AIDS in Los Angeles during the height of the epidemic. She visited Ruth's brother "every time he was in the hospital after that," Ruth remembered. She was also Ruth's introduction to MCCLA.

Ruth's brother passed away in 1993, the third of Ruth's immediate family to die. Like many in West Hollywood in the early and mid-1990s, Ruth found herself overwhelmed by the horror of living in the midst of the AIDS epidemic. Losing a family member to the disease, in addition to friends and on top of the trauma of losing her father and sister at an early age, was too much for Ruth. "I picked up a drink again," she told me somberly. "I think I remember thinking at the time, 'Well, my God, it's been about twelve years. What could it do to me now?' And I picked up a wine cooler, because I didn't want to cry anymore." Ruth's partner at the time tried to get her into treatment, and even suggested she attend MCCLA, but Ruth remembered "feeling too guilty" to go. "I couldn't go to church and be drinking," she told me wryly. "The place I needed to be."

Ruth eventually entered a residential treatment program, through what she firmly believes was "a miracle." She told me, "God puts angels in your life when you're in that kind of pain. . . . Angels were all around me during that time." During the treatment program, she went with the household to the Self-Realization Temple's Lake Shrine, Carmen's favorite spiritual site, and Ruth conducted a small ritual to release the memory of her brother.

> *And . . . I saw my brother. . . . He was sitting next to me, and at the same time there was, it was like . . . another dimension that opened in front of my eyes, like a tear or a rip or something. . . . And there were all of these . . . they were sort of rounded forms and they were all excited . . . it was like a very happy, very busy party going on, and foom! Like that, my brother was gone.*

"These things tell me," she added, "that there is a spiritual world. There is a higher being. There is a greater power."

After completing the treatment program, Ruth sought out MCCLA and quickly became deeply involved. When I interviewed her, she was considering running for the board of directors at the church, and she was very clear about her commitment to Christianity. "You can't keep me from being a Christian," she says. "That's who I am. . . . I know in my heart I'm a Christian. I couldn't tell you that any other time in my life. But I can tell you that today." Ruth also maintains her connections to AA, which she believes is "a program that was handed to us from God," and which serves as another source of spiritual practice for her.

Linda was one of the four participants who continued to identify with their childhood religion but had elected at the time of the study not to attend any religious organization. Although she wanted to return to a congregation, she had not yet found a suitable one; at times, she doubted that she would ever find a church again. Linda was raised a Southern Baptist, but like several others in this study, she had an apostate mother. Calling her mother the "black sheep of the family," Linda explained that "she kind of stood out on her own and said, you know, 'I don't need to go to a particular building to worship.' . . . She basically believed that she could be, I guess, spiritual in her own way at home, didn't need the organized religion."[33] Though Linda's mother allowed Linda's aunt to take her to church, Linda feels that she grew up "being given the freedom from my mom that it's okay to question and to wonder." When she was a teenager this freedom to question, along with a reduction in the amount of time she spent with her aunt, led Linda out of the church. She felt that there was too much fear in her church, and she found some members of the church hypocritical, espousing Christian teachings but refusing to put such beliefs into practice in their daily lives.

In her early twenties, Linda began looking for a new church. "I felt that there was some sort of voice, that there was something missing," she recalled. Restricting her search to Southern Baptist churches and a few nondenominational congregations, she tried to find a group that felt less hypocritical and rigid than her childhood church. "I also think that at that period of time in life I was going through a coming-out process," she told me. "So I'd get to the point [with a congregation] where I'm like, 'Okay, I like what you're saying. I hear it. Now how are you going to feel if I tell you that I'm gay?'" She found no church that met her needs. Looking back, she observed, "Even though I was saying, 'I don't like what I hear,' I was still searching for what I wanted to hear within that organization [the Southern Baptist Convention]. . . . I didn't have the strength or the confidence to step out of that [denomination], because it was a very scary transition."

By the end of her coming-out process, around the age of twenty-seven, Linda had realized that she would not find within her home denomination a church that would accept her as an out lesbian. "And too, at that time I was gaining a lot more confidence, I was feeling more comfortable with who I was, there was a lot of stuff that was going on that enabled me to be more open to things that were nontraditional." She and her partner began church shopping together. They attended MCCLA, and Linda liked the service, "but I kept saying to myself, 'Why should I have to go to a church that revolves around gay, lesbian, transgendered, the whole deal? Why can't I go to just a regular church for everybody and be accepted there? . . . You know, I'm not different. . . . My spirituality is the same as yours." They also tried Agape, a church that has interested Linda's partner for a number of years, but Linda was uncomfortable with it, at least at first. "I was just like, 'Okay, this is weird.' . . . You know, 'Are they going to try to hypnotize me?' I mean, just all the stuff I was taught as a kid started to come back."

When we spoke in 2001, Linda told me that she still considered herself Christian, "probably only because I don't have any other name to give myself. . . . So yeah, I can call myself Christian, but I don't align myself with all of the Christian beliefs." She added that she still believed in God, but "I don't know if that's the name, . . . I'm certain that there's something." When I asked how she would describe God now, she responded, "that's part of the process, I think, that I'm in right now, you know, what *is* God? I'm not sure that I know." She had been reading books on subjects as diverse as Buddhism and biblical interpretation, and considered her reading "spiritual." Of herself, she said, "I feel that I'm spiritual, but I'm searching. I haven't yet come up with a label for myself, but I consider myself a spiritual person." While she was still interested in finding "a group or an organization that I would want to align myself with," she told me, "I don't know that I ever will."

Like Linda, Cynthia and Lara still identified as Christians when I interviewed them, but were without a congregation. Also like Linda, they had looked for a church but had not found one that was suitable, and they clearly did not feel any urgent pressure to find a congregation with which to worship on a regular basis. Together for two and a half years and married for just over two, Cynthia and Lara believed that they were meant to be together, and they had worked hard to blend their two families. Both had children when they met; Lara had a long-term female partner at the time, and Cynthia had only recently come out and left her husband. They elected to interview with me as a couple, so I discuss their experiences together here.

The two partners could scarcely be more different in their religious and familial backgrounds. Though Lara was baptized Catholic, she was raised within the Assemblies of God. Despite the strict conservatism of this denomination, Lara's family was supportive of her from fairly early in her coming-out process. And although she remembered worrying about what God might think of her being a lesbian, Lara also told me that she was aware of her attraction to other girls so young (around fourth or fifth grade) that she simply knew she would never marry a man. She remembered her strongest concern being not God's opinion, but the opinions of other churchgoers. This was one of the reasons she drifted away from her family's church during high school, and she later spent some time in college seeking a church where she would be accepted and comfortable. "I think that there's one time," she remembered, "where God really told me to, you know, 'trust yourself. . . . Lead a good life, do right, and trust yourself. I'll always be there. I'm not going anywhere.'"[34] With this message to rely upon, Lara mostly stopped attending church. Before she met Cynthia she was drawn to All Saints Episcopal Church by a national conference on same-sex marriage and returned to services for a few years. From where the family lives now, however, getting to All Saints would take about an hour even without traffic, so Lara no longer attends.

Cynthia, too, knew early on that she was attracted to other girls. But as a devout Catholic schoolgirl, "you know, just 'It's wrong, it's wrong, it's wrong.' . . . If I even thought about a girl I started praying. . . . I was finding myself praying a lot." Cynthia and Lara both recalled being unaware, during their high school years in the mid- to late 1970s, that people lived as out gay men and lesbians. Cynthia went on to study at a Catholic college in the Los Angeles area, and began sneaking out at night to go to West Hollywood. She remembered dating both women and men, unsure still that her attraction to women could lead to a viable future even though she was becoming increasingly certain that the attraction was real and quite strong. After college she moved to New York City, and eventually prepared to rent an apartment together with her first serious girlfriend. "I believe it was a two-year sublet lease," she explained. "And I'm thinking, 'Two more years.' I mean, this is not Fantasy Island anymore. This is turning into a life with somebody. You know, where's my kids going to come from?'" Unable to see how she could have the traditional family she wanted with a woman rather than a man, Cynthia backed out of the relationship and returned to Los Angeles, only to follow the same girlfriend to Florida six months later. Religious doubts continued to nag her, though, and she asked God for a sign. "One day I said, 'You know, God, if you want me to go home and this isn't right for me, . . . send two white birds right by me, right now.' And two white birds come by!" Cynthia returned once more to Los Angeles.

She maintained contact with her girlfriend at first, and soon convinced her to move to L.A. Then, when her girlfriend was visiting before the move, Cynthia's mother caught the two together. Cynthia reflected, "I think the moment when my mother found out was when it really hit me. Reality is here, you know, the scary part is really now here. . . . I just had all the shame, fear, all of this hit me, and [I] ended up hooking up with a guy that liked me all these years and, you know, got pregnant, got married." She was married for ten years, but despite constant prayer for God to take away her desire for women, that desire never lessened. "I really had a day," she told me, laughing, "where I said to myself, 'You know, you're a lesbian. That's it. Just, you are.' It took me a long time to figure out that *I* didn't make myself that way. So once I figured it out that it's just gay from day one, well, then I figured out, well, God made me gay." She began divorce proceedings, contacted her old girlfriend, and began preparations to move to Florida. Then she met Lara.

Lara and Cynthia both remain firm believers in God, and they would like to have a church to attend. Because their two younger children continued to attend Catholic school for some time after their marriage, the family used to attend the church with which the school was affiliated. As Cynthia put it, "The Catholic church is my home. They welcomed me when I was baptized, therefore they can continue welcoming me till the day I die. . . . When God comes down and tells me I can't go to this church, then I'll stop going." Yet since they withdrew their youngest daughter from Catholic school, the two generally go only occasionally, to pray when no one else is there. The faculty at the school, Cynthia reported, had been supportive of their children, "but there's a little sect of the school that's part of, sort of like a very extremist-right wave of Christians." Some of her daughter's friends could not attend her birthday party because their parents refused to allow their children to enter Cynthia and Lara's home. "My daughter's a pretty outgoing person," Cynthia told me, "and I didn't want it to affect her, so I made the decision to pull her out." Cynthia now says that she and her family no longer "have a place that we consider our [religious] home." Both women enjoy formal services, and they tried attending MCCLA as a way of having an accepting church. They found MCCLA to their liking, but like All Saints Episcopal the church is too far from their home for a weekly trek with children in tow. As a result, they continue to explore both within and beyond Christianity, seeking a more permanent religious home.

Religious Pathways: Conversion

Of the nineteen women in the study who had definitively abandoned the religion of their childhood, seven had done so through conversion. For one this meant a conversion to atheism and a deep aversion to all things religious; for six others it meant conversion to a smaller, often lesser-known, and LGBT-supportive religion. Furthermore, five of the participants—mostly converts—spoke of the importance of twelve-step programs like Alcoholics Anonymous in their spiritual journeys. Although twelve-step principles continue to inform the beliefs and practices of these five women, they are but one piece in a larger and more complex picture of spiritual continuity, conversion, and innovation.

Converting to Irreligion

In stark contrast to women like Lara and Cynthia, Silva wants nothing to do with a permanent religious home: though she believes in souls, spirits, and reincarnation, she is a dedicated atheist. From age three to eight, what she called her "informative years," Silva lived in a Catholic orphanage. She described the nuns there as being severe, unloving, and abusive. "'cause they were frustrated beings, man," she opined. "You know what I mean? I mean, these were nasty women. They were. You know? They would hurt you, they destroyed you."[35] By the time an aunt took Silva and her younger brother in, when they were eight and five, respectively, Silva already had little patience for Catholicism, though she continued to believe in God. She attended church once a year, on Palm Sunday, out of respect for her aunt, who kept the palm fronds in the house, but "I didn't touch no water . . . I wasn't going to sit through mass."

"I was a very angry child," Silva recalled, and that anger, along with the accompanying violence, lasted until her brother committed suicide when she was thirty-two. "For the next few years," she told me, "I felt something was wrong. I wasn't compassionate enough. I wasn't there for him. You know, I felt I was empty, and maybe this is what I needed, that I needed God and I needed religion. So that's when I started studying the Bible." When a pair of Jehovah's Witnesses appeared on her doorstep one day, Silva invited them in and committed to a year of Bible study. "Boy, did I frustrate them," she recalled. "Boy, 'cause I had questions." The Bible study sessions did not have the result for which either Silva or her teachers were hoping. "I found out," Silva told me, "that . . . the Bible was worse than I was. . . . I was kinder and nicer than the people in the Bible." Before starting the Bible study, she explained, "I believed that there was a God, and he was a good God. Okay? That all these people [who commit atrocities in the name of God] were just messed up. Okay? But all these people are going by the Bible. Inspired by God. . . . I say, B.S.!" She laughed. "You know, I mean, why would you follow somebody like this?" When two elderly Witnesses came to Silva's door more recently, she sent them away with these words: "I'm sorry, there's just too much sex and violence in religion. You have a nice day."

In addition to her objections to the Bible, which include a narrow portrayal of women, Silva was also incensed by what she saw as the widespread hypocrisy of religious people. She did not restrict this criticism to Christians, either. "Right now, as we sit here talking," she told me, "people are being murdered because of their religion. The same god, but their religion. How odd! . . . The Protestants and the Catholics, the Muslims and the Sikhs . . . they're all committing murder, atrocities, in the name of this god." She conceded that there might indeed be some sort of higher power, because "something happened for us to get here." But if that higher power "is God, I don't want no part of him, okay?" She added, "Maybe there is a God and he's a good guy, you know what I'm saying? But what humanity has done, oh boy, it's just destroyed it." Silva said that she believed simply in the power of individuals to be caring and compassionate. "I believe in the human being."

Converting to Other Religions

Kathleen McGregor's journeys from Catholicism to Unitarian Universalism and from heterosexual identity to lesbian identity are deeply intertwined; one might even call them parallel conversions. Kathleen was raised in Nogales, Arizona, on the border between the United States and Mexico. Her parents met in Catholic school and married immediately after graduating, "so Catholicism was sort of a big part of my life," she told me.[36] Her grandmother, she remembered, was very religious. Kathleen walked to church with her on Sundays as a child and learned from her how to pray, especially to the Virgin Mary, whom Kathleen continues to associate with her grandmother. Kathleen's parents divorced when she was eight, and she remembers finding "a lot of comfort in the church [when] it was pretty chaotic at home." By her teen years, however, Kathleen was developing anxieties about her beliefs. "I thought, 'What if Jesus is the wrong guy? What if he really isn't the Messiah, you know?'" These fears were exacerbated by conversations about Satan with her Mormon babysitter. "After that I started really having nightmares, and having this fear that hell was just going to come and swallow me up any time." These fears grew until 1987 when there was widespread popular discussion, especially in New Age circles, of a "harmonic convergence" that would bring about major changes in the world.

Kathleen was nineteen at the time, and although most who believed in the harmonic convergence expected positive outcomes from it, she was nonetheless unnerved by their predictions. Overwhelmed by her own fears, she decided not to believe in a devil any more. Her boyfriend at the time asked her, "'Well, how can you believe in an ultimate good and not believe in an ultimate bad?' And so I thought about that," she told me, "and I thought, 'Okay, I'm not going to believe in anything.' And, you know, in that, the fear was gone. . . . But then, you know, I was also without an anchor."

Kathleen married in her early twenties; her husband turned out to be alcoholic and abusive, and she eventually divorced him and joined Al-Anon. "And there," she told me, "I started to gain some spirituality." However, "even though they say it's open to anybody, still some of the principles were very Christian, and I had a problem with that." Seeking something positive in her life, and remembering how much of a positive force religion had been for her grandmother, Kathleen decided to try a religion other than Catholicism. "Because I had sort of, you know, an inkling that I might be a lesbian or might want to go in that direction," she remembered, "I had this litmus test to look for a church that would be open to that." She discovered All Saints Episcopal Church, and began attending. She found it familiar and comforting, and she liked the church's "focus . . . on social action." However, she told me, "they were still saying the Nicene Creed every week . . . , and while they were challenging us to come to our own conclusions and believe what we wanted to believe or needed to believe, I still felt that . . . having to go in every week and . . . say the Nicene Creed was just, I couldn't be true to what I needed to find in spirituality."

The final straw at All Saints came when Kathleen decided to marry again. Still uncomfortable with her attraction to women, for both social and religious reasons ("deep down, I had this sense that [the Virgin Mary] would disapprove,"), Kathleen became engaged to another man. In deciding where to hold their wedding, she came to the realization that despite two years of attendance at All Saints, she had not come to know any of the priests there particularly well. Again she went in search for a church, now knowing that she "had to look outside of Catholicism and Episcopalianism," and, she concluded with a laugh, she "became a Unitarian because of the internet." A co-worker encouraged her to investigate the Unitarian Universalist Association, and though Kathleen resisted attending, she decided she would at least learn about the organization's principles. "And I found that they were really very closely aligned with my philosophy about life. And, you know, I wanted to become a Unitarian Universalist before I found a church."

Kathleen eventually visited both Unitarian Universalist congregations near her, and chose to begin attending Neighborhood Church because of how much she liked the minister. She married her second husband there and began attending regularly, but after a year and a half, the minister whom she had liked so much moved away. Kathleen maintained her affiliation with Neighborhood but began to spend more time in committee work than in church services. Five years after her second marriage she and her husband divorced, and Kathleen began to come out as a lesbian. Important in this process, she told me, was the LGBT group at Neighborhood; this group's members were among the first people she told about her feelings for women. "So, just sort of in the cocoon of that group I started to search for my identity," she recalled. "And it took a couple of years"—until quite recently before our interview, in fact—"to just truly become comfortable with myself."

Comfort with a church was Kathleen's next challenge. With a different minister in place at Neighborhood, she took the advice of a friend that she might be more comfortable at the smaller and more working-class Throop Church across town. She met with the minister and liked him a great deal; soon, she switched churches. Having been at Throop for a few years by the time she met with me, Kathleen spoke at length about the aspects of the church that appealed to her. These included a traditional building that reminded her of the comforts of her childhood church without requiring that she adhere to beliefs she no longer felt to be true; the small size of the congregation and an accompanying sense that the people and services were not "pretentious"; an informality in the services that stemmed in part from the small size; a feeling that Throop's services were more "spiritual" and less "intellectual" than Neighborhood's; and a sense that she was needed in this small, somewhat struggling congregation.

Kathleen appreciated the opportunities available in Unitarian Universalism to explore a wide range of beliefs. Some aspects of her Catholic upbringing remained important to her, she said, especially her interest in Mary and specifically in Our Lady of Guadalupe. At the time of our interview she was working to develop a broader sense of God: "I can't get rid of the Papa God," she told me in some frustration. Her church, however, referred to "God and Goddess and sometimes just all-unifying love," and she found these images to be helpful even as she wished "that I could just give in to that [the more inclusive image of God]." She also felt a strong spiritual connection to nature, especially through the moon and the ocean, and recent coursework in women's studies had led her to explore feminist spirituality and feminist theology as well.

A very different conversion story comes from Christie Tuttle, who was raised in a devout Mormon family and is one of two children in that family to have come out. "Even when I was a child," Christie recalled, "I never felt like I made contact with the religion. Never even wanted to go to church or felt like I believed in it."[37] By her early teens Christie was questioning the role of women in the church as well as the expectation of tithing, and once she turned eighteen and was allowed to make her own choice about attending services, she quit. Looking back, she said, "It was always 'The church tells us this, the church tells us that' . . . and I never felt the connection of your heart and dictates of your heart in it. It was too structured for me, I think." Though Christie said she was aware of an attraction to other girls as a child, she also remembered suppressing that attraction because of the LDS condemnation of homosexuality. A few years after she stopped going to church, Christie came out as a lesbian. Yet, she told me, she retained the belief (reinforced by her mother after she came out) that gay men and lesbians are destined for hell. "Whenever your life is so consumed with religion, day in and day out," she reflected, "you can't just, like, step away from it because it has such an impact on you. And so I have had a hard time reconciling with myself that I'm okay, that I'm still a good person, that my lifestyle doesn't dictate that I'm a bad person."

Christie went on with her life after leaving the church, but for a variety of reasons, she said, she "rejected" all religion and "even questioned whether I believed in God or not, basically until maybe three years ago." Christie was living in Seattle when a back injury prevented her from continuing with her job at an organic bread company. She and her partner both found job opportunities in Salt Lake City, where Christie's gay brother also lived, and they moved there. When doctors had difficulty diagnosing and treating Christie's injury, her brother recommended she see a friend of his who "does emotional release bodywork." He also offered to pay for Christie's treatments. Christie told me that she believed "the true meaning of going back to Salt Lake" was an opportunity to meet her brother's friend, who turned out also to be what Christie calls a "shaman." When I asked Christie what this meant, she replied simply, "She's studied shamanic rituals. She's studied Native American rituals." Christie's shaman is not Native herself, but of European descent; the practices Christie has undergone with her include a variety of New Age techniques such as "soul retrieval" (calling back portions of the soul that have left one's body) as well as aspects of Native ritual practices that have been widely adopted and altered by New Age practitioners, such as sweat lodge ceremonies.

Having discovered that her healer was also a shaman, Christie became intensely curious. "I started asking her questions," she told me, "because I was so intrigued by it all. . . . The more questions I asked, the more questions I had, and it excited me. And I could feel within me that this was what I needed to explore." She expanded on this perception a little later in the interview:

> *I could just feel within myself that I was on the right track for me, that this is what my spirit needed to help me evolve and move forward, because I didn't work good within the structure of organized religion, and I couldn't go into even a Unitarian church, that I needed something broader for me that allowed me to do my own exploring and be more independent. . . . And now, two, three years later, I see how I've evolved. And my brother even comments, the change in me. And I'm more in tune with myself, and listen to my heart.*

When Christie moved to Los Angeles, a year and a half before our interview, she remained in touch with her shaman in Utah. She had been exploring local New Age resources since her move, and when we spoke she was considering traveling to Northern California to study with one of her shaman's teachers. She had been working on retrieving aspects of her soul, and on expressing and affirming her sense of freedom. Of this work, she said, "I feel like it's just really something I've just cracked the door on, and have so much to learn."

Spirituality and Twelve-Step Programs

Five participants explicitly credited twelve-step programs—generally Alcoholics Anonymous and Al-Anon—with setting them back on a "spiritual" path. These include one woman who currently attends an LGBT-focused Christian church; one whose religiosity is best classed as "bricolage," and three who converted to lesser-known religions. Trish's and Regina's stories serve as illustrations for this pattern both because of the similarities they share with the other three participants who spoke openly about twelve-step programs and because of the differences in their interactions with these programs.

Trish was baptized Catholic, but was raised in a Presbyterian church because her mother "was rebelling against the Catholic church at the time."[38] For her, though, church was mostly a social and musical outlet. "I don't really recall having an understanding of God or the faith," she told me. Though she was in contact with the chaplain at her college through her involvement in social justice organizations on campus, Trish remembers that "I didn't really continue to think of myself as in a particular religion, or as having any particular faith." Furthermore, "I really didn't think of myself as either a religious or a spiritual person for most of my young adulthood." When Trish joined Alcoholics Anonymous, she discovered that, as she put it, "it's a very spiritual program. And God is mentioned in many of the steps." This bothered her at first; looking back at the time of the interview, she told me that she thought this "hostile" reaction to any talk of God came from not having developed a concept of God earlier in her life. "I'd had a good experience in church," she explained, "but I just didn't really have a concept of what God was all about, or having a God in my life. And I think that which I don't know anything about, I fear and loathe."

In order to remain in AA, Trish knew, she needed to work on developing a concept of God. This became an ongoing process; she joined a Unitarian Universalist (UU) church several years before our interview and had been studying a variety of religions through her involvement there. However, Trish credited AA with helping her "gain an understanding of what God is to me." When I met with her, Trish remained highly involved with her UU church, and was continuing to attend AA as well. She told me that she considered the latter "a very spiritual community and spiritual activity." Along with church and AA, her other main spiritual practice was "being out in nature."

Like Trish, Regina was raised with regular involvement in a religion—Catholicism, in this case—yet did not remember developing a deep sense of religiosity or an understanding of God during her years in the church. Also like Trish, she found the church to be a social and musical outlet rather than a religious one. Regina remembered reflecting on the meaning of her experiences when she became sexually active. "I was not raised with admonitions about saving sex until you got married," she told me. However, "I also knew, somehow, that having sex and going to church was a hypocritical thing to do if you were not married."[39] Therefore, Regina stopped attending church. She elaborated later in the interview that because she had no sense of God at that point in her life, she was not concerned about divine disapproval; she simply felt that extramarital sexual activity and the social space of the church were mutually exclusive.

"I never even thought about religion and its place in my life for a long time" after leaving the church, Regina said, "until I turned twenty-three and got sober in AA. And, you know, right away I hear that I've got to develop a conscious contact with God as I understand him." Dedicated to the goals of the program, Regina felt that if finding God was a prerequisite for recovering from alcoholism, then find God she would. "I didn't go to church," she remembered, "but I went to AA meetings, and to me it was equivocal." She began journaling, always addressing her entries "Dear God," and she prayed every night, using language for God that she had learned in AA. Then she began a career in women's studies. "When I turned thirty," she explained,

> *I took a women's history class. I'm developing a [feminist] language, I'm realizing the language that I was speaking in AA in terms of a God consciousness was not fitting any more. And it sounded very male, and very masculinized, and very dogmatic, and very preachy, and very patriarchal. So I kept taking women's studies and women's history courses and stopped going to meetings. And I realized that the fellowship that I needed in AA I was getting in school.*

Regina "left a God consciousness in the dust" and turned to her studies full-time. She continued journaling, and began addressing the entries to "Great Spirit," "'cause I didn't know what else to call this." In lieu of prayer, she developed what she calls a "mantra," which "for the last couple years . . . has sustained in me a sense of spiritual connection."

Religious Pathways: Innovation

Regina was still interested in spirituality at the time of our interview, but also continued to feel that she had not yet found the "language" she needed to describe the divine, or even to practice her spirituality in ways that did not feel patriarchal to her. Like four other participants, she was a seeker: aware of a sense of the divine and of "being spiritual," interested in some sort of religious practice, but not yet satisfied with the answers she had found to her religious questions. While ten of the women in this study continued as adults to identify in some way with their childhood religions and another seven converted in adulthood to atheism or to less mainstream religions, twelve found themselves at the time of the interviews in a space of religious innovation. Roughly half of this group were what I am here calling "seekers"; the other half engaged in a practice of religious bricolage, or mosaic making, of which more below.

Seeking

Vanessa, who was struggling with the compatibility of Jewish and lesbian identities when I first interviewed her, seems to have become a seeker during the course of this study: by the time of her e-mail contact with me two years after our interview, she had drifted away from Judaism and was reading books about Buddhism. Others in the study had been seekers at times in the past, such as Coco with her foray into the New Age movement during her twenties. Furthermore, as with the other religious patterns, the women whose experiences are described in this section might well have moved on to another pattern—to a form of continuity or to other forms of innovation—by the time this book is published. Not only are their identities and their daily beliefs and practices often fluid, the strategies through which the participants explore and maintain their spirituality have shifted over time.

Tami may have been in the process of moving from seeker to convert during the course of this project, though because that process was clearly incomplete when the project concluded I have included her here as a seeker. A Catholic from birth who "did all the sacraments except for marriage,"[40] Tami began to pull away from the church as a teenager. In retrospect, she said, "I think I was always turned off by the fact that somebody told me that this man was watching me, and if I did wrong he was going to burn me. I wasn't *afraid* of being burned; I was *mad* that somebody was going to do this to me." When she got her first job and was rewarded with a tithe request from the bishop, Tami recalls being taken aback. "So that kind of pushed me away." Once she had left the church, though, she found that she missed the ritual. "It was the incense, and the oils and the chanting, and I always thought that was so beautiful."

By the time Tami was seventeen or eighteen, she said, she had left Catholicism behind entirely. "But there was always a spiritual yearning, and I didn't know what it was." She became interested in Wicca through two college friends who were themselves Wiccans and who gave her a copy of Starhawk's *The Spiral Dance*. "I felt really drawn to it," Tami remembered, "but I never really did anything." Unsure whether Wicca was the right religion for her, and wary of stereotypes about witches, Tami continued searching. She explored Buddhism and other branches of Christianity through books, and learned about Judaism through friends. "It's all based on the same thing," she explained to me in an almost uncanny echo of Sheila Larson in *Habits of the Heart*. "I mean, you just want to be treated right, and you want to treat other people right, and if you don't, it'll come back to you. You know, it's that simple, and I just take from all the different ones [religions] and then kind of made my own, I guess." At the same time, she said, "I'm looking for the comfort, I'm looking for that one niche, I guess, that other people think the way I think."

Tami was missing religious community and tradition when we spoke, and she told me that a community of women, and especially of lesbians, was important to her. She had also begun focusing her personal theology around the Goddess. But the experience that had most rekindled her interest in Wicca was a concert she had attended the week before our interview. The group was Godsmack, whose lead singer is openly Wiccan. Tami was impressed with his stage presence, and was awestruck by a music video she saw at the concert, which included footage from a Wiccan ritual. "It was just really beautiful. And I'm sitting there staring, everybody's dancing around me, and I'm just like, 'Oh! I want to be there!'" Between a strong sense of spirituality in nature, an attraction to Goddess-focused religion, and a need for a religious community that empowered women and in which she could be out as a lesbian, Tami was suspecting when I interviewed her that the time was right for her to explore Wicca further. "I made the first couple steps by reading different books," she told me. "So I know I want to see groups and classes and different things, and see if that's really where I want to go." Just the day before we spoke, Tami had discovered the website for ReWeaving, and she was very interested in finding out more about the circle. A year later, when I conducted fieldwork with ReWeaving, Tami had not only started attending but had reached a level of comfort where she was willing to bring her eight-year-old son to rituals with her.

Tami was the only one of the seekers to have found a potential spiritual home at the time of the interviews; the others were all still searching. Lisa, who like Tami was raised Catholic, grew up an independent thinker in religious matters. Because her extended family members were heavily involved in the church and her immediate family attended with some regularity, Lisa was thoroughly exposed to Catholicism. "But we were never made to study the Bible, or to go to church or anything. And I think that predominantly had to do with my mom. She was somewhat of a feminist. . . . And if you wanted to become spiritual, then as a scholar she wanted to take you to the library and show you all your options."[41] Her mother believed in reincarnation and was interested in the writings of metaphysical author Edgar Cayce. "So," remembered Lisa, "my mom was more into just teaching us spirituality, from less of a structured, religious kind of perspective." Lisa also remembers being very interested in science as a child, "preferring to believe in things that I could rationalize and understand and explain." So while she remains open to the idea of God, she said, she is also skeptical.

"I still maintain that openness today," she added. Suspicious of the ways in which human interests have shaped religion, she saw spirituality as "the root, what *is* going on. It's a connection and an awareness and a striving for growth and understanding by my soul." Religion, to her mind, is "the manifestation of that concept of spirituality in a business sense. I really do view *religion* as a business. . . . A marketing tool to control people." Not all religions are like this, she said, especially the small ones, and it is still possible to be "spiritual," by her definition, within religious organizations. This is perhaps why Lisa remained interested in religious organizations as well as in developing her individual sense of spirituality. At the time of the interview she was a regular meditation practitioner, and she had been reading about a number of different religions.

She had also been studying the work of people she termed "prophets," such as Edgar Cayce. "We don't live in a vacuum," she noted. "And learning about other people's perspectives and experiences is how I form my own. . . . Spirituality, for me, is a lifelong pursuit."

An agnostic with a belief in reincarnation, Lisa found the Agape International Spiritual Center attractive not only because the ideas behind Religious Science were compatible with her own but also because "it appeals to my sense of personal responsibility and control." Though Agape was located far from Lisa's home and she had not attended regularly in some time, she had explored a Science of Mind organization closer to her and had found it promising. She also continued her seeking by attending any religious service to which someone invited her—"especially weddings," she added with a laugh. She was particularly impressed by what she termed the "inclusiveness" and "genuine realness" of the Jewish services she had attended. Because Linda, Lisa's partner at the time and also a participant in this study, was reluctant to explore too far beyond Christianity, the two had also attended MCCLA and West Hollywood Presbyterian Church. "They're really good," Lisa told me.

Although I got the sense during our interview that Lisa was interested in finding a religious organization to attend regularly, she and Linda had not yet settled into routine attendance anywhere. "Why haven't we done it?" Lisa asked rhetorically, with reference to attending West Hollywood Presbyterian. "I don't know. Life kind of gets in the way of life, you know, and you kind of forget that this *is* life."

Bricolage

Nearly a quarter of the study participants combined seeking and conversion to create unique mosaics of religious beliefs and practices drawn from a variety of different religions and teachers. This mosaic strategy, whether used in religion or in other contexts, is often referred to in academic circles as bricolage.[42] A *bricoleur* (or *bricoleuse,* to use the feminine form) is someone who makes do with the materials on hand, bringing disparate elements into new combinations in order to create an innovative whole. This is an undercurrent in many of the stories discussed above, but it becomes a prominent stream in the lives of seven of the participants.

Lauren came to New Age beliefs and practices as a part of her religious mosaic making. Although Lauren was raised a Protestant, she recalled being a skeptic from very early on:

> *From birth, essentially, from my earliest childhood, I had a sense that my physical being was incorrect. You know, that I was manifesting in a way that was contrary to my heart and my soul's feeling of the way I should be manifesting. And so, that immediately set up*

a conflict, you know, that things weren't right. When it goes down to that basic sense of personal identity, you begin to question everything. And so I was never able to just swallow things that people told me. I would have to, you know, go more for this almost unidentifiable sense of awareness, of feeling what was true.[43]

Protestantism failed this test, and around the age of twelve or thirteen, Lauren remembers writing a letter to her mother, explaining her objections to church and asking to be permitted not to attend. Her parents acquiesced.

Lauren, who was assigned male at birth, told me that gender was the main source of her sense of incongruity between her physical body and her soul. Yet the persistence and deep-rooted nature of this tension seems to have provided an important key for her religious beliefs and practices, as well. For instance, when she was twenty-one Lauren was experimenting with astral projection, "attempting to take my spiritual form out of my body, and release it to explore whatever was out there." Looking back, she explained, "I was very unhappy, and looking for something beyond the physical existence." She believes that her efforts drew "a spiritual being from another plane of existence" to her, an experience that she remembers as both terrifying and energizing. Though at the time she asked the being to leave, Lauren told me that she now hopes for its return, feeling that her practice and her spiritual self-awareness have advanced to the point where she is ready for such a visit.

Lauren's spiritual beliefs and practices developed through the influence of a variety of sources, most of them associated with the New Age movement. Recently, she has become interested in the writings and audio recordings of an entity named Kryon, whose teachings are "channeled" and published by a Southern California group.[44] She likes to meditate, especially near the ocean. "Oddly enough," she told me, "I love to meditate in my car. I have favorite CDs that I play, so that the outside world doesn't intrude on me. There's a place out by Santa Monica I go. I can park right at the beach, and just look out at the ocean, and play this CD, and just be in another world." A national billiards competitor, Lauren also considers that activity to be a form of meditation. She goes to events at local New Age bookstores, and she has sporadically attended several different New Age groups, though she admitted that concerns about being mistreated because she is transgendered have kept her from seeking out groups for spiritual practice to the extent that she might have otherwise. "Any time that you're wishing to grow [spiritually]," she reflected, "or any time that you're wishing to gain insight, a support system is helpful. . . . So, yeah, I've thoroughly limited myself as far as opportunities to grow."

Since the late 1990s, one of Lauren's most important forms of spiritual practice has been writing poetry, and she brought a collection of her poems to share with me during our interview. The poems come to her at certain times, during which, she said, she receives "a rather spontaneous influx of energy. . . . My whole energy level goes up, I need very little sleep, and I start getting these urges to write these poems. And basically I sit down, and they just dictate out of the place in my head where the poem was." One of her poems, "Through the Looking Glass," contains the following telling lines: "It becomes clear that I'm not the one you think you see when you think you see me."[45]

Importantly, Lauren believes that the physical form is an illusion masking a deeper (or perhaps higher) spiritual reality. She believes that individual souls tend to be more comfortable living in one gender than the other, but also that before birth one chooses one's human form in order to maximize one's learning, subsequently forgetting about that choice while on earth. Lauren sees human forms as extremely limiting, to the point that "God is incomprehensible to the biology of humans." Yet, to her, the human form is one stage of spiritual evolution, from which souls go on to more advanced learning and greater insight. Because of her enduring interest in discovering what realities lie beyond the human form, Lauren believes that she may be in her final human incarnation, "ready to go on, to graduate into a different plane of existence." Speculating on the future of humanity, Lauren observed, "I've often thought evolution would bring androgyny. You know, that rather than the genders splitting off further and further from each other, that they would be coming farther together. And so eventually we'd be a relatively androgynous species." This theory fit with Lauren's sense of being near the end of her own human incarnations, so I asked whether she saw transgendered people as a step forward in that evolutionary process. "Yeah," she responded, adding that she felt her own gender to be "along a gray scale" and "a blend," but that "society sort of requires you to sign on to one or the other." "So I picked the one that felt more true," she added.

Adesina, like Lauren, began her religious mosaic making with a fairly early rejection of her childhood religion. Adesina was brought up in the Baptist Church, "which I didn't really take to," she told me.[46] "As a child it was just something that was kind of forced on me." When she began learning the history of her African American ancestors, "I was totally turned off of Christianity because they supported the slave trade, and they supported a lot of abominations to women, you know, the Inquisition, things of that nature. So . . . I stopped going to church." During her senior year of high school, she saw a performance of Arthur Hall's Afro-American Dance Ensemble. Some of the dances drew on Yoruba tradition, and Adesina remembered that "my heart just, like, went out to it. I could feel tears rolling down my face as I saw these dances to Dambala and to Oshun and Yemanya." She sought out a Yoruba priest, and received the name she now bears.

In her early twenties Adesina left her hometown of Philadelphia and moved to San Diego. "I was running from the cold," she told me, laughing. Here she encountered some difficulty with continuing her Yoruba practices, since most of what she found in Southern California was the diasporic tradition of Santería. "I don't speak Spanish," she explained, "so it was a little bit hard for me, because I wanted it from an African American perspective." Then she began a nearly twenty-year stint of working at the Prophet, a vegetarian restaurant founded by Makeda Cheatom that became a landmark in the San Diego alternative scene as well as a hub of the reggae movement. The restaurant fostered not only healthy eating among its patrons but also cultural exchange. Adesina remembered that "we would have religious groups bring their pictures and information . . . to the restaurant and we would get a chance to explore them." Though Adesina first became a vegetarian for "purely cosmetic" reasons, she later became convinced that a vegetarian diet had health benefits not only physically but also spiritually. At that point, she decided she could not progress further in her involvement with Yoruba religion, because she could not condone animal sacrifice.

At the same time, though, she was exploring a wide variety of other religions through the constant stream of visitors at the Prophet. She learned about Soka Gakkai, Thich Nhat Hanh, the Dalai Lama, Taoism, Paramahansa Yogananda's Self-Realization Fellowship, Krishna devotion, Transcendental Meditation, yoga, and Science of Mind—among others. "And what I've found," she explained, "was that the religion in its pure form was wonderful, but then as you got into it, the organization and the people kind of corrupted it. . . . So what I found was that for me, spirituality was a stepping-stone to finding my own self. And each religion was a different level that I would go through."

In the mid-1990s Adesina moved north to Los Angeles. During Adesina's last few years in San Diego, an acquaintance made the two-hour drive north to Culver City twice a week to train as a Religious Science practitioner at the Agape International Spiritual Center. "And when she told me she did that, I couldn't believe it. . . . And she says, 'Yeah, you know, I'm really into this.' So that struck my curiosity." After she moved to L.A., Adesina visited Agape. "And I could see what she meant, you know, it's a driving force. It's a place where, in the city, for that Sunday, for that two hours, we have unity of all people." Though she had not joined the center at the time of our interview, Adesina was attending nearly every Sunday. She also was involved with TLC, the lesbian group at the Agape.

Yet despite her dedication to Agape, Adesina's story is not that of a convert; her lack of membership may be one indication of this. When asked how she would introduce herself to people interested in this study, Adesina said the following:

> *I'm an African American lesbian, vegetarian gourmet chef, and kripala yoga teacher, and I think that religion plays a major part in my life, and that it is threefold, where I use diet (which is vegetar-*

ian), meditation, and yoga to be my spiritual base. I've studied various religions from around the world, and I kind of take bits and pieces from each part of them to have my own source of spirituality. I lean towards Science of Mind right now, and that could change whenever, because I like having positive affirmations and being able to experience the Goddess within.

With such a summary, there can be little doubt that Adesina is a religious *bricoleuse.*

The final "mosaic maker" to be discussed in depth here is Dean Bramlett, whose range of spiritual practices may not be as numerous as Adesina's, but is definitely broader. "I guess I'm kind of a 'one from column A, one from column B' kind of religious person," she reflected during our interview. "You know, I choose what I like to believe, and I discard what I don't believe."[47]

Dean grew up experiencing a broad range of Protestantism—what she called "Heinz 57 Christianity."[48] Her mother was a New Jersey Episcopalian, her father a Georgia Southern Baptist. The two were married in a Moravian church, and baptized their children there as well, but on Sunday mornings when they drove into town from their farm, they attended whichever Protestant church had a service starting soon. Dean recalled, "That was kind of where I got started with the idea that religion isn't necessarily about one church. That religion is a dogma. Religion is a set of parameters around which people develop different kinds of beliefs." When Dean was in high school her parents decided to settle in a single congregation. They required her to go through confirmation classes in the local Lutheran church, despite the fact that she was older than all of the other students. This experience left her "resentful towards the church," and once she was confirmed she stopped going to church at all. However, she told me, "that was when I actually started looking at spiritual things."

Dean paid little attention to religion until after she moved to California in her twenties. In the meantime, trying to suppress her desire for women, she married and then divorced three times. "Every time I would become really involved with a woman," she explained, "that there was a relationship there, and I could really feel good about it, I would quickly go and marry a man." She came to California with "Husband Number Two." Then she began reading spiritual books, listening to spiritual audiotapes, and attending spiritual seminars. "I was basically a books-seminar-tape junkie," she recalled. She was especially involved with the Southern California–based Movement of Spiritual Inner Awareness, led by a man known as John-Roger. "I finally had a friend who introduced me to John-Roger, and brought me and started telling me about different things that I could look at. And different ways that I could look at my life, and why I was unhappy in my life."

Coming to believe that God is within each person, Dean said, allowed her to begin coming out as a lesbian during her thirties. When she finally came out at the age of forty, she remembered, "although I had taken some spiritual steps, I decided that I needed to look at some religious steps." I asked her to explain her distinction between religion and spirituality. "Religion is the dogma," she responded. "Religion is, you go and you say the words the way they're expected to be said, and you follow the dogma. Because religion is, to me, having to do with the church, and everything that goes into the church. Spirituality is what you find in yourself." Both are important to her; "dogma" provides a comforting sense of continuity and predictability, but does not "satisfy . . . my spiritual needs. Because I don't feel that I have found a church of any religion that speaks to me, and looks at my needs, as a woman."

Feeling ready to bring religion and "dogma" back into her life, Dean began church shopping and eventually found St. Thomas the Apostle Episcopal Church through a friend. At the time of our interview, she attended St. Thomas fairly regularly. She preferred the small size and introspective atmosphere of the early morning spoken mass, as well as its brevity. Laughing, she explained, "I can go to eight o'clock mass, go to the farmers' market, come home, have my breakfast, and be reading the paper before the people have even gone into the ten thirty mass! So for me it's also a time saver." While St. Thomas filled her need for "religion," for "spirituality" Dean listed several other practices. "I meditate, I burn candles and incense. I actually practice a little Wicca. I go to an ashram with a friend of mine, where we go to one-hour chants and two-hour chants and things like that." Her Wiccan practice, Dean elaborated, was generally solitary; she did not work with a coven or a public circle. Her best friend was Wiccan, though, and the two had conducted a number of "very spiritual kinds of ceremonies together." Chanting at the ashram, she told me later in an informal conversation, was a new practice when I interviewed her. After the terrorist attacks of September 11, 2001, she explained, she went to a service at St. Thomas but found it too noisy and active; she was seeking quiet and tranquillity. A friend invited her to chant at the Siddha Yoga Meditation Center of Los Angeles; not only did the chanting sessions meet her needs at the time, but she enjoyed them immensely and continued to go, backing off instead on her involvement with St. Thomas.

All of these sources of religious and spiritual fulfillment, however, came nowhere near the crux of Dean's spiritual practice. At the time of our interview Dean was also known as Sister Vibrata Electric of the Order of the Flaming Labia in the Sisters of Perpetual Indulgence, Los Angeles House. The Sisters, for her, were a source of both spirituality and religion, a source of community, a source of self-confidence, and an expression of her most important beliefs. "Their main mission statement," she explained, "says that we expiate stigmatic guilt and promulgate universal joy. No guilt. Which says a lot about how I believe, and what I feel." Furthermore, she felt celebrated by this nearly all-male group for being female, and that was an unusual experience for her.

Dean first met the Sisters when she was volunteering at a benefit bingo night at AIDS Project L.A. She "thought they were such great fun," and she began talking to them. "And I really liked what they told me." She stayed in contact with the group, got to know all of the members, and soon was presented as a postulant. "I know *exactly* how religious people feel a call," Dean told me intensely. "Because I had *such* a call. I was going to be a Sister—that was all there was to it." Though the Sisters are not a religious organization, they include people from a wide variety of religious backgrounds and persuasions. Dean saw her involvement with them as a central part of her religious and spiritual practice; also worth noting is that her work as a Sister was the only practice Dean mentioned that included both religious and spiritual aspects—an important distinction for her. "I take my Sisterhood extremely seriously," Dean explained, "because it ties right into my religious feelings, and it ties into my spirituality feelings. It is *me* giving to the community. It is of my heart. It is of my soul. It is of what I believe, and it is of who I *am*." The Sisters were a reflection of the mosaic Dean had created in her wide-ranging explorations of religion, spirituality, and identity.

Conclusions

This chapter has explored a variety of life stories in order to show the significant complexity in the beliefs, practices, and experiences that participants in this study consider relevant to their religion and spirituality. From marrying men and bearing children to avoid social stigma, religious stigma, or both, to coming out through the influence of Mother Teresa, to rejecting religion because of its sexism or racism and coming out after that, these women have followed a wide variety of paths in relating religion and spirituality to their sexual and gender identities, and in relating coming out to other aspects of their lives. Likewise, despite having nearly all begun their lives in fairly traditional religious settings—ten Catholic, twelve Protestant, one Christian Scientist, two Mormon, two Jewish, and one New Age—they traveled widely divergent routes before arriving at the diverse and complex beliefs and practices they shared with me.

In the breadth of their stories the women in this study represent, as I argued in chapter 1, an exemplary case study of religious individualism in the contemporary United States. In some ways, their religious and spiritual paths have been strikingly similar to those studied elsewhere: Tami sounds like Sheila

Larson when she speaks of her religious beliefs; several participants find their spirituality in part through the therapeutic models offered by twelve-step programs; and the effects of Roof's "spiritual marketplace" and Wuthnow's "spirituality of seeking" are everywhere to be seen. Where these women diverge from the general population is in the frequency with which they draw on seeking and bricolage in pursuing their spiritual journeys. In L.A., as in most major cities in the United States, lesbian, bisexual, and transgendered women have widespread access to supportive mainstream religious organizations: MCC churches, LGBT synagogues, welcoming Protestant congregations, Dignity, and the like. Unlike women in the general population, however, the women in this study attend religious organizations relatively infrequently and are far less likely than other women to be members of a religious group. Except for Silva, they all defined themselves as deeply spiritual, but nearly all have broken ties to their childhood religion at some point in their lives, and the majority continue to be estranged from it. Furthermore, even when compared to the religious LGBT populations that scholars have studied to date, this group is unusual: a full one-third of the participants reported coming out as bisexual, transgendered, or lesbian with no religious qualms whatsoever. This is in marked contrast to the findings of studies involving only those LGBT people (usually, by default, more men than women) who attend LGBT congregations of traditional religions: Shokeid speaks for a number of such studies, both past and future, when he explains that Congregation Beth Simchat Torah helps in "repairing a cracked identity."[49] Perhaps these "cracks" are more common for men, or perhaps they are more common for those who remain in traditional religions; indeed, perhaps these two factors are linked. The following chapter will consider this question, among others, in greater depth.

The routes that participants in this study traveled to arrive at their current spiritual, sexual, and sometimes gender identities were influenced by a number of different factors, few of which were predictable. Some participants were sensitive to racial dynamics or the importance of ethnic heritage; others were quite frank about disregarding such issues. Some placed women's community or sexism at the top of their list when it came to religious decision making; for others, inclusion as a lesbian, a bisexual, a polysexual, or a transperson was more important. In many cases, these identity factors themselves took a backseat to chance (or what some participants would prefer to call divine intervention): a friend's recommendation, an internet search, an evening spent volunteering at a bingo game. Interestingly, nearly all of the participants used travel metaphors ("journey," "path," and so on) to refer to their religious life stories, and many of them used the language of quest to describe both the development of their sexual and/or gender identities and the development of their religious and/or spiritual identities. This identity work is the focus of analysis in chapter 6; having finished the present chapter by discussing participants' involvement in religious organizations, however, I move next to consider more closely the nature and utilization of those organizations, and their roles in participants' identity negotiations.

5 *Tiles in the Mosaic*

ORGANIZATIONS AS RESOURCES

In the mid-1990s, theologian Mary Hunt wrote, "'Where have all the women gone?' is an oft-sung hymn" in LGBT church groups.[1] Academics, too, have sung this refrain since the early 1990s, and have been humming a similar tune since 1974—in the context of not only church groups but synagogues as well. The stories of the women who participated in my research indicate that there is not a single or simple answer to this question. The women with whom I spoke described a wide range of relationships with explicitly religious organizations, from active avoidance to avid and nearly lifelong commitment. What is consistent in their descriptions, though, is an understanding of such organizations as resources for their personal spiritual development. Those who saw such resources as being of little use, as "not working for me," avoided religious organizations. Those who found great spiritual support or sustenance in an organizational setting were committed attendees and sometimes members as well.

As I argued in chapter 1, the women whose stories form the core of this book are in many ways unremarkable in the broader context of religious patterns in the twenty-first-century United States. The idea that religious organizations in the United States function as competitors in an unregulated buyer's market is widespread within the sociology of religion, and in a recent study of post-baby-boom Americans, Robert Wuthnow describes a common pattern of religious identity formation as "tinkering."[2] So approaching religious organizations as resources to be drawn upon when needed as part of a larger identity negotiation process, rather than as "package deals," is not particularly unique to the women in this study. What *is* unique, however, is the extent to which they handle religion in this way, compared to the broader population and especially to women overall in the United States. Understanding, at least in the context of these twenty-nine women in L.A., where lesbian, bisexual, and transgendered women are religiously, and why they are where they are, thus accomplishes two goals: it sheds light on a striking pattern of religiosity in LGBT communities, and, as a magnified version of a common pattern, it allows for detailed exploration of an important national trend.

At the end of chapter 4, I wrote of bricolage as mosaic making. Not only the obvious *bricoleuses* were engaged in the process of building and maintaining a religious (or "spiritual") mosaic; in fact, each woman in this study did so, with some mosaics being more monochromatic and others more colorfully diverse. The religious organizations described in chapter 3 provide tiles of varying shapes and sizes for some of these mosaics, and don't appear at all in others. Yet even here the picture is more complicated than it first appears, because which aspects of a religious organization a particular woman found useful were inevitably influenced by her own heritage, personal history, previous experiences, and self-understanding. The development of these women's "spiritual" identities—the subject of the next chapter—and the roles of congregations in that development—the subject of the following pages—are thus not processes that can be easily mapped, categorized, or predicted. They exemplify "religious messiness" and "multiplicities," which Robert Orsi sees in religious spaces but which are also a central aspect of religious beliefs, practices, and identities.[3] Like mosaics, identities may appear disjointed when viewed only in sections, even though when they are viewed in their entirety the disjunctions often meld into a cohesive whole.

Invisibility

To return to Mary Hunt's "oft-sung hymn," where *are* all the women? One answer to this question is that queer women have been involved in congregations all along, but they have been invisible because they are involved in ways that fail to register in most studies. A good illustration of this point is a sociological study published by Darren Sherkat in 2002 that aimed to evaluate the religiosity of "non-heterosexuals" relative to heterosexuals.[4] Since there are no nationwide surveys in the United States that ask well-defined, in-depth questions about both sexual identity and religious beliefs and practices, the study's author attempted to extrapolate from a national survey that asked questions about sexual *behaviors* and about religion. Assuming that anyone who had reported having a same-sex sexual partner some time in the past five years was "non-heterosexual" (bisexual if there had also been opposite-sex partners, gay or lesbian if not), the study then calculated such respondents' religiosity through several measures, including "apostasy" (here defined as having grown up in a religion but not claiming a religious affiliation at the time of the survey), frequency of attendance at religious services, and belief that the Bible is the actual or inspired word of God. The study concluded that gay men were "more religious" than lesbians—an inversion of the gender pattern in the broader culture—and suggested that this might be because lesbians are masculine whereas gay men are feminine.

Beyond the more obvious problems of assuming that sexual behavior in the past five years correlates well with sexual identity,[5] and beyond the stunningly anachronistic revival of long-disproven theories of gender inversion, the difficulties with this study are rooted in an issue that has troubled the study of religion for some time now: how does one define the term "religious"?[6] In this particular study, religion was defined primarily through institutional commitment and biblical literalism: those appearing as most "religious," by these criteria, would be mostly conservative Protestants and Catholics who attended Sunday services without fail and also went to Bible study every week. LGBT congregational studies have already shown that lesbian, bisexual, and transgendered women are generally not in such spaces. But does this make them irreligious? The complex life stories described in the previous chapter strongly suggest that this is not the case. On the other hand, by the criteria of the study described above, these women's religiosity is nearly invisible. While thirteen of the core participants in this book would register (but not necessarily strongly) in the 2002 study's measure of religious attendance, no more than six or seven would likely claim that the Bible is the actual or inspired word of God. And the percentage of apostates—those claiming no official religious affiliation—would be large indeed. If "unaffiliated" and "irreligious" are equivalent, then lesbian, bisexual, and transgendered women are not religious. But changing the lenses through which we view religion reveals that real lives are much more complicated than this.

What is the explanation for the dearth of women in the LGBT-specific studies of religion that have been conducted to date? In a study like those conducted in LGBT congregations such as MCC, Dignity, and Congregation Beth Simchat Torah, only three of the women involved in my research would register. They would be Ruth Tittle, who is heavily involved in MCCLA; Ronni Sanlo, who attends Beth Chayim Chadashim with some regularity; and Emile, a committed member of Christ Chapel of Long Beach. Twenty-six of the women whose stories fill this book would be invisible. In a study of LGBT members of mainline Protestant denominations like the one conducted by Gary David Comstock in the early 1990s, two participants would appear: Carmen, who attends West Hollywood Presbyterian, and Margaret Jensen, at the (Episcopal) Chapel of St. Francis. Twenty-seven of the women in this book would be invisible. Thus, all of the studies so far conducted about LGBT people in religion, when taken together, would capture the experiences of just five of the women in this book. Though women are clearly present in these highly organizational settings, and while there are no doubt significant numbers of gay, bisexual, and transgendered men whose religious lives sound a great deal like those described in the last chapter, it would appear that Mary Hunt is right to argue that women's experiences differ from men's in LGBT communities, and that different research methods may be necessary even to register, much less study, such differences.

Making Use of Congregations

Where, then, are *these* particular women? Fewer than half of them—thirteen, to be exact—were regularly attending an explicitly religious (or "spiritual") organization at the time of this study. Six of those thirteen were involved with smaller, alternative religious organizations such as Unitarian Universalism and Religious Science. Three other women were actively seeking a single religious organization to attend regularly, but here too the focus veers away from more traditional religions: two of the three were looking for alternative religious groups (recall that Tami was drawn to a Reclaiming Wiccan circle; another participant, Ruth Sebastian, found even Unitarian Universalism too straitlaced). The third, Linda, still identified as Christian and was hoping to find a suitable Christian church, but she too had begun to branch out into alternative religions, in part out of discouragement.

One-fifth of the study participants were sporadic attendees at religious organizations, for a wide variety of reasons. Cynthia McCann had mostly given up attendance at her Catholic church because of lay members' bigotry against her children; her partner, Lara Sowinsky, found the churches that interested her to be too far a drive from their home. Lisa Taylor was a committed seeker, attending any service to which she was invited but unwilling to devote much of her valued weekend time to religious attendance. Vanessa was drifting, fearing homophobia in the Conservative synagogues that attracted her and turned off by the Reform style of the LGBT synagogues in the area. Cassandra was a *brico-*

leuse for whom several different religious organizations provided important but far from exclusive resources, and Corrine was involved with Santería, whose rhythms of ritual generally do not follow the regular weekly pattern adopted by many religions in the United States. Finally, for nearly a quarter of the participants, explicitly religious organizations played no role at all in their religious practices at the time of the interview, although three of these women actively pursue what they term their "spirituality" through other types of gatherings—Sue Field with the Gay and Lesbian Sierrans, Lauren at New Age book readings and billiards tournaments, and Christie Tuttle through meetings with her shaman.

Though these participants in no way constitute a statistically representative sample that could be used to extrapolate to the broader population of lesbian, bisexual, and transgendered women in the United States, it is nonetheless instructive to compare their experiences to patterns in the U.S. population as a whole. Because this project was advertised as focusing on religion and spirituality, if anything the women who volunteered to speak with me are *more* likely than the average LBT woman to be actively involved in such matters. Yet they are still *less* likely than the average woman in the United States to attend a religious organization. In the 2004 General Social Survey (GSS), conducted by the University of Chicago's National Opinion Research Center,[7] a little over half of the female participants between the ages of twenty-four and sixty-six (the age range of the women in this book) said they attended "religious services" once a month or more. Just over two-fifths of the women in this study would likely have given the same answer. In the GSS, one-third of the female participants between twenty-four and sixty-six years of age attended less than once a month; just over one-fifth in this study would likely have chosen this answer. And while around a tenth in the GSS were non-attendees, in this study that figure climbs to nearly a quarter. So, even among a population self-selected for its interest in spirituality and religion, lesbian, bisexual, and transgendered women fall quite a bit below the national average in attendance at religious services.

One answer, then, to Hunt's "oft-sung hymn" is that lesbian, bisexual, and transgendered women *are* attending congregations, but they attend sporadically or choose alternative rather than traditional religions. Another is that they do indeed attend less than is the average in the United States. And yet, despite these lower attendance rates, all but one woman in the study identify as religious, "spiritual," or both. Perhaps the more interesting question, then, is *why* these women are where they are. One way to tease apart possible answers to this larger question is to consider some of the factors that typically affect religious attendance and affiliation.

Family

One such factor is family structure. In a study of the religious beliefs and practices of baby boomers, for instance (a demographic group that includes a fair number of this study's participants), Wade Clark Roof notes that many people left religion during their teenage years, but "many parents returned to church, synagogue, and temple when their children were young."[8] When asked their reasons for this return, the participants in Roof's study made it clear that they had come back to religious organizations in order to give their children a religious education or at least to introduce them to religion. Adding that "even irregular churchgoers became more active as their children reached school age," Roof notes that this pattern of children's influence on parents' religious decisions is not confined to the baby boomer generation but was demonstrated as early as the 1950s.[9] Furthermore, Roof found that once children were in their twenties, their parents' religious involvement dropped again. Thus, having children who are between the ages of six and nineteen seems to be a powerful factor in increasing a parent's religious attendance.

My interview with the Reverend Daniel Smith at West Hollywood Presbyterian seemed to confirm that such dynamics might be coming into play in LGBT communities as well. Describing the recent increase in the number of women attending his church—a number that had hovered around 20 percent through the 1980s and part of the 1990s—Smith explained that "as gay and lesbian families started having children, that was the major change point for us, in getting women in here."[10] The church, he recalled, "had done everything under the sun to try to attract women," including hiring a female associate pastor, but to no avail. "It was the children that brought about that transformation," he concluded. Thus, both national data and anecdotal evidence from one of L.A.'s oldest LGBT-centered congregations suggest that the presence of children in the household may have something to do with the religious attendance patterns of the women in this study.

The matter is complicated, however, by the life changes brought about by coming out. Twelve of the twenty-nine women in the study mentioned children during our interview; all but three of them identified as heterosexual when their children were born. Some lost custody of their children as a result of coming out, and some did not come out until their children were adults. Although mothers are more heavily represented among the regular and sporadic attendees than they are among the seekers or the non-attendees, this fact may be misleading because only five women in the study—two of them a couple, so in effect four families—had children who were of school age and living with them at the time of the interviews. Of these four families, one falls in the regular attendee group, two in the sporadic group, and one with the seekers. The fabled "lesbian baby boom" of the late 1990s is largely absent from this study, for reasons that may be as simple as the time constraints and priorities of parents, and the influence of children on religious attendance is therefore unclear.

Several mothers did talk about the importance of religious education for their children. Tami, for instance, was teaching her eight-year-old son religious perspectives on her own, leaving the option open for him to attend religious services if he wished. "I want him to explore, himself, when he's older," she explained. "He knows *my* views on things, but I also express that you can have your own views."[11] A public school teacher taught Tami's son to say "Oh my dog" instead of "Oh my God," and the boy had also begun asking questions about life after death. In general, though, Tami's efforts at religious education so far had been focused on general morality: "You gotta do what feels right to you. But there's always consequences for what you do. So if you do something bad, it *will* come back to you, one way or another. One *day* or another. . . . I think as long as he lives by those standards, he'll find what he needs."

Emile, too, was concerned with building a moral foundation for her sons' lives, but she went about that process quite differently than Tami. "The Bible says you train a child in the way they should go, and they will not depart from it," she told me. "My parents showed me the way. And I'm forty-one years old, and I have not departed from it. Matter of fact, I continue to run to it each and every day. And that's what I teach my children, to run to it."[12] Some of this teaching came from Sunday school; Emile and her family attended Glory Tabernacle MCC, which has a Sunday school program, for some time. Yet the benefits of Sunday school seemed to be mainly intellectual—concerned with knowing particular facts—whereas when Emile discussed teaching her children adherence to Christian practices and faith she spoke far more about her own and her wife's influence:

> *God forbid, if he was to take me right now, my children already have that foundation in Jesus Christ. Because my faith, their faith, my parents' faith, it's like a lineage that goes on, you know. And my older children may have children one day in the future . . . And they will pass that on to their children also, about the love that God has for you and the love that you give to one another and the people around you, and not to be so selfish, not to just harbor all the blessings that you receive, but to give, give out to people.*

Cynthia McCann's children, whom she bore while she was married to a man and trying to make a heterosexual life for herself, were simply expected to go to Catholic school as their mother had done. "I was pretty much [thinking], 'Well, of course *my* children are going to go to Catholic school,' you know. And they're going to go to Catholic high school, and hopefully my daughter will go to the [Catholic] college that I went to."[13] When Cynthia made the decision to leave her husband and begin identifying as the lesbian she feels she has always been, the children stayed with her, and they stayed in Catholic school. This had consequences for her; when she first told her son that she was a lesbian, "he said, 'Well, you know I think that's wrong, Mom.'" But ongoing commitment to Catholic school also had consequences for Cynthia's children. Though her son left Catholic school fairly soon after Cynthia came out because he no longer wanted to attend, her daughter was still in that school system when Cynthia and Lara moved in together. Lara described the faculty at their daughter's school as "incredible in their support,"[14] but a small group of parents made it clear that they did not welcome lesbian mothers at their children's school. Concerned for their daughter's well-being, Cynthia and Lara transferred her to a public school.

Like Emile and Tami, Cynthia and Lara had come to concentrate on the ways in which they could teach their children religious perspectives in the home. "We do talk about God," Cynthia said, "but I don't talk about it how I was raised. You know, just sinning and church and God's with us and saying ten Hail Marys and how many Our Fathers that they tell you to say. . . . It's more just about God and be good to people, be good to everyone, you know." She knew that her son was confused by her departure from Catholicism, and she shared her changing beliefs with him but also encouraged him to seek out his own, just as Tami did with her son. "I'm just saying, 'You know, you'll figure it out as you go along, but just don't forget there is a God, you know. . . . Just be your own little guy. Love God your own way.'"

Many years ago, Ruth Tittle also brought her daughter to church. Like Cynthia and Lara, she withdrew again upon encountering homophobia in a setting that was supposed to introduce her daughter to her Christian heritage and help her to build a sense of values.

> *I would hear the minister start saying terrible things about homosexuals. And I was always out, I was out to my daughter from the time she was two or three years old. And how could I sit and take her to church and have the minister saying terrible things about who I am? So I felt like there was no place that I could go that I could take her. And I didn't want her to go there and hear that.*[15]

Such challenges, Ruth reflected, "make it very difficult for gay parents, lesbian parents to pass on ritual, traditions, values." Thus, although some of the women in this study might in other circumstances have increased their religious attendance on account of their school-age children, their concerns about their children's exposure to religious homophobia largely kept them from doing so. In some cases, then, the presence of school-age children in a same-sex household might actually have the opposite effect from that seen in the broader culture: it might *deter* parents from religious attendance.

Childhood Religious Attendance

Religious upbringing, in terms of both the religion itself and the intensity of the family's commitment to it, has been much debated among sociologists of religion as a potential influence on adults' patterns of attendance and affiliation.[16] Yet the stories traced in chapter 4 indicate that neither of these factors is particularly important in determining the role of congregations in the lives of most women in this study: only six participants were active in the religions of their upbringing at the time I interviewed them. Four of these women were raised in families that regularly attended religious events, and they remained strongly committed to the same religion as adults; the other two had weaker commitment patterns in childhood. On the other hand, only nine participants in all were raised attending religious services regularly *and* were also regular attendees—within or beyond their childhood religion—when I interviewed them. Seventeen of the twenty-nine women were raised with fairly regular religious attendance, yet had little or no commitment to congregational attendance when we spoke. Interestingly, only one respondent was raised with little religious attendance and continued that pattern in adulthood, whereas two others raised with little attendance were relatively frequent attendees at the time of the interview. So if childhood religious attendance has any influence at all in this group of women, it seems to lie in convincing the adult to do the opposite: to attend more if one's family attended little, and to attend little if one's family attended more. But with twenty-six of the twenty-nine women having been raised with some sort of regular religious attendance, it is difficult to see any significant pattern here. The type of religion in which participants were raised also has little influence; those participants raised in moderate or liberal religious traditions were only slightly more likely to be regular religious attendees at the time of the study than those raised in conservative traditions. As has been found elsewhere, then, childhood religious attendance seems to have little influence on adult patterns of religious involvement.[17]

Race, Ethnicity, Culture

There is good reason to believe that ethnic identity influences religious commitment, even among LGBT populations. In *Say It Loud: I'm Black and I'm Proud,* a wide-ranging survey of black LGBT people conducted in 2000, the Policy Institute of the National Gay and Lesbian Task Force (NGLTF) found that 85 percent of the respondents indicated a religious affiliation.[18] While this is strikingly high in contrast to the apparently low affiliation rates of white LGBT people, the report also notes that 97 percent of blacks in the United States overall report a religious affiliation. Although the survey unfortunately did not ask about religious attendance, participants were familiar enough with their religions to be able to describe those religions' views on homosexuality (though it is unclear how accurate those descriptions are), and 42 percent, primarily those whose religions were accepting of LGBT people, indicated that such views influenced their daily lives.[19]

While there are no contemporary studies of religion in the broader LGBT population with which to compare the NGLTF study, of some interest are the results a 1969 study of gay men and lesbians in San Francisco.[20] Here, black respondents were much more likely than white respondents to attend religious "functions" (defined as both services and "church activities") on a regular basis. Though San Francisco may be an unusual case because of the prominence of the Council on Religion and the Homosexual (CRH) in the 1960s, this study is still instructive. By 1969, condemnation of gay men and lesbians had already begun to shift from the realm of medicine to that of morality. Most religious bodies would release their first official statements on homosexuality in the early 1970s. Thus, it is likely that religious leaders were not focusing as much on the topic as they would for the next three decades, but it is also possible that they were beginning to discuss it. Certainly the presence of the CRH indicates that homosexuality was on the minds of at least some religious leaders. So in some ways the religious setting for many Christians might not have been all that different from what it is today. In other ways, of course, there are significant differences, with the opening up to LGBT people of the more liberal churches within both predominantly black and predominantly white denominations, and the spread of movements like MCC and Unity Fellowship. Nonetheless, there are hints in both the older study and the NGLTF black pride survey that race makes a difference in religious patterns within LGBT communities as well as beyond them. On the other hand, in both studies male participants predominated, so once again there is much less clear information on the religious patterns of women.

The influence of race is also less than clear among the women in the present study. Of the seven women who were complete non-attendees with respect to religious organizations, two were women of color, and two women of color were also among the six sporadic attendees.[21] Just over a third of the eleven women of color in the study therefore reported little or no involvement with religious organizations; among the white women, this figure rises to half. Conversely, one-third of the white women in the study attended a religious organization with some regularity at the time of the interview; over three-fifths of the women of color did so. From the numbers, then, one would suspect that race plays a role in the religious choices of the women in this study, as it does for many people in the U.S. population as a whole. But individual stories complicate this conclusion. For example, Latinas fall almost equally into every category of attendance and non-attendance, and even of the two women of Mexican descent who are regular religious attendees, one, Coco Gallegos, remains committed to the Catholicism of her childhood while the other, Kathleen McGregor, has left Catholicism to experiment with Neopaganism and feminist theology through the Unitarian Universalist church.

Perhaps it is more significant that all three of the African American women in the study were regular religious attendees at the time of our interviews. Yet, again, the details of their stories complicate matters significantly. Discussions of the high rate of religious affiliation and attendance among African Americans usually center around the historic importance of churches (especially black churches) in African American communities. Thus, one might predict that the African American women in this study would have been raised in historically black denominations, and would at the time of the study have been involved with liberal black churches such as First AME or an LGBT black church such as Unity Fellowship. Instead, while this pattern holds for all three women's childhoods—Betty Walker and Adesina were both raised Baptist, and Emile was raised in the Church of God in Christ—it fails entirely in the context of their lives at the time of the interviews.

Though Adesina's first religious exploration after leaving Christianity took her close to her African roots through Yoruba religion, she had in recent years become most heavily involved with the Agape International Spiritual Center. Agape is a Religious Science church, and thus is rooted in a movement that is predominantly white. On the other hand, its high-profile and highly charismatic founder is African American, and the church draws a multi-ethnic crowd each Sunday. Though much of what Adesina considered to be her spiritual practice was individual ("It's meditation, it's yoga, and it's also diet," she explained), regular attendance at Agape balanced this individualism for her.[22] "Going to church," she told me, "gives me the group feeling that I need, because, you know, doing the meditation and stuff you're isolated. So when I go there it's a different feeling. It's a different high, if you want to say it like that. The group thing helps to reinforce and to prepare me for my week."

Adesina continued to see important connections to her African American identity within her spiritual practice, but she created these connections in innovative ways and did not rely on religious organizations to do it. For instance, her elekes, the beads she received upon being initiated into Yoruba religion, were important symbols of both her spirituality and her pride in her African roots. "I have to be connected to my African roots, because that's where I came from," she explained.

> *You know, it's horrible to think that we are the only people who don't have a flag, who don't have a culture. I mean, we have an American culture, we have an African American culture, but we can't trace that, we can't trace our lineage back, you know what I mean? So there's a lot that we have lost. And then we've been brainwashed, that Africa is backward and savage, and why would you want to go there, when Africa was the cradle of civilization, you know? . . . So for me just having my elekes, which are the necklaces that I wear that represent the different gods and goddesses, is a vital part of me. And even though I tend more towards the eastern culture, that part is still there.*

Another way in which Adesina linked her spirituality to her identity as an African American was through her interest in bringing yoga and metaphysical teachings to other African American women in the Los Angeles area. She was especially concerned with offering services to HIV-positive women. Though she worked with a Los Angeles AIDS organization, she felt that the group's methods reflected its founding by white men, and that these methods were far less effective in serving women of color. "I think that part of your spirituality is finding your unique plan for your life, where you fit in and where you can help," Adesina told me. Her own "unique plan" was "to work with women who are either HIV positive or have some kind of disease . . . to incorporate my yoga with my health and nutrition with my positive affirmations from an African American point of view." She wanted "to help women find their self-esteem again, help women to find their self-worth, help women to know that, okay, this is happening, but where do I go from here?" She explained further that because her metaphysical beliefs stress that disease (which she pronounced "dis-ease" to emphasize this point) is rooted in emotional imbalance, alleviating emotional stress can also alleviate illness. Thus, even though Adesina's chosen religious organization was a far cry from the traditional black churches, her sense of spirituality was threaded through with strong connections to African American communities—especially women—and African American histories.

Betty Walker was also attending Agape at the time of our interview, though she had become seriously involved more recently than Adesina and her route to the church was different from Adesina's. Betty stopped attending her family's Baptist church once she was allowed to make her own religious decisions. However, her first religious destination after she came out was still Christian: she began attending Unity Fellowship Church of Los Angeles. She had continued to identify as a Christian throughout a long-term relationship with a man who was an atheist, but she was also aware of the conservative stance that many heterosexual-dominated churches took on homosexuality. Turning to Unity Fellowship allowed her to rekindle her relationship to the religion while at the same time feeling affirmed rather than condemned for her new sexual identity. When we spoke in late October of 2001, Betty described Archbishop Carl Bean warmly as "a religious leader that I felt like was really coming from the place that I was at, and could really understand the shoes that I was in."[23] She found "comfort" in Bean's persistent message, "that God didn't make any mistakes, God didn't do anything wrong. That if I'm made in the image and likeness of God, then how could I be a mistake, or how could what I'm doing or who I am be wrong?"

Though Betty remembers attending Unity Fellowship Church "probably for about five, six years," and though she enjoyed having the support of the church and of Archbishop Bean's affirming messages, it was also during this time that Christian co-workers began to question her morality by pointing out passages in the Bible that they believed were condemning of homosexual acts. Never having understood the King James version very well, Betty bought a more contemporary, vernacular translation and quickly confirmed for herself what her co-workers had been saying. At that point, she recalled, "I didn't feel like I could pick up a Bible, because the Bible said something different than what I was hearing in church. So I really couldn't pick up a Bible and feel comfortable about what I was reading, although I felt comfortable about what I was hearing, because it was different from what was in the Bible." An illness that took the archbishop out of the pulpit for a time proved to be the final straw for Betty, who left Unity and tried the meditation and chanting of the Buddhist movement Soka Gakkai. Finding this insufficiently "spiritual" and "a little too disciplined for me," Betty next went to Agape, perhaps influenced at least a little by the metaphysical undertones at Unity Fellowship Church. She was so impressed with the center in 1995 that she immediately joined, but then her interest flagged and she attended "maybe once or twice a year" until 2000, when she began taking introductory classes on Science of Mind. When we spoke, Betty was excited about these classes and was considering becoming a Religious Science practitioner. She considers Agape a source of spirituality and also is interested in the lesbian and bisexual women's group at the church. She did not mention (and I did not ask) whether she ascribed any importance to Agape's African American leadership and the multi-ethnicity of its congregation. But in leaving Christianity behind and choosing Agape instead, Betty also left behind her attendance at black-dominated, explicitly Afrocentric religious organizations.

While Betty defines Christianity as "organized religion" and attaches negative connotations to such a term, Emile clearly views Christianity as the one true way. Yet she too has followed an organizational path that engages her African American identity in complex ways. Raised like Betty and Adesina in a socially conservative, historically black church—the Pentecostal denomination known as the Church of God in Christ, or COGIC—Emile "accepted Christ into my heart" at sixteen but left the church in her midtwenties after the death of her mother.[24] A few years after coming out as a lesbian, Emile felt drawn to attend church again. She believes that God guided her in her choice of congregations, and at first he sent her to a black church.

> *The Lord spoke to me one day and he was like, "I want you to go to Unity." He said, "I want you to go, but I don't want you to join." And I said, "Okay." So we [she and a friend] went there, and it was good, I liked it. And we ended up going like every Sunday for about a month and a half. But after a while I see what he was talking about, you know: he said, "I want you to go, but I don't want you to join."*

"There was something that wasn't right for you about the church?" I asked Emile. "Well," she answered, "when I go to church, the building where other believers are, I just purely want to worship him. I want to clap my hands and sing praises to him, and I don't really want anything political. Anything political, you can go to the sinners, you know what I'm saying? It just wasn't for me at that time." Emile was also uncomfortable with Unity Fellowship's openness to transgendered people; she felt that she was not ready to explain transgender identities to her young children.[25] Furthermore, Unity Fellowship was also a significant drive from Long Beach, where Emile was living at the time. Thus, she began asking people in local gay clubs about churches that were closer. She was referred to Christ Chapel of Long Beach, which greatly impressed her, and since then her allegiance has shifted between that church (along with Christ Chapel of Denver, during the few years she lived in Colorado) and Glory Tabernacle MCC. Both Christ Chapel and Glory Tabernacle have predominantly white congregations, a fact that Emile noted wryly at one point in our interview. "Unity," she said, is "more African Americans and we get a little bit more beat going on, but I mean, they're all praising God the same, you know. Basically singing the same songs. Different tempo!" She laughed.

The stories of Adesina, Betty, and Emile indicate that the connections between racial or ethnic identity and religious commitment, especially among lesbian (and probably bisexual and transgendered) women, are not as straightforward as some of the existing literature on the topic might suggest. Although all three grew up in families that regularly attended historically black churches, and although all three were also regular religious attendees at the time of the interviews, in this case the simple explanation—that the importance of church in African American communities predisposes people raised in such communities to continue to take part in religion, and especially in predominantly black religious organizations—is insufficient. None of these three women attends a predominantly black church, and only one of the three identifies as Christian;

in fact, the other two explicitly identify as *not* Christian. Though two attend Agape, which has a black minister, Agape's congregation is multi-ethnic, its parent tradition is largely white, and the services follow a traditional black church style much less than those at Unity Fellowship. Two of the three women tried Unity Fellowship Church and found it attractive but ultimately wanting—because of its Christian roots in one case, and because of its commitment to politics in the other.

Furthermore, these stories are no more dominated by any other single aspect of identity than they are by race and ethnicity. Lesbian identity played a role in Betty's and Emile's decisions to attend Unity Fellowship rather than a Baptist or COGIC church, but it was not the sole determinant, and while none of the three would attend a church that was not welcoming of them as lesbians, that criterion alone would hardly help them to distinguish between Agape, which Adesina and Betty attend, and Christ Chapel or MCC, Emile's churches. Likewise, identifying as a woman is a factor in some ways but not a determining one; Adesina left Christianity because of her perception that the religion had historically encouraged the persecution of both blacks and women, whereas Betty believes that her religious and spiritual life has not been affected in any way by her being a woman. This complex interaction of identities in shaping participants' religious practices and beliefs will be a central issue in the following chapter; at this point, it is sufficient to note that racial and ethnic identities have some influence, in some cases, over participants' use of religious organizations.

Gender and Leadership

Another intriguing possibility, mentioned above, is that gender itself plays a role in lesbian, bisexual, and transgendered women's choices about religious attendance—not so much through their own identities as women or through some sort of gender inversion, as Darren Sherkat would have us believe, but through their identification (or lack thereof) with a religious leader. Moshe Shokeid raises this issue explicitly in the context of one of the oldest LGBT synagogues in the United States, New York's Congregation Beth Simchat Torah (CBST). After nearly two decades of lay leadership, the congregation voted in 1992 to hire Rabbi Sharon Kleinbaum. The man who coordinated the hiring process passed away just a week before Rabbi Kleinbaum's inauguration, but he warned his friends prophetically from his deathbed: "The women are coming!"[26] CBST had until that time struggled to include women, and to attract them to the congregation. Just three years before Rabbi Kleinbaum was hired, Shokeid reports, "women accounted for a third of the synagogue membership.

At regular Friday night services, however, most sat clustered together in a few rows in the center of the sanctuary, a disproportionately small presence. That underrepresentation of women characterized most CBST activities, committees, and leadership positions."[27]

Such underrepresentation seems to have an interrelated set of causes, including the divergence between lesbian and gay male cultures that widened during the 1970s and early 1980s (though the involvement of lesbians in AIDS care began to narrow this gap), resistance among male religious leaders and congregants to critical women's rights issues such as the equal inclusion of women in religious services, and some women's interest in feminist theology and feminist ritual practices. Demographics may also exacerbate this pattern. Since LGBT religious organizations are generally dominated by gay men and lesbians, most members who have partners are with someone of the same sex. Furthermore, the politically fraught gay and lesbian histories of the past several decades have made it fairly common, at least in the age groups that tend to be religious attendees, for gay men to have predominantly male friendship circles and for lesbians' friendship circles to be predominantly female. Whereas in a heterosexual-dominated religious organization the alienation of one woman or one man may mean the loss of her male partner or his female partner from the membership rolls, leaving the gender balance of the congregation intact, the alienation of a lesbian from a congregation may mean the loss of her female partner and perhaps even some of their female friends. Thus, the gender balance of LGBT congregations may be far less stable than that of predominantly heterosexual ones. Yet, interestingly, while male-dominated LGBT congregations can run to 80 percent men or more, female-dominated LGBT congregations seem to level off at around 60 percent women.[28]

Given that LGBT congregations with a predominance of female members do in fact exist, why do women join and remain in these congregations more than in others? The words of the CBST member may offer a clue: women's leadership. When Rabbi Kleinbaum took over the leadership of the synagogue, this member expected a surge in women's participation. And indeed, Shokeid reports that in 1998 the synagogue's membership was between 55 and 60 percent women—a major increase over the 33 percent of ten years earlier.[29] Though some men in the synagogue were delighted by the new rabbi and by the increase in the number of women, others were put off—not just by women's growing leadership but by the idea of having a rabbi at all, and by aspects of Rabbi Kleinbaum's leadership style. Thus, while part of the shift in favor of women at CBST was clearly due to women's increased attendance, some was also due to the same pattern that had kept women's participation low for so many years: departing men took their partners and sometimes their friendship circles with them.

But women have been in the leadership of LGBT religious organizations for decades; why, then, is there still such a predominance of men in most congregations? The Reverend Daniel Smith, longtime pastor of West Hollywood Presbyterian Church, noted when I spoke with him that hiring a woman as associate pastor had not made a significant change in the female membership of the church, and that such change had only come about more recently, with the rise of the "lesbian baby boom." Though Smith had been working for years to provide inclusive-language services with feminist ritual and theology as well as women's leadership, the story he told of his own church stressed demand over supply: women returned when they felt they needed a church (and then, presumably, they were attracted to WHPC because of the feminist underpinnings already in place). Just a few blocks away, however, MCCLA's congregation had been women-dominated for some time already when WHPC began to increase its female population. Both churches had both men and women in leadership positions, but the significant difference between them lay in the women's status: while the senior pastor of WHPC is male, the senior pastor at MCCLA for many years was the Reverend Nancy Wilson.

The key, then, to increasing female membership in an LGBT congregation may not lie in feminist theology and ritual or in having women associate pastors, as important and influential as these developments are. The key seems instead to be at the top: perhaps it is only when a woman holds the senior position at an LGBT synagogue or church that the congregation's gender balance tips significantly in favor of women. An informal conversation I had with Reverend Lori, a part-time associate pastor at MCCLA, further supported this hypothesis. Reverend Lori told me that the church had been approximately 50 percent men and 50 percent women, or even at times 55 percent women and 45 percent men, under Nancy Wilson's leadership. Yet, she continued, in the year or so since the church returned to male leadership, the number of women in attendance had dropped noticeably.[30]

It seems clear that having a woman in the highest leadership position makes it likely that an LGBT religious organization will draw at least equal numbers of men and women, and it may even draw more women than men. For some women, then, female leadership influences congregational choices. Does this pattern hold true among the relatively few women in this study who regularly attended events at LGBT-focused religious organizations? Only five women fit in this category: Carmen, who attended West Hollywood Presbyterian at the time of the interview; Ruth Tittle, who attended MCCLA; Emile, who attended Christ Chapel; Dean, who went to St. Thomas Episcopal whenever she needed more "dogma" in her life; and Ronni, who went to Beth Chayim Chadashim. Four of these five congregations were led by gay men at the time of the study, and of those only MCCLA had women in secondary leadership positions. BCC is the only female-led, LGBT-focused congregation attended by women in this study. Furthermore, even among the non-LGBT religious organizations attended by study participants on a regular basis, none were female-headed. On the other hand, two of these congregations—Neighborhood Unitarian Universalist and the Chapel of St. Francis—were formerly led by women, and the participants who chose these two congregations did so in part because of the female leadership. Both became disaffected when the subsequent (male) pastor arrived. A third participant left MCCLA when Nancy Wilson departed. None of these three, however, attributed their dissatisfaction specifically to the new pastor being male; rather, they criticized stylistic aspects of his leadership.[31]

It might be worth noting that, of the three women who were searching for an organization to attend at the time of the interviews, both Tami and Ruth Sebastian were explicitly seeking feminist and female-led organizations. However, overall the influence of female leadership that shows so clearly in the broader patterns of LGBT congregational studies had little relevance for the women in this project—possibly because so few of the participants attended LGBT congregations. Yet if women's religious leadership played a minor role in the religious decision making of the women in this study, women's religious equality was clearly far more significant.

Feminism

Feminism and feminist issues, such as women's equality in religious settings, were important topics for the women in this study and were mentioned by twenty-four of the twenty-nine participants. Though I did ask in most interviews whether participants felt that their religious and spiritual experiences had been affected at all by their being women—thus potentially raising the number of respondents who would discuss women's equality—several women simply answered "no," and many others raised the issue of women's inclusion long before I asked this question. Furthermore, some women saw the question about being a woman as an opportunity to talk about their belief in the unique spiritual abilities or perspectives of women, so while the question certainly contributed to the large number of women who raised feminist issues, it is by no means a sufficient explanation for this phenomenon. For the most part, the women in this study were highly interested in women's equality and women's inclusion in religious settings. They expressed this concern in both positive and negative ways. Several women openly identified themselves as feminists, and explained their religious beliefs and practices at least in part through this identification. Some spoke negatively, of their disgust with religious organizations that refused ordination to women, that decried feminine images of the divine, or that held to a gendered double standard on issues of morality. Others focused more positively on their search for a women-centered or women-affirming religious organization, on their perceptions of the divine as Goddess, or on their interest in feminist theology and feminist spirituality.

Of those whose discussion of feminist issues in religion focused on negative aspects of traditional religions, most striking are the four participants for whom sexism was a major factor in their decision to leave the religions of their childhood. Adesina was quite straightforward about this concern, which was interwoven for her with the history of racism she saw in Christianity: "I was totally turned off of Christianity because they supported the slave trade, and they supported a lot of abominations to women, you know, the Inquisition and things of that nature. So I kind of just left it."[32] A few minutes later, she added, "I just couldn't get with the Christian 'Fear God' . . . and 'Women are born in sin.' You know, I don't believe that! . . . I think that men use that to control women. And so, being the lesbian that I am, I couldn't condone that." Even at Agape, which she generally found supportive of her commitment to women, Adesina had experienced problems. The monthly lesbian group she attended at the church, she told me, had just recently been threatened with cancellation. "[By] the church itself?" I asked Adesina. "Yes!" she responded indignantly. "They were going to cancel the lesbian group. Instead, they had a vision where we would join The Circle [a gay-lesbian-bisexual group at Agape], and The Circle would be male and female, and so from this date on, TLC [The Lesbian Connection] would be disbanded. . . . And I hit the roof!" Agape's leadership responded to the women's objections and kept the group active, and though Adesina is not completely satisfied with the deal that was struck, she has remained in this church—unlike the Baptist church of her childhood. She summed up her story with the following conclusion: "So even in places like that [Agape] where they're supposed to be really cool and really progressive, they still try to control and dominate us, men over women! So that's one of the things that I don't like."

Lisa Taylor, who grew up with a feminist mother, said that "from a young age I've been very skeptical of religion because of the way it's treated women." Throughout her life, she explained, "my feminist awareness and feelings about women's rights and equality and value and place in life hugely has impacted my attitude toward religion and spirituality." Raised in an extended Italian American family that was strongly Catholic, Lisa had a great deal of exposure to Catholicism through her cousins' commitment to the faith. Her family went to mass on religious holidays, but otherwise "we were never made to study the Bible or to go to church or anything." With her skepticism of religious sexism and her belief that organized religion makes people into mindless "followers," Lisa was never drawn to her family's Catholicism. "As I've gotten older," she continued, "my feminism has definitely steered me away from organized religion." She still considered herself spiritual at the time of the interview, and yet despite her general condemnation of organized religion, she did see a role for it in a balanced spiritual life. "It's not just spirituality on your own," she explained, "and it's not just religion in the organized sense. There's a lot of middle ground that can be developed and experienced." The challenge, for Lisa, lay in finding a religious organization that did not feel too much like "organized religion," that was anti-sexist and was firmly committed to the support of LGBT people. For the time being, Lisa remained an active seeker.

Like Lisa, Christie Tuttle remembered becoming suspicious of the sexism she saw in organized religion at an early age. Raised in the Church of Jesus Christ of Latter-day Saints (LDS), Christie recalled that "even when I was a child, I never felt like I made contact with it, with the religion. Never even wanted to go to church or felt like I believed in it." When I asked how old she was when she realized she did not believe in Mormon teachings, Christie told me that she was five or six years old, and then elaborated on the teachings (mostly practices) with which she disagreed. One of the first on her list was attitudes toward women. "I questioned the role of women in the church," she told me, "and that the men were placed so much higher and they were given so much authority that women didn't have. I always questioned that. It never sat right with me."[33] Ultimately, she said, the treatment of women in the LDS church was the main reason she "tuned out" of the religion. When at the age of eighteen she was allowed to make her own decision about whether or not to attend church, Christie promptly stopped going, and she never returned.

Though Ronni Sanlo also left her childhood religion over issues of sexism, unlike the other three women who did so she returned to that religion much later in her life—but with an interesting twist. Ronni grew up with a blend of Conservative and Orthodox Judaism, and with a grandfather who was a rabbi. Judaism was a central part of the family's life, and unlike Christie, Ronni was just as dedicated as the rest of her family. She attended Hebrew school, had a bas mitzvah, attended Hebrew high school, and spent much of her free time with other children from the family's synagogue. As a child, Ronni recalled, "I didn't think about *not* having religion in my life. It simply was part of who my family was. From a religious perspective, culturally, traditionally, it permeated every aspect of my life and my family's life in my adolescence."[34] Devoted to the religion and the culture, and following in the footsteps of her grandfather, Ronni decided as a young girl that she wanted to be a rabbi. "And when I would say that, people would say, 'Oh, isn't that nice, isn't that cute?' And as I got older and became a teenager I realized that I was just being patronized, and . . . that I could never be a rabbi because I was a girl, and girls can't be rabbis. And I was brokenhearted. I was absolutely devastated." That devastation simmered throughout her teenage years, and came to a boil when she was in college. Once she started college, Ronni told me,

> *I just so much questioned my role in the synagogue as wanting to be something really important that I thought would be helpful and useful, and wasn't being valued. And that's probably pretty much when I realized also that women weren't particularly valued in Judaism, certainly not in the Conservative to Orthodox brand that my family practiced. So in much dismay and much disillusionment I left the synagogue. I left the synagogue for thirty years.*

When Ronni finally returned to the synagogue a few years before our interview, it was to Beth Chayim Chadashim—not only a synagogue focused on serving the LGBT Jewish community, but a Reform synagogue with two women at its head: one as rabbi and one as cantor.

LGBT Rights

For many of the women in this study, discussion of sexism in religion flowed easily into talk of heterosexism. Theologian Mary Hunt makes clear that this blending of concerns holds true for lesbians more broadly as well. "For example," she writes, "as a lesbian feminist I am equally troubled by the Catholic Church's position on abortion as on homosexuality. . . . I do not need to choose between the two issues, but I expect cooperation on both." Elsewhere in the same article, she adds, "that many of us [lesbians] have voted with our feet [by leaving religious organizations] is due as much to these broader issues as to the exclusion of lesbian/gay people."[35] This, then, is an important point: the lower attendance of lesbians, relative to gay men, in traditional religious organizations may be explained at least in part by the tendency of lesbians to be concerned with feminist issues as well as with LGBT rights issues. The preceding section makes it clear that the women in this study are indeed interested in feminist issues; though the four women discussed in depth are exemplary cases because they left their childhood religions over concerns about sexism, such concerns appeared in some way in twenty-four of the twenty-nine interviews. But what of concerns with LGBT rights? Here the numbers are even higher: though I only asked explicit questions about LGBT issues in religion at the very end of each interview, all but two participants raised these issues on their own.[36] Dean Bramlett made the link between sexism and homophobia explicit: "I think that religion is one of the last great bastions of the male-dominated society, where they can still step upon a woman and feel righteous about it. And so I rail against it. And between the way that the homosexual community is treated, and the way women are treated, I mean, lesbians get a double whammy."[37] Furthermore, the number of participants who left a religion—usually that of their childhood—because of homophobia or transphobia far outstrips the number leaving because of sexism.[38] While four participants fell in the latter category, nine—nearly one-third of the participants—fell in the former.

As in the case of sexism, participants responded to religious homophobia and transphobia in both positive and negative ways. Importantly, though, and unlike the discussions of feminist issues, even the positive discussions were generally underlaid by negative concerns with homophobia (those concerned with transphobia all responded to it in negative ways). In other words, some participants spoke in a positive tone about seeking or finding religious organizations that affirmed lesbians, gay men, and bisexuals, or that had LGB support groups, but in most of these cases the implicit context was the need to avoid or escape the homophobia they had found in other religious organizations, rather than to celebrate LGBT identities or to practice their religion with LGBT people. Other participants spoke more directly about experiencing homophobia and transphobia, and about taking steps to avoid such experiences in religious contexts. For some people, these issues became important before they came out; for others, afterward.

Christine Logan's first direct experience with religious homophobia came before she began to identify as a lesbian. A third-generation Christian Scientist whose grandmother had been a Christian Science practitioner, Christine spent much of her adult life deeply involved in her local church. At one point she served on the interview committee that screened applicants for membership. When two gay men applied for membership, she recalled, "people got afraid . . . that homosexuals were going to take over the church. And so they started asking questions about that."[39] The interview committee began asking potential members their opinion of homosexuality, and asking whether they knew that homosexuality was not in accordance with Christian Science teachings. Though the question was later removed (and the accordance of homosexuality with Christian Science teachings is actually debatable), Christine said that this period was "when I got to know that they [her church] didn't accept gayness." She found the fears of gays taking over the church to be "petty," and in our interview she used this story as an example of the difference between "religion" and "spirituality": "Religion," she summed up, "can get very rigid and judgmental and throw people out for the wrong reasons." Christine remembered the discovery of such rigidity and judgment in her own church as the beginning of her departure. She began to withdraw from church activities, though she retained her membership until after she came out.

Like Christine, Danielle remembered being intensely involved in her childhood religion and is the third generation of her family to be a member; in fact, she claimed in our interview to have been the most religiously involved person in her family while she was growing up. A committed Mormon who was assigned male at birth, Danielle attended church weekly, became involved with the Mormon priesthood, and joined a Mormon Boy Scout troop. In her later teens she also played piano and organ for the church. Though she remembers wanting to be a girl from the time she was small, and though she faced classism in her ward as a youth, the closest Danielle came to transphobia in the LDS church before she came out was a blank silence. "I didn't know that there were people out there that were like me, that you could get help, or any of that stuff," she recalled, "because being in the Mormon church you're really not exposed to the world out there."[40] And during Danielle's youth in the 1960s and early 1970s, the LDS church had no information available, positive or negative, on transgender identities. Once she began living as a woman, however, the church's position became quite clear. "One of the reasons that stopped me from going to church," Danielle explained, was that "so many people in the churches are so hostile." She told me that she had received a vision telling her "to leave the church, because the church is not following what Joseph Smith's original visions were of finding a true church that would be open to people." Yet the church remained important to her, and she hoped to be able to return one day. Though Danielle identified as a lesbian, she rarely mentioned homophobia in discussing her church's reaction to her; as with the other transgendered people in the study, transphobia was more present and pressing an issue than homophobia, at least in a religious context.

Linda's story provides an interesting counterexample to Danielle's and Christine's experiences, because although Linda left her Southern Baptist upbringing in her late teens for reasons having little to do with homophobia, she began to come back to the church in her early and mid twenties. Exploring a variety of conservative and fundamentalist congregations, she initially sought a church that was nondogmatic. "A lot of what I heard was 'This is what you shall believe.' And I just thought, you know, 'You're just a human. How dare you say that!'"[41] But in addition to her aversion to having her beliefs dictated to her, Linda was also beginning to realize that she needed a church that was affirming of LGBT people. "I'd get to the point where I'm like, 'Okay, I like what you're saying, I hear it. Now how are you going to feel if I tell you that I'm gay?'" Though she never asked this question aloud, the answers that Linda inferred meant that, ultimately, homophobia drove her out of the churches of her childhood. "I think that [the need for a supportive church] was the breaking point for me, because I knew that I was not going to find a church within the churches that I was raised in that was going to acknowledge the [same-sex] relationship." Thus, though Linda was also concerned with issues of dogmatism, the definitive break came as a result of her commitment to seeking a church that would be comfortable for her while also being LGBT-affirming. At the time of our interview, she was still searching.

Coming Out *of*, Coming Out *as*

Linda's story points to a particularly intriguing explanation for some of the patterns of organizational involvement among the participants in this study, as well as for the gender differences observed in studies of LGBT congregations. This explanation has to do with the temporal overlap between the process of identifying and naming oneself as lesbian, gay, bisexual, or transgendered, on the one hand, and the common pattern of leaving one's childhood religion during one's mid or late teens.

While there are some variations by denomination, research has consistently shown a dip in religious attendance in the United States starting in the late teens and continuing until one has children—if one does. In two successive waves of a study on religion in the baby boom generation, Wade Clark Roof found that over 60 percent of respondents "dropped out" of involvement in organized religion for at least two years during their youth. Men were "only slightly" more prone to drop out than women, and the pattern holds for both conservative and mainline Protestants, for Catholics, and for Jews.[42] Exposure to the cultural changes of the 1960s clearly influenced the frequency with which the participants in Roof's study dropped out, but even those with the lowest levels of such cultural exposure dropped out at a rate of 56 percent (for those with high levels of exposure, the dropout rate was 84 percent).[43] Roof also found that the age of dropping out seemed to be decreasing over time; the average age at which older baby boomers dropped out of organized religion was 21.1 years, while for the younger boomers it was 18.2 years.[44]

More recent research bears out these conclusions and confirms that, just as the young adult dropout pattern was not new with the boomers, it also has not ended with them. Studies based on the Monitoring the Future survey of high school students, conducted annually by the University of Michigan, show that religious attendance, especially among high school seniors, dropped fairly steadily from the survey's first administration in 1976 until the late 1980s, then stabilized for the rest of the twentieth century. These studies also show a clear pattern of decline in religious attendance between the eighth and twelfth grades. Since the late 1980s, fewer than 35 percent of high school seniors have reported attending religious functions on a weekly basis; shifting the measure to monthly attendance brings the number of participants to around 50 percent.[45] Furthermore, these studies concur with Roof's findings that gender differences in attendance, while present, are minor.[46] By themselves, then, the findings of such studies are insufficient to explain the gendered attendance patterns among gay men and lesbians.

Gender differences do consistently appear, however, in studies of lesbian, gay, and bisexual identity formation.[47] While people follow many different routes in developing a conscious LGB identity, psychologists have long held that some generalizations can be made about these routes in terms of the events involved (sometimes called "stages" but not always occurring sequentially) and in terms of the average age at which and the typical order in which each event occurs. Though psychologists debate what exactly the "stages" are, when they occur, in what order they occur, and how important each is, in examining the influence of gender they have found fairly consistent distinctions.

Some of the recent literature on LGB identity development focuses on the incidence and timing of certain "milestones" such as awareness of same-sex attraction; sexual experience with someone of the same sex; conscious identification as gay, lesbian, or bisexual; and disclosure of sexual identity to others. While all of these can have a significant impact on religion, the most significant, at least for western religions, is probably identification. Attractions, if considered sinful or a temptation to sin, can be (more or less) suppressed; a single sexual experience, again, if considered a sin, can be excused as a grave but nonetheless remediable error. However, in most western cultures the decision to self-identify beyond the heterosexual norm signifies a much more enduring and deeply rooted state of being than do attraction or the occasional one-night stand. In religions that condemn same-sex eroticism, or even those that are ambivalent about the topic, a decision to self-identify as bisexual, lesbian, or gay may place the religious and sexual aspects of one's identity in deep tension. The strength of religious identity at the time of LGB self-identification, and the intensity of exposure to social settings where religious identity and anti-LGB beliefs are simultaneously reinforced, may be significant factors in shaping how sexual and religious identities interact.

In 1990, Ritch Savin-Williams could already note that "a nearly universal finding in empirical research is that males recognize their homosexuality and come out at an earlier age than do females." He cited five previous studies in support of this claim; furthermore, his own data from a study conducted in 1983 found men more likely than women to have "first felt homosexual" between the ages of fourteen and nineteen, and women more likely than men to place this milestone between twenty and twenty-one.[48] Later studies became more detailed; for instance, a study co-authored by Savin-Williams and Lisa Diamond found men in the mid-1990s self-labeling as "not heterosexual" at an average age of 16.4, as opposed to 17.6 for women.[49] A recent study that included a wide age range (and thus reflected later self-identification in older LGB people, balanced by earlier self-identification among more recent generations) showed that the average age at which male participants self-identified as gay or bisexual was 18.8; for lesbian and bisexual women, the average age of identification was 20.7.[50] Such research has also shown little effect of race or ethnicity on age of self-identification or on age of disclosing one's sexual identity to others, although race and ethnicity have a clear effect on whether or not people come out to their parents.[51]

Though the distance between these average ages of self-identification may seem small despite their statistical significance, they may be extremely important in the context of religion. With religious attendance dropping dramatically between eighth grade (thirteen to fourteen years of age) and twelfth grade (seventeen to eighteen years of age), and continuing to fall during the rest of the teen years and into the twenties, those who self-identify as LGB later than others are less likely to be involved with organized religion when they come out. Given that the gender difference in age of self-identification places women quite a bit further into the religious disaffiliation period than men when they come out, it is possible that women, on average, self-identify as lesbian or bisexual in very different religious circumstances than those in which men identify as gay or bisexual.[52] If more lesbian and bisexual women than gay and bisexual men self-identify after they have disaffiliated from their childhood religions, for example, then men are more likely to come out within an organizational religious context and women outside of such a context.

What consequences might this difference in context have for the relationship between religious and sexual identities? A number of studies have shown that among LGBT Christians, Jews, and Muslims who come out within their religions, many (though definitely not all) go through a period of struggle during which they must reconcile their new identities with religious condemnations of same-sex eroticism and gender-crossing.[53] Some leave their religions entirely as a result of this process; others leave in order to develop their sexual or gender identities unhindered by religion but later return; another, smaller group sets LGBT identity aside and attempts to live cisgendered, heterosexual lives for a period of time; and some complete their negotiations within their religions, at most moving to a more LGBT-supportive congregation.

One might expect those who stay within their religions and negotiate an identity that is both LGBT and religious to be fairly committed to their religions, having often put a great deal of emotional and mental energy into creating this blended identity. But what of those who have already given up their religious affiliation by the time they come out? In this case, though a moral struggle may still ensue and there is much socially inculcated internalized prejudice to grapple with, there is little incentive for creating a blended LGBT/religious identity. If religion is of little importance in someone's life, and if she is rarely in contact with people who might reinforce a religious identity and point out the potential tensions between her religious and sexual/gender identities, then she might very well focus solely on developing the latter identities. In such cases, someone who was interested in religion might eventually seek out a religious setting that fits comfortably with her established sexual and gender identities. This *could* be her childhood religion, but if she believes that religion to be hostile to certain aspects of who she is, she may well seek out another religion entirely—or a blending of several. The temporal overlap between the ages of sexual self-identification and religious disaffiliation suggests that men are more likely to develop a blended identity from within a religion, and women are more likely to develop a sexual identity outside of any religious context. If this is indeed the case, it provides a very convincing explanation for the predominance of men and the relative absence of women in LGBT and welcoming congregations of traditional religions, as well as the mosaic-like nature of lesbian, bisexual, and transgendered women's religious and spiritual identities.[54]

Only seven of the twenty-nine women in this study are regularly involved in traditional religious organizations (including both LGBT-focused and mainline organizations), and only three of these women have a fairly consistent history of lifelong involvement in these religions. Therefore, it is logical to suspect that most of them, or at least those who identify as lesbian and bisexual, fall into the pattern that I have suggested may be most common for women: leaving organized religion in their late teens and coming out some time afterward, thus negotiating a secular lesbian or bisexual identity and subsequently choosing religious beliefs, practices, and affiliations that mesh well with the already established sexual identity. This in fact turns out to be the case, and in no small way. Of the twenty-six women who left the religion of their childhood for more than a short time, nineteen—nearly three-quarters—left their religion before self-identifying as lesbian or bisexual. Only seven, notably including all three transgendered women, self-identified before leaving their childhood religion. Moreover, six of these seven listed religious homophobia or transphobia among their main reasons for leaving their religion, and the seventh (Christine Peña, who is bisexual) left because of religious disapproval of sex in general. This very clear pattern not only substantiates the argument advanced above; it also helps to explain some of the ways in which these women's processes of identity negotiation differ from those found in studies of identity negotiation among LGBT Christians, Jews, and Muslims. This is the topic of the next chapter, but suffice it to say here that one significant difference is the infrequency with which participants talked about struggling with a sense of sinfulness; when they faced internalized homophobia, biphobia, or transphobia, these typically came from secular rather than religious sources.

Summary: Where and Why?

The variety of stories told by the women I interviewed suggests that a highly complex set of factors influences the ways in which contemporary lesbian, bisexual, and transgendered women—at least in L.A., and possibly in much of the United States—engage with religious organizations. It is also important to note that such patterns are dynamic: had I interviewed the same group of women five years earlier there would have been changes in several women's sexual and religious identities. Four lesbians, for instance, would have been in the throes of coming out, two would have identified as heterosexual, and a bisexual woman would have identified as lesbian. Some would not have been affiliated with the religious organizations they attended in 2001; others would have been affiliated with groups they had left by the time of our interview. Five years ago, all of the firm non-attendees in this group were still not attending any official religious organization, but the membership of the "regular attendees," "sporadic attendees," and "seekers" groups would have been shuffled. Nevertheless, within these fluid dynamics of contemporary sexuality and spirituality, some overarching patterns appear to be fairly stable. One of these is the relative dearth of women in LGBT-focused congregations. So where are they, and why?

A fair number of them, including one-third of those in this study, are not in religious organizations at all. Importantly, though, this by no means implies that they are not religious (though they might prefer the term "spiritual," and one participant, Silva, would most definitely identify as neither religious nor spiritual). Rather, they find their religious inspiration in private forms of practice and individually constructed belief systems—Danielle's visions from God; Christie's shamanic soul retrievals; Mary Jane's golden rule ethics, Greek mythology, and love of nature; Lauren's inspired poetry; Sue's involvement with the Gay and Lesbian Sierrans. Some of the non-attendees are in search of organizations that can anchor their individual beliefs and practices, but they have put together very clear criteria that the successful organization must meet in order to match their personal sense of spirituality. In economic terms, they are seeking a very specific product.[55]

Other women, including two-fifths of those in this study, are sporadic attendees. They often maintain an active private religious life, whether through regular individual practices such as meditation and reading books on spirituality or through an undercurrent of awareness. Congregations serve as resources for these women, filling a variety of needs. Cynthia, for instance, still seeks out a Roman Catholic church in times of trauma. After the September 11 terrorist attacks, she "want[ed] to go sit somewhere." Laughing, she added, "personally,

I want to go on my knees. You know, I'm Catholic, I want to pray. That's my thing. And so we went to church."[56] Lisa, on the other hand, uses congregations as sources of information in her quest to learn about a variety of religious traditions. Cassandra is a *bricoleuse* who likes meditating at centers, whether Buddhist or Hindu, but also maintains a certain connection to Christianity and finds beauty in many religions. For Corrine, involved in Santería and peripherally in pan-Indian religious events, communal gatherings are only one of many different routes to contact with the sacred.

Finally, some women, including thirteen of those in this study, are involved in religious organizations on a regular basis. Even in this group, though, there is a great deal of complexity. Only two participants attend organizations that are not officially LGBT-affirming, only four attend explicitly LGBT congregations, and nearly half of the regular attendees are part of less traditional religions such as Unitarian Universalism and Religious Science. Though these particular findings are specific to the relatively small group of women included in this study, the inability of previous studies to track down significant numbers of LBT women in mainline Protestant and LGBT congregations suggests that similar patterns may be in play on a national level. There may also be sizable numbers of LBT women, or of LGBT people in general, who do not consider themselves either religious or spiritual; clearly, such people would generally not have volunteered for a study with the word "spirituality" in the title, and thus, with the exception of Silva, they are unrepresented here.

The reasons for these patterns of religious affiliation vary as much as the individual life stories of the women I interviewed; in explaining the ways in which different religious organizations (or avoidance of such organizations) shaped their religious identities or filled particular spiritual needs, participants spoke of their individual belief systems, their preferences in religious practice, their heritage, the religion's leadership, and many other factors. In addition to primarily individual factors such as beliefs and personal tastes, several factors that have been shown to affect religious affiliation and attendance in the broader U.S. population may also play a role in lesbian, bisexual, and transgendered women's decisions about religious attendance. Some of these factors make sense in theory and have been shown to hold elsewhere, but were not clearly or significantly evident among the women in this study: family structure, for instance, and female leadership in LGBT religious organizations. Ethnicity and cultural heritage play some role among these women, as seen in Ronni's sense that there was "something missing" until she returned to a synagogue, and as hinted at by the strong attendance patterns of the African American women in the study, which replicate national distinctions in the United States between black and white religious attendance patterns regardless of sexual orientation. On the other hand, the influence of ethnicity and culture on religious decision making remains somewhat ambiguous for the women in this study.

Not at all ambiguous is the importance of feminism and especially of LGBT rights issues; not only these women's attendance at a particular congregation but even their identification with an entire religion was often fundamentally shaped by concerns for women's and LGBT equality. In combination, sexism and homophobia/biphobia/transphobia may be even more potent than they are alone, since those in this study who did not leave their childhood religions because of sexism did so because of bigotry around sexual or gender identities. Finally, there seems to be an intriguing overlap between women's age at coming out, at least among lesbians, and the age of young adult disaffiliation from organized religion. In a previous study of LGBT Christians, I found that leaving religion before one self-identified as LGBT was a relatively rare pattern;[57] here, it predominates. By focusing on Christians, my earlier study may have excluded by default these "early leavers," who seem relatively unlikely to return to their religions. As the early leavers may also be disproportionately female, this is one of the strongest potential explanations for the dearth of women in studies of LGBT congregations.

Conclusion: LBT Women and Religion in Postmodern Cultures

"If it hadn't been lesbianism, . . . it would have been a different thing," said Sue Field of her motivation to leave the Catholic Church. "I think that was only the catalyst to make me look at my own spirituality, versus the membership in a church. It could have been instead something like the abortion issue. It could have been birth control."[58] Had Sue been heterosexual, her spiritual journey might still have taken the same general course: increasing questioning of church authority, pointed exploration of different denominations' approaches to an issue important to her, and eventual rejection of organized religion in favor of personal spiritual development. The idea of moving or even graduating from religion to spirituality, where "religion" means an authoritative, dogmatic, static tradition that one must accept as dictated and "spirituality" means an intensely personal, individual, fluid, and generally autonomous interaction with the sacred, is an important theme in modern western discourse on religion and especially in the contemporary United States; LBT women simply happen to have found it more useful, or perhaps more necessary, than most.

Following Steven Tipton,[59] Paul Heelas calls this autonomous, personal approach to religiosity "expressive individualism" and describes its adherents as concerned with "the quest for creativity, personal 'growth,' 'meaningful' relationships, being in tune with oneself," and "one's authentic nature."[60] In a more recent work, Heelas and co-author Linda Woodhead expand this concept into what they term the "subjectivization thesis," arguing that contemporary England and the United States are experiencing growth in "subjective-life spirituality," a form of religiosity that centers on "life lived by reference to one's own subjective experiences (relational as much as individualistic)," and decline in "life-as religion," which focuses on "life lived in terms of external or 'objective' roles, duties, and obligations."[61]

Heelas and Woodhead suggest that the growth in subjective-life spirituality is currently most evident in contexts of culture and consumption, rather than in measurable (and especially organizational) religious practices. Yet, as I suggested earlier, this shift toward a subjective focus is likely also responsible both for the spread of LGBT identities (along with the rapidly proliferating riffs on those identities—"genderqueer," "heteroflexible," and the like) in western cultures and for the spread of LGBT theologies, religious organizations, religious autobiographies, and certainly individual spiritual "journeys."[62] While consumption is hardly irrelevant to contemporary gay and lesbian cultures, religious or otherwise, subjective-life spirituality stands out in much clearer relief among LBT women in the United States than it does in the touristy, semi-rural area of England studied by Heelas and Woodhead. It stretches far beyond New Age bookstores and yoga studios (though both certainly play a role here), affecting women's religious beliefs and identities as well as women's relationship to the religious and quasi-religious organizations in which they are involved.

What is most useful about Heelas and Woodhead's shift away from such terms as "expressive individualism," "religious individualism," and the like is that it allows us to look more closely at the altered roles of communities, which are still very much present in the "subjective turn" but are often elided by commentators' sometimes anxious focus on "individualism."[63] Even staunch religious individualists generally draw in some way from existing religious traditions. As David Lyon notes, postmodern religion serves as "a dynamic cultural resource."[64] Communities are a part of this resource. "In a very real sense," writes Wade Clark Roof, "the quest for community is a defining feature of our time."[65] For lesbian, bisexual, and transgendered women this quest becomes particularly important because so many religious organizations fail to provide the sort of community they seek; they need either to cobble their communities together from a variety of sources, or to search particularly carefully for a single group that meets their needs. Most central in this search for many women is not the *content* provided by a particular organization; rather, it is the *community.* For instance, the women who were actively seeking congregations when I interviewed them were looking not for a particular denomination or religious tradition, but for communities in which they might practice their already formed subjective spiritualities. Some of the regular attendees also mentioned the importance of their congregations as a source of community, and a few of the sporadic attendees missed the community they had lost when they left congregations that proved to be homophobic and thus unwelcoming. The primary function of religious organizations in these women's lives had to do not with dogma, but with a community of relatively like-minded people from whom they could learn and with whom they could share their own spiritual insights.

Another clue to the roles of congregations in "subjective-life spirituality" comes from Wuthnow's observation about the popularity of twelve-step groups, which play an important role in the spiritual lives of several women in this study. "Alcoholics Anonymous," Wuthnow observes, "and related twelve-step groups, such as Al-Anon and Adult Children of Alcoholics, have offered one of the clearest ways for pursuing self-understanding"[66]—such organizations, in Heelas and Woodhead's terms, serve as resources for "subjective-life spirituality." Indeed, Wuthnow makes explicit that a central role of religious organizations in what he terms the "spirituality of seeking" is to function as "supplier[s] of spiritual goods and services."[67] In a culture where the validity of religious beliefs and practices is measured by "finding out 'what works' by way of the truth of one's experience," religious organizations (and related material artifacts, such as books, audio recordings, and multimedia programs) offer some of the tiles from which the participants in this study have built the mosaics of their lived identities.

"Religion in its most basic sense," Roof observes, "is a story involving symbol, metaphor, and language, all having the power to persuade and fan the imagination. Symbol, metaphor, and language are in fact the means by which human beings come to self-awareness and articulate a sense of self in relation to others."[68] Religion, therefore, can be a critical source of both community and identity. But as Kimberlé Crenshaw and other theorists of intersectionality have taught us, no aspect of identity stands alone either.[69] This is why I use the metaphor of the mosaic here: religion (or irreligiousness, or active opposition to religion) may provide tiles in the mosaic of identity, but upon stepping back to view the larger picture, one realizes that those tiles can only be understood in the context of the others around them. Sexual orientation, gender, race, class, personal history, and other factors not only fill in different parts of the picture, but shift our interpretations of the other aspects of identity, just as a navy blue tile looks black next to a sky-blue one but blue next to a black one, and as a red tile that makes up part of a flag holds a different meaning from a red tile that helps form a rose.

Hervieu-Lèger makes a similar observation in the context of contemporary religion in the west:

> It is impossible to grasp the logic of spiritual do-it-yourself composition without taking into account both the social conditions of an individual's access to symbol resources of unequal availability and the cultural conditions of the use of these resources. It is true that relaxation of institutional control over belief favors individualistic dispersion of beliefs. But one should not overlook the fact that this dispersion still falls within a mechanism of social and cultural restrictions, the resonance of which remains extremely important.[70]

As this chapter has shown, the "mechanism of social and cultural restrictions" is especially relevant to the religious beliefs, practices, community involvement, and identities of the women in this study; indeed, this is true for LGBT people more generally, making these communities an important focus for the study of religion in "high modern" or "postmodern" cultures. The subjective turn has offered LGBT people new options for identity and community as well as new ways of maintaining religion (or "spirituality") in their lives. While social constraints and geography continue to shape the available choices, the cultural shift toward creating and seeking identities and communities that "fit" or "work" has allowed for the creative construction of a wide variety of new and intersecting mosaics. It is to the construction, alteration, and maintenance of those mosaics that the story now turns.

6 *Building a Mosaic*

THE SACRED (AND THE) SELF

It's all very spiritual, it's all God. It's the divine Goddess, the divine Mother, it's all of this universe working together to help one be who they really are. And I'm a fucking lesbian!
—Cassandra Christenson

Self-identity has become central to the partnership of individualism and consumerism that drives much of contemporary U.S. popular culture. Not only clothes and means of transportation, but cell phone covers and even candy can be personalized to display "who" the consumer "really is." Claiming and proclaiming less visible identities has become a political rallying cry, exemplified by ACT UP's slogan, "Silence = Death." At the same time, "identity politics," described by detractors as exclusive, noncoalitional, single-issue organizing around a socially significant (and usually nondominant) identity such as race, sexuality, or disability, has become the source of much controversy across the political spectrum. As the term "identity" has come into widespread usage, it has also come to hold a wide range of meanings, from group membership to demographic characteristics to sense of self.

As U.S. cultures have shifted across the twentieth century and into the twenty-first, it is not only religious practices that have moved away from "dwelling" and toward "seeking"; it is identity itself. While sociologists have long distinguished between ascribed (given) and achieved (earned) identities, the nature of these and the balance between them have undergone significant change. Fewer identities are ascribed in the early twenty-first century than in the early twentieth; some of those that are still ascribed have narrower consequences and less permanence. Achieved identities have broadened in scope, quantity, and variety, and the lessening importance of many (though certainly not all) ascribed identities leaves greater room for individual negotiations—a situation simultaneously influenced, capitalized upon, and constrained by the plethora of products bidding the buyer to "be yourself" through consumption. David Lyon, in exploring the convergence of religion and postmodernity, goes so far as to suggest that ascription and achievement have been replaced as modes of identity development by production and discovery.[1]

While popular culture and marketing agencies encourage us to "seek," "find," "express," "create," and "be" ourselves, this process is not as easy in reality as it seems in the dys/utopia of advertising, because some aspects of identity remain not only ascribed but also seriously constrained. Socioeconomic status often reproduces itself across generations, for reasons having little to do with individual choice and much to do with social structures. Race continues to be such a significant and essentialized marker of identity that the 2006 season of the reality TV show *Survivor* divided contestants into racial "tribes" (a turn of events with extremely troubling implications), and race continues to be associated with significant differences in average income, life expectancy, rates of incarceration, and other measures of collective well-being or lack thereof. Furthermore, different aspects of identity interact in ways that make it impossible to describe a single, fixed set of constraints upon and choices available to any particular group (a phenomenon often referred to as intersectionality).[2] Thus, even self-identity reflects a complicated combination of constraint and freedom, decisions made and options foreclosed.

Existing studies of LGBT religious identities, themselves implicitly intersectional, seem to support Lyon's argument that ascription and achievement are insufficient for conceptualizing postmodern identities. Yet rather than stressing the production and discovery of identity, these studies have portrayed something more like negotiation, bringing two apparently discordant and preexisting identities—religion and sexual orientation—into harmony or at least into a truce. However, such studies have focused entirely on specific religious traditions. The clear agreement among them is that there is no single pattern of identity negotiation, though several typical patterns seem to hold at least for Christians and Jews, and possibly for Muslims as well. In most studies these include suppressing one identity or the other, compartmentalizing the two identities and bringing only one out at a time (for instance, being Jewish in the synagogue and gay at the bar), integrating the two identities, and living with the two in tension.[3] Some studies also include strategies for addressing the sacred texts or theologies that call into question the validity of LGBT identities within traditional religions; interestingly, these strategies appear to be similar in many ways across the three monotheistic religions of Judaism, Christianity, and Islam. The primary strategies generally include downplaying the importance of the religious text, reading the text metaphorically, interpreting it through historical and cultural context, explaining it as the product of flawed human interpreters or scribes and therefore secondary in importance to direct communication with the divine, and finding positive examples in the text of gender diversity and same-sex love. Importantly, in the case of both Judaism and Islam, studies have shown that some LGBT people connect their ethnic identities to their religious identities, which complicates the need for identity negotiation while also allowing them to separate "ethnic" Jewish or Muslim identity from a belief in God and the attendant potential for religious identity discord.[4]

As I have noted throughout this book, what scholars have not previously considered in any depth is the complexity of religious identities among those LGBT people who do not adhere strictly to a single religious tradition or organization—and there is good reason to believe that these represent a large portion of the LGBT population, at least in the United States. Also not considered, with the exception of the aforementioned studies on ethnic and religious Muslim and Jewish identities, is the influence of *multiple* intersecting identities on the religious beliefs and practices of LGBT people. And yet, such complexity and multiplicity are central to postmodernity. In the twenty-first-century United States the people formerly known as "gays" have expanded their identities to the point that acronyms can no longer keep up and the vaguely defined or even intentionally undefined "queer" is replacing any attempt to name precisely one's sexual orientation or gender. In the twenty-first century United States the solidly bounded religions of the previous century have turned fluid to the point that many people identify as "spiritual but not religious" and consider religious traditions more as resources to be mined than as strictly defined identities. These phenomena of fluidity also intersect in the lives of the women in this study. This chapter explores participants' narratives of the sacred and the self, arguing that they exemplify postmodern religiosities through reliance on "everyday sacralogies," narrative self-construction, queer intersections of identities and spaces, the search for a "true self," and the experience of what I call "enselved bodies."

Everyday Sacralogies

In introducing her study of contemporary spiritualities in California, Ruth Frankenberg explains that her use of "detailed life history interviews" allows her to grasp "the inseparably visceral, discursive, experiential, and practical dimensions of religious and spiritual life."[5] Though the social dimension is conspicuously absent from this list, Frankenberg adds it on a secondary level later in her introduction. Though her focus, she explains, is on "inner spiritual journeys," such journeys do not stand alone. "Interviewees are members of 'communities of memory,' participants in 'networks of meaning' that help to make sense of their experiences" of the sacred.[6] Such networks, often referred to as "plausibility structures" by sociologists of religion,[7] offer narrative frameworks or scripts through which to interpret experiences of the sacred, and they reinforce beliefs shared by the network while delegitimating other beliefs.

Frankenberg's use of the term "journeys" also implies that one might drift away from some networks of meaning and toward others, if one's own trajectory differed from that of the rest of the network—thus turning the plausibility structure, one might say, into a structure of implausibility. Likewise, if Frankenberg's descriptions of religious and spiritual life hold true for identity more broadly, then the potential exists for one aspect of a self-identity to drift from or conflict with the plausibility structure even as that structure validates another aspect of the same identity. Frankenberg does indeed find such challenges, which she describes metaphorically as two identity spaces "crashing." Such crashes necessitate negotiation with the group or, if the group is not amenable to negotiation, redirection of one's spiritual journey.[8]

Notable in Frankenberg's nuanced exploration of intersectionality in spiritual practice is the fact that she allows for experiences that interviewees describe as relating to the sacred. While religious identity and participation play a role in some considerations of postmodern identities and communities, rarely is the sacred itself taken into account. Yet, a sense of the sacred does indeed seem to play an important role in identity, and may do so far more often than is generally noted.[9] In an earlier study of LGBT Christians, for instance, I encountered several stories of direct experiences of the sacred—visions, voices, a sense of the presence of God—that participants recalled as turning points in their self-acceptance.[10] As these examples suggest, and as Frankenberg points out as well, experiences of the sacred are often bodily; they can also become "commonplace" and be integrated into one's "networks of meaning" and sense of self, producing what Dawne Moon and others have referred to as "everyday theologies" that are central to many people's sense of self and of their location in the world.[11] Identity, then, cannot be thoroughly understood without taking everyday theologies into account. Since some of these "theologies" are in fact atheistic (ranging from "there is no sacred" to "there are sacred aspects to the cosmos, but they are not deities") or agnostic, I will refer to them here as "everyday *sacralogies*"—individual understandings of the sacred. Among participants' everyday sacralogies, the most prevalent themes were nebulousness and mystery, immanence, limitation, love, and the female divine.

Nebulousness and Mystery

Each participant in this study spoke in some way about the sacred. With Silva, the atheist in the group, this part of the conversation was predictably quite different than with other participants. Even Silva, however, was willing to elaborate somewhat on her beliefs when pressed. While she is a deeply committed atheist who believes "in the human being . . . in myself and in you," Silva does believe that souls or spirits survive death and experience reincarnation.[12] "Bottom line is," though, "I have a hundred and one reasons to dislike the Bible and God. For all we know, this world was created by aliens, you know?" Silva was not always so firm in her beliefs. "I always wanted to believe that God was good, okay? And he was merciful. Mm-hmm. Once I read the Bible, and you're telling me that the Bible was inspired by God, there went God out the window." On the other hand, Silva reflected at one point in the interview, "something happened for us [humans] to get here. So it has to be something bigger than us." She added firmly, "But it's not God." It is not, at least, the God of the Bible, whom Silva sees as violent, uncaring, and irrational—similar to her dim view of his followers.

The rest of the study participants felt more positive about the sacred, even if many were just as uncertain as Silva about its actual nature. In fact, the most central theme in participants' understanding of the sacred was mystery. For some this meant a concrete statement that the nature of the sacred was to be mysterious; for others, it was a way of expressing a certain agnosticism. Trish, for example, had recently attended a series of classes at Neighborhood Unitarian Universalist Church called "Building Your Own Theology," and had therefore been reflecting quite a bit on the nature of the sacred. She told me, "I like the word 'God' a lot because I don't know what it means, and it doesn't have any other connotation to me. . . . I don't really understand what God is or who God is, and I don't think I ever will, and I'm okay with that."[13] Accepting uncertainty was an important part of her involvement in Alcoholics Anonymous, where Trish first became comfortable with the idea of God, and the willingness to be "happy with not knowing" about God was clearly a part of this same mindset for her.

Although Regina Lark also connected with God through her participation in AA, and although she shared with Trish a deep uncertainty about the nature of the divine, she was less willing to simply accept this uncertainty. She balanced a somewhat frustrated lack of knowledge with a description of the sacred as "nebulous." Having become a committed feminist in college, Regina came to the realization that "the language that I was speaking in AA in terms of a God consciousness . . . sounded very masculinized, and very dogmatic, and very preachy, and very patriarchal."[14] Though she felt uncomfortable with both her childhood Catholicism and the understanding of religion she found in her AA group, Regina recalled that "I wanted something [religious] but didn't have a language for it. But I didn't know what else to do. I didn't know where to go." Her central connection to what she calls "God" had for years been through her journal, which she addressed "Dear God." When Regina left AA, seeking a more feminist understanding of and connection to the sacred, "the only thing

I held on to was my journal writing. And instead of addressing it 'Dear God,' I changed the language to 'Great Spirit,' 'cause I didn't know what else to call this. And I know it's something. I don't know what *it* is." Reaching for more detail later in the interview, Regina mused, "If I were to really envision some*thing*, it would be a smoky haze." "It's not a single person," she added. "It's everything right and good and just, according to what I believe justice and morality is." Even with her disillusionment about Catholicism and about the God of AA, even with her feminist critique of the religions she had revisited or experienced, Regina maintained a belief in the sacred, but lacked the language to conceptualize that belief.

Lara Sowinsky, in contrast, offered a clear conception of God, but one that was no less nebulous than Regina's. "I'd have to say," she told me, laughing, "that the mysterious part of God is the better part."[15] Unsure how to interpret her adjective, I asked, "You mean the most part, or 'better' as in good-better?" "For me," she responded, pausing, "both." She illustrated by explaining that humans are often unable to comprehend seemingly unfair and painful events in our lives, but that she believes God has reasons for all of these events—thus the mystery of God. Yet while Lara was willing to go so far as to envision a "being" who is responsible for or at least knows the reasons behind adverse events, she resisted assigning many other characteristics to the divine. "I understand God to be a being that's neither male or female, or black or white, or anything. I think there's a being that is about love and understanding and—" She paused. "That would be it." Lara suggested that an awareness of the divine is a universal human characteristic: "I would venture to say that every person alive has a sense of God, what God is. I think that people are born with that as part of their nature. And therefore that supersedes religion or education or culture or ability to read or write." Thus, the mystery of God, for Lara, is infused with a universalism, albeit one shaped by her own background in a contemporary, western, monotheistic religion.[16]

Lauren's concept of God was also shaped by western cultural patterns, but far from the conservative Protestant (and, more recently, Catholic) influences on Lara's beliefs, Lauren's worldview can be traced instead to western esotericism. Like many other participants, Lauren held to a concept of the sacred as mysterious—in fact, she believed humans to be literally incapable of comprehending the divine. "I think that God is incomprehensible to the biology of humans," she told me. "Certain transcendent beings may approach the understanding of what God may be, but I don't think you can really understand what God is in this form of biology. You have to transcend this form of biology to understand."[17] Despite these severe restrictions, Lauren could offer a few thoughts about what God might be like. "I picture God as part of everything and part of nothing," she explained. "To me, God is the center of all existence, of many, many levels of dimensional existence. Not just the physical dimension but, you know, innumerable dimensions beyond that." Such vastness that is also, paradoxically, "part of everything" evinces an intriguing combination of immanence and transcendence.

Immanence

For Coco Gallegos, unlike for Lauren, the emphasis is strictly on divine immanence. In her eyes, too, the sacred is nebulous, but this is because she feels such a close connection to the divine that she is unable to articulate her understanding of it. A devout and sometimes charismatic Catholic for whom God is an important part of everyday life, Coco choked up when she began to talk to me about her understanding of God. Her explanation is worth quoting in its entirety in order to capture the way she moves between metaphors and frustration with her inability to explain what she senses:

> *How I understand God? It took me also a long time to verbalize it. And this year I'm finally understanding why it has taken me a lot of time to verbalize a lot of things, because they are such an integrated part of me that I don't have the words, you know. It just is! But my concept of God is like the wind. I don't see it, but it moves my clothes, it moves my hair, it moves the leaves, God is present. And I know he's holding me. [She paused.] I'm going to cry. Because that integration part is what has been kind of like a confusing part. It was like there was something wrong with me because I couldn't put it in words. But it was because it has been an integrated part of me. It's like the blood, you know. It's so integrated that it's in the bloodstream.*[18]

Integrated in the bloodstream, part of everything yet part of nothing, a universal human characteristic, a smoky haze, an unknown: the sacred, for these participants and for many others, is ineffable. Yet Coco's sense of integration, of God being so close to her as to be indescribable, points to the other aspect of the sacred that dominates, somewhat paradoxically, in these descriptions: immanence and indwelling.

Coco's description of God as being so integrated as to be part of her bloodstream is among the more radically immanent sacralogies represented in this group. But it is not the only example of radical immanence. For Cassandra Christenson, no single term is adequate to express the sacred indwelling that she understands to be within each person. "I *really believe* that I am everything I am," she stressed to me. "I mean, that there isn't anything out there. But I use 'invite in,' or I use 'the Goddess' or 'God' or other symbols and such, because it helps me to express what I want to express."[19] At the same time, the sacred also has external roles in Cassandra's life. It guides her, for instance, to new experiences and opportunities for deeper thought. "Since I was about thirty-five, forty, I walk through life and I just watch for the universe to give me clues of, 'Oh, look at this,' or 'Think about this,' or 'Here's a place that's really magnificent. Come and connect with the great energy.'" For Cassandra, such opportunities do not arise only in traditional religious or spiritual settings. They can be nearly anywhere, including in an AIDS hospice organization like the one Cassandra ran in the 1990s. "I know God's inside [the self]," she told me, "but God is also there [with the hospice workers]. You know, that's where Jesus would be. This is where all of those great beings that come to teach us to be who we are . . . this is where they would be."

Radical immanence was also an important part of the sacred for all four participants who were involved in the Agape International Spiritual Center. While some, like Religious Science practitioner Christine Peña, had a clearly developed and nuanced sense of the divine as internal, Betty's thoughts are instructive because she had recently studied this perspective in her introductory class on Religious Science. Having grown up in a Baptist church, Betty was accustomed to "God being a person."[20] "But with Religious Science," she explained, "God is 'it,' and it's different, and that's a lot to work on." Another new perspective that Betty had to work on was her concept of herself as a "child of God." "When you speak of being a child of God, you are separating yourself from God. So I had to change my prayer [in class] because God and I are one." She then explained her current perspective: "I see God everywhere. I see God in you. I see God as everything now."

Limitation

In contrast to, and sometimes in combination with, the theme of immanence and often of panentheism (the belief that the sacred is *in* everything, in contrast to pantheism, which refers to the belief that the sacred *is* everything), some participants spoke of the divine as limited in its comprehension of or engagement with the world. Christine Peña, for instance, spoke of God as a part of her, evident in her sense of intuition; yet, she also described God as a "benevolent presence" and even as an "impersonal substance."[21] As immanence, Christine believes, God is in every human being. As impersonal substance and benevolent presence, though, "God doesn't know anything about suffering or pain. . . . God is just all good. And it's only our perceptions of what is bad and what is evil and what is wrong, you know. . . . I don't think God has opinions. I think God just *is*."

Vanessa also had a conception of God as somewhat out of touch with human experiences; this is not particularly surprising given the "identity crash" with which she was struggling at the time of our interview. Though she used the term "God," Vanessa noted that she was an agnostic, believing in a "higher power" but not necessarily in the God of her upbringing.[22] "I believe there's somebody there to look over us," she observed, "or else we'll have chaos and, you know, tragedy. But I don't believe he really does anything. I just believe that he's there." This higher power, in fact, is so distanced from the human realm that Vanessa believed he was unprepared for the development of gay and lesbian identities. She imagined God coming to earth (thus also implying that God is not already here) and seeing same-sex couples. "He would be like, 'Well, why are these men together? And why are these women together? That's not how I set out the world.'" At the same time, Vanessa also suggested that God would be unable to do anything about the development of LGBT communities. She thought that God (unlike the Conservative Jewish communities that were her reference points for her religion) would eventually come to accept gay men and lesbians because "I don't think he has a choice."

Love

In addition to nebulousness, immanence, and limitation, a fourth aspect of the sacred that was commonly invoked by participants—and one that is popular in the United States as a whole—was love. This theme was relevant regardless of whether participants saw the divine in alternative or traditional ways, as immanent, transcendent or both. "Love, love, love," intoned Emile with a benevolent smile when describing her relationship with Jesus. "You just can't say it enough, you can't give it enough, you can't receive it enough. That may be the thing, a lot of people not receiving enough. If you receive Jesus Christ, it's all that you need."[23]

Sue, although a self-described "ex-Catholic," still believes in Jesus because "it's the best deal going. He offered me a free gift! . . . You'll get eternal life if you believe in Jesus."[24] Yet her concept of God is considerably more complicated, involving both mystery and love. "I think God is everything we don't know," she explained to me. "But combine that—what we do know, but *more* than what we know. Combined somehow with love. Love and forgiveness are in that concept." So is universalism; though she personally has decided that Jesus is "the best deal going," she also feels that other religions are valid routes to the sacred. "Maybe we need all these different religions in the world," she mused, "because if somebody could computerize them, and find out what they had in common, that's probably the only truth there is."[25]

Sue referenced Hinduism as an example of an alternate route to sacred truth, and suggested that maybe the figures of Christ and Krishna might have something in common. Adesina also referenced Hinduism, speaking specifically of love, and also used it as an example of a route to a broader truth. An initiate of Yoruba religion and a practitioner of Religious Science, vegetarianism, yoga, and meditation, Adesina read voraciously on spiritual topics, and was especially drawn to Asian religious exporters: those who primarily address western converts and potential converts. Of Self-Realization Fellowship founder Paramahansa Yogananda, Adesina said, "I like his books, because he writes about God as a lover and his beloved, and I think that is just so sweet, to think of God that way."[26] She is also fond of Vietnamese Buddhist author Thich Nhat Hanh, and specifically mentioned his book *Teach Love*. Furthermore, the centrality of love in the divine is important for Adesina's self-understanding. When coming out as a lesbian, "I was very secure in the fact that God wasn't going to punish me because I loved a woman," she recalled. "I mean, hello! To me, God and love is one. And so if I'm finding love in another person, then that is helping me to find myself. . . . If God and love are one, then how could God condemn me for loving?"

The Female Divine

Perhaps tellingly, for Adesina this "God" who is love and who would not condemn her for loving a woman "is a Goddess." She told me, laughing, "Nobody's going to turn that around for me, you know what I mean?" Goddess, to Adesina, is made visible in the world through human actions; this further strengthens the ties between Adesina's vision of the divine as love and her belief that Goddess supports her loving relationships. But Adesina is not the only one in the study to explicitly conceive of the divine as Goddess; though some participants made it clear that the divine is neither male nor female, and some preferred to speak of a force rather than an anthropomorphic entity that might have gender, others found clear affirmation of themselves as women, and often of their feminist beliefs, though a sense of the divine as female.

For Tami, such a sense links to her concept of the divine as immanent and as rooted in nature. When I asked her whether she had a word for "what you consider to be sacred," Tami responded, "I'd say 'Goddess.' I mean, unfortunately there's like a thousand names that she goes by, but I just like to say 'Goddess' and incorporate it all."[27] When I asked Tami to explain how she understands the Goddess, she responded simply, "I'd say she's everything. Everything *living*. She's not some thing sitting on a cloud . . . and judging you, which is *unfortunately* how I view God. . . . The Goddess loves you no matter what." Because Wiccan beliefs generally include both a goddess and a god, I asked Tami whether she also believed in a god. She hesitated, and then said somewhat reluctantly, "Yes, I guess *a* god exists, but not the, quote, 'man-God' of the Bible. . . . Because it takes a man and a woman to give life, it would take a god and a goddess to also give life. But I think she's just a little bit more prevalent, because we give birth." Willing to acknowledge masculine as well as feminine aspects of the divine, Tami was nonetheless far more committed to the latter.

For Kathleen McGregor, the distinction between feminine and masculine aspects of divinity was a point of struggle. As a former Catholic, she had a strong conception of God as masculine. Having had several unpleasant men in her life and having recently come out as a lesbian, she wanted to distance herself from those masculine aspects of God. And with her growing interest in feminism, she found herself increasingly drawn to the feminine divine. Yet old habits are hard to break. "I can't get rid of the Papa God," she told me ruefully. "I want to get rid of him *so* bad. And it's just like, I guess it's so ingrained in my psyche, I can't seem to get rid of it." She explained, "I associate certain bad feelings with the male god. I associate all the terrible things that people do in the name of religion with the male god." One long-standing alternative to this masculine deity is Kathleen's "fascination with Our Lady of Guadalupe," whom she saw all around her during her girlhood in Nogales, Arizona. Yet despite fondly associating Mary with her grandmother, Kathleen also had an uneasy relationship with Guadalupe: "whenever I start being really attracted to her, things go really badly in my life. . . . When I think back on it, it's sort of like she's carrying me through." Thus, although she felt that Guadalupe was an important source of support, Kathleen was also wary of being drawn to her, fearing that such attraction was an indication of trouble on the horizon. She turned instead to images of the sacred that had been nurtured by her recent association with the Unitarian Universalist group CUUPS (Covenant of Unitarian Universalist Pagans). "I find myself praying to the moon," she explained, "and the earth. . . . It's like a healing or nurturing that comes from the earth." And she saw the connection between the moon and the ocean as "something so cosmically miraculous that I see that as an embodiment of all that's good in spirit." She also interpreted both the moon and the earth as feminine, and thus found these images to be important feminist alternatives to the "Papa God." Most recently, she had been focusing on imaging the divine as the aurora borealis.

As is already evident from the foregoing discussion, the consequences of participants' sacralogies for their identity negotiations are often profound. The predominance of nebulous conceptions of the sacred may seem theologically unfocused, but it would be a mistake to dismiss these concepts as simply lacking in rigor; the very fluidity of participants' sacralogies resists the rigid identity boundaries that can be constructed by more formalized and systematized theologies. Even in the absence of such fluidity, an emphasis on love has a similar effect: if the sacred is represented by a being whose foremost aspect is love, it is difficult (though possible) to argue that such a being responds to the humans it loves with anything other than warmth and acceptance. Immanence further reinforces this effect, and for women, receiving love from a feminine divine figure provides a sacred model for love relationships between women. As previous chapters have noted, all three transgendered women in the study also identified particular resonances between their conceptions of the sacred and the various ways in which they understand their gender identities. Thus, it should be unsurprising that many of the participants in this study saw explicit connections between their sacralogies and their own sexual or gender identities.[28] These connections are particularly apparent in participants' construction and expression of their identities through narrative.

Narrative

One of the better-known theorists of the self in what he alternately calls "high" and "late" modernity, sociologist Anthony Giddens stresses the theme of reflexivity in his understanding of self-identity. Rather than being either given or earned, he argues, in late modernity "the self, like the broader institutional contexts in which it exists, has to be reflexively made."[29] The late modern self, in other words, is an ongoing, lifelong project. Self-construction and self-maintenance, Giddens suggests, rely heavily on narrative; thus, the importance of "telling one's story" both to oneself and to others.[30] Importantly, Giddens also links this narrative element to what Philip Rieff earlier termed the "triumph of the therapeutic."[31] "Therapy," Giddens argues, "should be understood and evaluated essentially as a methodology of life-planning."[32] Creating a sense of order through the narrative linking of past, present, and future selves, therapy in Giddens's eyes is not only a tool but even a hallmark of the high modern self.[33] This may account in part for the central role played by therapeutic twelve-step groups such as Alcoholics Anonymous during what several participants identified as turning points in their own narratives of self and spirit.

If participants constructed their identities through narrative, both over the course of their lives and in the very moment of the interview itself, then two important questions arise. The first has to do with the nature and structure of time in narrative; the other concerns narrative solutions to "ungrammatical" identities.

Narrative Time

A notable, if subtle, aspect of Giddens's conception of the narratively constructed self is its linearity. The self is constantly under construction, and even if there is no clear telos here, there is at least a clear direction: forward. Yet queer identities, and sometimes queer religious identities, are constructed at least as much in reverse as forward: one looks back to an earlier time in one's life and says, "I should have known then that I was gay," or "I wanted to be a boy from the time I was three, but I didn't yet know what that meant." If one were to insist on a linear map of identity construction one might see an oscillation or spiral here, but perhaps there is something less directional going on. As anthropologist

Tom Boellstorff points out, linear time is also "straight" time—with the double entendre most definitely intended.[34] In developing his argument about time and narrative, Boellstorff draws from the work of queer theorists Judith Halberstam and Lee Edelman, who point to the reproductive ethos of linear, "straight time": an ethos in which generations are supposed to succeed each other in clearly marked, uncomplicated ways, in which there are expected life courses for all humans and many nonhuman animals as well, in which reproduction, despite its deceptively circular "re" prefix, is ultimately about *pro*duction and therefore about progress.[35]

"Queer time," these authors argue, has the potential to disrupt straight time and therefore to undermine social structures based on this linear model. While, as Boellstorff notes,[36] simply identifying as queer or even writing queer theory does not automatically effect a departure from straight time, the forced disruption of one's expected life path that often accompanies the coming-out process seems to catalyze this departure. Suddenly one's life course is no longer driven by accepting or refusing culturally expected, time-bound roles (high school graduate, productive worker, bride, father); instead, each of these roles comes into question or foreclosure. Such an anomic experience can be simultaneously paralyzing and freeing; identity is now more reliant on narrative than ever before. This means that queer identities in general are heavily reliant on narratives—some borrowed, some thoroughly reframed, and some freshly constructed. And while these narratives may be linear, they may also take an entirely different shape. In many queer identities, for instance—including those related within these pages—time seems both to cycle and to meld. Looking back on interviews conducted in another time and place, I discuss meetings wherein participants brought past events to the present in order to construct a cohesive narrative, a cohesive identity for the duration of the interview.

While having linear elements, these stories themselves are rarely linear. Often told (likely at my prompting) as tales of how participants got "here" from "there" (the sexual and religious identities of adolescence, for instance), when the stories focused on identity most participants refused the linear narrative. Events experienced one way in the past became in the present signs of the (past) future, unnoticed indicators perhaps of one's "true" sexual orientation or unrecognized communications from a deity of one's future faith. Though these overlaps of time—the past reinterpreted in the more recent past and both pasts rearticulated in the present for the sake of an interview that would be analyzed in the future—are hardly the exclusive province of the nonheterosexual, they produce a kind of narrative "wrinkling" of time (with apologies to author Madeleine L'Engle) that seems at the very least unstraight because of its refusal of linearity. While purportedly supporting the vision of an eternal self ("even though I didn't know it at the time . . . "), these queerly atemporal narratives in fact reinforce the perpetual construction and reconstruction of identity. In this, they may be playing less with "queer" time than with the postmodern, even if the "post" implies in some way a return to linearity.

"Ungrammatical" Identities

The perpetual narrative project of identity becomes clearest in contexts where aspects of one's identity are, as Boellstorff puts it, "'ungrammatical' with each other,"[37] where established social categories—even stigmatized ones—fail to match one's sense of self. Several stories from participants in this project highlight this ontological dilemma and its narrative resolutions. Vanessa, for instance, was convinced at the time of our interview that Judaism and lesbianism could not go together, yet she was equally convinced that in some way she was a part of both those categories. Lauren and Danielle had similar experiences—Danielle with firmly identifying as both Mormon and transgendered; Lauren with seeing herself on a gendered "gray scale" that was not recognized in the society around her, and with believing herself to be at the end of her human incarnations and ready to advance to a higher spiritual plane. But each of these stories represents a grammatical failure in two dimensions; when multiple identities fall outside of the available scripts, then the temporally queer, postmodern narrative seems to come most strongly into play. This is the case with Corrine.

The "ungrammatical" nature of Corrine's identity and experiences was evident from the time of my initial telephone interview with her. This was primarily a screening interview in which I determined volunteers' eligibility for the project, but I also used the opportunity to collect basic demographic data in advance of the in-depth interview. "What is your current gender identity?" I asked. "Female," Corrine replied. When I asked whether she identified as transgender/transsexual, she responded, "Transgender." She then added that she was "female-to-male," and that she identified as a woman but lived as a man. This aspect of her identity immediately demonstrated the inadequacy of my next stock question: "How do you identify in terms of sexual orientation?" Since the concept of sexual orientation is predicated on fixed gender identities, such a question loses its logic in the context of people who identify as both female and male. Corrine answered, "Bisexual or polysexual."[38]

While Corrine valued her gender fluidity, it had provoked hostility among both heterosexual and lesbian/gay communities. "Because the gay community and lesbian community have been so focused on being gay and lesbian that anything outside of that gay and lesbian perspective is like, '*Ohhh!*'" she gasped dramatically:

> *"Wait a minute, we've fought to be a gay and a lesbian person! And now you're going to come in here and confuse everybody with your idiotic way of thinking!" And what they tend to forget is that when*

> *we go back to history, and we study Stonewall, it was the butch women and the transgender males to females who got the ass-whuppings, to be able to open the door for the lesbians and the gays to walk through. . . . So we're marginalized in our own community. And that was a hard lesson for me to learn.*[39]

In fact, Corrine felt more accepted in her Latino community in East Los Angeles than she did in gay and lesbian communities in the L.A. area. She was aware that others often did not correctly perceive the identity she was expressing (a woman who lived as a man, or a person with both genders); instead, she was often perceived as "a butch lesbian." However, having arrived at this complex gender identity, she was sometimes willing to live with others' assumptions in order to conserve her own energy, and she took opportunities when she could to educate others about the varied realities of transgender identities.

Yet being transgendered had not been Corrine's only struggle with inadequate social categories. Though she was raised in East Los Angeles and considered the city her home and her community, she recalled being aware as a child that she was ethnically different from other children. "I'm looking around," she recounted, and "I'm not like anybody. I don't have anybody's background. Everybody has this common, you know, Mexico thing going on, and I don't. 'New Mexico? Ha, ha, ha, you mean Mexico.' 'No, I mean *New* Mexico.' 'There's no such place as *New* Mexico!'" Corrine's Pueblo grandmother had moved from New Mexico to East L.A. and had raised her granddaughter as a Latina; Corrine's grandfather on that side was Spanish. Corrine had no connection to her Native identity until she was sixteen and accompanied her grandmother back to the reservation. She had her first child with her when her uncle met them at the train station. "And my uncle said, 'You could take this baby and throw him with a bunch of Navajos, and you wouldn't be able to find which one is yours.' And that's when I realized . . . that someone in my family was acknowledging that I was Native." This experience sparked an "inner hunger to find out who I really was," and Corrine began learning all she could about Pueblo history.

She also developed an interest in Pueblo religious practices, but here she again fell between categories. "I'm a city Indian," she explained to me. "So I couldn't really go into the Native community and be able to practice their religion without everybody always saying, you know, 'She's from the city.' . . . I was always an outcast because I wasn't part of my culture." One solution to this problem was the pan-Indian movement, in which Corrine had occasionally been involved. Yet there she had encountered sexism and transphobia. So she focused most of her energies on a religion that is strongly rooted in the community of her upbringing, but that she also connected with her indigenous heritage. Santería, having both African and Hispanic overtones, reflected the cultures of Corrine's two grandfathers. Having developed in response to colonization and severe oppression, the religion also resonated with her sense of her Pueblo ancestors' history. Furthermore, with her strong connection to Changó—a deity Corrine understood to be both male and female—and having found a *padrino* who also expressed a fluid gender, she was supported in her gender and sexual identities by the religion as well. Though Corrine constantly created, recreated, and explained these connections through narrative, in many ways it was Santería that provided her with the basic elements from which to build a cohesive identity from so many pieces that fell between the cracks in pre-existing narratives. "All things are spiritual to me," Corrine observed.

> *Because I live my life in the spiritual. So when I get up, I get up just thanking the world that I have another day. And challenges that come into my life, I always look at them in a positive way, and how can that improve me as a person? As negative as they may be, you know. I just turn them around and try to work on the self. Because I can only come from the perspective of the self. All other things are just lessons in life to teach me the lesson for the next battle that I'm going to be going through. Because I am a warrior spirit. Through my indigenous roots, and also through Changó. So my spirit is a warrior spirit, that will always be fighting the battle of life.*

In the midst of ungrammatical identities, Corinne found her own grammar through Changó and the narrative of the warrior.

Queer Intersections

Intersectionality: Coincidences of Identity

Introduced by legal scholar Kimberlé Crenshaw and developed most fruitfully in the area of critical race theory, the term "intersectionality" encapsulates for theoretical purposes a situation long observed by feminists who did not share the dominant social identities of most mainstream feminist leaders—most notably feminists of color but also working-class feminists, lesbian feminists, and feminists with disabilities.[40] Noting that the concerns raised by the mainstream feminist movement as "women's issues" were not always *their* issues, these authors were among the first to point to the fact that different social identities impact and alter each other. Crenshaw, in a highly influential article, brought these ideas together with analyses of structural power to consider the intersectionality of race and gender in violence against women of color. Importantly, she also notes in the introduction to this article that her "focus on the intersections of race and gender only highlights the need to account for multiple grounds of identity when considering how the social world is constructed."[41] Crenshaw's analysis focuses on three types of intersectionality: structural intersectionality, which she defines as "the ways in which the location of women of color at the intersection of race and gender makes our actual experience . . . qualitatively different than that of white women"; political intersectionality, which centers on the marginalization of race in feminist politics and of gender in antiracist politics; and representational intersectionality, or "the cultural construction of women of color."[42]

In exploring the lives and stories of *gay* Indonesians (a term he italicizes to stress its differences from western concepts of gayness), Boellstorff discusses intersections of race, region, and sexuality, but rather than write of intersectionality he relies instead on the theme of coincidence—identity coincidence, temporal coincidence, disciplinary coincidence—as a strategy for avoiding the linearity and singularity of many narratives of identity, religion, and discipline.[43] Boellstorff finds one use of this metaphor in discussing the "ungrammatical" nature of *gay* and Muslim identities; rather than analytically forcing the two to come together in some way, he sees them as literally coinciding, existing simultaneously in the same life and affecting each other without becoming melded. I find this a particularly provocative addition to the concept of intersectionality.

What happens when coincidence and intersectionality impact the narrative project of the self? Though analyses of intersectionality focus more on experience than on identity, the two are interrelated, and thus any consideration of the self must also take intersectionality into account. In practice, intersectionality can make all the difference in religious affiliation and participation: in a Church of God in Christ (COGIC) congregation, for example, the same woman may be either a respected (though not ordainable) "Mother" in the church, or she may be a pariah—depending solely on her sexual orientation. Within a Metropolitan Community Church, a lesbian may feel more or less welcome depending on whether she is white or Latina. And a Mormon woman may feel embraced or excluded by her ward on the basis of class, or by virtue of having originally been blessed in the church as a son before she transitioned to living as a woman. All of these social experiences may influence self-identities.

Writing of the identity negotiations of young women, Shelley Budgeon captures this interaction particularly well.[44] Budgeon's study warrants a brief digression here, as her theoretical work on the tension between choice and constraint in postmodern identities is incisive; it is especially valuable for understanding the identity negotiations of the lesbian, bisexual, and transgendered women at the center of this book. Examining the self-concepts and life narratives of young urban women in northern England, Budgeon argues for a highly complex and fluid conception of identity as "a mode of being, a practice of making sense that is intimately connected with experience, subjectivity, and social relations,"[45] and she maintains that "the process of identity construction is simultaneously about stability and flux."[46] Likewise, it is simultaneously (and inseparably) about mind, body, and power: "Meanings do not simply become inscribed on the body as though it were a blank surface," Budgeon argues. "Instead, they enfold, merge, split apart, mingle, detach, and reattach in a constant process of becoming, in which the body is not an object separate from the subject but an event constituted by its connections with other bodies, practices, knowledges, devices, techniques, and relations."[47] The reflexive subject is simultaneously a socially embedded subject; the self is relentlessly embodied; and little about this social, reflexive, embodied self is stable for long—except, perhaps, for its very instability.

These themes of creative tension, and especially of instability, play an important part in queer theoretical understandings of sexuality and gender, though as Budgeon herself notes, such theoretical work is rarely grounded in empirical observations.[48] Its impact, however, is clear in smaller scale, more detailed studies of lesbian and gay identity. Cohler and Hammack's brief study of gay men's autobiographies, for instance, argues that "gay identity" is not "an achieved status"; rather, it is "a narrative rooted in sexual desire but motivated by social practice."[49] Another study of lesbian and gay identities, Dana Rosenfeld's *The Changing of the Guard,* stresses the importance of age and cohort in the development and forms of identity among older gay men and lesbians in the United States. Arguing that "identities are interpretations made with an awareness of (and, often, in conflict with) competing discourses and categories of the self,"[50] Rosenfeld notes the importance of choice and negotiation in the development of sexual identities while at the same time reminding readers that any exercise of choice is limited by the options available. Those gay men and lesbians who developed their sexual identities prior to the late 1960s, Rosenfeld suggests, produced a qualitatively different identity and set of values than did those who came out after the Stonewall rebellion in 1969. In addition to being influenced by social networks and webs of social power, identity is also, in Rosenfeld's words, "historically contingent."[51]

In considering the intersections of multiple identities, it is worth noting that I focus here on women who hold nondominant identities in areas other than sexual orientation and gender. This is not because dominant identities such as whiteness, Christianity, or cisgender (nontransgender) are irrelevant to the understanding of intersectionality—far from it, as dominant identities position people within social systems of power in ways that often make it easier for them to negotiate their other, nondominant identities. However, because of the "unmarked," or socially invisible, nature of dominant identities, they generally must be studied indirectly, by observation. Interviews, which turn primarily on self-perception, are a difficult tool to use in unpacking the intersectionality of unmarked identities.

A second important point to make about identity intersections is that some interviewees saw identities that clearly intersect at a structural level as being mutually irrelevant at other levels of their lives. Even Coco, who spoke so movingly about the deep connections between the sacred and her sexual and ethnic identities, rejected the idea that such connections were relevant on a public level. She told me a story about revealing her interest in the Catholic charismatic movement to someone in the archdiocesan office. That person, aware that the charismatic movement tends toward theological conservatism, asked Coco whether the organizers of the charismatic conference she attended "know that you are gay." Coco chuckled. "And I go, 'Do I need to tell them that I'm Mexican, too?'" On a personal level, being gay, Mexican, and a charismatic Catholic are tightly interwoven for Coco; on a public level they do not necessarily have any reason to interact.

Christine Peña felt that her sexual orientation was irrelevant on an even deeper level. In an e-mail she sent to me after reading the transcript of her interview, she noted that "I don't think the main point I would want to say about my spirituality/sexuality was touched on at all. The main thing I would want to say is that my sexual preference has almost nothing to do with my spiritual life." She explained that although being bisexual was definitely a part of who she was, "the need to even think of myself as 'different' has long been healed." "Science of Mind," she concluded, "is about Oneness and wholeness and sexual preference is irrelevant from that whole soul point of view."[52] Betty, another Agape member, was even more succinct (and emphatic) when toward the end of the interview I asked her, "Do you think that your experiences with religion and spirituality have been affected at all by your being a woman?" "I don't feel that," she replied. "Not at all. I sure don't. I really don't."[53] Yet other aspects of Betty's identity—her being a lesbian, especially—*had* impacted her spiritual and religious experiences. In each of these cases, some aspects of the participants' identities had interacted in important ways to shape their religious decision making and their sense of self, while others had remained generally irrelevant. For some, those interactions have been so diverse and complex that their experiences are worth discussing in depth as case studies of religion and intersectionality.

The role of intersectionality in Adesina's religious life began early, when she became "totally turned off of Christianity" both because of the religion's role in supporting the slave trade and because of its leadership in the witch trials and other "abominations to women."[54] When she watched Yoruba dances in high school and felt a deep connection to them, she knew she had found an important religious path, and that aspect of her religiosity remained important to her at the time of our interview even though she had largely ceased active involvement in it. "Just having my elekes, which are the necklaces that I wear that represent the different gods and goddesses, is a vital part of me," she explained. This was because of the importance of remaining "connected to my

African roots, because that's where I came from." But there was, to her mind, a limitation to Yoruba religion—as was true of all religions, for Adesina believed that "[any] religion in its pure form was wonderful, but then as you got into it, the organization and the people kind of corrupted it." In the case of Yoruba religion, though she identified as heterosexual during her main period of involvement with it, Adesina explained that even had she identified as a lesbian at the time, "I wouldn't have really been out . . . , because . . . everything is patrilineal, and . . . they condone the union of the man and female."[55]

Though by the time of our interview Adesina had become involved in a religious organization that was open to gay men and lesbians, she continued to be uneasy with incidents that she perceived as sexist. "Yet again, it's the patrilineal line, that are trying to force us [women] to fit into a mold that we don't want to fit into. And so I think that's why women as gay tend to go away from the institutions. . . . We have to create our own things, because we're not wanted." Furthermore, Adesina had to struggle for welcome in a number of different communities: "The African American community accepts you as long as you're not visible, you know, you're not espousing that 'Oh, I'm gay.' But then, on the other hand, the gay community doesn't really accept you if you're African American, so you're kind of like caught between a rock and a hard place." As a woman in a religious group that honored both sexual and racial diversity, she experienced sexism. As a lesbian and a woman in a religious group that affirmed her African roots, she imagined that she would have encountered both sexism and homophobia. But as someone "totally turned off of Christianity" she likely could not have found comfort in a black LGBT church like Unity Fellowship. Perhaps it is not surprising, then, that Adesina engaged enthusiastically in religious bricolage. "I think that I take from the different religions the things that are going to make me progress as a woman and develop to my fullest potential," she reflected. "The things that I can't use I discard, and so it narrows me down to this spiritual entity that I have created, not that has created me, or that I joined a sect that says this is the way I'm supposed to be."

The most important coincidences in Ronni's identity had been between sexuality and Judaism, although she also offered interesting reflections on whiteness during our conversations. To complicate matters further, though, Ronni understood her Jewish identity to have four different aspects, each of which had played different roles in her sense of self over the past several decades.

Judaism in all its aspects was extremely important to Ronni when she was growing up. So was her plan to be a rabbi. But she was a girl, growing up in the 1950s and 1960s in an Orthodox household. This was the first of her "identity crashes," and her growing awareness of the exclusion of women in the forms of Judaism to which she was exposed was the central factor in her rejection of the religion in college. It would be thirty years before Ronni returned to "the religious part" of her Judaism. However, she explained, "I still had the cultural part, I still had the traditional part. I think the spiritual part . . . waxed and waned throughout my life."[56] I asked what she thought of as the cultural part of her Judaism, and she replied, "You know what's funny? I used to think that what I retained—because I was raised in Miami Beach, everybody was from New York. And so I felt like I retained all the affect from that . . . and I used to think it was the characteristics and the affect of Jewish people, and I came to realize it was the characteristics and affect of New York people." She laughed, and then added, "But I did retain all the traditions. When the holidays would come around I might not go, in fact I didn't go, but I *thought* about it. And knew that I missed it." She also mentioned retaining a deep awareness of relatives who had died because they were Jewish, as well as a love of Israeli dancing and a smattering of Yiddish—all of these, to her, were the cultural and traditional parts of Judaism that she retained despite her rejection of the religion and its perceived sexism.

As a child, Ronni became aware that she was attracted to other girls. A scholar even then, she looked up the word "homosexual" in the family's *Encyclopaedia Britannica*. "And it told me how sick I was." But the entry also added to Ronni's confusion. "If you were queer, if you were homosexual, according to the *Encyclopaedia Britannica*, you were also a man. Who wanted to be like a woman. . . . And . . . I felt like a female person attracted to female people. So I thought I was even queerer than queer, actually." Furthermore, although Ronni remembered learning most of her internalized homophobia from social rather than religious influences, she did note that sexism and heterosexism went hand in hand in the Judaism of her childhood. Ronni could not be a rabbi, she was told, but she could be a rabbi's *wife*—implying that women were not rabbis, that men were, and that men and women belonged in relationships together in a proper Jewish family (a perspective that also deeply influenced Vanessa's identity struggles a generation later).

Though she had not yet reconnected with the religious side of her Judaism when she interviewed for a job in Los Angeles, Ronni nonetheless thought her Jewish identity important enough to mention it in that job interview. In discussing identities during our interview, Ronni also added that she had recently come to a conscious awareness of being white and of the ways in which her whiteness affects both her work and the other aspects of her identity. For instance, she noted that "I own the words 'lesbian' and 'gay' as white constructs. Lots of people believe that they are white constructs. And there are terms that other cultures use that we as the white, dominant people just don't even ask other people what they use." Thus, Ronni was in the midst of a relatively rare process of exploring the influences of a dominant identity in her life. Yet clearly (and logically, given the social near-invisibility of dominant identities) the aspects of her identity that she recalled as most profoundly affecting her life were those that, especially in their intersections, had closed doors and constrained choices. In this way, Ronni's story is a particularly good example of the ways in which constraint and choice coincide in the journeys of postmodern selves.

Queering Sacred Space, Sacralizing Queer Space

If participants' narratives of the sacred (and the) self are examples of queer time, in some cases their enactment of those narratives represents a queering of space. As with queer time, the queering of sacred space is not an activity exclusive to queer identities. Although its resonance with the theme of coincidence does seem to suggest a particular affinity, the queering of sacred space is also a part of a much broader pattern in the contemporary United States: the leaching of the sacred into secular spaces (for example, the grilled cheese sandwich with the Virgin Mary's image that sold on eBay a few years ago) and the leaching of the secular into sacred space.

Participants in this project took part in the queering of sacred space in several ways. One was through their repeated presence in sacred spaces designed for heterosexuals. This could be a more brash or a more quiet experience, depending on the participant. Coco Gallegos attended mass regularly with her partner, and felt that the two had even been recognized positively as a couple during a Catholic charismatic conference. Though she felt no need to be blunt about her sexual identity, Coco also made no effort to hide it. Vanessa, on the other hand, was almost stealthy in her attendance at Conservative synagogues, often attending outside of service times or attending with a male friend in order not to attract attention. Yet bold or surreptitious, the presence of queer bodies in straight spaces, and especially in straight sacred space, enacts in some way a queering of sacred space.

Some of the spaces in which participants brought and negotiated their senses of self were "pre-queered," as it were: they were groups that accepted or even specifically sought out LGBT people. But while some such spaces were religious congregations, in other cases these LGBT spaces were not explicitly constructed as sacred space: here, the presence of queer sacred selves made the queer space sacred. One example of this phenomenon is the Gay and Lesbian Sierrans (GLS), the Sierra Club group of which Sue Field was an active member. As a self-identified "ex-Catholic," Sue found her sense of the sacred in nature, and spent as much time there as she possibly could through her involvement and leadership in GLS. Because nature was intrinsically a sacred space for Sue, every GLS expedition took place in sacred space—whether or not the other participants were aware of it. Making the familiar unfamiliar, Sue was queering sacred space in a wholly different way from Coco, even though for both such queering ultimately came from their expressions of sacrality in the context of the self.

Perhaps the most obvious example of the queering of sacred space comes through Dean Bramlett's involvement with the Sisters of Perpetual Indulgence. Apparently an organization of contradictions, the Sisters may be better understood as a conglomeration of coincidences. Parodying a religious organization they feel has caused irreparable harm to LGBT people, the Sisters at the same time are an expression of spirituality for people like Dean. Campy, outrageous, and rarely serious, they were among the first on the scene when the need arose for AIDS care and education, and they continue to support often deadly serious causes in LGBT communities through their charity work. As a parody of the Roman Catholic Church, gleefully intoning their rallying cry—"Go forth and sin some more!"—the Sisters' playful queering of religious space intersects with searing critique. Yet as a secular organization, the Sisters become sacralized queer space when members like Dean find in them a deep expression and source of spirituality. Just as religious institutions can shape queer (sacred) selves, then, so too can such selves shape religious institutions—and herein lies a powerful coincidence, indeed.

True Selves and Enselved Bodies

The Postmodern Self

"Braiding," Robert Orsi explains in the context of historical narratives, "alerts us to look for improbable intersections, incommensurable ways of living, discrepant imaginings, unexpected movements of influence and inspiration existing side by side—within families and neighborhoods, as well as psychological, spiritual, and intellectual knots within the same minds and hearts."[57] Reading Orsi through the social-identity theories already discussed, here we have intersectional identities, identity crashes, and sacralogies. Sometimes this all works into a coherent whole, but as Tova Hartman Halbertal and Irit Koren point out in the case of Orthodox Jewish gay men and lesbians, identity negotiation does not have to end in consonance—sometimes, as in Boellstorff's work, it ends in coincidence instead.[58] Selves, like histories, can end up braided. So too, perhaps, can the sacred. The spiritual lives and sacred selves of the women in this study are the result of the braiding, or coincidence, of at least three contemporary cultural factors in the United States: sexual selfhood, religious individualism, and advanced consumer capitalism.

In his study of postmodern religion, David Lyon asserts that "the meaning-routes through the postmodern are characterized by consumer choice in identity construction."[59] At one level, this refers to the absurdist mass individualism marketed by businesses from coffeehouses to fashion designers to confectioners: "Buy our product, and you'll be expressing your true self and your individualism!" At another level, Lyon is pointing to the profound influence of consumer capitalism upon both identity and religion. This influence results, he claims, in two models of selfhood. One, the "'plastic self,' is flexible, amenable to infinite reshaping according to mood, whim, desire, and imagination."[60] The other is the "expressive self," an "authentic self" which "retains some sense of its own story, its own narrative, even though it is found in the same detraditionalized milieu as the 'properly' postmodern plastic self."[61] Among the women I interviewed, one could interpret the "plastic self" as the *bricoleuse,* who draws what she needs from a variety of religions rather than finding a home in any particular one. And yet, at least in this case the plastic and expressive selves seem difficult to separate, because the women in this study who are *bricoleuses* engage in such "infinite [spiritual] reshaping" because of an inner sense of truth, an inner sacred self for which they understand themselves to be on a quest.

True Selves

Although the idea of the self as a reflexive project or journey was an important theme in these stories of self, there is a twist here that reflects Lyon's claim that "a careful sociological listening to contemporary voices reveals a trend towards the more general sacralization of the self."[62] The women I interviewed not only spoke of their selves in multiple or fragmented ways; they also described their reflexive journeys less as projects than as quests for truth. In the contexts of both sexuality and spirituality, many women spoke of "seeking myself," or "finding who I really am." This implies, first of all, that the "I" who is seeking and finding is not identical to the sexual and spiritual "true self" that is sought. Second, it presents the sought self as a pre-existing truth—a treasure to be found at the end of a quest, rather than the end product of a construction process. While these themes were especially clearly articulated by those women who were influenced by the New Age movement (which uses quest language liberally and whose participants thus have such language readily available to describe their own experiences), they appeared in the narratives of participants from a wide range of backgrounds and current identities.

Christie Tuttle, for instance, was raised in a devout Mormon family. She remembers being resistant to the religion as a child, disbelieving many of the teachings and being reluctant to attend church. "I tried to believe in it," she told me, "because that was my upbringing, and tried to do things that I was told. But as I got older I realized it really wasn't my path."[63] Christie's language here evokes the idea of a preordained spirituality, different from the LDS church, that she needed to discover. It took her a long time to find this path, she explained to me, because she "rejected" religion for many years. Then, a few years before our interview, she met and began working with a white shaman. "The path I feel like I'm on today," she observed, "is exploring my spirituality and my heart and getting to know myself, where I'd shut myself down through everything from my past." Christie never explained the difference between the "I" who had done the shutting down and reopening and the "self" that had been shut down and rediscovered. However, this theme of multiple selves wove throughout her interview, becoming explicit when she discussed the "soul retrievals" her shaman had been conducting with her. When I asked Christie what these were, she elaborated: "I believe that there's many different aspects to your spirit. . . . Your spirit is comprised of all these multilayered personalities and dimensions." She added a few minutes later, "The belief is, certain things happen in your life, and how you react to them or shut down, if you don't have room for that piece of your soul, they'll leave." Christie believed that at least two of these personalities had left her own soul. One was a rebellious spirit, and the other was "a very young little girl" who helped her to appreciate beauty. The rituals she undertook to retrieve these pieces of her self were designed to prove that she was worthy of their return.

As she worked to retrieve parts of herself that had left, Christie also sought an occluded "true self" in terms of both sexuality and spirituality. She recalled that "I had these feelings [of same-sex attraction] in me as a child, even, and rejected the thought of it." In her early twenties, having left the LDS church and having begun to shed its influence on her beliefs, Christie also began to come out as a lesbian. When I asked where she currently stood on the debate over the roots of sexual orientation, Christie answered simply, "I choose to honor myself." She then elaborated: "My sexuality is just honoring who I am, so if people want to say that's choosing a lifestyle, I mean, people are going to put labels on it and say whatever it is. I just choose to honor who I feel like I am inside." She used similar language to speak about her spiritual journeys of the past few years: "Now, two, three years later [after meeting her shaman], I see how I've evolved. . . . I'm more in tune with myself and listen to my heart, where I didn't even know how to listen to my heart, or what was in my heart. . . . Because I never took the time, or knew how, to be still enough to know who I truly am inside." Though she spoke separately of discovering her spiritual self and her sexual self, Christie used closely parallel language to describe both discoveries: "who I feel like I am inside" (sexuality) and "who I truly am inside" (spirituality). Both, in other words, seem to reflect an unchanging, true self that Christie had to discover.[64]

Dean Bramlett's story is also woven with themes of denying, seeking, and expressing the true (and sometimes multiple) self. She referenced this sense of self in explaining why she had not officially become an Episcopalian, despite regularly attending an Episcopal church: "going to classes and having the bishop say words over my head is not going to *change* what's in my heart. And I think that's the biggest issue, is what's in your heart."[65] While Dean was clear that any beliefs or practices with which she engaged must conform to her inner sense of self, rather than the other way around, she described the origin of that sense of self in different ways. On the one hand, in speaking of a point in her life where she felt she had reconnected with spirituality, Dean explained that "I was looking for that connection, that place within myself that I had so given up when I gave myself to the corporate gods, sacrificed myself on the altar of money." On the other hand, there is also a sense of intentional construction of "that place within myself." "I have been searching for spirituality for years," Dean told me. "I pick up bits and pieces and glue them together, and have created the spirit that I have in my heart today, that I can give and be generous with." Thus, the inner space that Dean identified with her spirituality was both a space she had built and one that she had to seek out; it was also both a part of her (a "place within myself") and somehow separate, something that "she" must find.

This balance between innateness and seeking characterized Dean's descriptions of her sexual identity as well, which was linked with her sense of spirituality. "The Bible," she reflected,

> *says that God created all of us in his image. Well, if that's the case, then God lives in each of us, and therefore, we have to find what the God is within us. And how that God relates with us, and with the world around us. . . . And I think that when I came to that conclusion, I was able to start making headway, to admit first of all to myself and then to people around me that I was a lesbian.*

Dean also spoke of her lesbian identity as innate. "Everything that I had been shown in my life," she recalled angrily, "said, 'What you feel and what you're sure you are is *wrong.* And you'd better make it right.' So I tried." It was only years later that she was able to "be comfortable with who I am, and what my life is." This is less an identity that had to be sought than one that vied for expression, only to be suppressed at great cost. Nevertheless, the theme of one part of self allowing another part to exist or be acknowledged is central to the sexual aspects of Dean's story as well as to the spiritual aspects.

In addition to her spirituality and her sexual identity, Dean also spoke of her work with the Sisters of Perpetual Indulgence as reflective of an inner sense of self—or perhaps two inner selves. "I take my Sisterhood extremely seriously," she told me, "because it ties right into my religious feelings, and it ties into my spirituality feelings. It is *me,* giving to the community. It is of my heart. It is of my soul. It is of what I believe, and it is of who I *am.*" So is Sister Vibrata herself, whom Dean described in the third person as "very different from Dean." Yet, "Vibrata and Dean have become very woven together. We're different, but we're very much tied together. I don't want to say it's a split personality, because it's not. It's a different part of my personality that I use." Thus, for Dean, the self is something that develops, is sought, *and* is built—sometimes simultaneously.

Unlike Dean and Christie, Tami was still in the process of a spiritual search when I spoke with her, although she reflected back on a process of sexual discovery as well. In both searches, Tami's clue when she was on the right track was a sense of wholeness and comfort, but also a sense of being "myself." Like many lesbians, gay men, and bisexual people who retrospectively reinterpret youthful experiences of attraction in light of their current sexual identities, Tami told me, "Now that I look back, I should have figured it out [her sexual orientation] *way* back in high school, but I was naïve and ignorant."[66] "Once I started dating [men]," she explained, "I was never happy. I was never comfortable. I was like, 'Well, okay, I'll move on to the next one.' And they'd ask me out and, like, 'Nnn, this isn't right,' and so I'd try somebody else and, 'Nnn, that's not right,' and I was just never completely happy, never completely myself." In college, though, armed with greater knowledge and experience, Tami began to realize that she was attracted to other women. She talked a friend into going to a gay bar with her, and she told her current boyfriend that she thought she might be a lesbian. "And he understood. I mean, we were in college, you know, he's like, 'Go for it.' So I went out with a girl, and I was like, 'Ahhh, yeah, this is cool. I'm really *comfortable.*' I don't know, I just felt like I could be myself more."

Tami used similar terms to describe the spiritual search in which she had been engaged for the past few years. She had explored different religions, "and it was all very interesting. But I want to find something that makes me feel whole, I guess." She explained that "I'm looking for the comfort, I'm looking for that one niche." Though a seeker, Tami was hoping to find a single religious organization in which she could become a long-term member, part of a group whose shared beliefs reflected those she already had developed. Such a group would also have to be accepting of her as a lesbian and affirming of her as a woman: "I want to be accepted for me. I don't want to have to lie, or not even lie, but I don't want to have the whole truth not be told." Thus, though Tami's story places less emphasis on the quest for an inner sexual and spiritual self, it does stress the discovery of a whole or inner "true" self, and the search for a religious organization and a sexual practice that allowed her true self to be "wholly" present.

Enselved Bodies

In the work of many contemporary theorists, identity appears as primarily verbal and cerebral, a process of narrative, dialectic, interpretation, and reflection. Some also grant that "the self . . . is embodied," and Giddens devotes significant sections of his analysis to unpacking the interactions of self and body.

Important among these are bodily discipline (in the Foucauldian sense) and the role of the body as a medium for self-expression. Yet while Giddens focuses on the self's use or even management of the body, he misses an aspect of bodily experience that plays an important role in the identity negotiations of the women whose voices weave throughout this book: the unruly body.

In contemporary analyses, selves most often act on bodies; the role of the body acting on the self is in need of much greater attention. This issue is raised frequently by theorists of disability, but it applies as well to postmodern narratives of non-normative sexual and gender identities. The disciplined, "docile" body is expected to represent one of two clearly distinguished sexes, to present a gender that is culturally coherent and that matches the body's socially assigned sex, and to experience desire solely for the "opposite" sex. Historically, bodies that refuse to conform to these standards have been disciplined both externally, through means as varied as mob violence and reparative therapy, and internally, through efforts to "hide," "change," or otherwise manage difference.[67] Yet some bodies seem stubbornly to refuse such discipline: despite suppression, they insistently respond sexually to the "wrong" bodies, or persist in producing intense discomfort when attired and comported "properly" according to the gender standards of the surrounding society. It is on the basis of such refusals of discipline that some LGBT people renegotiate their identities; thus, the relationship between self and body is multidirectional.

While examinations of sexuality and gender might be expected to take embodied experience into account, such has not historically been the case for studies of religion. Here too, though, attention to the body has been growing in depth and significance in recent decades. A leading commentator in this area is anthropologist Thomas Csordas, who argues in his study of religious healing that the body functions not "as an object to be studied in relation to culture, but . . . as the subject of culture."[68] This pushes beyond the "embodied self" discussed above, positing instead what I term an "enselved body." The concept of an enselved body places the body, rather than the self, in the foreground of this pairing, a move particularly important for those aspects of selfhood—like sexuality, gender, and, arguably, religion—that are fundamentally grounded in and shaped by the body. Csordas reminds us, furthermore, that expressions and negotiations of identity are inescapably grounded in the body, when he describes speech as "an *act* or phonetic *gesture* in which one takes up an existential position in the world."[69] Though Csordas is most interested in ritual speech such as glossolalia, the links here to self and narrative—which are sometimes constituted in tension with an unruly desiring and gendered body—make for an increasingly intricate interweaving of the body, the self, the sacred, and the social.

Sacrality and Sexuality

For Cynthia and Lara, this interweaving showed most profoundly when they spoke about their relationship together. Both had been in other relationships when they met; Lara had a partner and children, and Cynthia had just left her husband and was in the process of preparing to move to Florida with her children, to live with the girlfriend she had rejected years earlier. "I know that there's a reason why Lara and I are together," Cynthia told me. "God's directing us somehow." She explained that the two had met through mutual friends who had convinced both of them (apparently with no ulterior motive) to go out that night; neither had been particularly inclined to do so. "If I hadn't met her that one night, I wouldn't be here. . . . So it's like, you got to believe that there's something out there that's kind of like helping us along the way."[70] Lara added, "I think I've relied more on God in these past few years than I probably ever have, because it has personally been very trying." Though both women speak of their meeting as finally finding the person they were meant to be with, the process of forming their family entailed separating from long-term partners, negotiating custody of children in both relationships, moving, and for Cynthia, coming out to an often rejecting natal family. "So I think I've leaned on God more than ever these past two years," Lara repeated. "And the good thing is that, you know, God has responded to me. And God's always there for me." Cynthia and Lara held a small, private wedding not long after they became partners. "Do you feel like God was there at your wedding?" I asked. Both women replied in the affirmative, and Cynthia added that because of God's presence, "I feel that I was married—not legally, but spiritually."

Coco, whose sense of God was so integrated into her sense of self that it was like blood in her veins, felt the same sense of sacred integration when speaking of her sexual orientation and her ethnicity. When I asked whether she saw any connection between sexuality and spirituality, Coco paused, then commented, "That's a very profound question." Her answer, which ties closely to her understanding of the divine, is worth quoting at length:

> *I think I'm created also in his image. And I don't know if God is asexual or homosexual, but it's a spiritual experience even making love. It's more than sex, it's making love. And I do invite God to be a part of it. And it is a spiritual connection. I don't think that I could see it any other way. God made us, like I said, in his image, and that's who we are, and that's who I am. And God is definitely a part of my sexual orientation. I don't think that he's making any changes or anything like that. I would like to even have my spiritual walk be deeper so that I invite him more in my relationship, in my*

> *sexual relationship, in my sexual orientation. Again, because I don't make an issue out of it. It's just an integration. He is integrated in my life, and wherever I go, there he is, or she is, or it is. It's a definite integration. I don't ever separate it. I would think that if I ever separated it, then I would have to go to confession. I would consider it a sin if God was not part of my sexual orientation. It would be like if I pretended that God was not part of my Hispanic heritage. It's the exact same thing.*[71]

What makes her perspectives particularly interesting is that Coco is a devout Catholic who attends mass regularly and is an award-winning volunteer in her parish. Yet, unlike many devout Catholics who are attracted to persons of the same sex, Coco saw cause for confession not in acting on her desires, but in the idea that she might separate God from that aspect of her life.

Lauren's integration of the sacred with her gendered sense of self drew heavily on the nebulousness and, for her, the ineffability of sacred realms—perhaps because she was living with a gender identity that itself was more nebulous than contemporary social boundaries are capable of recognizing. Because she believed that human biology was incapable of comprehending the divine, Lauren focused more on the sacred in general, bringing in not only fluidity but also a dispersed or fractured self. While she believed that her own location along the "gray scale" of gender was not recognized by limited human society, Lauren told me that she was "thoroughly convinced that we're eternal beings, that this is a brief moment in our awareness that we're spending here [on the human plane]."[72] She theorized that such eternal beings might even be "fragmented beings—that a fragment of our soul essence is on this planet, a fragment of our soul essence may be elsewhere, a fragment of our soul essence may be in another plane of existence, and that gradually those fragments are brought together."

How do these ideas work with her sense of gender, I wondered, especially given Lauren's focus on the illusory nature of material existence and on the limited nature of human existence? "Well," she replied, "the main concept that I've adopted about transgender is that at your core essence there is a sense of gender. At your soul level you have a sense of gender . . . Those veiled memories of past lives, you had genders at which you felt more comfortable, more appropriate. . . . And so . . . it goes beyond, prior to birth." I asked, "And that's a binary identity, then, that you think is at the soul level? *Either* male or female?" Lauren hesitated. "I mean, ideally, soul level should transcend gender. But it's one of those quandaries. I think it may have more to do with genders at which you were comfortable in past lives. That may have to do as much with that as with soul-level identity." Having been aware from early childhood that her body and her internal sense of self were discordant, Lauren soon grew suspicious of the traditional Presbyterian teachings of her upbringing, becoming interested instead in spiritual beliefs and practices that offered greater potential for separating bodily experience from the soul's inner sense of self. Working with ideas of past lives and "comfortable" genders, as well as theories of soul fragmentation, planes of higher existence beyond the biologically limiting human realm, and an evolution toward androgyny, Lauren negotiated spiritual and gender identities that shared the same logic and therefore were able not only to inform each other but also to help her understand her own restlessness and perceived lack of fit in her current human existence.

In some ways, Lauren's experiences epitomize the patterns discussed in this chapter. Her approach to the sacred works very much on the model of everyday sacralogies. She explores alternative (queer?) understandings of time in developing a narrative and a sense of self that can grapple with "ungrammatical" identities, and she lives at the center of coincidence—of feminine and masculine, sacred and profane. She queers sacred space when she finds spiritual sustenance in billiards competition. And in seeking a sense of true self, she grapples with an enselved body that does not fully match her own idea of self—matches so little, in fact, that she would not allow me to record any images of her during our interview. As much as LBT women like those in this study exemplify postmodern, capitalism-driven approaches to the self and the sacred, it is important to remember that they are most interesting exactly because they are exemplars of a much more widespread pattern. None of the approaches to the sacred and the self described in the preceding pages is solely about queerness—indeed, contemporary queer identities themselves have postmodernism and capitalism to thank, in part, for their existence. In the final chapter, then, I return to considering these women as exemplars of much larger patterns—exemplars that offer clues about not only national trends in queer religiosities, but postmodern trends in religion itself.

7 Queer Women, Religion, and Postmodernity

The religious (and irreligious) life stories of these twenty-nine lesbian, bisexual, and transgendered women in Los Angeles offer windows onto several different vistas. They provide perspectives on the religious life of Los Angeles in the late twentieth and early twenty-first centuries, LGBT communities—both sacred and secular—within the city and its environs, contemporary spiritualities, postmodern identities, and the roles of communities in the lives of those whose religious choices are constrained by (at least) nondominant gender and/or sexual identities.

This book opened with a question that has plagued scholars and religious leaders alike in LGBT religious communities: Where are all the women? The elaboration in chapter 3 of the various organizations on which the women in this study rely for spiritual sustenance provides one answer to that question: women are taking part in a wide variety of organizations. They are in traditional LGBT congregations such as MCC Los Angeles, Beth Chayim Chadashim, Glory Tabernacle MCC, Unity Fellowship Church, Christ Chapel of Long Beach, and West Hollywood Presbyterian, as well as support groups such as Affirmation. They are also in mainstream congregations that welcome LGBT people: parishes within the openly affirming Episcopal diocese of Los Angeles, for instance. One surprise in this study was how welcoming some found the Los Angeles archdiocese of the Roman Catholic Church, with its outreach to gay men and lesbians and its focus on the primacy of conscience. Less surprising was that a few study participants were interested in the feminist Wiccan groups in the area, such as the Circle of Aradia and ReWeaving. Other women relied on theologically universalist organizations, including two Unitarian Universalist churches and a Religious Science megachurch (the Agape International Spiritual Center). With the prominence of Latinas in L.A., it was perhaps predictable that Santería would be in the mix as well. Likewise, L.A. has long been known for the diversity of its religious exports and imports, and two of those—the Siddha Yoga Meditation Center and the International Buddhist Meditation Center—also made it onto the list of organizational resources. Finally, and perhaps the most interesting finding on the organizational level, a few women practiced their spirituality in groups that generally do not intend to offer spiritual resources: the Gay and Lesbian Sierrans and the Sisters of Perpetual Indulgence. One answer to "Where are all the women?," then, is that they are everywhere—or at least everywhere that is accepting and that they see as offering spiritual resources. But if some women are everywhere, others are nowhere. Whether atheist, agnostic, or "believing without belonging," more than half of the women in this study were not regularly involved in any organization for the provision of spiritual goods and services.

Yet, institutional involvement or lack thereof is not a reliable indicator of religious belief or identity among the women in this study. Their religious histories generally fell into six patterns: staying the course, tradition with a twist, rejecting tradition, conversion, seeking, and bricolage. Importantly, only two participants followed the first pattern, remaining involved in mainstream congregations within the religion of their childhood. Eight remained identified with their childhood religions but either attended an LGBT congregation or practiced their religion solely in private. Only one had simply left all religion and spirituality behind, but given that this study was advertised as a project on religion and spirituality, atheists are quite likely to be severely underrepresented here. On the other hand, six participants converted to less traditional religions from those of their childhood. Five became "seekers," looking for a religious organization that would reflect their beliefs and values but not yet having found one, and seven participants were practicing religious bricolage at the time of our interview. Thus, while approximately one-third of the participants retained their connections to their childhood religions (but nearly half of these did so without attending any religious organization), the strongest pattern among those in this study is that of religious innovation, whether tied to organizational involvement or not. Converts, seekers, and *bricoleuses* made up approximately three-fifths of the participants in this study.

The reasons for participants' religious identities and levels of institutional involvement varied greatly, as is true in the broader U.S. population. Chapter 5 suggested some of the influences that might be at play here. One is family structure, although among the women in this study that factor's influence was the opposite of that found in the general population: the presence of young children in an LBT household seemed more often than not to keep parents *away* from religious organizations as part of an effort to shield their children from religiously based homophobia. Race and cultural heritage had some influence, but these too were complicated, as they intersected persistently with other factors in participants' lives and thus produced somewhat unpredictable results. Female leadership has been suggested elsewhere as a possible influence on lesbian, bisexual, and transgendered women's attendance in LGBT congregations, but with few study participants in female-headed congregations it was difficult to determine whether this pattern had much influence.

Feminism and women's rights, on the other hand, were clearly influential. Twenty-four of the twenty-nine participants mentioned feminist issues as being important to them, and four named sexism as a central reason for leaving the religion of their childhood. Even stronger, and sometimes interacting with concerns over sexism, was the issue of LGBT rights. Twenty-seven of the twenty-nine participants mentioned this as an important issue in their spiritual decision making; nearly a third of the participants said they left their childhood religions because of homophobia, biphobia, and/or transphobia. Finally, chapter 5 suggested that a particularly intriguing explanation for the apparent gender differences in LGBT religious involvement may have to do with the interaction of sexual and religious identity negotiations during the late teenage years. While the pattern of "dropping out" of religion during the late teens does not appear to be gendered, the age at which one identifies as gay or lesbian is gendered, with women self-identifying on average several years later than men—just far enough apart that men would be more likely to negotiate their sexual identities before dropping out of religion and women afterward.[1] This distinction alone could go a long way toward explaining the apparent gender differences in religious identity and participation within LGBT populations.

Participants in this study had widely varying "sacralogies," as I have called them. But regardless of participants' names for the sacred or their religious self-identities, several patterns emerged in their sacralogies that had implications for their identity negotiations as well. The sacred, to many participants, was nebulous, mysterious, immanent, and often indwelling. For some the sacred was explicitly *not* omniscient or omnipotent, but it was compassionate and loving, and often at least partly female. Many participants saw explicit connections between their concepts of the sacred and their own sexual and/or gender identities. Some felt that the divine had blessed their sexuality and their relationships, others that their identities reflected broader patterns in the sacred universe. Overall, though, they were strongly inclined to speak of both religious and sexual identities not only as journeys (a theme often noted in contemporary western spiritual discourse) but also as a sort of treasure hunt, in which one journeys on a quest for one's own "true" identity. Finally, intersectionality is a critically important part of identity for these women. No single identity factor can adequately predict or explain their religious decision making; rather, who they "are" religiously is the product of a lifetime of multiple, interacting identities and experiences.

Spirituality and Religious Individualism

The obvious question in a study of twenty-nine women that attempts even to begin to answer questions of national or international import is whether there is any possibility that the study's conclusions might apply beyond the population studied. More specifically, it is worth asking to what extent the findings summarized above may be part of a broader U.S. phenomenon, an urban phenomenon, or an L.A. phenomenon; to what extent we might find similar patterns among gay men; whether studies focusing on bisexuals or transgendered people might come to different conclusions regardless of gender; and whether we might see similar patterns among any populations outside of LGBT communities.

To what extent might the patterns delineated in this study be indicative of broader patterns of gendered religiosity in LGBT communities across the United States? While generalizing beyond the United States is risky because of significant national differences in patterns of both religiosity and sexuality, within the United States there are good reasons to believe that these twenty-nine women are one tip of a much larger iceberg. This is not to say that the relative weight of the patterns identified here will necessarily hold—there are bound to be more atheists in LGBT communities across the United States than in this study, for instance, and the actual number of seekers may be greater or smaller in a similar study conducted elsewhere or, for that matter, in a similar study conducted in L.A. with different participants. However, the importance of alternative organizations and religious innovation, and the impact of concerns with women's rights and LGBT rights, are likely to hold beyond the L.A. context.

One important basis for the argument that this small study may be indicative of much broader, national patterns is the fact that none of the studies indicating a dearth of women in LGBT religious organizations comes from Los Angeles. Most, in fact, are from populations in the Northeast (New York, Philadelphia) and the Midwest (Chicago). Like Los Angeles, such cities host a wide variety of religious organizations, including alternative religious groups, so there is ample opportunity for the conversion and religious innovation practiced by so many of the women considered here.

What about the southern states? Patterns found in L.A. may be likely to replicate farther north along the west coast, and there may be evidence suggesting similar patterns in the northeast and Midwest, but shouldn't the Bible Belt be different? Perhaps, but again, there is at least supply-side evidence that the same patterns hold here too. *If* lesbian, bisexual, and transgendered women in southern states (or at least in the larger southern cities, of which more below) are inclined toward leaving their childhood religions, the ethnic and religious diversity in the larger southern cities offers plenty of alternatives, even if they are not as widespread as in L.A. But would LBT women across the country be equally prone to leaving their childhood religions? The main influences on religious identity and involvement, as shown in chapter 5, are not regional. They include such factors as race and cultural heritage, the need to protect children from religious homophobia (which, if anything, might be more important in the Bible Belt), female leadership in LGBT congregations, and concerns with women's and LGBT rights. While there might be some regional differences in the relative weight of these factors, it is hardly the case that they are irrelevant in some areas of the United States. Thus, there are ample reasons to believe that studies like this one, if conducted elsewhere in the country, would yield similar results.

Conducted in *cities* elsewhere in the country, that is. The metropolitan/rural distinction[2] is likely to be far more relevant in these patterns than any regional distinctions (leaving out the exception of rural communes, which are unique communities in which the group itself and not its rural nature is the most important factor in determining LBT women's participation). There are several reasons for this relevance. First, rural areas generally have few, if any, LGBT religious organizations. Other options favored by the women in this study are also usually restricted to larger metropolitan areas: Asian export religions, metaphysical and universalist organizations, new and alternative religions, and even welcoming congregations within mainline denominations. Assuming that the reasons for LBT women's religious choices remain unchanged across metropolitan/rural lines (an assumption which itself would need to be confirmed), in a rural setting with restricted religious options LBT women might be more likely to make all-or-nothing choices: either remain within one's childhood religion, for example, or leave religion entirely. For those raised in conservative Christian contexts in rural areas, switching from one's childhood religion to a more liberal Christian denomination may also be an option.

Then again, even this hypothesis must be tempered by the complexities of real life. Upon moving to my current home in a rural town of thirty thousand people, I was surprised to find an Open and Affirming Congregational church with a lesbian associate pastor, a small metaphysical church, a handful of (rather underground) Neopagans, an Orthodox Christian church, and a synagogue—

among, of course, the overwhelming number of telephone-book listings for evangelical and fundamentalist Protestant churches. Even more surprising to me at the time was the presence of a Unitarian Universalist church, an Islamic center, and even an MCC in the larger cluster of cities (total population around 150,000) about forty-five minutes away. The LGBT community in this area is small, struggling, and largely invisible except to its members and allies, and yet even here a number of religious options exist outside of the all-or-nothing choice between tradition and atheism.

Despite the potential applicability of these findings to metropolitan areas across the United States, it is also important to consider the extent to which they are specific to the Los Angeles area. After all, I have made the argument that the stories and experiences of these women are interwoven with the specificities of L.A.'s queer spiritual marketplace and of its religious and queer histories. Furthermore, Los Angeles is in the unique position of being the birthplace of most of the major LGBT religious movements: MCC, BCC, Dignity, Affirmation, Unity Fellowship, Christ Chapel, and even Dianic Wicca. So how might local and national patterns balance here?

One way in which this study is actually specific to L.A. has to do with the LGBT-specific and LGBT-welcoming organizations available in that city. In only a few other places in the United States, for example, could Dean be involved with the Sisters of Perpetual Indulgence or Sue with the Gay and Lesbian Sierrans. Not every Episcopal diocese is as openly welcoming as the one in Los Angeles, and L.A.'s Roman Catholic archdiocese is definitely unusual in its ministry to gay men and lesbians. On the other hand, many of the national LGBT-focused organizations founded in L.A. soon spread to other metropolitan and sometimes even rural areas around the country, and regional movements like Christ Chapel have arisen in other metropolitan areas. While such organizations are thus fairly widely available, in L.A. they are the most established, and this may also influence their effect on lesbian, bisexual, and transgendered women's lives.

Then, too, L.A.'s religious and queer histories (as distinct from its queer, religious histories) also have an influence. The city's history of religious innovation, for example, has affected the lives of a number of participants in this study. This is especially true of those who lived as adults in the L.A. area during the height of religious innovation in the 1970s, but it has also made L.A. particularly hospitable to innovative religious movements. In another city, for example, there might be no metaphysical megachurch to inspire and welcome women like Christine Peña, Betty Walker, Adesina, and Christine Logan. It might further be argued that L.A.'s mainstream culture promotes religious innovation more than the cultures of most cities, but in fact the studies of religious individualism and bricolage that were cited in earlier chapters show that such innovation is widespread, not only in the United States but in other western countries as well.

L.A.'s queer histories and cultures are also relevant to understanding the ways in which these women's stories reflect local as well as national patterns. The city has been home to active gay and lesbian communities for over a hundred years, and yet it does not have an activist focus of the same intensity as cities like New York and San Francisco. Self-fulfillment seems often to be the rallying cry of Angelenos. This could produce a greater focus on religion and spirituality in LGBT communities in L.A., *or* the activist focus of cities like New York and San Francisco could lead to greater agitation for LGBT religious rights and women's religious rights in those cities. In some ways, both of these have been true. Thus, even the fabled "navel-gazing" of the City of Angels can have a variety of effects on LGBT patterns of religious participation and identity. So, while these women's stories are intertwined with L.A. histories and communities, this does not mean that L.A. is unique in how its LGBT residents negotiate their religious or spiritual identities; it simply means that those identity negotiations are distinctly *located.*

Are they also gendered? This is a knottier question. On the one hand, existing research makes clear that men, and especially gay men, predominate in LGBT religious organizations, so at one level the patterns identified in the present study are clearly gendered. On the other hand, with the largest LGBT religious organization—MCC—claiming forty thousand members worldwide while the *Advocate* claims a circulation in the millions, it seems likely that traditional religious patterns cannot account for the majority of men in LGBT communities, either. Alternative religious organizations certainly are available for gay, bisexual, and transgendered men as well; most of the organizations described in chapter 3 are open to all genders, and for men seeking Neopagan religious spaces with other men, the Radical Faeries are an option.[3] Among Dean's fellow (male) Sisters were several Wiccans and Faeries as well as a practitioner of Siddha Yoga meditation, so clearly alternative religions are appealing to at least some GBT men. How far that pattern carries, the extent to which it differs from the patterns followed by LBT women, and the extent to which both populations are atheist, remains to be seen.

But it should be asked again: Are these patterns gendered? Asking that question in the general context of communities that include relatively small numbers of transgendered people effectively restricts the answer to the cisgendered. Studies such as this one that have included transgendered people have noted a number of similarities to gay men and lesbians in terms of the negotiation of religious identities and experiences. This is likely due in part to the fact that transgender and bisexual/lesbian/gay identities are so intertwined in the perceptions of the broader U.S. culture that religious organizations often conflate transgender identities with homosexuality (and bisexuality) and respond in similar ways to all LGBT people. The patterns identified here may also hold for other populations that are forced into religious individualism by bigotry, and transgendered people would be no exception in that case.

On the other hand, there are also significant differences between the religious experiences of gay men, lesbians, and bisexuals and those of transgendered people. While some transgendered people may also, upon transitioning, have to negotiate a gay, lesbian, or bisexual identity, religious gender identity negotiation seems to be more significant and difficult than religious sexual identity negotiation. And psychological literature as well as autobiographical narratives make abundantly clear that there are some significant differences between the development of a nondominant sexual identity and the development of a transgender identity. So transgendered people face fundamentally different challenges in negotiating religious identities—regardless of their gender or sexual orientation—from those faced by cisgendered bisexuals, gay men, and lesbians. They also face transphobia in some LGB gatherings, so spaces that provide important resources for those negotiating sexual orientation and religion may be inadequate for those negotiating gender identity and religion. Yet, because some people identify as gay or lesbian before identifying as transgendered, there may be overlap in these patterns of religious beliefs, practices, and identities. Thus, it is important to recognize the connections here while simultaneously refusing to efface key differences.

A similar argument can be made in the case of bisexuals. Only two of the women in this project identified as bisexual; one had moved directly and at a relatively young age from assuming she was heterosexual to identifying as bisexual, while the other identified as a lesbian for a number of years before falling in love with a man and deciding that she must instead be bisexual. Neither deviated significantly from the patterns of identity negotiation and organizational involvement that characterized the participants as a whole, and both felt that sexuality in general (for Christine Peña) and sexual orientation specifically (for Trish) had influenced their religious choices. As with transgendered people, there is reason to believe that the similarities in this study between the experiences of lesbians and those of bisexuals are more than coincidence. Some, like Trish, identify as gay or lesbian before identifying as bisexual, and thus may experience the same religious identity negotiation process during their late teens and early twenties as do gay men and lesbians. Popular culture, when it is not portraying bisexuals as promiscuous and "playing the field," often portrays them as people in transition to more permanent lesbian or gay identities; thus, heterosexual-dominated religious organizations are likely to treat bisexuals in the same ways as they treat gay men and lesbians.

This similarity does not always hold true, though. In the Roman Catholic

Church, for instance, where sexual orientation is officially regarded as innate, but sexual activity—*acting* on one's orientation—is proscribed, bisexuals are subsumed into heterosexuality. Perceived by both heterosexuals and gays and lesbians as having the option of an opposite-sex relationship, bisexual Catholics occupy the same position that gays and lesbians occupy in conservative Protestantism. As people with a "choice," they are expected to choose heterosexuality and a different-sex partner. At least, they are told, lesbians and gay men can't help it if heterosexual attraction isn't in their nature; but it *is* in the nature of bisexuals, who therefore should follow that aspect of their inclinations and suppress their same-sex desires. Not only does this attitude make some welcoming Catholic parishes distinctly *un*welcoming to bisexuals, but it may also make lesbian and gay social networks uncomfortable or inaccessible to them. Indeed, gay and lesbian biphobia is widespread, and is yet another reason why, despite the clear similarities and overlaps between the religious identity negotiations of bisexuals and those of lesbians and gay men, it is also logical to expect significant differences to emerge in research focused specifically on bisexuals. However, bisexuals' religious life stories may also be gendered like those of lesbians and gay men, since bisexuals are likely to have many of the same experiences with coming out, negotiating issues of women's and LGBT rights, and so on.

The final question raised earlier takes the applicability of this study a step further: Might other religiously excluded groups have similar patterns of identity negotiation and organizational involvement? The answer is both yes and no. Some aspects of the participants' life stories clearly relate to the negotiation between sexual and religious identities, and in this case, of course, groups negotiating other identities would have different experiences and different strategies. But gender and another nondominant, religiously salient identity should still be additive in some ways; in other words, people with concerns for both women's rights and the equal inclusion of another group to which they belong should be more likely to leave religions discriminating against both groups than are those with concerns for one or the other. And it stands to reason that groups experiencing religious discrimination would engage more in religious seeking and bricolage than those at the center of (positive) attention in their religious organizations. Seen from this perspective, the stories in this book tell of the collision between religious discrimination and postmodern selves. As Shelley Budgeon notes, "Individualization, as a defining characteristic of late modernity, translates into an enhanced potential of individuals to be freed from external forces that limit the kinds of identities possible."[4]

The stories contained in these pages weave together self and community in complex ways, leaning at times more toward one, at times toward the other.

But they are above all stories of the postmodern, and in some ways explicitly of the postmodern United States; in other eras and in other cultures these stories would be different, and in some contexts they would be literally unthinkable. This book is not, then, simply a story of twenty-nine women in Los Angeles; it is a portrait in miniature, an exemplary case study, of postmodern religiosity, sexuality, gender, and self.

Postmodern Selves: Identity and Community

The fluidity of sexual and gendered selves, and the importance of sexuality and gender for the self-concept, are both recent developments that have taken shape with the rise of the postmodern. If the idea that desire indicates an aspect of identity (e.g., heterosexuality, bisexuality, homosexuality) is a modern development, those understandings of sex and gender that transcend binary concepts such as male and female, heterosexual and homosexual, are far more postmodern—as is the slow disentangling of gender and sexuality from social roles and stigmas. As chapter 6 showed, many participants in this study viewed their sexual and/or gender identities as occluded "truths" about themselves to be sought, discovered, or revealed just as much as religious "truths" or personal spiritual paths. At the same time, these truths are very clearly individualized; few, if any, of the participants would claim that their sexual orientation or gender identity should be held by everyone.

Almost exactly the same things could be said about participants' religious identities. These were distinctly fluid and in many cases were constantly negotiated, but like sexual identities they appeared to most participants as an inner "truth" that needed to be discovered. The theme of relativism was also strong in participants' discussions of religion and spirituality. Charles Taylor has argued that both relativism and the sense of an inner "true self" are important aspects of religion in contemporary western cultures. Noting "a steady spread of . . . the culture of 'authenticity,'" Taylor describes this culture as rooted in "the idea that each of us has his or her own way of realizing one's own humanity, and that it is important to find and live out one's own [way]."[5] Likewise, he adds, "the [cultural] injunction would seem to be: let everyone follow his or her own path of spiritual inspiration. Don't be led off yours by the allegation that it doesn't fit with some orthodoxy."[6] At least in the religious context, this "true self" seems to be elusive for participants in this study, needing to be perpetually sought or at least regularly adjusted. This produces the "Brownian movement" of the self that Zygmunt Bauman characterizes as uniquely postmodern.[7] Such "Brownian movement" is also found to a certain extent in sexual and gender identities, though most of the participants in this study settled into fairly fixed sexual and gender identities—moving from Bauman's "self-constitution" to his more stable "self-project"—after a period of often intense negotiation.

Among the plethora of written works on "postmodernity," "high modernity," "late modernity," and the like, there are a number of clear themes regarding the changing nature of the self. These include a dialectic between fragmentation and wholeness, the growth of self-construction as opposed to ascribed or even earned identities, and fluidity. The participants in this study not only share such constructions of the self; their stories would in fact be fundamentally different *without* such ideas. Outside of postmodern contexts, queer religiosities as I have described them here—fluid, intersectional, negotiated products of persistent bricolage—simply cannot exist.

Organizations and communities, too, served particularly postmodern functions for the participants in this study. Though few participants were any longer a part of the religious communities, or even the religions, into which they were born, some aspects of their childhood communities remained important to them either geographically (Corrine and East L.A., for instance) or as a source of identity (Ronni and "cultural" Judaism). As theorists of the postmodern remind us, the emphatic shift toward expressive individualism should not distract us into believing that communities and social contexts have become irrelevant. Even within an individualist culture of religion (or, to be more individualist, a culture of "spirituality"), Taylor notes that "many people will find themselves joining extremely powerful religious communities, because that's where many people's sense of the spiritual will lead them."[8] Religious communities, and those that are not religious but that participants see as spiritual resources, serve four key functions for the women in this study: they provide tools, tiles, community, and memory.

As sources of *tools* for negotiating between one's inner sense of self and the external world, religious organizations are part of what Ann Swidler has famously called a "cultural tool kit."[9] In a more postmodern sense, we might say that different religions provide different tool kits for the negotiation of identities. An example of such tools might be explicitly LGBT-supportive biblical hermeneutics, or experiences of the sacred as encompassing all aspects of oneself. Also important for the participants in this study may be tools like universalism, a belief promoted by several of the religious groups that participants attended. If one believes that all religions are reaching toward the same truth but in culturally distinct ways, then it is not much of a stretch to argue that homophobia, biphobia, transphobia, sexism, classism, and racism are all cultural accretions having little to do with authentic religious truth. Contained in the "tool kit" of religion, then, may be the keys that unlock doors between different aspects of identity, enabling people to negotiate intersections more easily.

As *tiles* in the mosaic of the self, religious organizations do not just open doors; to follow the metaphor, they are rooms in themselves. But importantly, in a culture of bricolage religion may contribute tiles of many different shapes, sizes, and colors to the same mosaic. Even those who draw on just one religion will focus on different aspects of that religion and will identify with it at differing levels of intensity, thus producing different effects in their mosaics. Furthermore, the "religion" tiles can be scattered throughout the image, clustered in one section, or distributed in small clusters throughout, depending on whether a person considers religion (or spirituality) as separate from other aspects of her identity or as woven throughout it. And lastly, because tiles of the same color look different depending on the colors surrounding them, the "religion tiles" influence and are influenced by other tiles in creating a larger picture. Given the fluidity of identity discussed above, of course, this larger picture is never finished or static; the mosaic is always shifting, gaining new tiles and losing others.

As much as religious organizations serve to enhance individual identities, though, it is important not to forget that they also sometimes serve as sources of *community*, for the participants in this study as for postmodern subjects more generally. Dean is an excellent example of this: she spoke passionately and at length about the importance of the community of Sisters. More traditional religious organizations did not serve this purpose for her; for Dean, St. Thomas the Apostle and the Siddha Yoga Meditation Center were both tools more than anything else. Coco, on the other hand, found tools, tiles, and community at St. Monica's, and Adesina found tools and tiles at Agape services but community in the Agape women's group, TLC. In a scattered, individualist, automobile-centered metropolis like Los Angeles, and in subcultures like LGBT communities that may not be located within specific neighborhoods, nonresidential sources of community take on even greater significance. For the participants in this study, organizations that could provide religious community, LGBT community, or both were particularly important.

Finally, religious organizations offer access to what Danièle Hervieu-Léger calls a "chain of memory."[10] Hervieu-Léger proposes that one of the defining aspects of religion is that it traces its beliefs to a historical tradition, or "chain of memory." Even new religious movements, she notes, appeal to such a history, which they often claim was undiscovered or neglected prior to the advent of the new movement. Thus, practicing a religion, exclusively or not, inscribes one into that tradition.[11] This was especially important for Ronni, for whom the connection to Judaism had significant historical, cultural, and familial ramifications. It also was a central reason for Adesina's adherence to Yoruba religion and for her rejection of Christianity, a chain of memory in which she wanted no part. Even Lauren's interest in channeled writings evinces this concern with history, since the "higher beings" whose wisdom is supposedly contained in such works often claim to be ancient.

Importantly, popular notions of sexual and, increasingly, gender identities also seek to inscribe LGBT people within chains of memory. In many cases these are secular; there are innumerable examples of texts and even material culture (from bumper stickers to mugs, T-shirts, and coffee-table books) claiming that today's gay men, lesbians, and increasingly also transgendered people and bisexuals, stand within an august, queer lineage. Other cases are specifically religious, such as when Jewish and Christian theologians read biblical characters as expressing same-sex love or gender variance.[12] LGBT religious communities thus offer a sort of double chain of memory, weaving together a religious lineage with an LGBT lineage. In this way they may serve as a grounding point, a source of stability for the rather flighty postmodern self, but they also offer a significant source of affirmation in the face of ongoing social and religious prejudice.

Twenty-first Century U.S. Religion: An Exemplary Case Study

Curious about religious individualism among those around me, I recently asked my mother about her own experiences with religion. Born in 1942 to parents who had been raised as mainline Protestants but had attended church rarely as adults until they had children, my mother was not baptized as an infant. She does remember, however, regularly attending church on Sundays to sit with her father and watch her mother sing in the choir. "To me," she recalls, "church was more than a place where you went on Sundays; church was a place where you had connections with other people whose values were similar to yours." Her family minister's response to her father's death when she was seventeen precipitated a crisis of faith that would affect her attitude toward religion for the rest of her life. When she asked the minister why her father had died, he responded that it was God's will. "Well, that's stupid," she remembers thinking. "What kind of God is this?" Although she continued attending for seven more years and later attended for another decade or so, her involvement had more to do with community and spiritual resources than with belief. Having become an agnostic, she made sure that the pastors in the churches she attended knew of her unorthodox beliefs, and she simply refrained from participating in certain rituals—such as the recitation of the Lord's Prayer—that violated those beliefs.

When she retired in 2004, my mother had not attended church regularly for about twenty years—a period she refers to as her "intentionally uninvolved in religion phase." "Religion is differentiated from spirituality," she clarified, "because there were still times [during this period] when I could feel the spiritual side of me but it didn't have anything to do with organized religion." Using the occasion of her retirement to take "stock of my life—what's missing, and what am I going to do," she realized that "just because I wasn't a part of organized religion didn't mean there wasn't a spiritual part of me that could use some more thinking." She began to wonder, "What if I did become involved in organized religion again, if I could find a way to do it that would help me in my own spiritual journey?"

Having been a lifelong Presbyterian regardless of doctrine, she went first to the Presbyterian church closest to her home. Though she enjoyed the organ music and the beautiful stained-glass windows that brought back fond childhood memories of church, she found in the hymns and the sermons little that matched her own beliefs. After several Sundays she left sadly, deciding instead to explore Unitarian Universalism—and by the end of her first UU service she was hooked. Because the ethos of the church matched hers, she was able to participate fully in the service. "The songs that they sang," she recalls with delight, "I could sing them! And the things that we said together resonated with me." During her years of involvement with the church, she has come to her own understanding of the denomination. "My interpretation of Unitarian Universalism," she explained, "is that it helps each individual to move along in their own spiritual journey." She is thrilled to attend a church whose minister is Buddhist and whose congregants come from a wide variety of religious backgrounds. "And we all come together believing that we're each on our own spiritual journey, and supporting one another on those journeys." Such diversity and support also mean that as she learns about others' religious heritage, she gains more food for thought—and for her own spiritual growth.

My mother is a confirmed heterosexual and is cisgendered. Save for these facts, however, her story fits perfectly with those discussed in the previous chapters. Disillusioned with her childhood religion and a decided agnostic from the age of seventeen, she alternated during much of her adult life between attending church for the community and the spiritual resources, and avoiding organized religion even while remaining at least occasionally aware of her spiritual side. Unitarian Universalism offers her resources for the bricolage that she now finds spiritually fulfilling. In addition to talking as intently as we do about religious consumerism, when scholars discuss individualism we should perhaps be speaking equally clearly about religious *production*.

Traumatic as it was to have her father's death explained away as "God's will," my mother did not experience the kind of deep trauma that drove some of the women in this study from their childhood religions. Nor, during her first period of non-attendance, did she develop an identity that was fundamentally incompatible with that childhood religion. The doctrinal incompatibilities were acceptable to her ministers, so she continued to attend. On the one hand, my mother's story offers yet another example—and one that can be traced carefully across changing eras—of religion in the contemporary United States. On the other hand, because much of her identity connects her to dominant groups in the U.S. power structure (race, religion, education, sexual orientation, social class), the patterns of religious individualism are subtler in her life than they are in the lives of most of the queer women in this study. This is exactly why I have argued that this book presents an exemplary case study of religious individualism in the contemporary United States—or perhaps of postmodern religion itself.

Religious individualism is a critical development for LBT women, especially, for several reasons. First, it is a hallmark of a larger development—individualism in general, and especially individualism under advanced capitalism—that has fostered LGBT identities and has supported the growth of LGBT communities and enclaves. Second, individualism underlies many western feminist movements and is therefore partly responsible for women having the economic independence to live singly or with another woman (thus the feminist bumper sticker, 'A woman without a man is like a fish without a bicycle'). Third, religious individualism, and specifically patterns of seekerism and bricolage, offer options to those not accepted in traditional religions—including LGBT people generally, but especially including LBT women because of the sexism inherent in many traditional religions and because they may be more likely than GBT men to come out after leaving the religion of their childhood. In the face of discrimination, rejection, or even ejection from traditional congregations, rather than choose irreligion, the closet, or a battle for acceptance, LBT women can shop around for other religions, practice a combination of several, or find their own spiritual journeys in the most mundane or the most unexpected of places. Because LBT women are among those especially likely to benefit from religious individualism, they are an excellent target population for an exemplary case study of postmodern religiosities. But they are far from alone. These twenty-nine women from Los Angeles, each practicing religion (or spirituality) in her own complex, personalized way, demonstrate in concentrated form a phenomenon that is widespread in advanced capitalist societies—especially the United States, but other, less explicitly religious societies as well.

Religion is messy, Robert Orsi tells us,[13] and in the midst of this messiness is where one finds postmodern sexual, gendered, religious, and deeply queer selves. Refused by and refusing ascribed religious identities, generally disinclined to pursue earned religious identities, they draw on religion as tool kit and mosaic tiles, as community and chain of memory. They negotiate identities through their own life experiences, straddling intersections with both anguish and delight, seeking that authentic spiritual, sexual, and gendered (or gender-free) self that they envision at their own core. Each bringing order to the chaos of postmodern identity in her own individual way, they are *bricoleuses extraordinaires,* and at the same time, paradoxically, they are doing absolutely nothing out of the ordinary.

Appendix A

BIOGRAPHICAL SUMMARIES

These summaries are arranged alphabetically by first name. Ages and "current" identities are as of the time of the interviews (summer and fall 2001), unless otherwise noted. Identity terms such as race, ethnicity, and sexual orientation are in the participants' own words, and generally reflect their statements during the preliminary interviews; some are summaries of more nuanced identities reflected in the in-depth interviews and in the discussions of each participant in the book. (The pages on which each participant appears in the main text are listed in the index.)

Adesina—Fifty, middle class from a middle-class background, African American, cisgendered lesbian. Raised in a Baptist church, and describes her current beliefs and practices as an "eclectic mix." Identifies with Yoruba culture but has studied eastern religions and attends a Science of Mind church.

Betty Walker—Forty-four, upper middle class from an upper-middle-class background, black, cisgendered lesbian. Raised in a Baptist church, currently a member of Agape and a follower of Science of Mind.

Carmen—Forty-one, from a middle-class background but prefers not to make class distinctions about herself today. Multiracial Caribbean-Canadian, cisgendered lesbian. Raised Presbyterian and continues to identify with and attend that denomination, though she acknowledges and believes in the validity of other religions as well.

Cassandra Christenson—Sixty-six, middle class (but recently unemployed and living on Social Security), from a middle-class/upper-middle-class background. Caucasian, cisgendered lesbian. Raised in Disciples of Christ; currently describes an eclectic spirituality that she finds difficult to name. She feels she "belongs to Jesus" but has no involvement with Protestant churches; she meditates at the International Buddhist Meditation Center and at the Siddha Yoga Meditation Center; she goes to Catholic churches and to twelve-step groups; and she feels very close to God.

Christie Tuttle—Forty-one, lower middle class from an upper-middle-class background, white, cisgendered lesbian. Raised Mormon, now describes herself as having a much stronger spirituality but no classification for it. Currently works with a white shaman.

Christine Logan—Fifty-five, raised upper middle class and continues to see herself as upper middle class socially though she is no longer there economically following her divorce. Caucasian, cisgendered lesbian. Raised in Christian Science, currently identifies as spiritual but not religious. Explores different churches but also finds her spirituality eclectically, including through involvement in twelve-step programs.

Christine R. Peña—Forty-one, middle class from a middle-class background, multiracial (Mexican, German, French, and Chinese heritage), cisgendered bisexual woman. Does not place much emphasis on sexual orientation in her identity: "I'm technically bisexual," she says, "but I'm just me." Raised irreligious but chose to begin attending a Baptist church at thirteen; currently a Religious Science practitioner. Describes her beliefs as a "transdenominational philosophy and spirituality."

Coco Gallegos—Forty-eight, upper middle class from a lower-class background, Hispanic, cisgendered, gay woman. Raised Catholic, and currently describes herself as a strong and very active Catholic.

Corrine Garcia—Forty-four, working class from a working-class background, Native American (Laguna Pueblo and Blackfoot), transgendered (FTM spectrum), bi- or polysexual woman who lives as a man. Raised Catholic, currently practices a blend of Santería and Native religious traditions.

Cynthia McCann—Thirty-seven, middle class from a middle-class background, Mexican, cisgendered lesbian. Raised a devout Catholic; currently describes her beliefs and practices as "pretty far from Catholic" but has no name for them. "God is God," and she prefers not to set any boundaries on that. Partner of Lara Sowinsky.

Danielle—Forty-six, middle or working class from a middle- or working-class background, Caucasian, transgendered (MTF spectrum) lesbian. Raised Mormon, continues to identify as Mormon, "but with some disagreements."

Dean Bramlett—Fifty-four, middle class from a lower-middle-class background, Caucasian, cisgendered lesbian. Raised in "Heinz 57 Christianity," attending whatever church was open, but confirmed Lutheran as a teenager. Currently appreciates the ritual of her Episcopal church but also meditates at the Siddha Yoga Meditation Center, lights candles, practices solitary Wicca, and serves as a Sister of Perpetual Indulgence.

Emile—Forty-one, working class from a lower-middle-class background, African American, cisgendered lesbian. Raised Pentecostal Christian (Church of God in Christ); currently describes herself as a "strong, practicing believer in God and Christianity."

Kathleen McGregor—Thirty-three, lower middle class from a lower-middle-class background, biracial (white and Hispanic), cisgendered lesbian. Raised Catholic, currently a Unitarian Universalist with interests in Buddhism and meditation. Definitively not Christian.

Lara Sowinsky—Thirty-nine, middle class from a middle-class background, Italian/Polish American, cisgendered lesbian. Baptized Catholic, raised in Assemblies of God. Currently describes herself as "deeply religious" with an interest in many different religions—"similar to a theosophist viewpoint." Partner of Cynthia McCann.

Lauren—Fifty, lower middle class from a lower-middle-class but economically constrained background, white/Anglo-Saxon, transgendered (MTF spectrum) lesbian. Raised Presbyterian until she "bought out of it"; currently believes that religion is a political force that "leashes" the spirit, and she leans more toward spirituality and the New Age movement. Believes that humans are eternal beings "veiled to true reality" who live on earth as a form of education.

Linda—Thirty-three, middle class from a lower-middle-class background, Caucasian, cisgendered lesbian. Raised Southern Baptist, currently continues to identify as Christian but describes herself as "searching." Partner of Lisa Taylor at the time of the interview.

Lisa Taylor—Forty-two, middle class from a middle-class background, white (of Italian descent), cisgendered lesbian (but specifies that her sexual orientation is fluid). Raised Roman Catholic, though her family was not particularly committed to the religion; describes her current beliefs and practices as "strongly agnostic" and open to most possibilities. Partner of Linda at the time of the interview.

Margaret A. Jensen—Sixty-three, middle class from a middle-class background, Anglo, cisgendered lesbian. Raised Episcopalian and still identifies with that religion; describes her spirituality as "Christian but ecumenical."

Mary Jane—Thirty-four, lower middle class from a lower-middle-class background, cisgendered lesbian. Describes herself as "either Native American or Hispanic" but with "no cultural background." Raised Catholic; now says she has no belief in organized religion and considers herself simply moral and spiritual.

Regina Lark—Forty-two, lower middle class from a working-class background, Caucasian, cisgendered lesbian. Raised Catholic; currently believes in universal mind, positive thinking, trusting in the universe. She doesn't like the language of religion and describes herself as "metaphysical."

Ronni Sanlo—Fifty-four, middle class from a lower-middle-class background, white, cisgendered lesbian. Raised Jewish; currently describes herself as Jewish, but left the religion behind for a lengthy period of time before joining Beth Chayim Chadashim in Los Angeles.

Ruth Sebastian—Thirty-five, middle to upper middle class from a middle- to upper-middle-class background, white, cisgendered, and questioning her sexual orientation—probably lesbian, she says, but she is currently uncomfortable with labels. Initially raised Protestant, but heavily involved in the New Age movement for much of her youth through the influence of her mother. Currently describes herself as "exploring" her spirituality—interested in goddess worship, feminist spirituality, Zen Buddhism, Unitarian Universalism, and writing and art as forms of spiritual expression.

Ruth Tittle—Fifty, upper class from a middle-class background, white, cisgendered lesbian. Raised mostly irreligious but with some Baptist influence; currently identifies as Christian.

Silva—Fifty-one, working class from a lower-class background, Latin American, cisgendered lesbian. Raised Catholic; currently has no spiritual beliefs or practices and describes herself as "not a Bible person."

Sue Field—Fifty-two, upper middle class from a middle-class background, white/American, cisgendered lesbian. Raised Catholic; currently describes herself as a nonpracticing Catholic or ex-Catholic and a spiritual person. She says she saved the best parts of Catholicism and made her own spirituality.

Tami—Thirty, working class from a working-class/poor background, white, cisgendered lesbian. Raised Catholic, describes her current beliefs and practices as a "hodgepodge." Interested in Wicca and exploring ReWeaving.

Trish—Thirty-five, upper-middle to middle class from an upper-middle- to middle-class background, white, cisgendered, bisexual woman. Raised Presbyterian, currently a Unitarian.

Vanessa—Twenty-four, lower middle class from an upper-middle-class background, Caucasian, cisgendered, identifies her sexual orientation as "open" but leaning toward lesbian. Raised in a Conservative Jewish family but attended an Orthodox Jewish school for several years; currently describes herself as "probably agnostic" and as "shopping" spiritually. Still involved culturally in Judaism, but no longer believes in the religious tenets.

Appendix B

Methods and Methodological Considerations

Studying LGBT communities has become increasingly easy over the past few decades. A number of challenges remain, however, and these are potentially exacerbated by the challenges of studying religion. For instance, in order to obtain a reliably accurate picture of religion among lesbians, bisexual women, and transgendered people in the United States, one might wish for a nationwide survey, large enough and diverse enough for the results to be statistically significant and meaningful. Most surveys on religion, though, as well as most general surveys of the U.S. population, fail to ask questions about sexual and transgender identities. Sexual orientation has been estimated in some studies by using questions about sexual behavior in the General Social Survey or by tracing same-sex households in the census.[1] However, having sex with other women, or living with another man as one's "unmarried partner" (the census term), is neither a necessary nor a sufficient criterion for identifying as lesbian, gay, bisexual, or any of the other identity terms adopted by different same-gender-loving communities in the United States. Of course, such measures also come nowhere near identifying transgendered people.

Similarly, surveys that do ask well-researched, well-informed questions about sexual and/or transgender identity rarely ask questions about religion. When there are questions about religion, they are often limited to institutional measures such as religious membership and attendance. This seems to be exactly where queer women, whose "primary faith communities," as Gary David Comstock notes, are "outside of institutional and formal religious organizations,"[2] fall through the cracks. Some queer men also go unrepresented in such studies, since demographically balanced recruitment of participants is notoriously difficult in LGBT communities. As I often quip to my students, standard research methods do not work well in these contexts: one can hardly dial a random telephone number and then ask whomever answers whether anyone in the household is queer and whether the queer people can come to the phone. Those working on a national scale to research LGBT people are often limited to internet recruitment, recruitment at gatherings such as pride festivals, and recruitment through LGBT-identified organizations. Each of these approaches is feasible, but each also has its drawbacks, especially in terms of the potential skews introduced in the recruitment process.[3] Until now, those wishing to study religiosity in LGBT communities have recruited research participants from congregations, thus producing a growing body of research on gay and bisexual men's experiences and far less on the experiences of lesbians, bisexual women, and transgendered people.

In order to address some of these challenges, this study takes a different approach that is not based on survey methods. Since so little is known about the religious beliefs and practices of queer women, it seems that what is most needed at this point is in-depth research that can explore the richness and complexity of such women's spiritual lives and identities. To that end, in planning the present study I elected to adapt community studies methods, long a mainstay of the sociology of religion, to the study of a subculture (or rather multiple, intersecting subcultures): lesbians, bisexual women, and transgendered people in the Los Angeles area.

Community studies methods were developed by Robert and Helen Lynd in the 1920s and 1930s. Taking as their subject a small town they dubbed "Middletown," the Lynds approached the study of American culture at the microcosmic level in their two books, tracing patterns of institutional and individual interaction throughout the intricacies of small-town life.[4] Scholars of religion have adapted this approach to their field in more recent decades, studying the relationships among congregations, and between congregations and secular institutions, in small and midsize communities.[5] Indeed, the field of congregational studies itself could be considered an even smaller scale version of the community studies model, focusing as it does both geographically and socially on an interactive and self-identified group of people.

In large urban contexts, however, community studies becomes more challenging. There have been a number of successful neighborhood studies,[6] which adapt the community studies model to a geographic subset of the city, but what does one do with those communities that are more ideological than geographic, or are transitorily geographic, as with the large gathering of LGBT people in certain urban areas for pride festivals? These are community too, but they are a far cry from Middletown.

One challenge in using such an approach with an ideological community, and in Los Angeles especially, lies in defining "subculture" and determining whether queer women, or LGBT people in general, actually do constitute a subculture. It seems fair to argue that in urban areas some types of community are interwoven with, or overlaid upon, other types. Furthermore, in a sprawl-driven urban area like Los Angeles, residents—especially in the suburbs and so-called "bedroom communities"—may find little community in neighborhoods and far more in nongeographic, ideological, and potentially overlapping communities such as religious organizations, political groups, sports leagues, and the like. A colleague who has lived in L.A. for many years confirmed the validity of this perspective for Los Angeles:

> *We [people in L.A.] are a virtual community—it is extremely common for people to show up somewhere having driven an hour or so to get there, and to do that on a regular basis and to consider that part of their community—and not live geographically around "their community" at all—but to just live somewhere affordable/geographically desirable for their job, whatever—that is Los Angeles—we show up, we connect with those people, we leave and we probably will not see those people until we "show up" again.*[7]

Queer women in Los Angeles may belong to many of these evanescent communities, but a large number of them do "show up" for the L.A. Pride festival in June, especially for the Saturday morning Dyke March. A number of them also show up at religious organizations in the area. Neither an in-depth study of Pride nor a study of one or more of these religious organizations, however, can uncover the extent to which these sources of community overlap in such women's lives—for this, one must speak to women themselves. This book, therefore, adapts contemporary community studies and congregational studies methods to an examination of queer women's religious beliefs and practices in the specific urban setting of Los Angeles. It could be seen as a congregational study without a congregation, a community study without a small town or neighborhood, or simply, perhaps, an ethnography of people and patterns rather than groups.

The LAWS Project

In June of 2001, my partner and I spent a weekend sitting behind a table under an awning in the scorching Los Angeles sun. The occasion was the Los Angeles Pride Festival, and we were launching recruitment for the Los Angeles Women and Spirituality (LAWS) Project, which provided the ethnographic data on which this book is based.[8] We handed out flyers, discussed the project with potential participants and with a few local religious leaders who stopped at the table, and collected the names and contact information of those who were interested in taking part. Recruitment for the study also took place through print advertising in the locally published magazine *Lesbian News,* as well as through a limited amount of snowball sampling and targeted recruitment in communities that were underrepresented in the study.

Brochures that were available at the pride festival and were mailed to secular LGBT organizations in the Los Angeles area explained that the project's "goal is to explore the meaning and importance (or lack thereof) of religion and/or spirituality in the lives of lesbian, bisexual, transgender, and queer women in the greater Los Angeles area." Thus, it was made as explicit as possible that the project was not focused solely on institutionalized religion, but neither did it exclude such forms of religion. On the other hand, since the project obviously focused on religion and spirituality, people with little or no interest in such topics were unlikely to participate; the lives and experiences represented in this book are, therefore, those of a subset of women in L.A.'s LGBT communities who have an interest, mostly positive but occasionally negative, in religious and/or spiritual matters.

The lack of congregational ties that was so important for the project's goals ironically seems to have hindered the recruitment process. In my earlier study of two MCC congregations, over 70 of the 384 people who were initially contacted volunteered for interviews;[9] in the LAWS Project, with a much larger target audience including all of those at Pride and all of the readers of the *Lesbian News,* only fifty-seven potential participants volunteered. Thirty-five of these signed up for the project at L.A. Pride, approximately eighteen contacted me in response to the advertisement in the *Lesbian News,* and four heard about the project from a friend.

In July and August of 2001 I conducted initial telephone interviews, approximately ten minutes in length, with each potential participant.[10] The first part of these interviews was dedicated to a brief screening process that determined whether the volunteer was indeed part of the group I intended to target for the study. Because of the geographically bounded nature of the project and the existence of multiple hubs of LGBT activity within the gargantuan sprawl beyond L.A. itself, I limited the interviews to people who lived roughly within the Los Angeles city boundaries. For human subjects purposes and because I was interested in long-term negotiations of religious/spiritual identities, the study was limited to participants who were eighteen years of age or older. I also limited the study to those participants who identified as at least one of the following: lesbian, bisexual, transgendered, queer, or questioning.[11] Finally, given the importance of gender to the hypotheses driving the project, I limited the study to volunteers who either currently identified as women, or had identified as women at some point in the past. During the second part of the telephone interview, I collected basic demographic information and then scheduled a face-to-face interview.

Of the initial fifty-seven participants, ten dropped out of contact before interviews could be scheduled. Eleven lived beyond the targeted geographic area, and one identified as male, was neither transgendered nor transsexual, and had never lived or identified as a woman. One volunteer left town, two dropped out of the project for personal reasons, and three had repeated scheduling conflicts that prevented their participation. This left twenty-nine core participants in the project, all of whom currently identified, at least in part, as women.[12] Between August and November of 2001 I met in person with each core participant, at a location of her choice, for an in-depth, audiotaped interview. These interviews were episodic, using a combination of semistructured and narrative techniques,[13] and lasted anywhere from 50 to 190 minutes; the average length was 90 minutes. Two participants who were partners chose to interview together; all others, including another set of partners, chose to be interviewed singly. To begin an interview, I asked each participant to tell me a little about the roles that religion and/or spirituality had played in her life. Based on her response, I then asked other questions that followed up on issues the participant had raised or that gathered related information I needed for the project. Interviews were transcribed (producing 675 pages of transcripts for the core participants alone) and the transcripts were returned to the participants for comments; I also rechecked each transcript against the tape before beginning the analysis.

During each interview with a core participant, I asked whether there were any groups in which she participated as a part of her spiritual practice. If she said yes, I asked her to list the groups. Early in 2002, with the occasional assistance of several graduate students, I began conducting fieldwork visits with all of the groups currently or recently utilized by the core participants. These visits involved attending and participating in a service or meeting of the group, and interviewing at least one leader: either the senior leader of the organization, if that person was available, or an assistant leader, especially someone in charge of public outreach or LGBT issues. Print materials were collected during site visits, and because of the current popularity of the internet as a way for groups to advertise, I also printed out each group's website in the form it took at the time of the site visit. Especially extensive websites were printed selectively; some, if printed in full, would have produced more than fifty pages of text.

Methodological Questions and Caveats

Recruitment: Inclusions and Exclusions

Like most innovations, the recruitment strategies designed for this project solved some problems while creating others. On the one hand, recruiting participants outside of the traditional congregational framework did indeed allow me to pursue a wide variety of beliefs and practices that have not yet been considered in any depth by LGBT studies scholars. On the other hand, not only is a study of twenty-nine people not statistically reliable (nor was it intended to be, as the goal of the study was depth and detail rather than wide generalizability), but the core participants are not entirely representative of L.A.'s population as a whole. Whites are overrepresented by more than fifteen percentage points, making up 62 percent of the study participants but only 46.9 percent of the population in the City of Los Angeles, according to the 2000 census.[14] Though the representation of people of African descent in the study roughly approximates that in the city itself (10 percent in the study, 11.2 percent in the city census), Latinos, who make up 46.5 percent of L.A.'s population, are far underrepresented, and those of Asian and Pacific Islander descent are not included at all. Having more than one participant of Native American heritage would also have been a boon. Likewise, there are no Muslim participants in the study and very few Jewish participants,[15] and the only participants involved in Buddhism and Hinduism are converts to those religions. Bisexual and transgendered people are also small populations in this study.

Special recruitment efforts during the early months of the study attempted to address these problems of representation; I sent letters, flyers, and brochures to organizations representing the interests of many of the underrepresented groups, including gay and lesbian Asian/Pacific Islander groups, transgender organizations, LGBT synagogues, and the like. A lesbian friend of Arab descent contacted an e-mail list for Arab lesbians in Southern California to inform list members of the project and encourage their participation, but to no avail.

Some of the skewed representation in the study may have to do with the nature and variety of LGBT communities in Los Angeles; in other cases the likely explanation is more complicated, having to do with the roles of different religions in the lives of their natal followers and their converts. Many of the more visible LGBT communities in the United States are heavily white, and L.A. Pride is held in and near West Hollywood, the most famous gay (predominantly male) city in the L.A. metropolis and a predominantly white area. The development of a separate "Dyke March" at L.A. Pride and of Black Pride and Latino/a Pride celebrations—held, significantly, in other areas of the city—testify to the perceived whiteness and maleness of the main parade despite the participation of women and people of color in that parade as well. As I was unaware of the Black Pride and Latina/o Pride celebrations in Los Angeles at the time of the study, I did not recruit at these events. While bisexuals and transgendered people also participate in, organize, and attend events at the West Hollywood Pride festival, their less visible representation and the occasional hostility directed at both groups by some lesbians and gay men may lead some bisexuals and transgendered people to avoid pride events entirely.[16]

The relatively low number of Jewish participants in the study may have more to do with the noncongregational recruitment methods than with any other factors. It is worth noting, for instance, that Christians are also underrepresented in this study, relative to the general population: only 24 percent of the participants currently identify as Christian. The case of Islam is more complicated;

though there is some evidence for historical periods of acceptance of same-sex eroticism and gender fluidity in some Islamic cultures,[17] only quite recently have any positive contemporary discussions of such issues taken place.[18] Many LGBT Muslims remain closeted within their communities, and it is likely they would be more hesitant than LGBT people in general to participate in studies of this sort. Buddhism and Hinduism may be a contrasting case; although attitudes toward same-sex eroticism and gender diversity vary greatly across both of these religions,[19] many in the United States who are born into Hinduism and Buddhism are of Asian descent, and they may find that their communities question LGBT identities for cultural rather than religious reasons. Thus, LGBT identities and religious ones may overlap very little in such contexts, making a study such as this one seem irrelevant.

Despite the challenges of recruitment and representation, I believe it remains significant that the ethnic, religious, sexual, gender, and economic diversity included in this study in fact outstrips that in all other work published to date on LGBT religiosities. Furthermore, the problems of under- and over-representation are most critical in quantitative studies; qualitative studies such as this one can shift the analytical focus in ways that compensate for these problems to a certain extent. Here, as in previous work,[20] I place extra emphasis on the experiences of women of color, bisexual and transgendered women, women from non-Christian backgrounds, and other underrepresented groups, in order to bring into sharp relief both the complex divergences and the intriguing similarities in participants' beliefs and experiences.

Naming and Closeting in the Social Sciences

Social scientists have long made it common practice to protect the anonymity of their sources, believing that the data about research participants, and not the participants themselves, are the important factor in any study. Most ethnographies contain a footnote or paragraph somewhere in the introduction that explains that participants' names have been changed and potentially identifying features altered as well. Even when this is painfully transparent (I think of a dissertation from the University of Chicago that discussed congregations located in "Lake City"), anonymity is an almost-sacred ritual among social scientists. The Code of Ethics of the American Sociological Association (ASA) puts it quite clearly: "Sociologists do not disclose in their writings, lectures, or other public media confidential, personally identifiable information concerning their research participants."[21]

Feminist ethics might pose a counterquestion here: What are the consequences of erasing the human reality of research participants, of changing their identities? Is this positivism masquerading as social justice? Certainly there are cases in which anonymity is critical and highly ethical; some of the participants in my own previous research took part only in the survey aspect of the project and likely would not have taken part at all without the assurance of complete anonymity. Yet, an interview participant in a previous study posed a thought-provoking question to me. When I asked him whether he would like me to use any specific pseudonym when writing about him, he looked surprised, and then asked why I had to use a pseudonym. Having worked so hard to come out of the closet, he said, he was uncomfortable being forced back into it by the standards of social science.

This conversation gave me pause. Working with people whose identities are often quite consciously negotiated, and the level of their visibility carefully chosen and managed, why did I assume that I had the right to *hide* anyone's identity when I would never dare to assume the right to *reveal* it? Why did social scientific codes of ethics allow or even require me to control the representation of someone else's identity, effectively without his or her consent? The passage quoted above from the ASA Code of Ethics continues as follows: ". . . unless consent from individuals or their legal representatives has been obtained."[22] Why do social scientists not request consent for anonymity as well?

Finding no good answer to this question, I requested that participants in the LAWS Project determine their own level of anonymity, and I ensured that all participants understood that they could change their level of anonymity at any time up to the publication of the study. As part of an informed-consent procedure at the beginning of each interview, I asked participants to choose between total anonymity (including having all contact information in my records destroyed at the conclusion of the interview), anonymity in print (using a pseudonym), using a (real) first name only, or using a full, real name. I stressed that the study results would be published in articles and a book. No one chose total anonymity, and only four participants chose not to use their real names; all four selected their own pseudonyms. Ten participants elected to use only their first names in the study, and fifteen—just over half—asked me to use their full names. In order to further protect those who did wish to use pseudonyms, I have not revealed which of the names in this book are real and which are not. If a participant gave me a full name, either real or invented, I use her last name from time to time. For simplicity's sake, however, and since many of the participants wished to go by just a first name, whether real or pseudonymous, most of the references to the core participants are by first name. Because of the public roles played by the organizational leaders who contributed to the secondary interviews in the project, and because only one of them asked me to use anything less than her full name and title, these participants (with one exception) and all of the groups they represent are discussed using their real names.

Interpretation

Readers who are familiar with my work will know that, in general, I am an advocate of comparative work in gender studies—in other words, I usually prefer studies that include men, women, and everyone in between so that the gendered nature of a phenomenon can be examined from all sides. It may come as a surprise, then, to see a study in which I do nothing of the sort, and for that reason it seems important not only to explain my reasons for designing the study in this way, but also to discuss the role of gender in potential future studies.

The decision about how to include gender in this study was a difficult one, and choosing to focus on women, even in the broadest sense, has the consequence that there is still no work on the importance of noncongregational religious practices among gay and bisexual men. However, the majority of academic work to date on LGBT religiosities—even in studies designed to be gender-inclusive—has focused on men. At times this has been intentional, as with Mark Jordan's study of clerical culture in the Catholic Church; to examine the culture of priests *and* the culture of nuns would have given Jordan a completely different book.[23] At other times the skew toward men has been unavoidable. Historical works, for example, must grapple with the fact that in text-based, male-run religions, the voices and experiences of women are difficult to come by.[24] And, as discussed above, contemporary ethnographers' focus on LGBT congregations has unintentionally produced a male-centered genre of research.

Because there are so many data on men and so few on women in the study of LGBT religiosities, this book is intended as a corrective that can begin to balance out the cumulative "data set," so to speak; it is not intended to be a model for future studies, but rather to begin to level the data so that future studies have a more balanced grounding from which to explore the full range of gender dynamics in LGBT religiosities. By focusing specifically on women and highlighting a wide variety of beliefs, practices, and identities in their lives, this study begins to fill some of the gendered gaps in the existing literature and also raises a number of important questions about both women's and men's religious identities for future researchers to address. Because there are so few bisexual and transgendered people in the study, it also points to the pressing need for more research focused specifically on religion in the lives of bisexual and transgendered people.

A second important interpretive question for any researcher using interviews involves the reliability of memory and narrative, especially in studies of identity. On the one hand, I make no claim to be tracing any sort of objective reality through my interpretations of the interviews and fieldwork that make up the backbone of this book. Few contemporary qualitative researchers make such claims; indeed, even the objective reality of quantitative research can be called into question, as subjective processes are an important part of survey design, participant responses, data interpretation, and so on. In many cases I see no reason to doubt information from participants: there would be little reason, for instance, for a participant to err or deceive in explaining how she identifies her current religious beliefs and practices. Likewise, although human memory can always be called into question—and often is—simple facts like the denomination of one's upbringing or the age at which one ceased attending synagogue are generally reliable. Even when a recalled date is a year or two off, the general time span is the central concern here, so there is room for such small errors to intrude without altering the analysis.

Furthermore, this is primarily a study of identity, which is itself narratively constructed. This is especially true of contemporary western sexual identities,[25] which follow a familiar trope—the "coming-out story"—that bears an uncanny resemblance to the classic Protestant conversion narrative.[26] Narrative is a central component and carrier of religious identities, too; the role played by storytelling in the cycle of the Jewish year is an especially clear example of this. Thus the use of interview, which is essentially narrative, to examine a narratively constructed phenomenon seems amply logical. It does carry the risk that the interview process itself, as a narrative, will participate in the construction process: that is, that a participant might think of herself differently at the end of the interview than she did at the beginning. Participants have sometimes told me that an interview "made me think about this differently" or "made me think about questions I hadn't considered before." Frankly, I believe this is all but inevitable. Though researchers do have a responsibility to avoid putting words in participants' mouths, an interview is ultimately a social interaction and therefore can be expected to change both the interviewer and the interviewee, often in unanticipated ways.[27]

As a general rule, I take the narratives in these interviews at face value—if a participant tells me she left her church in 1989, I assume that she did so, or that any inaccuracy in her memory is slight enough not to be of any concern. However, I also attempt to read between the lines at times; if a participant tells me she left Christianity because of sexism, I will usually note that she *recalls* leaving that religion because of sexism. In other words, regardless of whether sexism was really her reason for leaving at the time, what is important for this study is that she remembers it that way; part of her religious identity is that she is an ex-Christian because she found the religion sexist. Such assertions are important because they often set up a later assertion that the religious practices in which the participant is now involved are not sexist, or at least are less so.

I also mark where I am using the terms "spirituality" and "religion" separately. By religious studies definitions, what most people refer to as "spirituality" can be considered a subset of "religion," and I generally use the terms as such. However, like many people in the United States today, the participants in this project often use "religion" negatively to refer to organizations they see as coercive, to dogmatic beliefs, to empty or meaningless ritual, and the like. By "spirituality," on the other hand, participants often mean a personal relationship with the sacred, more practice-oriented than belief-oriented. Spirituality, by this definition, can be practiced within religious organizations as well as outside them, but this happens through individual initiative. Thus there is a close link, in participants' definitions, between spirituality and what sociologists have termed "religious individualism."[28] However, many of the scholars who have commented on religious individualism have neglected to explore the extent to which, somewhat paradoxically, religious individualism may take place in communal settings.[29]

A final, important methodological question is that of intersectionality, the inextricable interweaving of socially relevant identity factors. In my analyses of identity construction, maintenance, interaction with communities, and so on, I take as one of my primary principles the insistence of many scholars—especially critical race theorists and feminists of color—that identity factors such as race and gender cannot be examined in isolation. Because, in a racialized society like the United States, one's race plays a part in determining gender norms, and because, likewise, in a gendered society one's gender plays a role in determining the details of racial identity (e.g., social expectations of Asian American women are different from those of both African American women and Asian American men), studying gender in isolation has the effect of erasing race. Likewise, and for the same reason, studying race in isolation has the effect of erasing gender. Moreover, the same could be said for a number of different, socially relevant identity factors, including sexual orientation, gender history, socioeconomic status, religious heritage, age, and so on. To ask questions about religion and identity alone, then, in a society that empowers and thus normalizes men, whites, the affluent, heterosexuals, the cisgendered, young adults and those in middle age, the able-bodied, the U.S.-born, and those of Christian heritage, is to offer answers that generally hold true for the above groups but may be irrelevant to women, people of color, queer people of all varieties, people with disabilities, non-Christians, immigrants, youth and the elderly, working-class people, and so on. Ambitious though it may seem to explore all of these identity factors in tandem, the analyses in this book refuse to take any identity for granted as long as information on the relevance of that identity is available from participants.

Appendix C

INTERVIEW SCHEDULES

Schedule for Telephone Interviews (Preliminary Screening; Structured)

ELIGIBILITY

1. Do you identify as lesbian, bisexual, transgender, queer, or questioning?
2. Do you identify as a woman, or have you identified as one in the past?
3. Do you live within roughly twenty miles [as the crow flies] of West Hollywood?
4. Are you eighteen or older?

DEMOGRAPHICS

1. What is your age?
2. What is your current gender identity?
3. Do you identify as transgender, or transsexual?
4. How do you identify in terms of sexual orientation?
5. How do you identify ethnically or racially?
6. Would you identify yourself as working class, lower middle class, upper middle class, upper class, or something else?
7. Would you identify your upbringing as being in a different class, or the same one?
8. What is your occupation?
9. What religion, if any, were you raised in?
10. How would you describe your spiritual beliefs and practices now?

Guidelines for Core Participant Interviews (Unstructured)

- Basic prompt: Ask participant to talk about the roles that religion and/or spirituality have played in hir[1] life.
- Guiding interests: First, how does the participant tell hir story? What is relevant to hir, and why? Then, after the story has taken shape, childhood (religious upbringing and level of involvement, beliefs, feelings about religion/spirituality, etc.), any shifts in teenage years (what and why), coming out (at what age; how long did it take or is it still ongoing; where was/is the partici-

pant religiously/spiritually before, during, and after coming out; did religion or spirituality play a role, and if so, what kind, through whom, was it personal, through an individual, a community, anonymous assistance [e.g., the internet], etc.), where is ze now with regard to religion/spirituality and how did ze get there? *Note:* This timeline (childhood—teenage years—coming out—present) may not be relevant or applicable to every participant; adjust as necessary.

- Further interests [added over the course of the project]: current resources and communities; self-definitions of religion and of sexual identity; the nature of the divine or the sacred; ontology of lesbian, bisexual, and transgender identities (born vs. became); current religious/spiritual practices.
- Before closing this portion of the interview, ask whether there is anything we haven't covered that the participant would like to talk about.
- Follow-up questions [Asked only at the conclusion of the interview so as not to skew the interview process; originally designed for an accompanying film, but occasionally useful for analysis as well. Participants were asked to respond in a few sentences to each question, or to skip a question if it was not relevant to their lives].
    1. Please introduce yourself as you'd like to be introduced for the film.
    2. How has organized religion affected your life?
    3. How has spirituality affected your life?
    4. If you could say one thing to a religious leader or religious leaders you knew as a child, what would it be?
    5. What would you say to a religious leader or religious leaders you knew while you were coming out?
    6. What about religious conservatives who believe that LGBT identities are false or sinful?
    7. Is there anything else that you would like to add?

Guidelines for Religious Leader Interviews (Semistructured)

ALL ORGANIZATIONS:

1. History of congregation or group; history of parent organization if relevant. How long has this congregation been in existence, how founded, what locations has it occupied, how long have current staff been in place, who are they (male, female, LGB, straight, trans- or cisgendered, race/ethnicity, religious background), etc.
2. If not a typical religious congregation: How often do you meet? What do meetings generally involve?
3. Congregants: Who comes? Why? How big is the congregation usually, how many members are there, does it tend to be mostly men? women? mixed? and

why does the interviewee think this is? Ethnic and class makeup of the congregation? How far do people come to participate? Does the congregation overall tend to be politically or religiously liberal? conservative? mixed?

FOR LGBT CONGREGATIONS ONLY:

1. Do you see this congregation/group as having a special focus on LGBT people (or "gays," "gays and lesbians," "the queer community"—whatever term the interviewee tends to use)? If so, how is that expressed in the daily or weekly life of the group?
2. Religious organizations: What is your own theological approach to homosexuality? bisexuality? transgender issues? (e.g., how do you approach the typical argument that homosexuality and "cross-dressing" are "abominations"?)
3. Do heterosexuals attend as well? Roughly how many? More men? women? mixed? Why?
4. What sorts of subgroups exist within the congregation (e.g. women's groups, men's groups, AIDS service organizations, Bible study, choir, etc.)? Roughly what percentage of the overall congregation tends to participate in these?
5. What do you feel are the most pressing needs of the individuals in your congregation? How are those needs addressed or not addressed by the group?

FOR NON-LGBT CONGREGATIONS ONLY:

1. What is your congregation's attitude toward LGBT people? Is there a difference between any official position the group might have and the overall "feel" of the group—e.g., is the congregation affirming overall but with a number of members opposed to that position or uncomfortable with it? (Another way to ask this: "What would you say to a gay man/lesbian/bisexual/transgendered person who inquired about the group?")
2. What is your own personal (especially theological, if relevant) take on homosexuality, bisexuality, transgender issues?
3. In what ways are your attitudes and those of the congregation expressed publicly? E.g., how are those positions communicated to newcomers, is there an LGBT (LGB? gay/lesbian?) group that meets, are there visual cues around the physical property, is the topic ever addressed during ritual, does the organization take part in LGBT-supportive events or activism?
4. If there is an LGBT group within the organization, how often does it meet? What does it do? How long has it been in existence? Roughly how many people attend? More men? women? mixed? Why?
5. How many LGBT people do you think attend this congregation regularly? Do they tend to be more men? women? mixed? Why?

6. What do you think are the most pressing needs of the LGBT individuals in your congregation? How are those needs addressed/not addressed here?

FOR ALL ORGANIZATIONS:

1. Do you feel that the women in your congregation have different needs from the men? If so, what are they?
2. What are your congregation's current positions on women's rights issues, and how are those positions expressed (e.g., in ritual, in publications, in hiring, etc.?)
3. Do you think that those women who are attracted to this group, *or* who avoid it, do so for different reasons from the men?
4. What are your visions for the future of this group, both immediate and long-term?
5. Is there anything I haven't touched on that you'd like to bring up?

Notes

1. Beyond the Congregation

1. Robert N. Bellah, Richard Madsen, William M. Sullivan, Ann Swidler, and Steven Tipton, *Habits of the Heart: Individualism and Commitment in American Life* (Berkeley: University of California Press, 1985).

2. On gender and individualism, see especially Michael S. Kimmel, *Manhood in America: A Cultural History,* 2nd ed. (New York: Oxford University Press, 2005).

3. Cf. Anthony Giddens, *Modernity and Self-Identity: Self and Society in the Late Modern Age* (Stanford, Calif.: Stanford University Press, 1991), 3.

4. A quick glance at the various groups hosted by the larger LGBT community centers, or the organizations represented at summer pride festivals, gives some sense of this proliferation of identities.

5. Grace Davie, *Religion in Britain since 1945: Believing without Belonging* (Oxford, UK: Blackwell, 1994).

6. R. Stephen Warner, "Work in Progress toward a New Paradigm for the Sociological Study of Religion in the United States," *American Journal of Sociology* 98 (March 1993): 1044–1093; Wade Clark Roof and William McKinney, *American Mainline Religion: Its Changing Shape and Future* (New Brunswick, N.J.: Rutgers University Press, 1987).

7. Robert Wuthnow, *After Heaven: Spirituality in America since the 1950s* (Berkeley: University of California Press, 1998).

8. Wade Clark Roof, *A Generation of Seekers: The Spiritual Journeys of the Baby Boom Generation* (San Francisco: HarperCollins, 1993) and *Spiritual Marketplace: Baby Boomers and the Remaking of American Religion* (Princeton, N.J.: Princeton University Press, 1999). I am indebted to the latter work for a number of conceptual insights.

9. See Claude Lévi-Strauss, *The Savage Mind* (Chicago: University of Chicago Press, 1966), 16–22. "Bricolage" means drawing upon available resources to create a coherent whole; it describes the sort of "found-art" approach to religious identity discussed earlier. See also Danièle Hervieu-Léger, "Bricolage Vaut-Il Dissémination? Quelques Réflexions sur l'Operationnalité Sociologique d'une Metaphore Problématique," *Social Compass* 52, no. 3 (2005): 295–308.

10. See Christian Smith, Melinda Lundquist Denton, Robert Faris, and Mark Regnerus, "Mapping American Adolescent Religious Participation," *Journal for the Scientific Study of Religion* 41, no. 4 (2002): 597–612; John M. Wallace, Jr., Tyrone A. Forman, Cleopatra H. Caldwell, and Deborah S. Willis, "Religion and U.S. Secondary School Students: Current Patterns, Recent Trends, and Sociodemographic Correlates," *Youth & Society* 35, no. 1 (2003): 98–125.

11. Michael Burawoy, "The Extended Case Method," *Sociological Theory* 16, no. 1 (1998): 5.

12. An exception to this lack of knowledge, and significantly also a book that uses a case study approach, is Ruth Frankenberg's *Living Spirit, Living Practice: Poetics,*

Politics, Epistemology (Durham, N.C.: Duke University Press, 2004). In a much broader study of literary and cinematic representations of Asian and Asian American women, Laura Hyun Yi Kang notes in passing the existence of resistance and self-construction within the boundaries of religious tradition. See *Compositional Subjects: Enfiguring Asian/American Women* (Durham, N.C.: Duke University Press, 2002), 223.

13. Ronald M. Enroth and Gerald E. Jamison, *The Gay Church* (Grand Rapids, Mich.: Eerdmans, 1974); see also Ronald M. Enroth, "The Homosexual Church: An Ecclesiastical Extension of a Subculture," *Social Compass* 21, no. 3 (1974): 355–360.

14. Paul F. Bauer, "The Homosexual Subculture at Worship: A Participant Observation Study," *Pastoral Psychology* 25, no. 2 (1976): 115–127.

15. E. Michael Gorman, "A New Light on Zion: A Study of Three Homosexual Religious Congregations in Urban America" (Ph.D. diss., University of Chicago, 1980).

16. This has been true for noncongregational groups, as well. Most recently, a small study of Mormons concluded that lesbian Mormons' experiences were so different from gay men's that the two should be studied separately. The author chose to study the men only. See Rick Phillips, *Conservative Christian Identity and Same-Sex Orientation: The Case of Gay Mormons* (New York: Peter Lang, 2005).

17. See Enroth and Jamison, *Gay Church;* Bauer, "The Homosexual Subculture," and Gorman, "A New Light on Zion." The quotation from Gorman's work in the epigraph is almost the only mention of gender tensions in his entire dissertation.

18. Leonard Norman Primiano, "'I Would Rather Be Fixated on the Lord': Women's Religion, Men's Power, and the 'Dignity' Problem," *New York Folklore* 19, no. 1–2 (1993): 89–103. Primiano's research was conducted in the early 1980s.

19. Moshe Shokeid, *A Gay Synagogue in New York* (New York: Columbia University Press, 1995).

20. Moshe Shokeid, "'The Women Are Coming': The Transformation of Gender Relationships in a Gay Synagogue," *Ethnos* 66, no. 1 (2001): 5–26.

21. For instance, the chapter on "the gender issue" in Shokeid's book is all of nine pages long (Shokeid, *A Gay Synagogue,* 174–182). Also interesting is that discussions of gender generally do not appear in this research until there is an explicit focus on women's roles. This betrays a common assumption that it is women who "have" gender, while men somehow do not.

22. Primiano, "I Would Rather"; see especially 91–93.

23. Gay men's and lesbian women's cultures in the United States, though long allies, have often been separate. This is less the case today than in previous eras, but when Primiano was conducting his fieldwork in the 1980s the separation was still quite strong. It remains in place today, albeit in weakened form. For more on this history, see chapter 2.

24. However, Dignity today vocally supports women's ordination in the Roman Catholic Church.

25. Melissa M. Wilcox, *Coming Out in Christianity: Religion, Identity, and Community* (Bloomington: Indiana University Press, 2003), 18.

26. Shokeid, "'The Women Are Coming,'" 7.

27. Wilcox, *Coming Out in Christianity,* 20–23.

28. When referring to groups of people, I sometimes will use "queer" as an umbrella term that includes a wide variety of sexual and gender diversity: lesbians, gay men, bisexuals, and transgendered, transsexual, genderqueer, and intersexed people, to name a few. When referring to individuals in this study, I use "queer" only for those people who describe themselves that way. When discussing previous academic work, I try to restrict my terms to those identities discussed in the study in question; thus, in some cases I may refer solely to "gay men and lesbians" or "lesbians, gay men, and bisexuals." This is an attempt to avoid the gratuitous and misleading (and ultimately false) inclusion that results from using the term "LGBT" as a simple replacement for "gay" or

"gay and lesbian."

29. Gary David Comstock, *Unrepentant, Self-Affirming, Practicing: Lesbian/Bisexual/Gay People within Organized Religion* (New York: Continuum, 1996), 182–183.

30. Shokeid, *A Gay Synagogue,* 174.

31. For a discussion of the methods used in this study, see Appendix B.

32. The use of the term "spirituality" here is intentional; see the discussion below on the differences between popular perceptions of "religion" and "spirituality," and see Appendix B for an explanation of this choice of terms.

33. Some interesting recent contributions to this discussion include Ralph W. Hood, Jr., "The Relationship between Religion and Spirituality," in *Defining Religion: Investigating the Boundaries between the Sacred and Secular,* vol. 10, *Religion and the Social Order,* ed. Arthur L. Greil and David G. Bromley (New York: JAI, 2003) , 241–264; Robert A. Orsi, *Between Heaven and Earth: The Religious Worlds People Make and the Scholars Who Study Them* (Princeton, N.J.: Princeton University Press, 2005), especially chapter 6; Penny Long Marler and C. Kirk Hadawaym, "'Being Religious' or 'Being Spiritual': A Zero-Sum Proposition?" *Journal for the Scientific Study of Religion* 41, no. 2 (2002): 289–300; and Frankenberg, *Living Spirit, Living Practice* (particularly the introduction).

34. Cf. David D. Hall, ed., *Lived Religion: Toward a History of Practice* (Princeton, N.J.: Princeton University Press, 1997).

35. Peter Berger, *The Sacred Canopy: Elements of a Sociological Theory of Religion* (New York: Doubleday, 1967), 175.

36. This is also Frankenberg's approach, in a study of identity that bears a number of similarities to my work; see *Living Spirit, Living Practice,* 1–5.

37. From an anthropological perspective, using the terms interchangeably could be seen as switching between "emic" or insider terms ("spirituality") and "etic" or outsider terms ("religion").

38. See Joanne Meyerowitz, *How Sex Changed: A History of Transsexuality in the United States* (Cambridge, Mass.: Harvard University Press, 2002).

39. Cf. Harry Emerson Fosdick, *On Being a Real Person* (New York: Harper and Brothers, 1943).

40. Will Herberg, *Protestant, Catholic, Jew: An Essay in American Religious Sociology* (Garden City, N.Y.: Doubleday, 1955). I have never forgotten a graduate class years ago, in which one of my friends asked pointedly whether any of our classmates had ever met a "Judeo-Christian." I use the term here because it came to have such widespread usage, which it still enjoys, following the publication of Herberg's book.

41. Wuthnow, *After Heaven.*

42. Giddens, *Modernity and Self-Identity.*

43. Wuthnow, *After Heaven.*

44. Giddens, *Modernity and Self-Identity* (cf. p. 5).

45. Gender identity disorder, or GID. There is some controversy in transgender communities over whether this designation is useful (because it recognizes the distress of transgendered people forced by parents or a stigmatizing society to present a false gender image, and may help to pave the way for health insurance coverage of sex reassignment procedures) or harmful (because it labels transgender identity "disordered").

2. Setting the Stage

1. Early sources, as well as the history of Spanish and later U.S. relations with the Gabrielino people, are summarized in Lowell John Bean and Charles R. Smith, "Gabrielino," in *Handbook of North American Indians,* vol. 8, *California,* ed. William C. Sturtevant (Washington, D.C.: Smithsonian Institution, 1978), 538–548; and a more

updated source, Amanda Beresford McCarthy, "Gabrieliño," in *The Gale Encyclopedia of Native American Tribes,* vol. 4, ed. Sharon Malinowski, Anna Sheets, Jeffrey Lehman, and Melissa Walsh Doig (Detroit: Gale, 1998), 65–68. As in most small-scale societies, the western term "religion" most likely fails to do justice to the role played by cosmological beliefs and their related practices in pre-invasion Gabrielino culture; rather than being one aspect of that culture, relationships with nonhuman and superhuman beings would instead have pervaded it.

2. Michael E. Engh, *Frontier Faiths: Church, Temple, and Synagogue in Los Angeles, 1846–1888* (Albuquerque: University of New Mexico Press, 1992).

3. U.S. Census Bureau, "American Indian and Alaska Native Tribes in the United States: 2000." Available online: http://www.census.gov/population/cen2000/phc-t18/tab001.pdf (accessed August 29, 2006).

4. Antonio Ríos-Bustamante, "The Barrioization of Nineteenth-Century Mexican Californians: From Landowners to Laborers," *Masterkey: Anthropology of the Americas* 60 (1986): 26–35.

5. See Engh, *Frontier Faiths;* Douglas Flamming, *Bound for Freedom: Black Los Angeles in Jim Crow America* (Berkeley: University of California Press, 2005), especially 109–117.

6. Korean Protestants, too, had established congregations in the city by this time.

7. Cf. Harvey Cox, *Fire from Heaven: The Rise of Pentecostal Spirituality and the Reshaping of Religion in the Twenty-first Century* (Reading, Mass.: Addison-Wesley, 1995).

8. Engh, Michael E., "'Practically Every Religion Being Represented,'" in *Metropolis in the Making: Los Angeles in the 1920s,* ed. Tom Sitton and William Deverell (Berkeley: University of California Press, 2001), 203–204. On McPherson, see also Cox, *Fire from Heaven,* 123–128.

9. Ron Kelley, "Muslims in Los Angeles," in *Muslim Communities in North America,* ed. Yvonne Yazbeck Haddad and Jane Idleman Smith (Albany: State University of New York Press, 1994), 135–167.

10. On the latter, see Lillian Faderman and Stuart Timmons, *Gay L.A.: A History of Sexual Outlaws, Power Politics, and Lipstick Lesbians* (New York: Basic Books, 2006), 9–14.

11. Ibid., 14–17.

12. Leila Rupp, *A Desired Past: A Short History of Same-Sex Love in America* (Chicago: University of Chicago Press, 1999), 94. See also Faderman and Timmons, *Gay L.A.,* 30–35.

13. See, e.g., John D'Emilio, *Sexual Politics, Sexual Communities: The Making of a Homosexual Minority in the United States, 1940–1970,* 2nd ed. (Chicago: University of Chicago Press, 1998), 23–39.

14. Coverage of the Mattachine Society can be found in nearly every gay, lesbian, gay/lesbian, or LGBT history of the United States. Useful sources include Faderman and Timmons, *Gay L.A.;* D'Emilio, *Sexual Politics;* Rupp, *A Desired Past;* and Nicholas C. Edsall, *Toward Stonewall: Homosexuality and Society in the Modern Western World* (Charlottesville: University of Virginia Press, 2003). See also Harry Hay, *Radically Gay: Gay Liberation in the Words of Its Founder,* ed. Will Roscoe (Boston: Beacon Press, 1996); and Stuart Timmons, *The Trouble with Harry Hay: Founder of the Modern Gay Movement* (Boston: Alyson Books, 1990).

15. According to Edsall, German homosexual organizers had previously invented the term, before Nazi forces obliterated the growing movement there. See *Toward Stonewall,* 273. The Mattachine Society attempted to involve women as well, but had difficulty persuading lesbian and bisexual women that their concerns were the same as those of gay and bisexual men. See Faderman and Timmons, *Gay L.A.,* 128.

16. The plaintiff was Dale Jennings, one of the founders of the Mattachine. Police

entrapment, which was common throughout the 1950s and 1960s, usually involved an undercover officer posing as a gay man, seducing another man, and then arresting him for lewdness or disorderly conduct. Lesbian and bisexual women were also entrapped.

17. *One* also became embroiled in a court case, when in 1954 the Los Angeles postmaster accused the magazine of obscenity and refused to distribute it. The case, which *One* eventually won, went to the Supreme Court. See Rupp, *A Desired Past,* 162; Faderman and Timmons, *Gay L.A.*, 116–120.

18. The Daughters of Bilitis was founded by Phyllis Lyon and Del Martin in 1955, in San Francisco. Its chapters generally held to the same politics of respectability evinced by the Mattachine after the 1953 mutiny. Cf. Faderman and Timmons, *Gay L.A.*, 128–133.

19. Faderman and Timmons, *Gay L.A.*, 386, n. 43.

20. Cf. Rupp, *A Desired Past,* 163–165; Edsall, *Toward Stonewall,* 307–308 and 328–330; Boswell, *Sexual Politics,* 184–186; and Lillian Faderman, *Odd Girls and Twilight Lovers: A History of Lesbian Life in Twentieth-Century America* (New York: Columbia University Press, 1991), 159–187. Rupp helpfully notes that these divisions were not without exception, and that they were more severe between lesbian communities than they were between gay male communities.

21. West Hollywood was incorporated as a city in 1985. Though this move was initially viewed with some suspicion by many of the neighborhood's LGBT inhabitants because of the relative safety provided by the lack of incorporation, and though a significant number of the city's inhabitants are not gay, West Hollywood has come to be known as a gay city. The city's current logo, which is even emblazoned on its police cars, incorporates the rainbow colors that many LGBT people have come to associate with their community.

22. Moira Rachel Kenney, *Mapping Gay L.A.: The Intersection of Place and Politics* (Philadelphia: Temple University Press, 2001), 165.

23. Kenney, *Mapping Gay L.A.*, 165–166.

24. Elizabeth A. Armstrong and Suzanna M. Crage, "Movements and Memory: The Making of the Stonewall Myth," *American Sociological Review* 71, no. 5 (2006): 724–751. Armstrong and Crage point out that though the protests resulted in an investigation of the officers involved in the raid, none of those officers were reprimanded, while six of those arrested in the raid were successfully charged with "lewd conduct."

25. D'Emilio, *Sexual Politics,* 227.

26. Armstrong and Crage note that only two other cities held pride parades that first year: New York and Chicago. See "Movements and Memory," 740–741.

27. Kenney, *Mapping Gay L.A.*, 43; see also 154.

28. Ibid., 10.

29. Ibid., 6. This is not to say that there were not separatist organizations in L.A.; lesbian feminists, for example, managed to sustain separatist goals for far longer than gay men did. Cf. Faderman and Timmons, *Gay L.A.*, 181–192.

30. See Eric C. Wat's oral history of these organizations, *The Making of a Gay Asian Community: An Oral History of Pre-AIDS Los Angeles* (Lanham, Md.: Rowman and Littlefield, 2002).

31. For the history of APLA, see Kenney, *Mapping Gay L.A.*, 92–96 and 105–110. For a broader history of responses to AIDS in L.A.'s LGBT communities, see Faderman and Timmons, *Gay L.A.*, 301–321.

32. There certainly have been street protests in Los Angeles since 1993. These have focused on a variety of issues, including immigrants' rights, workers' rights, and most recently the wars in Afghanistan and Iraq and the attendant civil rights concerns in the United States. In December 2002, for instance, rallies protested the arrest and disappearance of hundreds of men of Middle Eastern descent in Southern California who had responded to a request to register in person at immigration offices. LGBT people

have been involved in all of these protests, but as activists more generally rather than as activists for LGBT rights.

33. Kenney, *Mapping Gay L.A.*, 6.

34. Faderman, *Odd Girls*, 278.

35. On the history of the Eucharistic Catholic Church and its incorporation into the Orthodox Catholic Church of America, see the oral history of George Hyde, available through the LGBT Religious Archives Network. Available online: http://www.lgbtran.org/Interview.aspx?ID=6 (accessed December 10, 2008). On LGBT religious history through the mid-1970s, see also Heather R. White, "Homosexuality, Gay Communities, and American Churches: A History of a Changing Religious Ethic, 1946–1976" (Ph.D. diss., Princeton University, 2007).

36. Faderman and Timmons, *Gay L.A.*, 121.

37. See Boswell, *Sexual Politics*, 192–195; Faderman and Timmons, *Gay L.A.*, 162. An informative "virtual museum exhibit" on the San Francisco CRH is available on the LGBT Religious Archives Network website: http://www.lgbtran.org/Exhibits/CRH/Exhibit.asp (accessed September 6, 2006).

38. On Metropolitan Community Church history, see Melissa M. Wilcox, *Coming Out in Christianity: Religion, Identity, and Community* (Bloomington: Indiana University Press, 2003), 81–99, and White, "Homosexuality." Primary source materials on this history include Troy D. Perry, as told to Charles L. Lucas, *The Lord Is My Shepherd and He Knows I'm Gay* (Los Angeles: Nash, 1972); and Troy D. Perry with Thomas L. P. Swicegood, *Don't Be Afraid Anymore* (New York: St. Martin's Press, 1990). Historical information is also woven throughout Nancy Wilson's *Our Tribe: Queer Folks, God, Jesus, and the Bible* (San Francisco: HarperSanFrancisco, 1995).

39. See the interview with Freda Smith that is housed on the LGBT Religious Archives Network website: http://www.lgbtran.org/Exhibits/OralHistory/Smith/FSmith.pdf (accessed September 13, 2007).

40. See Perry and Swicegood, *Don't Be Afraid*, 76. The number of burned MCC churches had risen to twenty-one by the time the most recent UFMCC media fact sheet was assembled in 2003 (available online: http://www.mccchurch.org/Content/NavigationMenu/MediaRoom/PressKit/Press_Kit.htm; accessed September 6, 2006).

41. Aside from White's dissertation, there is little secondary material on Dignity's history. The organization has written its own history, however, which can be accessed at http://www.dignityusa.org/history (accessed December 10, 2008).

42. See the Dignity website, http://www.dignityusa.org/history/1969 (accessed December 10, 2008). The quotation is uncited.

43. National Conference of Catholic Bishops, *Principles to Guide Confessors in Questions of Homosexuality;* Congregation for the Doctrine of the Faith, *Declaration Regarding Certain Questions of Sexual Ethics.*

44. Congregation for the Doctrine of the Faith, *Letter to All Catholic Bishops on the Pastoral Care of Homosexual Persons.* An excellent discussion of these documents, and of official Catholic attitudes toward gays and lesbians in general, can be found in Mark D. Jordan, *The Silence of Sodom: Homosexuality in Modern Catholicism* (Chicago: University of Chicago Press, 2000).

45. Cf. Leonard Norman Primiano, "'I Would Rather Be Fixated on the Lord': Women's Religion, Men's Power, and the 'Dignity' Problem," *New York Folklore* 19, no. 1–2 (1993): 89–99.

46. See chapter 3 for a discussion of this organization.

47. On the history of radical feminism, see Alice Echols, *Daring to Be Bad: Radical Feminism in America, 1967–1975* (Minneapolis: University of Minnesota Press, 1989). One of the most persistent radical feminist writers in redefining derogatory terms is Mary Daly; cf. *Beyond God the Father: Toward a Philosophy of Women's Liberation* (Boston: Beacon Press, 1973).

48. Gerald Gardner, *Witchcraft Today* (New York: Citadel Press, 1955) and *The Meaning of Witchcraft* (London: Aquarian Press, 1959).

49. This is the division between "Gardnerian" Wicca (followers of Gardner) and "Alexandrian" Wicca (followers of Alex Sanders). Margot Adler's *Drawing Down the Moon* (Boston: Beacon Press, 1986) provides nearly encyclopedic coverage of these early movements.

50. Cf. Johann Jakob Bachofen, *Myth, Religion, and Mother Right: Selected Writings of J. J. Bachofen,* trans. Ralph Manheim (Princeton, N.J.: Princeton University Press, 1967). Bachofen published *Das Mutterrecht* in 1861. Along with Robert Graves's *The White Goddess,* published in a revised edition in 1966, Bachofen's text was influential in the development of an important feminist story of origins. By the early 1970s, cultural feminists had embraced the now-discredited idea that ancient Mediterranean (and, some argued, global) cultures were matriarchal and worshipped a Great Goddess. This concept exerted a powerful influence over the development of feminist spirituality. Cf. Faderman, *Odd Girls,* 226–229.

51. This policy continues to be in place, and like many women-only groups rooted in radical second-wave feminism, Dianic Wicca admits only "women-born women"—i.e., women who were assigned female at birth, were raised as females, and continue to identify as female. For an interesting twist to this policy, see the discussion of the Circle of Aradia in chapter 3. On early Dianic Wicca, see Zsuzsanna Budapest, *The Feminist Book of Lights and Shadows* (Venice: Luna Publications, 1976) and *The Holy Book of Women's Mysteries* (Berkeley: Wingbow Press, 1989). Ironically, Faderman and Timmons note that MCC's Los Angeles church hosted the Susan B. Anthony Coven No. 1 in its early years; see *Gay L.A.,* 262.

52. Perhaps even into corporate culture, if the Starbucks logo is any indication.

53. See Stephen J. Sass, "Our History," 2002, http://www.bcc-la.org/history1.pdf and http://www.bcc-la.org/history2.pdf (accessed July 5, 2006; not currently available online); Faderman and Timmons, *Gay L.A.,* 262–264.

54. The New York synagogue is Congregation Beth Simchat Torah; for its history see Moshe Shokeid, *A Gay Synagogue in New York* (New York: Columbia University Press, 1995).

55. See D. Michael Quinn, *Same-Sex Dynamics among Nineteenth-Century Americans: A Mormon Example* (Urbana: University of Illinois Press, 1996). Tragically, Quinn's work in this area has resulted in his being blacklisted in his field of Mormon studies, and by 2006 this had rendered him jobless despite his long and distinguished academic career and his notable scholarly innovation and talent. See Daniel Golden, "Higher Learning: In Religion Studies, Universities Bend to Views of Faithful," *Wall Street Journal,* Eastern Edition, April 6, 2006, A1.

56. Paul Mortensen, "In the Beginning: A Brief History of Affirmation." Available online at http://www.affirmation.org/memorial/in_the_beginning.shtml#1977_ad (accessed September 8, 2006).

57. See Timmons, *The Trouble with Harry Hay,* and Hay, *Radically Gay.*

58. Timmons, *The Trouble with Harry Hay,* 265.

59. Hay would have been familiar with Crowley through serving as the organist for the Los Angeles lodge of the O.T.O., the Order of the Eastern Temple, in his twenties. Crowley was closely involved with this occult movement, which Timmons claims "was known to have created homosexual sex-magic rituals" (p. 75). Gerald Gardner, the founder of Wicca, was also strongly influenced by Crowley. On Crowley and Gardner, see Hugh B. Urban, *Magia Sexualis: Sex, Magic, and Liberation in Modern Western Esotericism* (Berkeley: University of California Press, 2006).

60. Calamus root, also known as sweet flag, is used for medicinal purposes by several Native American cultures, according to the U.S. Department of Agriculture Plants Database (available online at http://plants.usda.gov/java/profile?symbol=ACCA4; ac-

cessed September 8, 2006). Hay maintained an interest in Native American cultures and Native American rights throughout his life.

61. Hay, *Radically Gay*, 239–241. The flyer apparently used the spelling "Fairy," which changed fairly early in the movement's history to "Faery."

62. Thanks to Catherine Garoupa for this term.

63. To the best of my knowledge there are no secondary sources on Christ Chapel. Because a study participant attended Christ Chapel–Long Beach, I interviewed Pastor Michael Cole in 2002 and ended up conducting an informal oral history (this can be accessed through the LGBT Religious Archives Network oral history project, available online at http://www.lgbtran.org/Interview.aspx?ID=2 [accessed December 10, 2008]). Cole's untimely death in 2005 underlines the critical importance of oral history projects among these founders.

64. Pastor Michael Cole, interview with the author, August 8, 2002.

65. Ibid.

66. Not to be confused with Calvary Open Door Worship Center, which is an ex-gay ministry; see Tanya Erzen, *Straight to Jesus: Sexual and Christian Conversions in the Ex-Gay Movement* (Berkeley: University of California Press, 2006).

67. To date, the only published secondary material on the UFCM is Pamela Leong, "Religion, Flesh, and Blood: Re-creating Religious Culture in the Context of HIV/AIDS," *Sociology of Religion* 67, no. 3 (2006): 295–311. Leong is writing a dissertation on the movement as well. The UFCM is also briefly mentioned in Faderman and Timmons, *Gay L.A.*: see pp. 265, 291–292, 318. A very brief summary of UFCM history is available on the organization's website at http://www.unityfellowshipchurch.org/site2009/?page_id=20 (accessed December 10, 2008).

68. Rev. Elder Alfreda Lanoix, interview with the author, March 19, 2002.

69. Though by no means all: First AME, for example, has been a leader in L.A. on issues of LGBT rights.

70. "MAP History," available online at http://www.map-usa.org/html/history.htm (accessed September 8, 2006).

71. Ibid.

72. Kenney, *Mapping Gay L.A.*, 1.

73. George Chauncey, *Gay New York: Gender, Urban Culture, and the Makings of the Gay Male World, 1890–1940* (New York: Basic Books, 1994) and Charles Kaiser, *The Gay Metropolis: 1940–1996* (Boston: Houghton Mifflin, 1997); Susan Stryker and Jim Van Buskirk, *Gay by the Bay: A History of Queer Culture in the San Francisco Bay Area* (San Francisco: Chronicle Books, 1996); Lillian Faderman and Stuart Timmons, *Gay L.A.: A History of Sexual Outlaws, Power Politics, and Lipstick Lesbians* (New York: Basic Books, 2006).

74. Faderman and Timmons, *Gay L.A.*, 361.

3. Queering the Spiritual Marketplace

1. Rev. Susan Russell, interview with the author, June 19, 2003.

2. Rev. Daniel Smith, interview with the author, June 17, 2003.

3. *Gay and Lesbian Community Yellow Pages: Southern California*, 2001, 16–20.

4. *Lesbian News* 26, no. 11 (2001): 2.

5. Ibid., 17.

6. Ibid., 45.

7. Rev. Daniel Smith, interview with the author, June 17, 2003. For earlier accounts of daytime, face-to-face meetings of LGBT people, see Lillian Faderman and Stuart Timmons, *Gay L.A.: A History of Sexual Outlaws, Power Politics, and Lipstick Lesbians* (New York: Basic Books, 2006).

8. Rev. Daniel Smith, interview with the author, June 17, 2003.

9. Ibid.

10. Ibid.

11. For studies of the debates over the status of lesbian and gay Presbyterian pastors, see James K. Wellman, Jr., ed., *Religious Organizational Identity and Homosexual Ordination: A Case Study of the Presbyterian Church, U.S.A.*, special issue of *Review of Religious Research,* vol. 41, no. 2 (1999). In 2006, the denomination adopted a policy allowing local churches greater power in decisions about ordination, effectively opening what the *Los Angeles Times* called a "loophole" for the ordination of LGBT clergy. See K. Connie Kang and Stephen Clark, "Churches Rule on Gays in Clergy," *Los Angeles Times,* 21 June 2006, A-11.

12. "WHPC History," http://www.wehopres.org/aboutdata.html (accessed August 19, 2002; no longer available online).

13. Rev. Daniel Smith, interview with the author, June 17, 2003.

14. "The History of the Parish," available online at http://saintthomashollywood.org/stthomas/page.php?ref=history&ts_hld=parish (accessed December 10, 2008).

15. Ibid.

16. Ibid.

17. Ibid.

18. "Book of Remembrance," http://saintthomashollywood.org/aidsbook.html (accessed March 12, 2002; no longer available online).

19. Father Ian Elliott Davies, interview with the author, March 19, 2002.

20. Ibid.

21. Father Ian Elliott Davies, personal communication with the author, August 5, 2004.

22. Reverend Lori (last name withheld by request), interview with the author, August 25, 2002. "Boystown" is a nickname of West Hollywood; Faderman and Timmons note that the nickname is "a reference to the 1948 Spencer Tracy film about a colony of orphaned newsboys" (*Gay L.A.*, 231).

23. Reverend Lori, interview with the author, August 25, 2002.

24. Ibid.

25. E.g., Donald Eastman, "Homosexuality: Not a Sickness, Not a Sin: What the Bible Does and Does Not Say" (Los Angeles: Universal Fellowship of Metropolitan Community Churches, 1990); Buddy Truluck, "Homosexuality: The Bible as Your Friend: A Guide for Lesbians and Gays" (Los Angeles: Universal Fellowship of Metropolitan Community Churches, 1991); Nathan L. Meckley, "Homosexuality and the Bible: Bad News or Good News?" (Los Angeles: Universal Fellowship of Metropolitan Community Churches, 1994); and my personal favorite, a simple tri-fold brochure that asks "What did Jesus say about homosexuality?" and is blank inside.

26. E.g., *Welcome to Glory Tabernacle Metropolitan Community Church* (Long Beach, Calif.: Glory Tabernacle MCC, n.d.). These "prooftexts" are also in the service bulletins and on the church's website: http://www.glorytabernacle.com/AboutUs_WorshipQuestions.htm (accessed October 4, 2007). In November 2004, Glory Tabernacle disaffiliated from the UFMCC because of objections to MCC's explicit focus on LGBT people and to its less evangelical theological orientation. Sandra Turnbull wrote to me in 2007: "We really wanted to be a congregation where people from all walks of life would feel welcome and be known for more than sexual identity. . . . On another note, besides the inclusivity issue, we wanted to maintain a very Christ centered or evangelical message as a church. It seemed to me and leaders of our church that the MCC organization was broadening its message where Jesus Christ was not as central" (the Rev. Sandra Turnbull, personal communication with the author, October 4, 2007).

27. Available online at http://www.glorytabernacle.com (accessed October 4, 2007).

28. Rev. Sandra Turnbull, interview with the author, April 14, 2002.

29. Ibid.

30. It may also be relevant that Long Beach is known for having a strong and prominent lesbian community. While this might have been an argument for locating the present study in Long Beach rather than centering it around West Hollywood, the prevalence of historic LGBT and welcoming religious organizations in and around the West Hollywood area made that city a better choice for the center point of a community studies–based project focused on religious institutions and practices.

31. This is Sandra Turnbull's estimate.

32. Pastor Michael Cole, interview with the author, August 8, 2002.

33. There is little written history of Beth Chayim Chadashim (BCC). Brief coverage of the congregation's first two years can be found in Thomas L. P. Swicegood, *Our God Too: Biography of a Church and a Temple* (New York: Pyramid Books, 1974), 348–362. A more thorough source, which includes a timeline, is Steven J. Sass, "Our History," June 2, 2002, http://www.bcc-la.org/history1.pdf and http://www.bcc-la.org/history2.pdf (accessed July 5, 2006; no longer available online). For a description of BCC's history, see chapter 2.

34. Lisa Edwards, "Rabbi Edwards Returns from Sabbatical," *G'vanim* 30, no. 9 (May 2002): 2.

35. Rabbi Lisa Edwards, interview with the author, August 8, 2002.

36. Jacki Riedeman, interview with the author, June 19, 2003.

37. Tere La Giusa, Jacki Riedeman, and Ben Jarvis, interview with the author, June 19, 2003. See also Rick Phillips, *Conservative Christian Identity and Same-Sex Orientation: The Case of Gay Mormons* (New York: Peter Lang, 2005).

38. Ben Jarvis, interview with the author, June 19, 2003. Proposition 22, which passed in 2000, added the following words to the California family code: "Only marriage between a man and a woman is valid or recognized in California" (see http://primary2000.ss.ca.gov/VoterGuide/Propositions/22text.htm; accessed June 29, 2006). On May 15, 2008, the California State Supreme Court declared that Proposition 22 violated the state constitution, thereby legalizing same-sex marriage in the state. In response, opponents of same-sex marriage introduced Proposition 8, which was included on the November 2008 ballot. This proposition, which added the text of Proposition 22 to the state constitution, passed with 52.3% of the vote. As of this writing, same-sex couples cannot marry in California.

39. Several articles on Affirmation's history can be found on the organization's website: http://www.affirmation.org/memorial/history.shtml (accessed December 10, 2008). See chapter 2 for a discussion of this history.

40. Jacki Riedeman, interview with the author, June 19, 2003.

41. See http://www.affirmation.org (accessed June 18, 2003).

42. See http://www.unityfellowshipchurch.org (accessed March 12, 2002). This pop-up message has since been removed from the site.

43. Frankie Lennon, "Who We Are: The Unity Fellowship Movement," http://www.unityfellowshipchurch.org/ufc-history.html (accessed March 12, 2002; no longer available online).

44. See http://www.ufc-usa.org (accessed December 10, 2008).

45. *Unity Fellowship Church* (Los Angeles: Unity Fellowship Church, 1989).

46. Rev. Gerald Green, interview with the author, February 10, 2002.

47. Rev. Elder Alfreda Lanoix, interview with the author, March 19, 2002.

48. Odds are very high that the denominational choices of participants in this project do not indicate that LGBT people prefer Unitarian Universalist, Episcopal, and Catholic churches over the United Church of Christ, the United Methodist Church, or other liberal and mainline denominations. It is likely significant, though, that there are no *un*affirming congregations represented here.

49. Marta Flanagan, *We Are Unitarian Universalists* (Boston: Unitarian Universalist Association, 1992), n.p.

50. See Gordon Melton, *The Churches Speak on Homosexuality: Official Statements from Religious Bodies and Ecumenical Organizations* (Detroit: Gale Research, 1991), 265–267.

51. Rev. Paul Sawyer, "A Brief History of Throop Church," http://www.throopuu.org/throophistory.html (accessed June 3, 2003; no longer available online).

52. Beth Leehy, interview with the author, June 19, 2003.

53. Ibid.

54. This process, available under a number of different names in different mainline and liberal Protestant denominations, offers a lengthy curriculum for congregational learning and self-study on topics related to diversity, especially sexual diversity. Curricula are developed by each denomination individually, and the process culminates in a vote whereby the congregation decides whether or not to declare itself "welcoming," "open and affirming," "more light," and so on. Central to the curriculum and the designation is a welcoming and affirmation of gay men and lesbians (and bisexuals and transgendered people, in more recent years) as full and integrated members of the congregation.

55. Beth Leehy, interview with the author, June 19, 2003.

56. Rev. Lee Barker, interview with the author, June 17, 2003.

57. Available at http://www.uuneighborhood.org/involved.html (accessed June 3, 2003).

58. Rev. Lee Barker, interview with the author, June 17, 2003. Barker left Neighborhood to become president of Meadville-Lombard Theological School.

59. See http://www.uuneighborhood.org/sjhistory.htm (accessed June 3, 2003). According to Lee Barker, the service was conducted partly as a protest against California's pending Proposition 22 (see n. 38).

60. Rev. Lee Barker, interview with the author, June 17, 2003.

61. Ibid.

62. Mary Mitchell, interview with the author, June 27, 2003. Telling the children that the picketers were saying God hates people is not an exaggeration in this case: Phelps's motto, as well as the URL of his inflammatory website, is "God hates fags."

63. Since about 2004, Phelps has increasingly targeted the funerals of military personnel who served in Iraq and Afghanistan. He claims that their deaths are a direct result of the acceptance of homosexuality in U.S. culture.

64. Ibid.

65. Rev. Susan Russell, interview with the author, June 19, 2003.

66. Available online at http://www.allsaints-pas.org/greetings/greetings.htm (accessed August 19, 2002).

67. These are outlined on the church's extensive website: http://www.allsaints-pas.org/site/PageServer?pagename=ministries_homepage (accessed December 10, 2008).

68. Rev. Susan Russell, interview with the author, June 19, 2003.

69. Ibid.

70. Mary Mitchell, interview with the author, June 27, 2003.

71. Rev. Susan Russell, interview with the author, June 19, 2003.

72. Father Juan Barragan, interview with Marcy Braverman, October 16, 2002.

73. Ibid.

74. Ibid.

75. "St. Monica Catholic Church, 1886–1986: The Centennial Chronicle," http://www.stmonica.net/historyb.htm (accessed March 12, 2002). At the time of this writing, the article was not available online, but a note at http://www.stmonica.net/archives/index.html says that the archives section of the website is under development.

76. *Ministry with Lesbian and Gay Catholics* (Los Angeles: Archdiocese of Los Angeles, n.d.), italics in original.

77. One striking example is that the handouts that reproduce in English and Spanish the pastoral recommendations to parents from "Always Our Children," a 1997 document produced by the U.S. Bishops' Committee on Marriage and Family, do not include the small but significant conservative revisions made by Cardinal Ratzinger (now Pope Benedict XVI) in 1998.

78. In which, it may be worth noting, there is no reference to same-sex relationships.

79. "Mission Statement," *Ministry with Lesbian and Gay Catholics* (Los Angeles: Archdiocese of Los Angeles, n.d.).

80. In 2003 the archdiocese withdrew the funding for a formal director for this program, for reasons that remain unclear. When I last spoke with Fran Ruth in the spring of 2003, she had left the ministry because she could not afford to run it as a volunteer. The ministry is still active, however, and in 2006 its web page (http://www.la-archdiocese.org/ministry/mlgc/index.php; accessed July 5, 2006) listed five participating spiritual advisors, six parish-based GLO groups and one non-parish group, twelve welcoming parishes, and three Spanish-language groups.

81. Fran Ruth, interview with the author, August 22, 2002. Ruth also noted that it was fortuitous that the ministry had a lay director during a period of conservatism in the Vatican, because unlike a nun or a priest, she could not be silenced. A lay leadership structure has worked for other LGBT Catholic organizations as well, most notably Dignity, which eventually separated from the church but was able to do so (instead of simply dying out) because of its lay leadership.

82. Ibid.

83. "About Agape," http://www.agapelive.com/aboutagape/index.html (accessed March 12, 2002). Current information is available at http://www.stmonica.net/archives/index.html (accessed December 10, 2008).

84. Agape International Spiritual Center, service bulletin, February 17, 2002.

85. Fieldnotes, Agape International Spiritual Center, February 17, 2002.

86. Rev. Sage Bennet, interview with the author, August 8, 2002.

87. There are no ministries at Agape that explicitly include transgendered people. Though Sage Bennet does not believe, given Agape's teaching that all people are an embodiment of the divine, that transgendered people would be excluded from any Agape ministry, they are also not explicitly welcomed.

88. I draw these terms from Catherine L. Albanese.

89. See http://www.ibmc.info (accessed March 12, 2002).

90. Ven. Dr. Karuna Dharma, interview with Dan Michon, March 10, 2002.

91. Ibid.

92. Ibid.

93. *Frequently Asked Questions and Common Sanskrit Terms* (South Fallsburg, N.Y.: SYDA Foundation, 1999).

94. Cf. http://www.siddhayoga.org/teachings-siddha-yoga.html (accessed December 10, 2008).

95. Daryl Glowa, interview with the author, June 27, 2003.

96. Ibid.

97. Almost no secondary literature exists on Dianic Wicca. For an overview of the history and beliefs of the Dianic movement, however, see Zsuzsanna Budapest, *The Holy Book of Women's Mysteries* (1980; Berkeley, Calif.: Wingbow Press, 1989).

98. On this history, see the oral history of Ruth Barrett at the Lesbian, Gay, Bisexual, and Transgender Religious Archives Network, available online at http://www.lgbtran.org/Interview.aspx?ID=3 (accessed October 16, 2008).

99. Letecia Layson, interview with the author, July 12, 2002.

100. See http://www.circleofaradia.org/mission.htm (accessed December 10, 2008).

101. Letecia Layson, interview with the author, July 12, 2002.

102. See Simone de Beauvoir, *The Second Sex,* trans. H. M. Parshley (New York: Alfred Knopf, [1952] 1980).

103. In the same vein, Dianic Wicca's moratorium on teaching magic to and practicing ritual with men holds only until men and women are fully equal.

104. Letecia Layson, interview with the author, July 12, 2002.

105. Ibid.

106. Starhawk, *The Spiral Dance: A Rebirth of the Ancient Religion of the Great Goddess,* 3rd ed. (San Francisco: HarperSanFrancisco, 1999). On Reclaiming, see Jone Salomonsen, *Enchanted Feminism: The Reclaiming Witches of San Francisco* (New York: Routledge, 2002).

107. Though it does not specifically address Reclaiming, Mary Jo Neitz's article, "Queering the Dragonfest: Changing Sexualities in a Post-Patriarchal Religion" (*Sociology of Religion* 61, no. 4 [2000]: 369–392) offers an example of this kind of fluidity.

108. Available online at http://www.reclaiming.org/about/directions/unity.html (accessed July 6, 2006).

109. ReWeaving leadership (Otter Coyote Moon, Firewalker, Flame, Kerry Thorne, and Anonymous), group interview with the author, August 3, 2002. Because ReWeaving follows Reclaiming's consensus model of leadership, those currently leading the circle deemed it inappropriate for any one of them to represent the group for this study. They requested instead that I conduct a group interview with several current leaders and long-time members of ReWeaving.

110. Ibid. Reclaiming groups sponsor Witch Camps in several locations each year; though they are open to people not affiliated with Reclaiming, they serve as an opportunity for Reclaiming witches to meet with others in the tradition.

111. For a good introduction to these religions, see Joseph M. Murphy, *Working the Spirit: Ceremonies of the African Diaspora* (Boston: Beacon Press, 1994).

112. *Church of the Lukumi Babalu Aye v. City of Hialeah.* At issue was a city ordinance that outlawed animal sacrifice. The Supreme Court decision, which struck down the ordinance, held that the city had violated the First Amendment by specifically targeting the practice of Santería.

113. See Randy P. Conner with David Hatfield Sparks, *Queering Creole Spiritual Traditions: Lesbian, Gay, Bisexual, and Transgender Participation in African-Inspired Traditions in the Americas* (Binghamton, N.Y.: Harrington Park Press, 2004), and Salvador Vidal-Ortiz, "Sexuality and Gender in Santería: LGBT Identities at the Crossroads of Santería Religious Practices and Beliefs," in *Gay Religion: Innovation and Continuity in Spiritual Practice,* ed. Scott Thumma and Edward R. Gray, 115–37 (Walnut Creek, Calif.: Alta Mira, 2004).

114. See http://www.angeles.sierraclub.org/gls/history.htm (accessed June 14, 2003).

115. "Women's Lake Extravaganza, Emigrant Wilderness," *Tracks* 16, no. 3 (2003): 10.

116. Sister Phyllis Stein the Fragrant and Sister Kitty Catalyst O.C.P., "A Sistory Blow by Blow." Available online: http://www.thesisters.org/sistory/spihistory.htm (accessed July 7, 2006).

117. Ibid.

118. Chapters of the Sisters, which exist in ten states and in six countries outside the United States, are sometimes called "houses," "missions," "abbeys," or "orders." I know of none that are actually residential communities. This is in line with the organization of some drag communities into nonresidential "houses" based on fictive kinship.

Cf. *Paris Is Burning,* VHS, produced and directed by Jennie Livingston (New York: Off White Productions, 1990).

119. The Sisters of Perpetual Indulgence of Los Angeles, "Sistory." Available online: http://www.lasisters.org (accessed July 7, 2006). It is worth noting that although the order is clearly open to all sexual orientations and genders, most of the Sisters in the L.A. house are white, gay men.

120. For an overview of negative reactions to the Sisters, as well as a theoretical consideration of the performative nature of their work, see Cathy B. Glenn, "Queering the (Sacred) Body Politic: Considering the Performative Cultural Politics of the Sisters of Perpetual Indulgence," *Theory & Event* 7, no. 1 (2003), n.p. This is, to my knowledge, the only secondary literature on the Sisters.

121. The Sisters of Perpetual Indulgence of Los Angeles, "Sistory." Available online: http://www.lasisters.org (accessed July 7, 2006). "Faerie paganism" is probably a reference to the Radical Faeries, although Wicca is also popular in this house of the Sisters. On the Radical Faeries, see chapter 2. Two San Francisco sisters, Sister Hysterectoria and Reverand [*sic*] Mother, attended the initial gathering of the Radical Faeries just a few months after the Sisters of Perpetual Indulgence began, and the New York City Sisters' web pages are currently housed on a Radical Faerie website (http://radicalfaeries.net/radicalfaeries/sisters.htm; accessed July 7, 2006). Harry Hay was elevated to sainthood by the Sisters in 2000, dubbed "Saint Harry Faerie Godfather" (Sister Phyllis Stein the Fragrant and Sister Kitty Catalyst O.C.P., "A Sistory Blow by Blow," cited above.

122. Wade Clark Roof, *Spiritual Marketplace: Baby Boomers and the Remaking of American Religion* (Princeton, N.J.: Princeton University Press, 1999), 9. See also *A Generation of Seekers: The Spiritual Journeys of the Baby Boom Generation* (San Francisco: HarperCollins, 1993).

4. Negotiating Religion

1. Christine R. Peña, interview with the author, August 30, 2001.

2. Wade Clark Roof, for instance, dubs the baby boomers "a generation of seekers" and understands their seeking as a personal quest for truth. Robert Wuthnow identifies a "spirituality of seeking" as the predominant religious pattern in the post-1960s United States, and understands such a spirituality as a radically individualistic and potentially isolating approach to religion. See Wade Clark Roof, *A Generation of Seekers: The Spiritual Journeys of the Baby Boom Generation* (San Francisco: HarperCollins, 1993) and Robert Wuthnow, *After Heaven: Spirituality in America Since the 1950s* (Berkeley: University of California Press, 1998).

3. See Claude Lévi-Strauss, *The Savage Mind* (Chicago: University of Chicago Press, 1966), 16–22.

4. Vassilis Saroglou, "Religious Bricolage as a Psychological Reality: Limits, Structures, and Dynamics," *Social Compass* 53, no. 1 (2006): 109–115; Danièle Hervieu-Léger, "Bricolage Vaut-Il Dissémination? Quelques Réflexions sur L'Operationnalité Sociologique d'une Metaphore Problématique," *Social Compass* 52, no. 3 (2005): 295–308 (translation mine).

5. Hervieu-Léger, "Bricolage," 298 (translation mine).

6. Christine R. Peña, interview with the author, August 30, 2001.

7. The passage to which Christine refers here is I Corinthians 7:9.

8. Ruth Tittle, interview with the author, September 20, 2001.

9. Mary Jane, interview with the author, September 12, 2001.

10. Betty Walker, interview with the author, October 21, 2001.

11. The biblical passages that some Christians interpret as condemning same-sex relationships and/or transgender identities are heavily contested for a number of reasons. Those arguing that such passages do not in fact condemn contemporary same-sex

relationships point to the historical context of the biblical texts, scholars' uncertainty as to the meaning of several key words, and the textual context, among other factors. Christian theologians also point out that none of Jesus' teachings mentions homosexuality, but that Jesus always had a concern for the downtrodden and for those unjustly injured by the pursuit of rules over compassion. Christian and Jewish theologians both note the importance of loving same-sex relationships (whose sexual status is not revealed in the texts) between such figures as Ruth and Naomi, and David and Jonathan. Key texts at the center of this debate include Genesis 19:4–11; Leviticus 18:22 and 20:13–14; Deuteronomy 22:5; I Corinthians 6:9; I Timothy 1:10; and Romans 1:26–27. The New International Version, or NIV, translates some of these contested passages as commentaries on "homosexuality."

12. Coco Gallegos, interview with the author, August 23, 2001.

13. Ronni Sanlo, interview with the author, August 30, 2001.

14. Even among those who became aware of such feelings later on in life, several have come to believe in hindsight that they were attracted to the same sex at an early age.

15. This is consistent with my findings in an earlier study on Christianity and LGBT identity. See Melissa M. Wilcox, *Coming Out in Christianity: Religion, Identity, and Community* (Bloomington: Indiana University Press, 2003).

16. Betty Walker, interview with the author, October 21, 2001.

17. Danielle, interview with the author, September 12, 2001.

18. When I tried to contact Danielle a few years after this interview to follow up on her plans, I was unable to reach her—evidence, perhaps, that she had been successful.

19. Emile, interview with the author, October 6, 2001.

20. "A Gay's Road to God." Accessed at http://www.outofthecube.com, October 22, 2001, hard copy in the author's possession. By 2006, this site was no longer in existence.

21. Sue Field, interview with the author, September 29, 2001.

22. James Mills, "Lesbians Try to Peddle Each Other: Activities in Times Square," *Life,* December 3, 1965, 98–99.

23. Vanessa, interview with the author, September 16, 2001.

24. Vanessa, personal communication with the author, November 13, 2003, and November 15, 2003.

25. Corrine Garcia, interview with the author, November 3, 2001. Because Corrine identifies as female and also lives as a man, because she elected to use her feminine name for the project, and because she used the feminine pronoun in our interview to refer to herself, I have chosen the feminine pronoun to represent her here.

26. Carmen, interview with the author, September 8, 2001.

27. Christine Logan, interview with the author, August 30, 2001.

28. Cf. Duane Noriyuki, "Finding a Place of Peace: The Carl Bean AIDS Care Center Specializes in Comfort—for the Dying and for the Volunteers of Project Nightlight Who Sustain Their Spirits," *Los Angeles Times,* October 11, 1995, E1.

29. Coco Gallegos, interview with the author, August 23, 2001.

30. Margaret A. Jensen, interview with the author, October 2, 2001.

31. Carmen, interview with the author, September 8, 2001.

32. Ruth Tittle, interview with the author, September 20, 2001.

33. Linda, interview with the author, September 29, 2001.

34. Cynthia McCann and Lara Sowinski, interview with the author, September 20, 2001.

35. Silva, interview with the author, August 26, 2001.

36. Kathleen McGregor, interview with the author, August 28, 2001.

37. Christie Tuttle, interview with the author, September 16, 2001.

38. Trish, interview with the author, September 29, 2001.

39. Regina Lark, interview with the author, September 8, 2001. Regina identified as heterosexual at this point in her life.

40. Tami, interview with the author, August 26, 2001.

41. Lisa Taylor, interview with the author, September 8, 2001.

42. The term originates with anthropologist Claude Lévi-Strauss; see *The Savage Mind* (Chicago: University of Chicago Press, 1966), 16–22. It was popularized by Michel de Certeau—see *The Practice of Everyday Life,* trans. Steven Rendall (Berkeley: University of California Press, 1984)—and has been widely used since then.

43. Lauren, interview with the author, September 16, 2001.

44. See http://www.kryon.com (accessed August 16, 2006).

45. These poems are unpublished. Because Lauren read them aloud to me I have no line divisions for them, and I have been unable to contact Lauren for further guidance.

46. Adesina, interview with the author, October 2, 2001.

47. Dean Bramlett, interview with the author, September 25, 2001.

48. Dean Bramlett, telephone interview with the author, September 19, 2001.

49. Moshe Shokeid, *A Gay Synagogue in New York* (New York: Columbia University Press, 1995), 238.

5. Tiles in the Mosaic

1. Mary E. Hunt, "Opposites Do Not Always Attract: How and Why Lesbian Women and Gay Men Diverge Religiously," in *Spirituality and Community: Diversity in Lesbian and Gay Experience,* ed. J. Michael Clark and Michael J. Stemmler (Las Colinas, Tex.: Monument Books, 1994), 147–163.

2. Robert Wuthnow, *After the Baby Boomers: How Twenty- and Thirty-Somethings are Shaping the Future of American Religion* (Princeton, N.J.: Princeton University Press, 2007). On economic readings of religion in the United States, cf. Roger Finke and Rodney Stark, *The Churching of America, 1776–1990: Winners and Losers in Our Religious Economy* (New Brunswick, N.J.: Rutgers University Press, 1992); R. Stephen Warner, "Work in Progress toward a New Paradigm for the Sociological Study of Religion in the United States," *American Journal of Sociology* 98, no. 5 (1993): 1044–1093; Wade Clark Roof, *Spiritual Marketplace: Baby Boomers and the Remaking of American Religion* (Princeton, N.J.: Princeton University Press, 1999); and Laurence R. Iannaccone, "Economics of Religion: Debating the Costs and Benefits of a New Field," *Faith and Economics* 46 (2005): 1–9.

3. Robert A. Orsi, *Between Heaven and Earth: The Religious Worlds People Make and the Scholars Who Study Them* (Princeton, N.J.: Princeton University Press, 2005), 167.

4. Darren E. Sherkat, "Sexuality and Religious Commitment in the United States: An Empirical Examination," *Journal for the Scientific Study of Religion* 41, no. 2 (2002): 313–323.

5. Indeed, studies of sexual identity development indicate that this assumption may also have introduced a gender skew into the project, as women are more likely than men to develop a nonheterosexual identity before having a same-sex sexual experience. Cf. Ritch C. Savin-Williams and Lisa M. Diamond, "Sexual Identity Trajectories Among Sexual-Minority Youths: Gender Comparisons," *Archives of Sexual Behavior* 29, no. 6 (2000): 607–627; Frank J. Floyd and Roger Bakeman, "Coming-Out across the Life Course: Implications of Age and Historical Context," *Archives of Sexual Behavior* 35, no. 3 (2006): 287–296.

6. Though there are numerous sources for this debate, Robert Orsi's musings on the topic are especially illuminating in this context. See *Between Heaven and Earth,* chapter 6.

7. James Allan Davis and Tom W. Smith, *General Social Survey, 2004* (machine-

readable data file). Principal investigator, James A. Davis; director and co-principal investigator, Tom W. Smith; co-principal investigator, Peter V. Marsden, NORC ed. Chicago: National Opinion Research Center, producer, 2004; Storrs, Conn.: Roper Center for Public Opinion Research, University of Connecticut, distributor. Microcomputer format and codebook prepared and distributed by MicroCase Corporation.

8. Roof, *Spiritual Marketplace,* 232.

9. Ibid., 233.

10. Rev. Daniel Smith, interview with the author, June 17, 2003.

11. Tami, interview with the author, August 26, 2001.

12. Emile, interview with the author, October 6, 2001.

13. Cynthia McCann and Lara Sowinsky, interview with the author, September 20, 2001.

14. Ibid.

15. Ruth Tittle, interview with the author, September 20, 2001.

16. For a brief overview of such debates, see Matthew T. Loveland, "Religious Switching: Preference Development, Maintenance, and Change," *Journal for the Scientific Study of Religion* 42, no. 1 (2003): 148.

17. Cf. Loveland, "Religious Switching." For similar findings among LGBT Christians, see Melissa M. Wilcox, *Coming Out in Christianity: Religion, Identity, and Community* (Bloomington: Indiana University Press, 2003).

18. Juan Battle, Cathy J. Cohen, Dorian Warren, Gerard Fergerson, and Suzette Audam, *Say It Loud: I'm Black and I'm Proud* (New York: Policy Institute of the National Gay and Lesbian Task Force, 2000).

19. Ibid., 51.

20. Alan P. Bell and Martin S. Weinberg, *Homosexualities: A Study of Diversity among Men and Women* (New York: Simon and Schuster, 1978).

21. I include as "women of color" those who identified as multiracial as well as those identifying as black, Latina, and Native American.

22. Adesina, interview with the author, October 2, 2001.

23. Betty Walker, interview with the author, October 21, 2006.

24. Emile, interview with the author, October 6, 2001.

25. Such uneasiness with transgendered people, or "transphobia," on the part of lesbians and gay men plays a significant role in the lives of all three transgendered people in this study—Lauren, Danielle, and Corrine—and has been a part of their religious decision making as well.

26. Moshe Shokeid, "'The Women Are Coming': The Transformation of Gender Relationships in a Gay Synagogue," *Ethnos* 66, no. 1 (2001): 8.

27. Moshe Shokeid, *A Gay Synagogue in New York* (New York: Columbia University Press, 2005), 174.

28. An exception to this pattern was Oceanfront MCC, which I discuss at length in *Coming Out in Christianity.* This congregation was made up almost entirely of lesbians, but it was extremely small and was located in a city long known as a lesbian haven (though not a Christian haven). It also closed within five years of the conclusion of my research.

29. Shokeid, "'The Women Are Coming,'" 18.

30. Christ Chapel of Long Beach seems to be an interesting exception to this pattern; though the church is male-led, Pastor Michael Cole reported that the congregation was approximately gender-balanced.

31. Criticisms of a pastor's style could certainly mask a gender-based complaint. However, I never heard such a complaint explicitly articulated by the women in the study who regularly attended LGBT religious organizations.

32. Adesina, interview with the author, October 2, 2001.

33. Christie Tuttle, interview with the author, September 16, 2001.

34. Ronni Sanlo, interview with the author, August 30, 2001.

35. Hunt, "Opposites Do Not Always Attract," 157, 156.

36. Certainly the topic of the study in general—LBT women and religion—may have led some women to bring up LGBT issues when they might not have done so otherwise, but given that I did not ask about religious homophobia or heterosexism until the very end of the interviews, and that several participants felt quite comfortable assuring me that being a woman had no impact on their religious experiences yet talked explicitly about religious homophobia, it seems that the high number of participants who discussed such topics indicates a real concern.

37. Dean Bramlett, interview with the author, September 25, 2001. An interesting indication of the complexity involved in these women's religious identity negotiations is that while Dean "rails" against organized religion as sexist and homophobic, at the time of our interview she was regularly attending St. Thomas the Apostle Episcopal Church whenever she needed what she called "dogma" (religious stability) in her life.

38. Though biphobia can also be an important factor, especially in the context of Catholic gay and lesbian groups that rely on a naturalistic, "we don't have a choice" argument to make the case for their equal status in the church, in this study even those participants who identify as bisexual spoke of religious opposition to same-sex eroticism rather than any explicit opposition to bisexuality. This is consistent with many religions' official statements on same-sex eroticism, which seem to understand bisexuals as partial homosexuals rather than as people with a separate sexual orientation.

39. Christine Logan, interview with the author, August 30, 2001.

40. Danielle, interview with the author, September 12, 2001.

41. Linda, interview with the author, September 29, 2001.

42. Wade Clark Roof, *A Generation of Seekers: The Spiritual Journeys of the Baby Boom Generation* (San Francisco: HarperCollins, 1993), 55; and *Spiritual Marketplace,* 122.

43. Roof, *A Generation of Seekers,* 57.

44. Ibid., 154–155.

45. Unfortunately, there are no data on the next two years of these teenagers' lives, when Roof's study and others would predict an even more precipitous drop in attendance.

46. See Christian Smith, Melinda Lundquist Denton, Robert Faris, and Merk Regnerus, "Mapping American Adolescent Religious Participation," *Journal for the Scientific Study of Religion* 41, no. 4 (2002): 597–612; John M. Wallace, Jr., Tyrone A. Forman, Cleopatra H. Caldwell, and Deborah S. Willis, "Religion and U.S. Secondary School Students: Current Patterns, Recent Trends, and Sociodemographic Correlates," *Youth & Society* 35, no. 1 (2003): 98–125.

47. I have left out transgender identities in this discussion both because the literature on transgender identities does not generally focus on age and because gender identity development differs from sexual identity development in significant ways. However, it is possible to speculate about the interactions between transgender identity and religion; see n. 52.

48. Ritch C. Savin-Williams, *Gay and Lesbian Youth: Expressions of Identity* (New York: Hemisphere, 1990), 156–159. All gender differences discussed in this section are statistically significant.

49. Ritch C. Savin-Williams and Lisa M. Diamond, "Sexual Identity Trajectories among Sexual-Minority Youths: Gender Comparisons," *Archives of Sexual Behavior* 29, no. 6 (2000): 607–627.

50. Floyd and Bakeman, "Coming-Out across the Life Course," 287–296. Furthermore, another recent study showed clear "cohort," or generational, effects in the age of self-identification, with by far the youngest self-identification (at 15.88 years) occurring among those born between 1979 and 1986. Those born between 1969 and

1979 self-identified at an average age of 18.86 years; those born between 1959 and 1969 at 21.06; those born between 1949 and 1959 at 23.09; and those born before 1949 at 24.9. See Christian Grov, David S. Bimbi, José E. Nanín, and Jeffrey T. Parsons, "Race, Ethnicity, Gender, and Generational Factors Associated with the Coming-Out Process among Gay, Lesbian, and Bisexual Individuals," *The Journal of Sex Research* 43, no. 2 (2006): 115–121.

51. Grov, Bimbi, Nanín, and Parsons, "Race, Ethnicity, Gender, and Generational Factors."

52. Furthermore, studies focused on bisexuality show that self-labeling as bisexual takes place a good deal later than self-labeling as gay or lesbian, and that bisexual women and men do not differ significantly in their ages of self-labeling. Thus, bisexuals generally come out even farther along the religious life cycle than lesbians or gay men, and may either be long gone from religion when they self-identity or (especially if they have children) have returned to religion. A further complication is also introduced by the fact that some bisexuals first self-identify as lesbian or gay, thus potentially interacting with religion from this perspective before later integrating bisexual identity into any religious sense of self they may have. Cf. Martin S. Weinberg, Colin J. Williams, and Douglas W. Pryor, *Dual Attraction: Understanding Bisexuality* (New York: Oxford University Press, 1994). Research on transgender and transsexual identity development is less widespread than research on sexual identity, and it has not focused on "milestones" and ages. However, it does indicate that an often inchoate sense of difference appears very early on in childhood for many who later come to identify as transgendered or transsexual. Developing these identities, claiming them, and living them out is a different process from developing, claiming, and living out a sexual identity (though the former does have implications for the latter); thus, the interactions between transgender/transsexual identities and religion are likely different from those between sexual identities and religion. On the other hand, given that some western religions explicitly condemn gender-crossing and that such religions (mirroring contemporary western cultures in general) sometimes inaccurately take gender-crossing and other gender-diverse behavior to be an indication of homosexuality, there may be some similarities in the interactions as well. We might expect, for instance, that someone who comes to identify as transgendered or transsexual while a regular participant in organized religion would be more likely to stay in that religion after the early-adult period of disaffiliation than would someone who had entered the disaffiliation period (and *had* disaffiliated) prior to identifying. On transgender/transsexual identity development, cf. Aaron H. Devor, "Witnessing and Mirroring: A Fourteen Stage Model of Transsexual Identity Formation," *Journal of Gay and Lesbian Psychotherapy* 8, no. 1–2 (2000): 41–67.

53. Cf. Leonard Norman Primiano, "Intrinsically Catholic: Vernacular Religion and Philadelphia's 'Dignity'" (Ph.D. diss., University of Pennsylvania, 1993), esp. chapter 7; Shokeid, *A Gay Synagogue*; Gary David Comstock, *Unrepentant, Self-Affirming, Practicing: Lesbian/Bisexual/Gay People within Organized Religion* (New York: Continuum, 1996); Kimberly A. Mahaffy, "Cognitive Dissonance and Its Resolution: A Study of Lesbian Christians," *Journal for the Scientific Study of Religion* 35, no. 4 (1996): 392–402; Andrew K. T. Yip, "Attacking the Attacker: Gay Christians Talk Back," *British Journal of Sociology* 48, no. 1 (1997): 113–127; Michele Dillon, *Catholic Identity: Balancing Reason, Faith, and Power* (New York: Cambridge University Press, 1999), chapter 5; Eric M. Rodriguez and Suzanne M. Ouellette, "Gay and Lesbian Christians: Homosexual and Religious Identity Integration in the Members and Participants of a Gay-Positive Church," *Journal for the Scientific Study of Religion* 39, no. 3 (2000): 333–347; Wilcox, *Coming Out in Christianity;* Andrew K. T. Yip, "Negotiating Space with Family and Kin in Identity Construction: The Narratives of British Non-Heterosexual Muslims," *The Sociological Review* 52, no. 3 (2004): 336–350; Andrew K. T. Yip, "Queering Religious Texts: An Exploration of British Non-Heterosexual Christians' and Muslims' Strategy

of Constructing Sexuality-Affirming Hermeneutics," *Sociology* 39, no. 1 (2005): 47–65; Omar Minwalla, B. R. Simon Rosser, Jamie Feldman, and Christine Varga, "Identity Experience among Progressive Gay Muslims in North America: A Qualitative Study within Al-Fatiha," *Culture, Health, and Sexuality* 7, no. 2 (2005): 113–128; Randal F. Schnoor, "Being Gay and Jewish: Negotiating Intersecting Identities," *Sociology of Religion* 67, no. 1 (2006): 43–60; and Tova Hartman Halbertal with Irit Koren, "Between 'Being' and 'Doing': Conflict and Coherence in the Identity Formation of Gay and Lesbian Orthodox Jews," in *Identity and Story: Creating Self in Narrative,* ed. Dan P. McAdams, Ruthellen Josselson, and Amia Lieblich, 37–61 (Washington, D.C.: American Psychological Association, 2006).

54. Further support for this hypothesis is offered by the gendered ordering of "milestones" in sexual identity development. A study conducted in the mid-1990s (Savin-Williams and Diamond, "Gender Differences") showed that women generally self-identify as lesbian or bisexual before they have a same-sex sexual experience, whereas men self-identify as gay or bisexual after such experiences. As women already self-identify later than men, this places women's first same-sex experience well into the religious disaffiliation period. On the other hand, it places men's first same-sex experience solidly within a period of high religious affiliation. This is one more reason for men to negotiate a blended sexual and religious identity, and for women to negotiate their sexual identities outside of religion, perhaps never returning to a religion they perceive as condemning. These patterns also may help to explain the apparent predominance of men in religious (mostly Christian) "ex-gay" movements.

55. David Lyon explicitly terms such approaches to religion "consumer religion." David Lyon, *Jesus in Disneyland: Religion in Postmodern Times* (Cambridge, UK: Polity Press, 2000), 85.

56. Cynthia McCann and Lara Sowinsky, interview with the author, September 20, 2001.

57. Wilcox, *Coming Out in Christianity;* see especially pp. 47–49.

58. Sue Field, interview with the author, September 29, 2001.

59. Tipton's work, published in full in *Getting Saved from the Sixties,* also contributed to *Habits of the Heart,* the classic text on contemporary U.S. individualism. See Steven Tipton, *Getting Saved from the Sixties* (Berkeley: University of California Press, 1982); Robert N. Bellah, Richard Madsen, William M. Sullivan, Ann Swidler, and Steven Tipton, *Habits of the Heart: Individualism and Commitment in American Life* (Berkeley: University of California Press, 1985).

60. Paul Heelas, *The New Age Movement: The Celebration of the Self and the Sacralization of Modernity* (Cambridge, Mass.: Blackwell, 1996), 156.

61. Paul Heelas and Linda Woodhead, with Benjamin Seel, Bronislaw Szerszynski, and Karin Tusting, *The Spiritual Revolution: Why Religion Is Giving Way to Spirituality* (Malden, Mass.: Blackwell, 2005), 2–9.

62. See also Melissa M. Wilcox, "When Sheila's a Lesbian: Religious Individualism among Lesbian, Gay, Bisexual, and Transgender Christians," *Sociology of Religion* 63, no. 4 (2002): 497–513.

63. Heelas and Woodhead, *The Spiritual Revolution,* 11.

64. David Lyon, *Jesus in Disneyland,* 32.

65. Ibid., 161.

66. Wuthnow, *After the Baby Boomers,* 153.

67. Ibid., 15.

68. Roof, *Spiritual Marketplace,* 297.

69. Kimberlé Crenshaw, "Mapping the Margins: Intersectionality, Identity Politics, and Violence against Women of Color," *Stanford Law Review* 43, no. 6 (1991): 1241–1279. "Intersectionality" refers to the implicitly interrelated nature of various aspects of identity. What it is to be "a woman," for instance, varies depending on whether one

is bisexual or lesbian, African American or Latina, working class or middle class, and so on. And these identities—middle-class, bisexual Latina, for instance—are further intersected by each other and by still other identities.

70. Hervieu-Léger, "In Search of Certainties," 62.

6. Building a Mosaic

1. David Lyon, *Jesus in Disneyland: Religion in Postmodern Times* (Cambridge, UK: Polity, 2000), 69.

2. The term originated in the work of Kimberlé Crenshaw; see "Mapping the Margins: Intersectionality, Identity Politics, and Violence against Women of Color," *Stanford Law Review* 43 (1991): 1241–1298.

3. Studies of LGBT religious identities have blossomed encouragingly in recent years. Among the earlier, landmark studies that focus specifically on identity are Scott Thumma, "Negotiating a Religious Identity: The Case of the Gay Evangelical," *Sociological Analysis* 52, no. 4 (1991): 333–347; Moshe Shokeid, *A Gay Synagogue in New York* (New York: Columbia University Press, 1995), especially chapter 12; Kimberly A. Mahaffy, "Cognitive Dissonance and Its Resolution: A Study of Lesbian Christians," *Journal for the Scientific Study of Religion* 35, no. 4 (1996): 392–402; and Andrew K. T. Yip, "Attacking the Attacker: Gay Christians Talk Back," *British Journal of Sociology* 48, no. 1 (1997): 113–127. More recent work includes Eric M. Rodriguez and Suzanne C. Ouellette, "Gay and Lesbian Christians: Homosexual and Religious Identity Integration in the Members and Participants of a Gay-Positive Church," *Journal for the Scientific Study of Religion* 39, no. 3 (2000): 333–347; Andrew K. T. Yip, "The Persistence of Faith among Nonheterosexual Christians: Evidence for the Neosecularization Thesis of Religious Transformation," *Journal for the Scientific Study of Religion* 41, no. 2 (2002): 199–212; Melissa M. Wilcox, "When Sheila's a Lesbian: Religious Individualism among Lesbian, Gay, Bisexual, and Transgender Christians," *Sociology of Religion* 63, no. 4 (2002): 497–513; Melissa M. Wilcox, *Coming Out in Christianity: Religion, Identity, and Community* (Bloomington: Indiana University Press, 2003); Andrew K. T. Yip, "Negotiating Space with Family and Kin in Identity Construction: The Narratives of British Non-Heterosexual Muslims," *The Sociological Review* 52, no. 3 (2004): 336–350; Andrew K. T. Yip, "Embracing Allah and Sexuality? South Asian Non-Heterosexual Muslims in Britain," in *South Asians in the Diaspora: Histories and Religious Traditions*, ed. Knut A. Jacobsen and P. Pratap Kumar (Leiden: Brill, 2004): 294–310; Andrew K. T. Yip, "Queering Religious Texts: An Exploration of British Non-Heterosexual Christians' and Muslims' Strategy of Constructing Sexuality-Affirming Hermeneutics," *Sociology* 39, no. 1 (2005): 47–65; Lori Peek, "Becoming Muslim: The Development of a Religious Identity," *Sociology of Religion* 66, no. 3 (2005): 215–242; Rick Phillips, *Conservative Christian Identity and Same-Sex Orientation: The Case of Gay Mormons* (New York: Peter Lang, 2005); Michelle Wolkomir, *Be Not Deceived: The Sacred and Sexual Struggles of Gay and Ex-Gay Christian Men* (New Brunswick, N.J.: Rutgers University Press, 2006); Randal F. Schnoor, "Being Gay and Jewish: Negotiating Intersecting Identities," *Sociology of Religion* 67, no. 1 (2006): 43–60; Pamela Leong, "Religion, Flesh, and Blood: Re-Creating Religious Culture in the Context of HIV/AIDS," *Sociology of Religion* 67, no. 3 (2006): 295–311; Tova Hartman Halbertal with Irit Koren, "Between 'Being' and 'Doing': Conflict and Coherence in the Identity Formation of Gay and Lesbian Orthodox Jews," in *Identity and Story: Creating Self in Narrative*, ed. Dan P. McAdams, Ruthellen Josselson, and Amia Lieblich, 37–61 (Washington, D.C.: American Psychological Association, 2006); and Wendy Cadge and Lynn Davidman, "Ascription, Choice, and the Construction of Religious Identities in the Contemporary United States," *Journal for the Scientific Study of Religion* 45, no. 1 (2006): 23–38.

4. These studies, which helpfully bring a greater complexity of identities (and the

concept of intersectionality) to the study of LGBT religiosities, are those of Yip and Schnoor, cited above.

5. Ruth Frankenberg, *Living Spirit, Living Practice: Poetics, Politics, Epistemology* (Durham, N.C.: Duke University Press, 2004), 4.

6. Ibid., 20.

7. Cf. Meredith McGuire's classic textbook in the field, *Religion: The Social Context*, 5th ed. (Belmont, Calif.: Wadsworth, 2002), 37–39.

8. Frankenberg, *Living Spirit*, 159–161. The "crash" Frankenberg describes involved a meditation group that welcomed a participant as a gay man but proved insensitive to his experiences as a person of color.

9. Note that this assertion is based not on any stance regarding the reality or unreality of the sacred itself, but rather on the fact that experiences that people associate with their understanding of the sacred often have a profound influence on their lives. One need not take a stand on the "reality" or causes of such experiences in order to consider their impact.

10. See Wilcox, *Coming Out in Christianity*.

11. Cf. Dawne Moon, *God, Sex, and Politics: Homosexuality and Everyday Theologies* (Chicago: University of Chicago Press, 2004).

12. Silva, interview with the author, August 26, 2001.

13. Trish, interview with the author, September 29, 2001.

14. Regina Lark, interview with the author, September 8, 2001.

15. Lara Sowinsky, interview with the author, September 20, 2001.

16. Hervieu-Léger considers such universalism a key pattern in contemporary religiosities: "Frequent reference to the convergence of different individualized spiritual quests (following the pattern of 'we are all saying and seeking the same thing,' 'we are expressing the different aspects of a common truth in a variety of forms,' etc.) allows the idea of a 'common core belief' to be authenticated" ("In Search of Certainties," 65).

17. Lauren, interview with the author, September 16, 2001.

18. Coco Gallegos, interview with the author, August 23, 2001.

19. Cassandra Christenson, interview with the author, August 23, 2001.

20. Betty Walker, interview with the author, October 21, 2001.

21. Christine Peña, interview with the author, August 30, 2001.

22. Vanessa, interview with the author, September 16, 2001.

23. Emile, interview with the author, October 6, 2001.

24. Sue Field, interview with the author, September 29, 2001. The undertones of consumerism in Sue's comment are worthy of note: she describes Christianity as a "deal," implying that one gets the best value for one's money (or commitment?) in this religion, as opposed to other religions. Offering free gifts in exchange for purchases or memberships is also a common marketing ploy.

25. Here again, Hervieu-Léger's comments on universalism are relevant; see n. 16 above.

26. Adesina, interview with the author, October 2, 2001. The Self-Realization Fellowship is an export religion based in Hinduism. I draw the terms "import religion" and "export religion" from historian Catherine L. Albanese.

27. Tami, interview with the author, August 26, 2001. Her monistic understanding of the Goddess reflects a common Wiccan perspective—a kind of gendered or binary monism—that holds that the Goddess and the God are each singular but are recognized by different names and with different aspects in the various religions of the world. This is similar to the belief expressed by Lara and Sue that all religions address the same god from different angles, and resonates again with Hervieu-Léger's suggestion that such monism or universalism is an important aspect of contemporary (western) religiosities; see n. 16 above.

28. This was not true entirely across the board, though. Mary Jane, for instance, succinctly summarized the opposing perspective: "Religion is religion and sex is sex. I don't think it should matter to anyone what your sexual orientation is. It's a whole nother topic" (interview with the author, September 12, 2001).

29. Anthony Giddens, *Modernity and Self-Identity: Self and Society in the Late Modern Age* (Stanford, Calif.: Stanford University Press, 1991), 3.

30. It is important to note from the outset that this narrative construction is not performed in a vacuum. One needs to tell a story that others consider plausible given one's social context, and thus the act of "giving an account of oneself," as Judith Butler puts it, is also an act of responding to another, figurative or real, who demands such an account. The narrative construction of the self, in other words, is always socially conditioned. See Judith Butler, *Giving an Account of Oneself* (New York: Fordham University Press, 2005). Thanks to Nicole Pexton for bringing this work to my attention.

31. Philip Rieff, *The Triumph of the Therapeutic: Uses of Faith after Freud* (New York: Harper and Row, 1966).

32. Giddens, *Modernity and Self-Identity,* 180. Therapy is also, of course, a prime location for the exercise of social norms; thus, Giddens's point here reinforces Butler's.

33. Indeed, it is worth pondering whether the life-history interview is also such a tool and hallmark, as interviewees work to put together a cohesive narrative that links past experiences with present realities and future expectations, presenting the resulting package to an interviewer who then assists with the reconciling of inconsistencies and the filling in of gaps in the narrative.

34. Tom Boellstorff, *A Coincidence of Desires: Anthropology, Queer Studies, Indonesia* (Durham, N.C.: Duke University Press, 2007), 23.

35. See Judith Halberstam, *In a Queer Time and Place: Transgender Bodies, Subcultural Lives* (New York: New York University Press, 2005); Lee Edelman, *No Future: Queer Theory and the Death Drive* (Durham, N.C.: Duke University Press, 2004).

36. Boellstorff, *A Coincidence of Desires,* 23.

37. Ibid., 140.

38. Corrine Garcia, telephone interview with the author, October 28, 2001.

39. Corrine Garcia, interview with the author, November 3, 2001.

40. One of the best-known and earliest compilations of such writings is *This Bridge Called My Back: Writings by Radical Women of Color,* ed. Cherríe Moraga and Gloria Anzaldúa (1981; New York: Kitchen Table Press, 1983).

41. Crenshaw, "Mapping," 1245.

42. Ibid.

43. Boellstorff, *A Coincidence of Desires.*

44. Shelley Budgeon, *Choosing a Self: Young Women and the Individualization of Identity* (Westport, Conn.: Praeger, 2003).

45. Ibid., 111.

46. Ibid., 127.

47. Ibid., 180.

48. In fact, Budgeon suggests that the entire debate over the nature of postmodern identity is often conducted with little connection to empirical research. See *Choosing a Self,* 2–3.

49. Bertram J. Cohler and Phillip L. Hammack, "Making a Gay Identity: Life Story and the Construction of a Coherent Self," in *Identity and Story: Creating Self in Narrative,* ed. Dan P. McAdams, Ruthellen Josselson, and Amia Lieblich (Washington, D.C.: American Psychological Association, 2006), 152.

50. Dana Rosenfeld, *The Changing of the Guard: Lesbian and Gay Elders, Identity, and Social Change* (Philadelphia: Temple University Press, 2003), 88.

51. Ibid., 82.

52. Christine R. Peña, personal communication with the author, October 7, 2004. Interestingly, Christine directly contradicts other participants when she argues that sexual orientation is irrelevant to wholeness.

53. Betty Walker, interview with the author, October 21, 2001.

54. Adesina, interview with the author, October 2, 2001.

55. Some branches of the African diaspora religions are quite welcoming of LGBT people, but this evidently was not the case in the communities of which Adesina was a part. Cf. Randy P. Conner with David Hatfield Sparks, *Queering Creole Spiritual Traditions: Lesbian, Gay, Bisexual, and Transgender Participation in African Traditions in the Americas* (New York: Harrington Park Press, 2004).

56. Ronni Sanlo, interview with the author, August 30, 2001.

57. Robert A. Orsi, *Between Heaven and Earth: The Religious Worlds People Make and the Scholars Who Study Them* (Princeton, N.J.: Princeton University Press, 2005), 9.

58. Halbertal and Koren, "Between 'Being' and 'Doing,'" 37–61.

59. Lyon, *Jesus in Disneyland,* 96.

60. Ibid., 92.

61. Ibid., 93.

62. Ibid., 18.

63. Christie Tuttle, interview with the author, September 16, 2001.

64. The implicit internal/external distinction is also interesting here, as it suggests that the real "truth" is internal and that the external, at some level at least, is false.

65. Dean Bramlett, interview with the author, September 25, 2001.

66. Tami, interview with the author, August 26, 2001.

67. In *The Changing of the Guard,* cited above, Dana Rosenfeld argues that such self-disciplining approaches characterize the identities and values of most gay men and lesbians in her study who developed non-normative sexual identities prior to the rise of the gay liberation movement in the late 1960s.

68. Thomas J. Csordas, *Body/Meaning/Healing* (New York: Palgrave Macmillan, 2002), 58.

69. Ibid., 76 (italics added).

70. Cynthia McCann and Lara Sowinsky, interview with the author, September 20, 2001.

71. Coco Gallegos, interview with the author, August 23, 2001.

72. Lauren, interview with the author, September 16, 2001.

7. Queer Women, Religion, and Postmodernity

1. As chapter 5 discusses, transgender and bisexual identity formation work differently from gay and lesbian identity formation, and thus their relationship to the religious dropout point is more tenuous—except in the case of those people for whom identification as lesbian or gay is a temporary phase in the process of developing a more permanent identity as transgendered or bisexual.

2. I use "metropolitan" here instead of "urban" because my argument is most relevant to larger cities and their suburbs and exurbs.

3. On the Radical Faeries, see chapter 2.

4. Shelley Budgeon, *Choosing a Self: Young Women and the Individualization of Identity* (Westport, Conn.: Praeger, 2003), 5.

5. Charles Taylor, *Varieties of Religion Today: William James Revisited* (Cambridge, Mass.: Harvard University Press, 2002), 83.

6. Ibid., 100.

7. Zygmunt Bauman, *Intimations of Postmodernity* (New York: Routledge, 1992).

8. Taylor, *Varieties of Religion Today,* 112.

9. Ann Swidler, "Culture in Action: Symbols and Strategies," *American Sociological*

Review 51, no. 2 (1986): 273–286.

10. Danièle Hervieu-Léger, *Religion as a Chain of Memory*, tr. Simon Lee (New Brunswick, N.J.: Rutgers University Press, 2000).

11. See also Danièle Hervieu-Léger, "Bricolage Vaut-Il Dissémination? Quelques Réflexions sur l'Operationnalité Sociologique d'une Metaphore Problématique," *Social Compass* 52, no. 3 (2005): 299.

12. Cf. Nancy Wilson, *Our Tribe: Queer Folks, God, Jesus, and the Bible* (San Francisco: HarperSanFrancisco, 1995), and Justin Tanis, *Trans-Gendered: Theology, Ministry, and Communities of Faith* (Cleveland: Pilgrim, 2003). The classic text here is John Boswell's *Christianity, Social Tolerance, and Homosexuality: Gay People in Western Europe from the Beginning of the Christian Era to the Fourteenth Century* (Chicago: University of Chicago Press, 1980). Also relevant as an example of both secular and sacred chains of memory is Leslie Feinberg's *Transgender Warriors: Making History from Joan of Arc to RuPaul* (Boston: Beacon, 1996). It is important to note that historical accuracy is not of great concern to chains of memory. This is obvious in the case of religions, since relatively little of the content of sacred texts can be proven (despite the valiant efforts of religious authorities in certain time periods and cultures), but it holds true for secular texts as well. For instance, academics have come to quite a clear agreement that the concept of sexual orientation as a central and innate aspect of identity was invented in the nineteenth-century west; nevertheless, outside of these academic circles the discussion continues about which well-known historical figures were "gay" or "lesbian."

13. Robert A. Orsi, *Between Heaven and Earth: The Religious Worlds People Make and the Scholars Who Study Them* (Princeton, N.J.: Princeton University Press, 2005), 167.

Appendix B

1. E.g. Darren E. Sherkat, "Sexuality and Religious Commitment in the United States: An Empirical Examination," *Journal for the Scientific Study of Religion* 41, no. 2 (2002): 313–323; Lisa K. Jepsen and Christopher A. Jepsen, "An Empirical Analysis of the Matching Patterns of Same-Sex and Opposite-Sex Couples," *Demography* 39, no. 3 (2002): 435–453.

2. Gary David Comstock, *Unrepentant, Self-Affirming, Practicing: Lesbian/Bisexual/Gay People within Organized Religion* (New York: Continuum, 1996), 183.

3. Most often underrepresented by these methods are "closeted" LGBT people and those who identify as LGBT but do not consider that identity primary or even particularly important in their lives. Other skews include region, class, race, immigration status, and physical dis/ability.

4. Robert S. Lynd and Helen Merrell Lynd, *Middletown: A Study in Contemporary American Culture* (New York: Harcourt, Brace, and Company, 1929) and *Middletown in Transition: A Study in Cultural Conflicts* (New York: Harcourt, Brace, and Company, 1937).

5. E.g., N. J. Demerath and Rhys H. Williams, *A Bridging of Faiths: Religion and Politics in a New England City* (Princeton, N.J.: Princeton University Press, 1992), and Nancy Tatom Ammerman, *Congregation and Community* (New Brunswick, N.J.: Rutgers University Press, 1997).

6. One excellent neighborhood study that involves religion is Omar M. McRoberts, *Streets of Glory: Church and Community in a Black Urban Neighborhood* (Chicago: University of Chicago Press, 2003).

7. Marie Cartier, personal communication with the author, May 23, 2001.

8. Given the apparent antipathy toward religion among many lesbian, bisexual, and transgendered women, and given the project's goal of investigating queer religion

beyond the congregation, I stressed the term "spirituality" over "religion" (assumed by many in the United States today to mean "institutionalized religion") in the recruitment material for the project.

9. Melissa M. Wilcox, *Coming Out in Christianity: Religion, Identity, and Community* (Bloomington: Indiana University Press, 2003).

10. For the questions used in both the telephone interviews and the in-depth interviews, see Appendix C.

11. The term "questioning" usually indicates that someone is exploring (or "questioning") her or his sexual orientation but does not currently identify as lesbian, bisexual, gay, *or* heterosexual.

12. I say "at least in part" because one transgendered participant identifies as "a woman who lives as a man." Those interested in tracking the stories of specific participants should find Appendix A, which provides brief biographies for each participant, helpful.

13. Cf. Claire Mitchell, "Behind the Ethnic Marker: Religion and Social Identification in Northern Ireland," *Sociology of Religion* 66, no. 1 (2005): 3–21.

14. U.S. Census Bureau, *Census 2000.* A summary of the demographics for the city of Los Angeles is available online at http://censtats.census.gov/data/CA/1600644000.pdf (accessed October 17, 2008).

15. Though the percentage of Jewish participants in this study is more than proportional to the national population, a small percentage of a small population yields very few actual participants.

16. Related issues are probably at work in the case of recruitment through the *Lesbian News.* Although its editorial staff makes an effort to cover stories that are of interest to women from a wide range of ethnic backgrounds, the magazine may be of less interest to transgendered lesbians, certainly to heterosexual transgendered women, and to bisexuals of any gender.

17. See Stephen O. Murray and Will Roscoe, *Islamic Homosexualities: Culture, History, and Literature* (New York: New York University Press, 1997).

18. Cf. Scott Siraj al-Haqq Kugle, "Sexuality, Diversity, and Ethnics in the Agenda of Progressive Muslims," in *Progressive Muslims: On Justice, Gender, and Pluralism,* ed. Omid Safi (Oxford, UK: Oneworld, 2003), 190–233, and Kecia Ali, *Sexual Ethics and Islam: Feminist Reflections on Qur'an, Hadith, and Jurisprudence* (Oxford, UK: Oneworld, 2006). Al-Fatiha, a U.S. organization for LGBT Muslims, also fosters quite a bit of this discussion; see http://www.al-fatiha.org (accessed October 17, 2008) for examples.

19. See (among others) Bernard Faure, *The Red Thread: Buddhist Approaches to Sexuality* (Princeton, N.J.: Princeton University Press, 1998), and Ruth Vanita, ed., *Queering India: Same-Sex Love and Eroticism in Indian Culture and Society* (New York: Routledge, 2002).

20. See Wilcox, *Coming Out in Christianity,* 28–29.

21. "Anonymity of Sources," American Sociological Association, *Code of Ethics and Policies and Procedures of the ASA Committee on Professional Ethics* (1999), 11.06.

22. Ibid.

23. Mark D. Jordan, *The Silence of Sodom: Homosexuality in Modern Catholicism* (Chicago: University of Chicago Press, 2000).

24. Cf. John Boswell, *Christianity, Social Tolerance, and Homosexuality: Gay People in Western Europe from the Beginning of the Christian Era to the Fourteenth Century* (Chicago: University of Chicago Press, 1980); Murray and Roscoe, *Islamic Homosexualities.*

25. See Ken Plummer, *Telling Sexual Stories: Power, Change, and Social Worlds* (London: Routledge, 1995).

26. Kenneth L. Cuthbertson, "Coming Out/Conversion: An Exploration of Gay

Religious Experience," *Journal of Men's Studies* 4, no. 3 (1996): 193–207.

27. Cf. Dana Rosenfeld, *The Changing of the Guard: Lesbian and Gay Elders, Identity, and Social Change* (Philadelphia: Temple University Press, 2003), 193–194.

28. Cf. Robert N. Bellah, Richard Madsen, William M. Sullivan, Ann Swidler, and Steven M. Tipton, *Habits of the Heart: Individualism and Commitment in American Life* (Berkeley: University of California Press, 1985); Wade Clark Roof, *Spiritual Marketplace: Baby Boomers and the Remaking of American Religion* (Princeton, N.J.: Princeton University Press, 1999).

29. I make this argument at some length in "When Sheila's a Lesbian: Religious Individualism among Lesbian, Gay, Bisexual, and Transgender Christians," *Sociology of Religion* 63, no. 4 (2002): 497–513. This idea is also apparent in the work of Paul Heelas; cf. *The New Age Movement: The Celebration of the Self and the Sacralization of Modernity* (Oxford, UK: Blackwell, 1996).

Appendix C

1. Hir (pronounced "hear") and ze (pronounced "zee") are among the more popular of the myriad of gender-neutral pronouns proposed over the years. Such pronouns become especially important when discussing transgendered people who fall between genders rather than identifying wholly with one or the other.

Selected Bibliography

Adler, Margot. *Drawing Down the Moon.* Boston: Beacon Press, 1986.

Armstrong, Elizabeth A., and Suzanna M. Crage. "Movements and Memory: The Making of the Stonewall Myth." *American Sociological Review* 71, no. 5 (2006): 724–751.

Battle, Juan, Cathy J. Cohen, Dorian Warren, Gerard Fergerson, and Suzette Audam. *Say It Loud: I'm Black and I'm Proud.* New York: The Policy Institute of the National Gay and Lesbian Task Force, 2000.

Bauer, Paul F. "The Homosexual Subculture at Worship: A Participant Observation Study." *Pastoral Psychology* 25, no. 2 (1976): 115–127.

Bauman, Zygmunt. *Intimations of Postmodernity.* New York: Routledge, 1992.

Bean, Lowell John, and Charles R. Smith. "Gabrielino." In *Handbook of North American Indians,* vol. 8, *California,* ed. William C. Sturtevant, 538–548. Washington, D.C.: Smithsonian Institution, 1978.

Beckford, James A. *Religion and Advanced Industrial Society.* London: Unwin Hyman, 1989.

Bell, Alan P., and Martin S. Weinberg. *Homosexualities: A Study of Diversity among Men and Women.* New York: Simon and Schuster, 1978.

Bellah, Robert N., Richard Madsen, William M. Sullivan, Ann Swidler, and Steven Tipton. *Habits of the Heart: Individualism and Commitment in American Life.* Berkeley: University of California Press, 1985.

Berger, Peter. *The Sacred Canopy: Elements of a Sociological Theory of Religion.* New York: Doubleday, 1967.

Boellstorff, Tom. *A Coincidence of Desires: Anthropology, Queer Studies, Indonesia.* Durham, N.C.: Duke University Press, 2007.

Boswell, John. *Christianity, Social Tolerance, and Homosexuality: Gay People in Western Europe from the Beginning of the Christian Era to the Fourteenth Century.* Chicago: University of Chicago Press, 1980.

Brekhus, Wayne. *Peacocks, Chameleons, Centaurs: Gay Suburbia and the Grammar of Social Identity.* Chicago: University of Chicago, 2003.

Budapest, Zsuzsanna. *The Feminist Book of Lights and Shadows.* Venice, Calif.: Luna Publications, 1976.

———. *The Holy Book of Women's Mysteries.* Berkeley, Calif.: Wingbow Press [1980] 1989.

Budgeon, Shelley. *Choosing a Self: Young Women and the Individualization of Identity.* Westport, Conn.: Praeger, 2003.

Butler, Judith. *Giving an Account of Oneself.* New York: Fordham University Press, 2005.

Burawoy, Michael. "The Extended Case Method." *Sociological Theory* 16, no. 1 (1998): 4–33.

Cadge, Wendy, and Lynn Davidman. "Ascription, Choice, and the Construction of Religious Identities in the Contemporary United States." *Journal for the Scientific Study of Religion* 45, no. 1 (2006): 23–38.

Chauncey, George. *Gay New York: Gender, Urban Culture, and the Makings of the Gay Male World, 1890–1940.* New York: Basic Books, 1994.

Cohler, Bertram J., and Phillip L. Hammack. "Making a Gay Identity: Life Story and the Construction of a Coherent Self." In *Identity and Story: Creating Self in Narrative,* ed. Dan P. McAdams, Ruthellen Josselson, and Amia Lieblich, 151–172. Washington, D.C.: American Psychological Association, 2006.

Comstock, Gary David. *Unrepentant, Self-Affirming, Practicing: Lesbian/Bisexual/Gay People Within Organized Religion.* New York: Continuum, 1996.

Conner, Randy P., with David Hatfield Sparks. *Queering Creole Spiritual Traditions: Lesbian, Gay, Bisexual, and Transgender Participation in African-Inspired Traditions in the Americas.* Binghamton, N.Y.: Harrington Park Press, 2004.

Cox, Harvey. *Fire from Heaven: The Rise of Pentecostal Spirituality and the Reshaping of Religion in the Twenty-first Century.* Reading, Mass.: Addison-Wesley, 1995.

Crenshaw, Kimberlé. "Mapping the Margins: Intersectionality, Identity Politics, and Violence against Women of Color." *Stanford Law Review* 43 (1991): 1241–1298.

Csordas, Thomas J. *Body/Meaning/Healing.* New York: Palgrave Macmillan, 2002.

de Certeau, Michel. *The Practice of Everyday Life,* trans. Steven Rendall. Berkeley: University of California Press, 1984.

D'Emilio, John. *Sexual Politics, Sexual Communities: The Making of a Homosexual Minority in the United States, 1940–1970.* 2nd ed. Chicago: University of Chicago Press, 1998.

Devor, Aaron H. "Witnessing and Mirroring: A Fourteen Stage Model of Transsexual Identity Formation." *Journal of Gay and Lesbian Psychotherapy* 8, no. 1–2 (2000): 41–67.

Dillon, Michelle. *Catholic Identity: Balancing Reason, Faith, and Power.* New York: Cambridge University Press, 1999.

Edelman, Lee. *No Future: Queer Theory and the Death Drive.* Durham, N.C.: Duke University Press, 2004.

Edsall, Nicholas C. *Toward Stonewall: Homosexuality and Society in the Modern Western World.* Charlottesville: University of Virginia Press, 2003.

Engh, Michael E. *Frontier Faiths: Church, Temple, and Synagogue in Los Angeles, 1846–1888.* Albuquerque: University of New Mexico Press, 1992.

———. "'Practically Every Religion Being Represented.'" In *Metropolis in the Making: Los Angeles in the 1920s,* ed. Tom Sitton and William Deverell, 201–219. Berkeley: University of California Press, 2001.

Enroth, Ronald M. "The Homosexual Church: An Ecclesiastical Extension of a Subculture." *Social Compass* 21, no. 3 (1974): 355–360.

Enroth, Ronald M., and Gerald E. Jamison. *The Gay Church.* Grand Rapids, Mich.: Eerdmans, 1974.

Faderman, Lillian. *Odd Girls and Twilight Lovers: A History of Lesbian Life in Twentieth-Century America.* New York: Columbia University Press, 1991.

Faderman, Lillian, and Stuart Timmons. *Gay L.A.: A History of Sexual Outlaws, Power Politics, and Lipstick Lesbians.* New York: Basic Books, 2006.

Feinberg, Leslie. *Transgender Warriors: Making History from Joan of Arc to RuPaul.* Boston: Beacon, 1996.

Flamming, Douglas. *Bound for Freedom: Black Los Angeles in Jim Crow America.* Berkeley: University of California Press, 2005.

Floyd, Frank J., and Roger Bakeman. "Coming-Out across the Life Course: Implications of Age and Historical Context." *Archives of Sexual Behavior* 35, no. 3 (2006): 287–296.

Frankenberg, Ruth. *Living Spirit, Living Practice: Poetics, Politics, Epistemology.* Durham, N.C.: Duke University Press, 2004.

Giddens, Anthony. *Modernity and Self-Identity: Self and Society in the Late Modern Age.* Stanford, Calif.: Stanford University Press, 1991.

Glenn, Cathy B. "Queering the (Sacred) Body Politic: Considering the Performative Cultural Politics of the Sisters of Perpetual Indulgence." *Theory & Event* 7, no. 1 (2003): n.p.

Gorman, E. Michael. "A New Light on Zion: A Study of Three Homosexual Religious Congregations in Urban America." Ph.D. diss., University of Chicago, 1980.

Grov, Christian, David S. Bimbi, José E. Nanín, and Jeffrey T. Parsons. "Race, Ethnicity, Gender, and Generational Factors Associated with the Coming-Out Process among Gay, Lesbian, and Bisexual Individuals." *Journal of Sex Research* 43, no. 2 (2006): 115–121.

Halberstam, Judith. *In a Queer Time and Place: Transgender Bodies, Subcultural Lives.* New York: New York University Press, 2005.

Halbertal, Tova Hartman, with Irit Koren. "Between 'Being' and 'Doing': Conflict and Coherence in the Identity Formation of Gay and Lesbian Orthodox Jews." In *Identity and Story: Creating Self in Narrative,* ed. Dan P. McAdams, Ruthellen Josselson, and Amia Lieblich, 37–61. Washington, D.C.: American Psychological Association, 2006.

Hall, David D., ed. *Lived Religion: Toward a History of Practice.* Princeton, N.J.: Princeton University Press, 1997.

Hay, Harry. *Radically Gay: Gay Liberation in the Words of Its Founder,* ed. Will Roscoe. Boston: Beacon Press, 1996.

Hayashi, Brian Masaru. *"For the Sake of Our Japanese Brethren": Assimilation, Nationalism, and Protestantism among the Japanese of Los Angeles, 1895–1942.* Stanford, Calif.: Stanford University Press, 1995.

Heelas, Paul. *The New Age Movement: The Celebration of the Self and the Sacralization of Modernity.* Cambridge, Mass.: Blackwell, 1996.

Heelas, Paul, and Linda Woodhead, with Benjamin Seel, Bronislaw Szerszynski, and Karin Tusting. *The Spiritual Revolution: Why Religion Is Giving Way to Spirituality.* Malden, Mass.: Blackwell, 2005.

Hervieu-Léger, Danièle. *Religion as a Chain of Memory,* trans. Simon Lee. New Brunswick, N.J.: Rutgers University Press, 2000.

———. "Bricolage Vaut-Il Dissémination? Quelques Réflexions sur l'Operationnalité Sociologique d'une Metaphore Problématique." *Social Compass* 52, no. 3 (2005): 295–308.

———. "In Search of Certainties: The Paradox of Religiosity in Societies of High Modernity." *Hedgehog Review* 8, nos. 1–2 (2006): 59–68.

Hood, Ralph W., Jr. "The Relationship between Religion and Spirituality." In *Defining Religion: Investigating the Boundaries Between the Sacred and Secular* (*Religion and the Social Order* Vol. 10), ed. Arthur L. Greil and David G. Bromley, 241–264. New York: JAI, 2003.

Hunt, Mary E. "Opposites Do Not Always Attract: How and Why Lesbian Women and Gay Men Diverge Religiously." In *Spirituality and Community: Diversity in Lesbian and Gay Experience,* ed. J. Michael Clark and Michael J. Stemmler, 147–163. Las Colinas, Tex.: Monument Books, 1994.

Jordan, Mark D. *The Silence of Sodom: Homosexuality in Modern Catholicism.* Chicago: University of Chicago Press, 2000.

Kaiser, Charles. *The Gay Metropolis: 1940–1996.* Boston: Houghton Mifflin, 1997.

Kelley, Ron. "Muslims in Los Angeles." In *Muslim Communities in North America,* ed. Yvonne Yazbeck Haddad and Jane Idleman Smith, 135–167. Albany: State University of New York Press, 1994.

Kenney, Moira Rachel. *Mapping Gay L.A.: The Intersection of Place and Politics.* Philadelphia: Temple University Press, 2001.

Kimmel, Michael S. *Manhood in America: A Cultural History.* 2nd ed. New York: Oxford University Press, 2005.

Kristeva, Julia. *Powers of Horror: An Essay on Abjection.* Trans. Leon S. Roudiez. New York: Columbia University Press, 1982.

Leong, Pamela. "Religion, Flesh, and Blood: Re-creating Religious Culture in the Context of HIV/AIDS." *Sociology of Religion* 67, no. 3 (2006): 295–311.

Loveland, Matthew T. "Religious Switching: Preference Development, Maintenance, and Change." *Journal for the Scientific Study of Religion* 42, no. 1 (2003): 147–157.

Lyon, David. *Jesus in Disneyland: Religion in Postmodern Times.* Cambridge, UK: Polity, 2000.

Mahaffy, Kimberly A. "Cognitive Dissonance and Its Resolution: A Study of Lesbian Christians." *Journal for the Scientific Study of Religion* 35, no. 4 (1996): 392–402.

Marler, Penny Long, and C. Kirk Hadawaym. "'Being Religious' or 'Being Spiritual': A Zero-Sum Proposition?" *Journal for the Scientific Study of Religion* 41, no. 2 (2002): 289–300.

McCarthy, Amanda Beresford. "Gabrieliño." In *The Gale Encyclopedia of Native American Tribes,* vol. 4, ed. Sharon Malinowski, Anna Sheets, Jeffrey Lehman, and Melissa Walsh Doig, 65–68. Detroit: Gale, 1998.

McGuire, Meredith. *Religion: The Social Context.* 5th ed. Belmont, Calif.: Wadsworth, 2002.

Melton, Gordon. *The Churches Speak on Homosexuality: Official Statements from Religious Bodies and Ecumenical Organizations.* Detroit: Gale, 1991.

Meyerowitz, Joanne. *How Sex Changed: A History of Transsexuality in the United States.* Cambridge, Mass.: Harvard University Press, 2002.

Mills, James. "Lesbians Try to Peddle Each Other: Activities in Times Square." *Life,* December 3, 1965, 98–99.

Minwalla, Omar, B. R. Simon Rosser, Jamie Feldman, and Christine Varga. "Identity Experience among Progressive Gay Muslims in North America: A Qualitative Study within Al-Fatiha." *Culture, Health, and Sexuality* 7, no. 2 (2005): 113–128.

Monroy, Douglas. *Rebirth: Mexican Los Angeles from the Great Migration to the Great Depression.* Berkeley: University of California Press, 1999.

Moon, Dawne. *God, Sex, and Politics: Homosexuality and Everyday Theologies.* Chicago: University of Chicago Press, 2004.

Neitz, Mary Jo. "Queering the Dragonfest: Changing Sexualities in a Post-Patriarchal Religion." *Sociology of Religion* 61, no. 4 (2000): 369–392.

Noriyuki, Duane. "Finding a Place of Peace: The Carl Bean AIDS Care Center Specializes in Comfort—For the Dying and for the Volunteers of Project Nightlight Who Sustain Their Spirits." *Los Angeles Times,* October 11, 1995, E1.

Orsi, Robert A. *Between Heaven and Earth: The Religious Worlds People Make and the Scholars Who Study Them.* Princeton, N.J.: Princeton University Press, 2005.

Peek, Lori. "Becoming Muslim: The Development of a Religious Identity." *Sociology of Religion* 66, no. 3 (2005): 215–242.

Phillips, Rick. *Conservative Christian Identity and Same-Sex Orientation: The Case of Gay Mormons.* New York: Peter Lang, 2005.

Primiano, Leonard Norman. "'I Would Rather Be Fixated on the Lord': Women's Religion, Men's Power, and the 'Dignity' Problem." *New York Folklore* 19, no. 1–2 (1993): 89–103.

———. "Intrinsically Catholic: Vernacular Religion and Philadelphia's 'Dignity.'" Ph.D. diss., University of Pennsylvania, 1993.

Quinn, D. Michael. *Same-Sex Dynamics among Nineteenth-Century Americans: A Mormon Example.* Urbana: University of Illinois Press, 1996.

Rieff, Philip. *The Triumph of the Therapeutic: Uses of Faith after Freud.* New York: Harper and Row, 1966.

Ríos-Bustamante, Antonio. "The Barrioization of Nineteenth-Century Mexican

Californians: From Landowners to Laborers." *Masterkey: Anthropology of the Americas* 60 (1986): 26–35.
Rodriguez, Eric M., and Suzanne C. Ouellette. "Gay and Lesbian Christians: Homosexual and Religious Identity Integration in the Members and Participants of a Gay-Positive Church." *Journal for the Scientific Study of Religion* 39, no. 3 (2000): 333–347.
Roof, Wade Clark. *A Generation of Seekers: The Spiritual Journeys of the Baby Boom Generation.* San Francisco: HarperCollins, 1993.
———. *Spiritual Marketplace: Baby Boomers and the Remaking of American Religion.* Princeton, N.J.: Princeton University Press, 1999.
Roof, Wade Clark, and William McKinney. *American Mainline Religion: Its Changing Shape and Future.* New Brunswick, N.J.: Rutgers University Press, 1987.
Rosenfeld, Dana. *The Changing of the Guard: Lesbian and Gay Elders, Identity, and Social Change.* Philadelphia: Temple University Press, 2003.
Rupp, Leila. *A Desired Past: A Short History of Same-Sex Love in America.* Chicago: University of Chicago Press, 1999.
Salomonsen, Jone. *Enchanted Feminism: The Reclaiming Witches of San Francisco.* New York: Routledge, 2002.
Saroglou, Vassilis. "Religious Bricolage as a Psychological Reality: Limits, Structures, and Dynamics." *Social Compass* 53, no. 1 (2006): 109–115.
Savin-Williams, Ritch C. *Gay and Lesbian Youth: Expressions of Identity.* New York: Hemisphere, 1990.
Savin-Williams, Ritch C., and Lisa M. Diamond. "Sexual Identity Trajectories among Sexual-Minority Youths: Gender Comparisons." *Archives of Sexual Behavior* 29, no. 6 (2000): 607–627.
Schnoor, Randal F. "Being Gay and Jewish: Negotiating Intersecting Identities." *Sociology of Religion* 67, no. 1 (2006): 43–60.
Sherkat, Darren E. "Sexuality and Religious Commitment in the United States: An Empirical Examination." *Journal for the Scientific Study of Religion* 41, no. 2 (2002): 313–323.
Shokeid, Moshe. *A Gay Synagogue in New York.* New York: Columbia University Press, 1995.
———. "'The Women Are Coming': The Transformation of Gender Relationships in a Gay Synagogue." *Ethnos* 66, no. 1 (2001): 5–26.
Smith, Christian, Melinda Lundquist Denton, Robert Faris, and Merk Regnerus. "Mapping American Adolescent Religious Participation." *Journal for the Scientific Study of Religion* 41, no. 4 (2002): 597–612.
Stryker, Susan, and Jim Van Buskirk. *Gay by the Bay: A History of Queer Culture in the San Francisco Bay Area.* San Francisco: Chronicle Books, 1996.
Swicegood, Thomas L. P. *Our God Too: Biography of a Church and a Temple.* New York: Pyramid Books, 1974.
Tanis, Justin. *Trans-Gendered: Theology, Ministry, and Communities of Faith.* Cleveland: Pilgrim, 2003.
Taylor, Charles. *Varieties of Religion Today: William James Revisited.* Cambridge, Mass.: Harvard University Press, 2002.
Thumma, Scott. "Negotiating a Religious Identity: The Case of the Gay Evangelical." *Sociological Analysis* 52, no. 4 (1991): 333–347.
Timmons, Stuart. *The Trouble with Harry Hay: Founder of the Modern Gay Movement.* Boston: Alyson Books, 1990.
Tipton, Steven. *Getting Saved from the Sixties.* Berkeley: University of California Press, 1982.
Urban, Hugh B. *Magia Sexualis: Sex, Magic, and Liberation in Modern Western Esotericism.* Berkeley: University of California Press, 2006.

Wallace, John M., Jr., Tyrone A. Forman, Cleopatra H. Caldwell, and Deborah S. Willis. "Religion and U.S. Secondary School Students: Current Patterns, Recent Trends, and Sociodemographic Correlates." *Youth & Society* 35, no. 1 (2003): 98–125.

Wat, Eric C. *The Making of a Gay Asian Community: An Oral History of Pre-AIDS Los Angeles.* Lanham, Md.: Rowman and Littlefield, 2002.

Weinberg, Martin S., Colin J. Williams, and Douglas W. Pryor. *Dual Attraction: Understanding Bisexuality.* New York: Oxford University Press, 1994.

Wellman, James K., Jr., ed. *Religious Organizational Identity and Homosexual Ordination: A Case Study of the Presbyterian Church, U.S.A.*. Special issue of *Review of Religious Research,* 41, no. 2 (1999).

White, Heather R. "Homosexuality, Gay Communities, and American Churches: A History of a Changing Religious Ethic, 1946–1976." Ph.D. diss., Princeton University, 2007.

Wilcox, Melissa M. "When Sheila's a Lesbian: Religious Individualism among Lesbian, Gay, Bisexual, and Transgender Christians." *Sociology of Religion* 63, no. 4 (2002): 497–513.

———. *Coming Out in Christianity: Religion, Identity, and Community.* Bloomington: Indiana University Press, 2003.

Wilson, Nancy. *Our Tribe: Queer Folks, God, Jesus, and the Bible.* San Francisco: HarperSanFrancisco, 1995.

Wolkomir, Michelle. *Be Not Deceived: The Sacred and Sexual Struggles of Gay and Ex-Gay Christian Men.* New Brunswick, N.J.: Rutgers University Press, 2006.

Wood, Matthew. "Kinship Identity and Nonformative Spiritual Seekership." In *Religion, Identity, and Change: Perspectives on Global Transformations,* ed. Simon Coleman and Peter Collins, 191–206. Aldershot, UK: Ashgate, 2004.

Wuthnow, Robert. *After Heaven: Spirituality in America since the 1950s.* Berkeley: University of California Press, 1998.

———. *After the Baby Boomers: How Twenty- and Thirty-Somethings Are Shaping the Future of American Religion.* Princeton, N.J.: Princeton University Press, 2007.

Yip, Andrew K. T. "Attacking the Attacker: Gay Christians Talk Back." *British Journal of Sociology* 48, no. 1 (1997): 113–127.

———. "The Persistence of Faith among Nonheterosexual Christians: Evidence for the Neosecularization Thesis of Religious Transformation." *Journal for the Scientific Study of Religion* 41, no. 2 (2002): 199–212.

———. "Embracing Allah and Sexuality? South Asian Non-Heterosexual Muslims in Britain." In *South Asians in the Diaspora: Histories and Religious Traditions,* ed. Knut A. Jacobsen and P. Pratap Kumar, 294–310. Leiden: Brill, 2004.

———. "Negotiating Space with Family and Kin in Identity Construction: The Narratives of British Non-Heterosexual Muslims." *Sociological Review* 52, no. 3 (2004): 336–350.

———. "Queering Religious Texts: An Exploration of British Non-Heterosexual Christians' and Muslims' Strategy of Constructing Sexuality-Affirming Hermeneutics." *Sociology* 39, no. 1 (2005): 47–65.

Index

Melissa M. Wilcox is Associate Professor of Religion and Gender Studies at Whitman College. She is author of *Coming Out in Christianity: Religion, Identity, and Community* (Indiana University Press, 2003) and co-editor of *Sexuality and the World's Religions.*

Printed and bound by CPI Group (UK) Ltd, Croydon, CR0 4YY

13/04/2025

14656543-0004